115010

D1616668

540 LITTLE KNOWN FACTS ABOUT THE BIBLE

540 LITTLE KNOWN
FACTS
ABOUT THE BIBLE

——:o:——

The 101st Anniversary Edition

EDITED BY ROBERT TUCK

WITH DRAWINGS BY ANTONY GROVES-RAINES

A DOUBLEDAY-GALILEE ORIGINAL
DOUBLEDAY & COMPANY, INC., GARDEN CITY, NEW YORK
1980

ISBN: 0-385-15807-6
LIBRARY OF CONGRESS CATALOG CARD NUMBER 79–8569
ILLUSTRATIONS COPYRIGHT © 1980 BY DOUBLEDAY & COMPANY, INC.
ALL RIGHTS RESERVED
PRINTED IN THE UNITED STATES OF AMERICA
FIRST EDITION

220
T793f

L.I.F.E. College Library
1100 Glendale Blvd.
Los Angeles, Calif. 90026

Editor's Note

———:o:———

This volume was first published in 1879 in London under the title *Biblical Things Not Generally Known*. In the one hundred years since then, the number of books on biblical themes has proliferated into the thousands. Yet much of what is included in this book remains "not generally known." Because of the immense social changes in countries of the East over the past hundred years, some "modern" illustrations here included no longer exist as described. Rather than revise or update the original volume, this new edition preserves the exact text of the original work, allowing today's reader to glimpse the Bible and its treasured contents through reverent nineteenth-century eyes.

On the following pages appear the Preface and Introduction as they were originally prepared by the editor, the Reverend Robert Tuck, B.A. (1836–1911). A minister of the Congregational Church in England and Wales, Tuck authored a large number of biblical and devotional books as well as readings for young people.

026457

Preface

TO THE ORIGINAL EDITION
1879

——:o:——

It is a pleasing characteristic of these modern times that the results of the widest research and the most profound study are brought within the reach of the general public, and accommodated to the average intelligence. Thereby knowledge is very extensively diffused, and many, having taste and abilities, are led on to the fuller pursuit of various branches of learning. The remark may be applied in an eminent degree to that increased knowledge of all matters of history, custom, legend, or criticism, which, in recent years, has almost made a new book of the Sacred Scriptures. It is the aim of this work to gather together such stores of knowledge from all quarters, and present them to the many students of the Bible who are engaged in accumulating knowledge of the Sacred Book, in short, simple paragraphs, free from learned references, and with such explanations only as may make the facts narrated or observed clearly intelligible.

There is a vast fund of information that would elucidate Holy Scripture hidden away in books of travel that have had their day, and passed into the upper or back shelves of libraries: in works of Biblical criticism that can only be wisely used by the advanced Bible student; in writings of Continental authors, which are hidden in a foreign tongue; in Oriental literature, which is known only to the few; and in modern works of too expensive a character to come within reach of the general reader. Such little known and valuable help in Biblical study is collected and classified for easy reference and in a readable form in the present work.

Every paragraph will be found either to elucidate or illustrate at least some one passage of God's Word; and by the aid of the copious indices, both of the subjects dealt with and of the texts referred to, the contents of the work are placed at the ready command of the Bible Student, the Teacher, and the Preacher, while every effort has been made to secure that the book shall be attractive to the General Reader; one that may be pleasantly and usefully taken up in leisure moments; one that Christian parents may wish to have lying on the family table; one that shall be regarded as essential by all who earnestly desire to enlarge their acquaintance with that great treasure of truth which God has given to man.

This work is not designed to supersede the use of cyclopaedias or other works of reference. It simplifies the information afforded by such works; directs those who may be interested in any particular topic to the further study of them; and supplements them with curious, quaint, and out-of-the-way information, such as is not usually found in modern literature.

Items of information which are known by some readers will yet be quite fresh to others; and in the case of familiar topics, new light has usually been thrown on facts that may be well known. In a few cases the same subjects have been dealt with more than once, but in these cases some additional information of importance is given in the second paragraph. Every effort has been made to secure accuracy; and in dealing with places of which the identity is disputed the name of the person whose judgment is expressed in the paragraph is usually given.

The Editor has endeavoured to furnish a broad, comprehensive and efficient treatment of the great range of subjects brought under consideration; and it is hoped that the work will prove of permanent value to all who would either *know* or *teach* the Word of God.

Introduction

————:o:————

The remarkable attention which has, during the last quarter of a century, been given to the lands and literature of the Bible, has put a vast mass of fresh information at the command of Bible students; and there are few portions of the Sacred Word which have not received elucidation, or gained new force, by an enlarged knowledge of ancient customs, or the closer observation of present Eastern habits. The Book of the Ages is becoming every day more precious to us as its treasury of truth and knowledge grows vaster to our view. But it is necessary that, to be of practical service to Bible students, the results of varied research and observation should be *collected* for the sake of the many who have not access to original sources of information. In "Biblical Things not Generally Known" is gathered together the results of many years' reading. It is a record of *bare facts* which appear to offer explanation of Scripture passages. It is not intended to give opinions, either those of the editor, or those of the authors from whom he may quote. Nor can a list of authorities be presented, as it would comprise all the Biblical works published in recent years, and most of those which have taken their place as standards. The paragraphs into which the work is divided are short, but they are not set in consecutive order as in a cyclopaedia; so that, while serving as a cyclopaedia by means of a very copious index, it is also a readable book to those who do not use it as a book of reference. Each paragraph is numbered, so that its subject may readily be found by the index, and a reference to it may be easily made in the margin of the reader's Bible. No pains have been spared to secure variety and sustain interest, and this collection of "Biblical Things not Generally Known" will, it is hoped, prove, in a remarkable way, helpful to Sunday-school Teachers and Preachers of the Gospel, as well as a work of general interest to intelligent Christian readers.

1.—CHRIST CRUCIFIED.
Matt. xxvii. 35.

❡ Some of the early heathen writers mention the crucifixion of Christ. Thus, Lucian, who flourished about A.D. 175, and ridiculed the Christians, says: "They still worship that great man who was crucified in Palestine because he introduced into the world this new religion" (*Peregrinus,* sec. 11). Still earlier, Tacitus the Roman historian, who was born A.D. 61 or 62, when reporting Nero's persecution of the Christians, says: "They had their denomination from Christ, who in the reign of Tiberius was put to death as a criminal by the procurator Pontius Pilate" (*Annals,* bk. 15, ch. 44). If any doubt had existed respecting the actual crucifixion of Christ as related in the Gospels, these writers would have known it.

2.—THE STAR OF BETHLEHEM AND THE WISE MEN FROM THE EAST.
Matt. ii. 1.

❡ In the annals of the Celestial Empire, there is historical evidence of ambassadors or "wise men" having been sent towards the West in search of the "Great Saint who was to appear." The following from the *Annals* narrates the circumstance:—

"In the twenty-fourth year of Tchao-Wang, of the dynasty of the Tcheou, on the eighth day of the fourth moon, a light appeared in the south-west which illuminated the King's palace. The monarch, struck by its splendour, interrogated the sages, who were skilled in foretelling future events. They then showed him books in which it was written that this prodigy signified the appearance of a great saint in the West, whose religion was to be introduced into this country. The King consulted the ancient books, and having found the passage corresponding with the time of Tchao-Wang, was filled with joy. Then he sent the officers Tsa-yn and Thsin-King, the learned Wang Tsun, and fifteen other men to the West to obtain information."

2.—The Star of Bethlehem and the Wise Men from the
East.

So sensible were these "wise men" of the time and place of the
Saviour's birth, that they set forth to hail the expected Redeemer.
The envoy encountered in their way the missionaries of Buddhism
coming from India, announcing an incarnate God: these the Chinese took for the disciples of the true Christ, embraced their teaching, and introduced them to their fellow-countrymen as the
teachers of the true religion. Thus was Buddhism introduced into
China in place of Christianity.

3.—THE LORD'S "PILLOW" IN THE SHIP.
Mark iv. 38.

⚐ The following description of the ships at present sailing on the
Black Sea, the Aegean Sea, and the Eastern end of the Mediterranean, will aid us in realising the boats and ships that are introduced in Bible narrative. "A narrow bow usually rises to a considerable height, while the sides are low and spreading out above, so
as to keep the deck dry. The stern is sharp like the bow, but rises
high, while the cumbrous rudder rises still higher, and has a very
long cross-pole, one end of which is held by the steersman. This
important personage—always the captain or his mate—sits cross-
legged upon a little quarter-deck, from which high position he can
best watch the course of the ship, which he steers, not by the compass, but solely with the eye. At the extreme end of the stern is
often seen a small low bench, upon which the steersman sometimes
sits for a change. Here the captain often rests his head, when, as is
his custom, he sleeps upon the quarter-deck. This little bench may
generally be seen in the fishing crafts, particularly those which ply
on the Sea of Galilee, a circumstance which explains the nature of
the 'pillow' upon which rested the head of our Lord during the sudden storm narrated in Mark iv. 38. Passengers of distinction alone
are allowed a place upon the quarter-deck."

4.—SWEET SPICES.
Mark xvi. 1.

⚐ On the subject of perfumed flowers and herbs, the Rev. Hugh
Macmillan says:—"Geologists inform us that all the eras of the
earth's history previous to the UPPER MIOCENE were destitute of
perfumes. Forests of club-mosses and ferns hid in their sombre
bosoms no bright-eyed floweret, and shed from their verdant

boughs no scented richness on the passing breeze. Palms and cycads, though ushering in the dawn of a brighter floral day, produced no perfume-breathing blossoms. It is only when we come to the periods immediately antecedent to the human that we meet with an odoriferous flora. God adorned the human period with labiate flowers, modest in form and sober in hue, but exhaling a rich aromatic fragrance at every pore. And so widely and lavishly did He distribute this class of plants over the globe, that at the present day, in the south of Europe, they form one-nineteenth part of the flora; in the tropics one-twenty-sixth; and even in the chill plains of Lapland, out of every thirty-five plants, one is a sweet-smelling labiate. In our own country the tribe is peculiarly abundant, and highly prized. Basil, marjoram and lavender, balm and mint, rosemary and thyme, are dear to every heart, and are as fragrant as their own leaves with the sweetest poetry of rural life. Banished now from the garden to make room for rich and rare exotics, they still linger in romantic old-fashioned places, and are carefully cultivated by the cottager in his little plot of ground. . . . The rosemary is still placed on the snowy shroud of the dead cottager, soothingly suggestive of the sweet and lasting perfume left behind in the dark tomb, by the Rose of Sharon, Mary's Son, who once lay there."

5.—CHALDEAN ACCOUNT OF THE FLOOD.
Genesis vi., vii.

ℭ One of the most remarkable of the recent Assyrian researches and discoveries of George Smith, is a new and more complete account of the flood, found upon Chaldean tablets at Konyunjik. There were twelve of these tablets, and the inscriptions upon them are known as the "Izdubar Legends," probably composed during the early Babylonian Empire more than two thousand years B.C. Of these inscriptions Mr. Smith says:—

"Izdubar, the hero of these legends, probably corresponds with the Biblical Nimrod. He is represented as a giant or mighty man, who, in the early days after the flood, destroyed wild animals, and conquered a number of petty kings, uniting their dominions into one monarchy, which stretched from the Persian Gulf on the south, to the land of Bitani or Bachtan, near Armenia, on the north. He is a representative of the beginning of empire, and a type of the great conquerors who succeeded him. Izdubar has a court, a seer or astrologer, and officers, like later sovereigns; and these tablets are of the utmost value, as showing the manners and customs and religious beliefs of his time. It appears that at that remote age the Babylonians had a tradition of a flood which was a Divine punishment for the wickedness of the world; and of a holy man, who built an ark, and escaped the destruction; who was afterwards translated, and dwelt with the gods. They believed in hell, a place of torment under the earth, and heaven, a place of glory in the sky; and their description of the two has in several points a striking likeness to those in the Bible. They believed in a spirit or soul distinct from the body, which was not destroyed on the death of the mortal frame; and they represent this ghost as rising from the earth at the bidding of one of the gods, and winging its way to heaven. This history of Izdubar appears to have formed a national poem to the Babylonians, similar in some respects to those of Homer among the Greeks. The centre of the story of Izdubar is the city of Erech, now represented by the ruins of Warka, on the eastern bank of the Euphrates. . . . Erech is one of the cities mentioned as the capitals of Nimrod in Genesis x. 10. In early times, according to an inscription which I recently discovered at Nineveh, it was called Unuk or Anak, the giant city, perhaps from its connection with the giant hunter Nimrod. Erech continued a great town down to the twenty-third century before the Christian era, when it was captured by Kudurnanhundi, king of Elam, B.C. 2280, who carried off the famous image of Ishtar or Nana, which was in the temple there. After this the city passed through the same changes as the rest of Babylonia, and at a later period formed part of the empire of Assurbanipal."

6.—ALMS-GIVING IN THE EAST.
Matt. vi. 1–4.

⁋ Various circumstances—prevalence of war, limit of trade, features of disease, and bad governments—have always tended to make a large proportion of Eastern peoples indigent and beggars. In every religious system the duty of caring for them has been commended; and our Lord affirmed the duty while He corrected the modes and spirit in which it had come to be performed. Few well-to-do people in the East can pass by a beggar without giving him the customary piece of copper, the five-para bit (equal to half a cent). Travellers tell us how exceedingly annoying is the perpetual

beggar's cry, *Backsheesh! Backsheesh!* The police do not interfere
with them. Many of them are really needy and deserving; but, as in
other lands, a great many are lazy impostors. They secure the best
positions for appealing to passers-by; and the disabled ones are laid
by friends at the gates of cities, entrances to mosques, and doors of
richer citizens. In some cities Saturday is beggar's day, and every
merchant, shopkeeper, and housewife lays by a store of coppers
and remnants of food. As the beggars go from door to door, and
from one shop to another, their voices are heard from morning till
night, crying, "It is Saturday today," and invoking blessings on
their benefactors, as well as upon their ancestors and their posterity.

7.—THE CURSE CONNECTED WITH ABRAM'S PROMISE.
Genesis xii. 3.

¶ As they stand in our version of the Bible, as well as in many
others, these words sound exceedingly harsh. A recent author asserts that the unpleasant aspect of the text, and of others like it, is
due entirely to the translation, the translators having "suppressed a
fact consistently marked in the Hebrew, viz., that though we may
say that wicked men, such as Goliath or Shimei, *curse,* we must
not, according to the Hebrew, say that God, or good men, ever
curse. Our translation ignores and obliterates a punctiliousness and
delicacy observed in the Hebrew, which confirms St. Peter's doctrine, that though the Lord is reviled, He revileth not. The Hebrew
employs two distinct words to designate respectively the act of God
and the act of the wicked. The wicked *curse* or *revile,* so the Hebrew *galal* or *kalal* implies; but God *degrades* or impoverishes, as is
implied by the Hebrew word *arar.*"

This may be illustrated by the passage referred to at the head of
this paragraph, which should read, "I will degrade (*arar*) him that
revileth (*galal*) Thee." See also Josh. ix. 22, 23. "And Joshua
called for the Gibeonites and said, Now therefore ye are cursed,
and there shall none of you be freed from being bondmen, and
hewers of wood and drawers of water for the house of my God."
Here *arar,* to curse, is fully explained by the context—the Gibeonites were degraded to perpetual bondage, but not reviled.

In sentences such as "cursed is the ground" (Gen. iii. 17),
"cursed be Canaan" (Gen. ix. 25); and without a single exception,
wherever the Lord, or good men, are the speakers, the word is *arar,*

to impoverish. Where violent men speak it is *galal,* to *revile.* Of these two words the former cannot be translated *curse,* though the latter reasonably may. The former is prophetic, the latter malevolent. This serious defect in the English nullifies St. James's saying (James iii. 10) that blessing and cursing should not proceed out of the same mouth, for it represents the Lord as cursing as well as blessing.

8.—"I Appeal unto Caesar."
Acts xxv. 11.

℗ An important protection of the rights of suitors and prisoners is found, under every legislative system, in the right of appeal to a superior court. Only by it can the examination of a case be removed from the sphere of public or judicial prejudice. Under the Roman law from the supreme criminal jurisdiction (both under the Republic and the Empire) was exercised by the governors, whether they were proconsuls, propraetors, or procurators. Against their sentences the inhabitants of the provinces had no appeal. But Roman citizens residing or travelling in the provinces were specially protected from the possible abuse of the governor's authority; they could stop his proceedings by an appeal to the Tribunes, under the Republic, or to the Emperor, under the Empire, and by so doing the trial was transferred to the ordinary tribunals at Rome, and the prisoner must be forwarded to the capital, together with all necessary legal documents, formal charge, depositions of witnesses, sentence of governor, etc., with the least possible delay. There were a few cases in which the right of appeal was not allowed: a bandit, or a pirate, for example, taken in the fact, might have his appeal refused, and be executed on the warrant of the provincial governor. In the case of Paul we find that Felix consulted with the assessors or magistrates sitting with him on the bench before deciding to accept Paul's appeal (chap. xxv. 12).

9.—The Anchor as the Symbol of Hope.
Heb. vi. 19.

℗ Because the anchor is often the sole hope and resource of the sailor, it came to be called by the ancients "the sacred anchor," and was made the emblem of "hope." By the early Christians it was naturally adopted, sometimes with regard to the stormy ocean of

9.—The Anchor as the Symbol of Hope.

human life, at other times in relation to the persecutions and dangers of the ship of the Church. It is found engraved on rings, and depicted on monuments and on the walls of cemeteries in the Catacombs. The symbols on sepulchral tablets often contain allusions to the name of the deceased. The Chevalier de Rossi states that he has three times found an anchor upon *tituli*, bearing names derived from *spes*, the Latin, or ἐλπίς, the Greek word for "hope," upon the tablet of a certain ELPIDIVS, and upon two others, in the cemetery of Priscilla, two women, ELPIZVSA and SPES. In some cases, above the transverse bar of the anchor stands the letter E, which is probably the abbreviation of the word ἐλπίς. Further, we find the anchor associated with the *fish,* the symbol of the Saviour. It is clear that the union of the two symbols expresses "hope in Jesus Christ," and is equivalent to the formula so common on Christian tablets, "Spes in Christo," "Spes in Deo," "Spes in Deo Christo." The fact that the transverse bar of an anchor below the ring forms a cross, may have helped towards the choice of this ring as a Christian symbol.

10.—"AMEN" SAID PUBLICLY BY THE CHURCH.
1 Cor. xiv. 16.

℘ From this passage it is plain that the "Amen," which was freely used in the services of the synagogues, was in the times of the Apostles transferred to the Christian assemblies. And the following early authorities confirm the fact, that the word was repeated aloud as a response by the congregation. Justin Martyr, A.D. 138, notices that the people present say the "Amen" after prayer and thanksgiving; Dionysius of Alexandria, A.D. 232, speaks of one who had often listened to the thanksgiving and joined in the "Amen" which followed. Cyril of Jerusalem, A.D. 320, says that the Lord's Prayer is sealed with an "Amen." And Jerome, A.D. 331, speaks of the thundering sound of the "Amen" of the Roman congregations.

11.—THE TRIBUTE-MONEY DEMANDED OF CHRIST.
Matt. xvii. 24.

℘ "From time immemorial there had been a custom among the Jews, at the recurrence of every census, of collecting a tax of 'half a shekel, after the shekel of the sanctuary,' from each Jew who had reached the age of twenty years. This half shekel was regarded as a 'ransom for his soul,' unto the Lord.

"The money thus gathered was devoted to the service of the Temple, and was expended on the purchase of the sacrifices, scape-goats, red heifers, incense, shew-bread, and other expenses of the Temple service. After the return from the captivity, this *be-ah*, or half shekel, became a voluntary annual tax of a third of a shekel; but at some subsequent period it had again returned to its original amount. This tax had to be paid by every Jew in every part of the world, whether rich or poor; and, as on the first occasion of its payment, to show that the souls of all alike are equal before God, 'the rich paid no more, and the poor paid no less.' It produced vast sums of money, which were conveyed to Jerusalem by honourable messengers."

12.—Engraved Gems in the High Priest's Breastplate.
Exodus xxviii. 15–20.

℃ How soon in history the engraver's art was invented cannot be ascertained. Seals were in existence long before the construction of the high priest's breastplate; but there is no reason to suppose that they consisted of precious stones with engravings upon them. The engraving of the stones of the Jewish breastplate cannot be considered the oldest instance of the engraver's art, since this is referred to in the passage, Ex. xxviii. 21, as something well known. There is, however, no reference to the engraving upon precious stones more ancient than the passage heading this note.

It is impossible to ascertain what were the precious stones with which the breastplate was adorned, as the names by which gems are now designated are very different from the names used in the Hebrew Bible. There seems, however, no reason to doubt the identity of some of them. In the second row a diamond is mentioned: the word in Hebrew is *yahalom*, which certainly does not, in this place, signify the diamond, which, though it can be cut and polished, has never been engraved, and never can be till a harder substance than itself is found.

Josephus relates that the stones were conspicuous for their size and beauty, and of incomparable value. The names of the tribes were engraven in Hebrew characters. "It will sound incredible to the ears of the uninitiated," says the Rev. C. W. King, in his *Antique Gems*, "but every one conversant with the nature of gems will admit that these most venerable productions of the glyptic art must still be in existence. No lapse of time produces any sensible effect upon these monuments, as is testified by the numerous seals, even in a softer material—vitrified clay—bearing the name of Thothmes III. Their intrinsic value also, as the finest gems that could be procured by a race trafficking all over the world, must have rendered them objects of care to all the conquerors into whose hands they fell; and though removed from their original arrangement, and reset in various ornaments, they must always have ranked amongst the most precious state-jewels of the captor of the Holy City. This, doubtless, is the reason why the breastplate belonging to the first temple is not mentioned in the list of sacred articles sent back by Cyrus to Jerusalem. The breastplate in use after the captivity, when worn by the high priest, shot forth, according to Josephus, brilliant rays of fire, that manifested the immediate presence of the Deity. This invaluable trophy was carried to Rome, together with the other spoils of the temple. Of the subsequent fate of these treasures there are two accounts—one that they were conveyed by Genseric, after his sack of Rome (A.D. 455), to Carthage, but that the ship containing them was lost on the voyage: the other account, and the more probable one, is that they had been transferred, long before that time, to Constantinople, and had been deposited by Justinian in the sacristy of Santa Sophia. Hence, there is a chance of the gems, at least, emerging from oblivion at no distant day, when the dark recesses of the Sultan's treasury shall be rummaged."

13.—MODES OF CARRYING WATER.
Genesis xxiv. 15, 46.

℩ So important in Palestine is the easy access to water, that the existence of a spring has often determined the site of a city or village. To this spring a woman from every family comes at least once a day to fetch the necessary supply for the house. The younger members usually perform this duty, which they greatly enjoy, as the fountain is the place for meeting their friends and indulging in social gossip. The jars used are of various shapes, some with and some without handles. Some of them have broad rounded bases, then they are carried on the head, the pressure being

relieved by a small circular cushion. Other jars have almost pointed
bases; these rest upon the cushioned shoulder. But sometimes the
bearer prefers to balance the vessel farther back, with its side
pressing against the shoulder-blade. It is not considered improper
for a man, on passing one of these water-carriers, to ask her to let
down her pitcher and allow him to drink. This she does by lifting
down the jar, resting the side of it upon one hand, while she bal-
ances it at a proper angle with the other. The man who drinks does
not touch the jar, except with his lips. These customs may be compared with those in English village districts, where there is only
one public fountain or well. Though the water-cans are not carried
on head or shoulder, a yoke is often borne on the shoulder, from
which the buckets or cans are hung.

14.—STONE WATERPOTS.
John ii. 6.

℟ Clark, in his *Travels,* says:—"In Cana, we saw large, massive
stone waterpots, not preserved nor exhibited as relics, but lying
about. From their appearance, and the number of them, it was
quite evident that a practice of keeping water in large stone pots,
each holding from twenty to twenty-seven gallons, was once common in the country."

15.—ROBBERS DIGGING THROUGH HOUSES.
Job xxiv. 16.

℟ In the fourth chapter of Job, Eliphaz speaks of men "dwelling
in houses of clay, whose foundation is in the dust." Clay or mud
houses have been common in many countries, including our own,
and they have not even yet disappeared. Houses of this description
must be referred to in the above text; for burglars would find it
difficult, especially with the tools known in the days of Job, to have
digged through a stone wall without prematurely rousing the inmates of the house. An extract from a work published in 1815, by
Mr. Alexander Fraser Tytler, entitled, *Observations on the Present
Political State of India,* will throw some light upon the text. The
writer says:—"The huts of the Bengalees afford no security against
the attacks of robbers. They are built with light bamboo frames,
covered with a kind of reed, bruised flat, and plaited into mats.

The floors are generally raised about a foot or two from the ground by layers of clay beaten down. The thieves, who are denominated *sindeals,* or hole-cutters, easily undermine these floors from without, or cut holes through the mats, sufficiently large to admit of their entering, and by these means carrying away property, generally to a very small amount. . . . In the earthen floor it is not uncommon for the Bengalee to bury in a clay vessel the little money or jewels he may possess; and sometimes the servants of the house give information of this to the *dacoits* (robbers). There are many instances of the dacoits having tortured the poor natives till they gave information of the place where the money was concealed. In one village in particular, which I entered after a dacoity had been committed, I recollect being shown two stakes, with a hollow pit dug between, over which they had suspended the master of the house, and had actually roasted him over a slow fire, until he pointed out the place where his little treasure was hid."

In the text from Job, put at the head of this paragraph, we have probably the most ancient existing description of burglary.

16.—UNDERGIRDING A SHIP.
Acts xxvii. 17.

℃ In ancient ships there was usually but one mast, and one large sail, fixed to an enormous yard, consequently the strain was concentrated on a small portion of the hull, instead of being distributed over it as in one, two, or three masted vessels, and there was great danger of leakage. Ancient writers testify that most of the vessels that were lost foundered at sea. Virgil speaks of the ships of the fleet of Aeneas, as lost in various ways, but "all with fastenings loosened." Some arrangement was therefore necessary to temporarily strengthen the hull in time of storm; so we find it was customary to take to sea, as part of the ordinary "tackling," ropes, which might be passed round the hull again and again at the point where the greatest strain would be, and these would help to prevent the planks from starting. These were called "undergirders," and this process, which in the English navy is called "frapping," is still taught to English seamen. The operation has been thus described in a Marine Dictionary:—"To frap a ship is to pass four or five turns of a large cable-laid rope round the hull or frame of a ship, to support her in a great storm, or otherwise, when it is

apprehended that she is not strong enough to resist the violent
efforts of the sea."

17.—SPECIAL INSIGNIA OF THE APOSTLES.
Matt. x. 2–4.

℃ The characteristic differences between the men whom our Lord
chose as His Apostles have been set forth in various ways, but in
none more succinctly and suggestively than by Leonard Limousin
in a series of enamels in the church of St. Peter, at Chartres. The
Twelve are there represented with the following insignia: St. Peter
with the keys, as commissioned (according to Roman Catholic
ideas) with the power to bind and to loose. St. Paul with a sword,
as a soldier of Christ, armed with the "sword of the Spirit." St.
Andrew with a cross, shaped as the letter X, the form of the cross
on which he is supposed to have been martyred. St. John with a
chalice, in allusion to Matt. xx. 23. St. James the Less with a book
and a club, in allusion to the supposed manner of his death. St.
James the Elder with a pilgrim's staff, a broad hat with scallop-
shells, and a book, he being regarded as the patron of pilgrims. St.
Thomas with an architect's square, as patron of architects and
builders. St. Philip with a small cross, the staff of which is knotted
like a reed, and indicates the traveller's staff, and marks the Apostle as the preacher of Christ crucified to *distant* nations. St.
Matthew with a pike (or spear); St. Matthias with an axe; St.
Bartholomew with a book and a knife; St. Simon with a saw; these
indicating the different modes of their death, according to the leg-
endary accounts.

18.—OFFEND ONE OF THESE LITTLE ONES.
Matt. xviii. 6.

℃ The word *skandalon*, the old form of the word *skandaletron*,
properly denotes a trap for ensnaring animals, then in general a
noose, a snare, the laying of nets. In the New Testament it is
transferred to spiritual things, and under *skandalon* everything is
included which can hinder the development of spiritual life, or
deter men from faith in the Divine. The verb therefore means, to
give offence, to prepare spiritual obstruction, and so, in another
form, to take offence.

19.—PASSING UNDER THE ROD.
Lev. xxvii. 32.

℃ A Christian missionary gives the following interesting explanation of this figurative expression:—"In Syria, just below my house, which stood facing the Mediterranean Sea, there was a sheepfold; a large area surrounded by high walls. It had but one entrance, a little gateway near the corner. It was low and narrow, and a man must stoop to get into it. Every night the shepherd brings home his flock from outside the city, or from the distant field, or the mountain side, to be gathered into this fold. And as they pass into this narrow gateway, they must go one by one. No huddling, and crowding, and jostling, as boys do sometimes at play; and as they pass in, the shepherd stands by the gate and holds his crook over them, to count them one by one as they go in. Every night the shepherd does this, and so he knows if any are left out in the field or on the mountains. And to this counting of the sheep as they pass under the rod, I wish to call attention. We have always supposed, and most people now think, that to pass under the rod means to pass under some affliction, to experience some great trial. Some one has written a touching piece of poetry, called, 'Passing under the Rod,' showing how one and another was afflicted, and made to pass under the rod of God's chastisement. It does not mean any such thing, as you will see by two passages of Scripture. Lev. xxvii. 32—'And concerning the tithe of the herd and of the flock, even of whatsoever passeth under the rod, the tenth shall be holy unto the Lord.' Jer. xxxiii. 13—'In the cities of the mountains, in the cities of the vale, and in the cities of the south, and in the land of Benjamin, and in the places about Jerusalem, and in the cities of Judea shall the flocks pass again under the hands of him that telleth (*counteth*) them.' This is a work of restoration, and the fields there shall have flocks in great number, and they shall pass under the hand of the shepherd, who tells them one by one as he gathers them into the fold."

20.—TROUBLING THE WATER AT BETHESDA.
John v. 4.

℃ This verse is probably the explanatory addition of some copyist, and embodies rather the tradition popularly received respecting the pool than the fact concerning it. There are several intermittent springs in Palestine, and these sometimes possess mineral qualities which render them healing to certain classes of disease. The Pool of Siloam has an intermittent ebb and flow, recurring every few minutes. Near Beirut is a fountain of the same kind, gushing forth from the foot of Lebanon in a strong stream; periodically it is dry for hours at a time. We know a spring of a similar character, at the roadside under Giggleswick Scaur, in Yorkshire. At irregular intervals it rises above its ordinary level, and flows over the top of the trough. The water at Bethesda was doubtless of this intermittent character, and the inflowings were popularly regarded as an angel's troublings. There is good reason for supposing that Bethesda was supplied from the same source as Siloam, and the character of the fountain at Siloam can be observed at the present day. Bethesda, however, is now dry.

21.—THE EXACT SITE OF THE CARMEL CONTEST.
1 Kings xviii. 20.

¶ Van de Velde gives a vivid delineation of the precise locality. He was, it is believed, the first traveller who identified the site of the "Burning;" his decision being fully confirmed by Dean Stanley and other recent travellers.

"One can scarcely imagine a spot better adapted for the thousands of Israel to have stood drawn up on than the gentle slopes around. The rock shoots up in an almost perpendicular wall of more than two hundred feet in height on the side of the vale of Esdrelon. On this side, therefore, there was no room for the gazing multitude, but, on the other hand, this wall made it visible over the whole plain, and from all the surrounding heights, so that even those left behind, and who had not ascended Carmel, would still have been able to witness, at no great distance, the fire from heaven that descended on the altar. . . . Here we were certain the place *must* have been, for it is the only point of all Carmel where Elijah could have been so close to the brook Kishon as to take down thither the priests of Baal and slay them, return again to the mountain and pray for rain, all in the short space of the same afternoon. Nowhere does the Kishon run so close to Mount Carmel as just beneath *El-Mohhraka* (the place of the Burning). . . . Two hundred and fifty feet beneath the altar plateau is a vaulted and very abundant fountain, built in the form of a tank, with a

few steps leading down into it, just as one finds elsewhere in the
old wells or springs of the Jewish times. Possibly the water of this
spring may have been consecrated to the Lord, so as not to be
generally accessible to the people even in times of fearful
droughts. In such springs the water remains always cool, under the
shade of a vaulted roof, and with no hot atmosphere to evaporate
it. While all other fountains were dried up, I can well understand
that there might have been found here that superabundance of
water which Elijah poured so profusely over the altar. . . . On the
west and north-west sides of the position of El-Mohhrakah the
view of the sea is quite intercepted by an adjacent height. That
height, however, may be ascended in a few minutes, and a full
view of the sea obtained from the top."

22.—THE SAMARITAN MODE OF OBSERVING
THE PASSOVER.
Exodus xii. 8.

℆ Dean Stanley witnessed the celebration of the passover on
Mount Gerizim, in April, 1862, and his description is of exceeding
interest. The travellers ascended Gerizim, and on arrival at the
rocky platform, found the whole Samaritan community of 152
persons encamped in tents, a few hundred yards below the summit. The women were shut in the tents; fifteen of the men, with
the priest Amram, were clothed in long white robes, but their feet
were bare. "Presently there appeared among the worshippers six
sheep, driven by six youths dressed in white shirts and drawers.
The sun, which had hitherto burnished the Mediterranean, now
sank to the ridge overhanging Sharon. The whole history of the
Exodus, from the plagues of Egypt, was then furiously chanted.
The setting sun touched the ridge (the passover was to be
sacrificed at the going down of the sun, Deut. xvi. 6), the youths
with a wild murmur drew forth long bright knives, and brandished
them aloft; the sheep were thrown on their backs, the knives rapidly drawn across their throats; a few convulsive, silent struggles,
'as a sheep, dumb, that openeth not his mouth,' and the six forms
lay lifeless on the ground, the blood streaming from them, the one
only Israelitish sacrifice lingering in the world.

"Two holes had been dug upon the mountain, and in one a fire
was kindled with dry heath and briars, such as are named in
Jotham's parable, uttered not far from this very spot. On this fire

two cauldrons of water were heated, while bitter herbs were handed round, wrapped in a strip of unleavened bread (Ex. xii. 8). The water, boiling, was poured over the sheep by the youths, and their fleeces plucked off. Certain parts of the animals were then thrown aside and burnt, and they were afterwards spitted, each on a long pole, at the bottom of which was a transverse stick to prevent the body from slipping off. In this act, Justin Martyr, in the second century, had seen the likeness of the Crucifixion. The sheep were then carried to the second circular pit, with a fire kindled at the bottom, and roasted together in this oven, by stuffing them in vertically and carefully head downwards. A hurdle was then placed over the mouth, covered with bushes and wet earth, to keep in the heat till the meat was done.

"Five hours or more now elapsed in silence, and most of the party retired to rest. The whole male community then gathered round the oven's mouth, the covering of the hole was torn off, and there rose into the still moonlight sky a vast column of smoke and steam. The six sheep were dragged on their spits and laid in a line between two files of Samaritans, still in white robes, but now with shoes on their feet, staves in their hands, and ropes round their waists (Ex. xii. 11). Recitation recommenced of prayer or Penta-teuch, soon as suddenly terminated by their all sitting down in Arab fashion and beginning to eat. The feast was conducted in rapid silence, as of hungry men. To the priest and women separate morsels were carried round. The remains, mats and all, were then burned on a hurdle over the hole where the water had been boiled; the ground being searched in every direction for each consecrated particle. By the early morning the whole community had de-scended from the mountain, and occupied their usual habitations in the town."

23.—ABRAHAM CALLED THE "FRIEND OF GOD."
Isaiah xli. 8.

℃ In three passages of Scripture Abraham is referred to as the Friend of God, viz., 2 Chron. xx. 7; Is. xli. 8; James ii. 23. The Mohammedans also, in agreement with Scripture, call Abraham the Friend of God, or simply, The Friend; and respecting him they tell the following story, which is not without interest:—

"Abraham, in a time of dearth, sent to a friend of his in Egypt for a supply of corn; but the friend excused himself, saying that, though there was a famine in their country also, yet, had it been for Abraham's own family, he would have sent what he desired; but he knew that he wanted it only to entertain his guests, and give away to the poor, according to his usual hospitality. The servants whom Abraham sent on this message, being ashamed to return empty, to conceal the matter from their neighbours, filled their sacks with fine white sand, which pretty much resembled meal. Abraham being informed by his servants, on their return, of their ill success, the concern he was in threw him into a deep sleep. And, in the meantime, Sarah, knowing nothing of what had happened, opening one of the sacks, found good flour in it, and immediately set about making bread. Abraham, awaking, and perceiving the smell of new bread, asked her whence she had the flour. 'Why,' said she, 'from your friend in Egypt.' 'Nay,' replied the patriarch, 'it must have come from no other than my Friend, God Almighty.' "

24.—WHAT IS CAMPHIRE?
Canticles iv. 13.

℃ The tree, bush, or substance here referred to, and translated *camphire,* is called in Hebrew, *copher;* and is the plant known in Arabia as *henna*. It is worthy of notice that the people in Nubia call the plant *kophreh,* a name almost identical with the Hebrew. The leaves of the plant are pounded, and made into a paste with water. The Egyptians bind this paste upon the nails of both their hands and feet, and keep it on all night. This gives their nails the yellow colour so much admired among the Orientals. One application of the colour will serve for two or three weeks. The custom of thus colouring the nails must be very ancient in Egypt, for it is said that mummies are yet found with their nails so dyed. From this fact it also appears that the dye is exceedingly permanent. It is further said that women dye their bosoms with henna-juice by applying the pressed leaves to the skin. This fact may explain Cant. i. 13, especially if *it* be substituted for *he.* Another explanation is equally probable; the blossoms of the henna are very fragrant, and for the sake of the odour, it is said, women are accustomed to place a handful in their bosoms.

The *henna* is a shrub rising five or six feet high, with fragrant whitish flowers growing in clusters (*Lawsonia alba*).

25.—The Father's Sins Visited Upon the Children.
Exodus xx. 5.

⟪ A recent writer points out that the word used in the original Hebrew is not *chatah*, the sin of man against man, but *avon*, sin against Jehovah in the form of idolatry. The word *avon* (including the sense of *vanity,* idols being regarded as vain things, 1 Sam. xii. 21) is restricted in Scripture to the sins of idolatry and adultery, which is taken as the synonym of idolatry (Ezek. xxiii. 37). Those guilty of the iniquity denounced are said to be those who *hate God*, and none are regarded as hating God save those who worship idols. In Bible passages that treat of religion, the fathers are the teachers, and their children are their disciples or followers. The Hebrew shows that the Lord forbade the acknowledging of any one but Himself as God, and also the worshipping of images. And then He declared that the duration of His forbearance with perverters of religion should be limited to the fourth generation of those who might continue so long to hold the heresies and idolatries taught them by their *spiritual fathers*. To "four generations" is the space given to communities to repent in and amend in; after this period the Lord's corrective and punitive forbearance is superseded by His judgments. This explanation may be illustrated in the Divine treatment of the houses of Ahab and Jehu. We are cautioned against entertaining the idea that the punishments of a father's *personal iniquities* are laid on his children by the precise language of Deut. xxiv. 16. There is, however, a sense in which the consequences of parental wrong-doing fall on the offspring, as we plainly see in the case of the drunkard; the laws of heredity have been carefully studied during late years with many remarkable results.

The belief in the transmission of penalty to offspring was in ancient times very widely extended, as may be illustrated by the following extract from the laws of Menu, the most ancient lawgiver of the Hindoos:—

> "*Even here below an unjust man attains no felicity:*
> *Nor he whose wealth proceeds from giving false evidence:*
> *Nor he who constantly delights in mischief.*
> "*Though oppressed by penury, in consequence of his righteous dealings,*

Let him (the good man) never give his mind to unrighteousness;
For he may observe the speedy overthrow of iniquitous and
*   sinful men.*

"Iniquity committed in this world produces not fruit immediately;
But like the earth, in due season, and advancing little by little,
It eradicates the man who committed it.

"Yes, iniquity once committed fails not of producing fruit to him
*   who wrought it;*
If not in his own person, yet in his sons,
Or if not his sons, yet in his grandsons.

"He grows rich for awhile through unrighteousness;
Then he beholds good things; then it is that he vanquishes his
*   fear;*
But he perisheth at length from his root upwards."

26.—EARLY PICTURES AND MOSAICS
OF ST. PETER AND ST. PAUL.
Acts xv. 7, 12.

❡ St. Peter is represented as a robust old man, with a broad fore-head, and rather coarse features, an open, undaunted countenance, short grey hair, and short thick beard, curled, and of a silvery white. Paul is represented as a man of small and meagre stature, with an aquiline nose and sparkling eyes: in the Greek type the face is long and oval, the forehead high and bald; the hair brown, the beard long, flowing and pointed.

These traditional characteristic types of the features and person of the two greatest Apostles were long adhered to. We find them most strictly followed in the old Greek mosaics, in the early Christian sculpture, and the early pictures, in all of which the sturdy dignity and broad rustic features of St. Peter, and the elegant contemplative head of St. Paul, who looks like a Greek philosopher, form a most interesting and suggestive contrast.

27.—PREVENT.
1 Thess. iv. 15.

❡ The word "prevent" is used in our English Bible as meaning *to go before*. "The God of my mercy shall prevent me;" "In the morning shall my prayer prevent thee." But the word is now commonly understood as meaning *to hinder*. It is not strange that that which is in advance has come to be spoken of as a hindrance. The

men who are before us on the street, going the same way we
travel, are commonly more of an obstacle to our progress than are
those who are going in an opposite direction. So in approaching
any public building, where it is for the time a centre of attraction,
those who go before us hinder us; they prevent us. So also in
many a work of Christian usefulness, those who are just in advance of us keep us back; not in every case because they cannot
move more rapidly, but because they do not. They move slowly, if
at all, and their delay hinders us in our best efforts at progress. It
may be said of very many who *prevent* religious activities in the
Church, in the Sunday-school, or in the community, by occupying
a foremost place and failing to move forward, "Ye entered not in
yourselves, and them that were entering in ye hindered."

28.—MOSLEM RULES RESPECTING SALUTATIONS.
illustrating Ruth ii. 4.

⚏ The salutations exchanged between Boaz and his reapers show
the simple courtesy of the ancient people, and indicate relations
between masters and servants which seem to have altogether
passed away.

Among the Moslems the salutation, "Peace be to you" (with the
response, "To thee be peace, and the mercy of God, and His blessing"), is used by all classes, and belongs to the courtesy of common life. Kitto gives the following account of the rules regulating
Moslem salutations:—

"We find in the Mohammedan books that the Jews of Arabia in
Mohammed's time always used a different salutation to Moslems
from that which was in use among themselves, often changing it
into a malediction. Hence Mohammed directs, 'When a Jew makes
a salaam to you, and he says *Al-sámo âlaica* (which sounds like
Al-salámo alaica; but the substituted word *sámo,* means May you
die), then do you answer, *O-alaica* (Be the same to you).' When a
Moslem discovers that he has inadvertently given the salutation of
peace to one not a Moslem, he usually revokes the salutation, saying, 'Peace be on *us,* and on the right worshippers of God.' The
giving of it by one Moslem to another is a duty, but one that may
be omitted without sin, though the returning of another's salutation is absolutely obligatory. The chief rules given by Mohammed
are—the person riding is to salute first him who is on foot; and he
who passes by, the persons who are sitting down or standing still;

28.—Moslem Rules respecting Salutations.

and a small party, or one belonging to such a party, should give
the salutation to a large party, and the young to the aged. These
rules are irrespective of the social difference between the persons.
The Orientals have modes of indicating such differences; but not
in the salutation of peace, which is the same for all. We have before us a book of the acts and sayings of Mohammed, as reported
by his associates, from which one or two illustrations of his own
views and practice, which regulate those of his followers, may be
drawn. A man asked his Majesty, 'What quality is the best of a
Mussulman?' He said, 'Giving food to others, and returning the
salutation of acquaintance or strangers.' Anas said, 'Verily, his
Majesty passed by some boys and made a salaam to them.' The
Khalif Ali reports that he heard Mohammed say, 'There are six
duties from one Mussulman to another—to salute each other when
they meet; to accept each other's invitations to dinner; to say, God
have mercy upon you, after sneezing; to visit the sick; to follow
each other's biers when dead, and for one Mussulman to wish for
another what he wishes for himself.' Jabir reports, 'Verily, his
Highness passed by a party of women and made a salaam to
them;' but on this the commentators add, 'This practice was peculiar to his Highness; for it is bad for a man to make a salaam to a
strange woman, or a woman to a strange man, unless it be an old
woman.' Abuhurairah reports that he heard Mohammed say, 'You
will not enter into Paradise until you believe, and you will not
complete your faith until you love one another, and that is shown
by making salaam to friends and strangers.' "

Eastern travellers speak of hearing among peasants in the fields
now, the identical words used by Boaz and his reapers. When a
master enters his harvest-field, he says, *Ullah makum* (God be
with you), and the uniform response from the reapers is, *Ullah
yubarekek* (God bless thee).

29.—THE KINDS OF CUSTODY RECOGNISED
BY ROMAN LAW.
Acts xxiv. 23.

℅ A Roman governor or judge was bound to permit no longer
delay than was absolutely necessary in the trial of a prisoner after
his arrest; but it was at his discretion to fix the time and place, and
also to settle in what form of custody the prisoner should be de-
tained. Roman law recognised three forms. 1. The prisoner might

be confined in the public gaol (*custodia publica*); this was the most severe kind, the common gaols being loathsome dungeons, where the prisoners were kept in chains, or even bound in positions of torture. We have an illustration of this kind of custody in the treatment of Paul and Silas at Philippi. 2. The prisoner might have some well-known person made responsible for his appearance when called on. This is like our liberation on bail, and was called free custody (*custodia libera*); but this kind of detention was reserved exclusively for men of high rank. 3. The prisoner might be committed to the charge of a soldier, who was responsible with his own life for the safe keeping of his prisoner. This was called military custody (*custodia militaris*), and was introduced at the beginning of the Imperial age. The prisoner was secured by a species of handcuff, a chain attaching the prisoner's right hand to the soldier's left. The soldiers would relieve one another, and the prisoner would live with them in their guard-room, or barracks, but in some cases a private house was allowed. To this species of custody the Apostle Paul was subjected at Cesarea.

30.—SHISHAK.
1 Kings xiv. 25.

⁋ The reign of this monarch, Sheshenk or Sheshonk of the Egyptian monuments, offers the earliest *data* for ascertaining the comparative chronology of the Hebrew monarchs. The first year of Shishak corresponds to the twenty-sixth of Solomon, and therefore the fifth year of Rehoboam would fall in about the twentieth of Shishak. The expeditions of this king are sculptured on the wall of the great temple of El Karnak, Shishak being depicted as leading to the god a train of captives with shields on their breasts containing the names of their respective nations. "Amongst these the student can readily recognise certain well-known Scripture names, which have been read as follows: 'Land of *Mahanna*,' which Rosellini considers to be the *Mahanaim* of Gen. xxxii. 2, an ancient city belonging to the tribe of Gad; 'land of *Baitaurhia*,' supposed to be the same as the two *Bethhorons*, which Solomon fortified, according to 2 Chron. viii. 5; 'land of *Maktu*,' interpreted as the *Megiddo* of 2 Kings xxiii. 29, where three centuries later Josiah, king of Judah, was defeated by another king of Egypt, who is mentioned as Pharaoh Necho. The fourth and most interesting name which the genius of Champollion detected is that of the

KINGDOM OF JUDAH, commonly but erroneously read as *Judah Melek*, which could only be rendered literally as Judah king, whereas the final hieroglyph, being the determination of a country, proves beyond all doubt that it means, not the reigning king, but the *kingdom* of Judah, which Pharaoh Shishak boasted of having subdued, and which exactly harmonises with what Scripture records concerning his capture of Jerusalem."

31.—THE SIGN OF THE LITTLE CLOUD
LIKE A MAN'S HAND.
1 Kings xviii. 44.

℃ To the Eastern, habituated to the signs of the sky, such a little cloud was the trustworthy token of approaching storm and rain; and in the Mediterranean such storms advance with great rapidity. Dr. Kitto gives the following very remarkable illustration:—

"One of the most graphic descriptions of such a sudden storm is given by Mr. Emerson, in his letters from the Aegean. He is at sea in a Greek vessel in the Levant. One morning, which had opened clear and beautiful, it was announced that a squall might be expected. No sign recognisable by European landsmen appeared; but, on attention being properly directed, 'a little black cloud' was seen on the verge of the horizon, towards the south, which was every instant spreading rapidly over the face of the sky, and drawing nearer and nearer to the vessel. Order was immediately given to strike sail, and to prepare the vessel for scudding before the hurricane. But scarcely an instant had elapsed ere the squall was upon us, and all grew black around; the wind came rushing and crisping over the water, and in a moment the ship was running almost gunwale down, while the rain was dashing in torrents on the deck. As quick as thought the foresail was torn from the yards, and as the gust rushed through the rigging, the sheets and ropes were snapping and cracking with a fearful noise. The crew, however, accustomed to such sudden visitants, were not slow in reefing the necessary sails, trimming the rigging, and bringing back the vessel to a proper course, and in about a quarter of an hour, or even less, the hurricane had all passed away; the sun burst out through the clouds that swept in its impetuous train; the wind sunk to its former gentleness, and all was once more at peace, with the exception of the agitated sea, that continued for the remainder of the day rough and billowy. To this Mr. Emerson adds the interesting fact that it is mainly the dread of

such sudden bourasques as the present that compels almost every
vessel in the Levant to shorten sail at the close of the day, since
in cloudy weather it would be next to impossible during the night
to discern the cloud which announces the approach of the tempest,
in time to prepare for its reception, and to a ship with all her
canvas spread, the effect might be terrific."

32.—THE USE OF THE SHOE IN CONNECTION
WITH MARRIAGE CUSTOMS.
Ruth iv. 7, 8.

℀ In a work, partly dealing with the custom of the Jews in Bar-
bary—Urquhart's *Pillars of Hercules*—occurs the following passage: "At a Jewish marriage I was standing beside the bridegroom
when the bride entered; and, as she crossed the threshold, *he
stooped down and slipped off his shoe,* and struck her with the
heel on the nape of the neck. I at once saw the interpretation of
the passage in Scripture respecting the transfer of the shoe to another, in case the brother-in-law did not exercise his privilege. The
slipper, being taken off indoors, or if not, left outside the apartment, is placed at the edge of the small carpets on which you sit,
and is at hand to administer correction, and is here used in sign of
the obedience of the wife and the supremacy of the husband. The
Highland custom is to strike for 'good luck,' as they say, the bride
with an old slipper. Little do they suspect the meaning implied.
The regalia of Morocco is enriched with a pair of embroidered
slippers, which are, or used to be, carried before the Sultan, as
among us the sceptre and sword of state."

S. Cox explains the transfer of the shoe in the passage above indicated thus: "As a symbol and attestation that he cedes all right
to the inheritance, he draws off his shoe and hands it to Boaz,
transferring to *him* the legal right to plant his foot on the parcel of
land left by Elimelech."

33.—JACOB'S BOWING HIMSELF
UPON THE BED'S HEAD.
Gen. xlvii. 31.

℀ The author of the Epistle to the Hebrews, referring to this act
of the aged patriarch, says that Jacob "worshipped, leaning upon
the top of his staff" (Heb. xi. 21). A *bed* and a *staff* are very

different things; and it would seem that one of the passages must be wrong as they now stand. The Hebrew word *matteh* signifies a stick, a rod, a staff, a sceptre; but *mittah* means a bolster, a bed, or a bier. The consonants of the two words are the same, and as the original Hebrew was read without marks for the vowels, it is probable that the one word has been put for the other, *matteh* for *mittah,* and hence the mistake of representing Jacob as bowing upon the "bed's head." Most likely, "bowed upon," or "bent over the tip of his staff," is the real meaning.

But the reference to the staff, and the significancy of Jacob's act, need to be explained. The following suggestion is worthy of consideration, though many may prefer to think that the staff which accompanied Jacob through all his wanderings is the staff on which in his feebleness he leaned; probably, seated in his chair, and leaning both hands on the staff, held thus between his knees, and bowing his head almost on his hands.

The staff was however, possibly, a sceptre, and not Jacob's, but Joseph's. For Joseph, though Jacob's son, was practically the King of Egypt, and when he visited his father it is not at all likely that his visits were private and unceremonious. He would be more likely to go *in state,* followed by his retinue, and accompanied by the insignia of his office. On the occasion referred to Jacob was old, and anticipating his speedy dissolution: in those circumstances he exacted an oath from Joseph that he would bury him in Canaan. In this transaction Joseph acted as much in the capacity of Egypt's ruler, as in that of Jacob's son; and in accepting the responsibility, and in pledging himself to the performance of the duty, he did to his father as he would have done to any other man,—stretched out his sceptre in token of good faith, and in confirmation of the oath; and Jacob bowed and touched the tip of the sceptre, to signify his entire satisfaction with a promise thus royally given.

It will be remembered that when Queen Esther ventured into the presence of Ahasuerus, to entreat him to save her doomed countrymen, the king extended his sceptre, and Esther went forward, and touched its tip. Probably the action of Jacob and that of Esther were identical, and both appear to have implied an act of homage. Joseph's dream (Gen. xxxvii. 10, 11) had long before indicated that Jacob should bow down to his favourite son; and it appears that his action on the above occasion was that dream's fulfilment.

34.—THE AGAPAE, OR COMMON FEASTS, IN THE EARLY CHURCH.
Acts ii. 42.

℀ The custom of meeting at fixed seasons for partaking of a common meal, as brethren, should be distinguished from the observance of the Lord's Supper, which was probably connected with such feasting times. We have no description of these meals, as they were conducted by the Apostles themselves, and the name Agapae was not attached to them until the close of the Apostolic age. The modes in which they were then arranged will, however, indicate their character as presided over by the Apostles, if we make some allowance for the growth of formalities and tendency to add to ceremonials.

The Christians of a given town or district came together on a fixed day, probably the first day of the week, in some large room, either hired or lent by some wealthy Christian. The materials of the meal varied according to the feeling or wealth of the society. Bread and wine were essential, because used in that more solemn commemorative act which came at some period in the service. But they provided also meat, poultry, cheese, milk, and honey; and early paintings in the Catacombs of Rome indicate that fish was also used. If the feast was of this kind we can well understand how gluttony and drunkenness became associated with it, and called forth the indignant reproaches of the Apostle Paul (1 Cor. xi. 20–22). The cost of the meal fell chiefly on the richer members of the church, but it is probable that each person was expected to bring his contribution in money or in food. The women and men were seated at different tables, perhaps on opposite sides of the room, and all waited until the presbyter or bishop pronounced the blessing. Then they ate and drank. At some time during the meal, one loaf was passed round, and one cup, the cup of blessing, and of these all partook. Then they washed their hands, and the more devotional part of the evening began. Reports from district churches were read, those having gifts expounded, collections were made for the poor, and with the kiss of charity the evening closed. Such meetings were designed to be a witness and bond of the common brotherhood of Christians; and their likeness to our modern tea-meetings will immediately appear.

35.—A Covenant of Salt.

35.—A COVENANT OF SALT.
Num. xviii. 19.

¶ "A covenant of salt" was intended to be perpetual and inviolable; and the term refers to an extremely ancient eastern custom,
which must have been observed over a very large portion of the
old world. Baron du Tott, who travelled in Turkey in the last century, gives an account of a "covenant of salt," in which he was
one of the parties. He relates, Moldovanji Pacha "was desirous of
an acquaintance with me, and seeming to regret that his business
would not permit him to stay long (when he called to see me), he
departed, promising in a short time to return. I had already attended him half way down the staircase, when stopping, and turning briskly to one of my (Turkish) domestics who followed me,
'Bring me directly,' said he, 'some bread and salt.' I was not less
surprised at his fancy, than at the haste which was made (by the
servant) to obey him. What he requested was brought, when, taking a little salt between his fingers, and putting it with a mysterious air on a bit of the bread, he ate it with a devout gravity, assur-
ing me that I might now rely on him." Unfortunately the same
pacha violated his "covenant of salt," though the Turks think it
the blackest ingratitude to forget the man from whom you have
received food.

Another story is told of Jacomb Ben Luith, founder of a dynasty
of Persian kings. He was of low extraction, and made himself no-
torious as the fearless leader of a large band of robbers. Among
other daring exploits, he entered the palace of the prince, and
collected a large quantity of booty; but before removing it his foot
struck against some substance in his path, which he imagined to be
something of value. The better to ascertain its character, he put it
to his mouth, and found to his chagrin that it was *salt*. He had
tasted the prince's salt, and however accidentally it might have
been done, superstition told him that he had now entered into a
"covenant of salt" with the prince. He refused to remove the
booty, though at the risk of offending his comrades. Some time
after he told the prince the whole story, and in consequence he
was appointed to a command in the army; eventually making his
way even to the throne.

36.—CHRIST FIGURED AS A LAMB.
Rev. v. 6.

℃ In earlier Christian art, symbolical representations of our Saviour are found, and it was at the Trullan Council (692 A.D.) that it was decreed the Lord should no longer be pictured in churches under the form of a lamb, but in human form.

It was an ancient custom to distribute to the worshippers, on the first Sunday after Easter, particles of wax taken from the Paschal tapers, each particle being stamped with the figure of a lamb. These were burned in houses, fields, or vineyards, to secure them against evil influence or thunder-strokes.

A waxen *Agnus Dei* is said to have been among the presents made by Gregory the Great to Theodelinda, Queen of the Lombards, but proof of this is wanting. One was found in 1725 A.D., in the Church of San Clemente, on the Canlian Hill at Rome, in a tomb supposed to be that of Flavius Clemens, a martyr.

A legend preserved by Robert of Mount St. Michael tells how, in the year 1183, the Holy Virgin appeared to a woodman at work in a forest, and gave him a medal bearing her own image and that of her son, with the inscription, *Agnus Dei, qui tollis peccata mundi, Dona nobis pacem*. This she bade him bear to the bishop, and tell him that all who wished the peace of the Church should make such medals as these, and wear them in token of peace.

The sentiments properly connected with this symbol of Christ are well indicated in the prayer of the English Church Litany: "O, Lamb of God, that takest away the sins of the world, Grant us Thy peace."

37.—THE BURNT-OFFERING.
Gen. xxii. 7, etc.

℃ This kind is known as the *whole-offering,* or can also be named the *splendour,* or more exactly the *glow*-offering, and Luther not improperly called it the *brand-opfer*. In this, man's share in the consumption of the offering, being connected with sensuality, altogether vanished. The sacrificer consecrated to the Deity alone the enjoyment of the whole, and this not to punish himself, or because he was punished, on account of a special consciousness of guilt, by deprivation of sensuous participation, but rather from free resolve and purest self-denial. The reciprocity, which originally existed at every offering of food, here totally disappears, inasmuch as man voluntarily withdraws his claim for sensuous participation, and consecrates to God alone that of which he might himself partake. Yet his entreaty for Divine favour is now all the purer, his soul bent more exclusively on spiritual nourishment, and his hopes stronger of winning the Divine favour. The whole-offering had no further aim than just to win the Divine favour and reconciliation generally, apart from special circumstances; but this it sought all the more strongly and intensely, with all the energy of which the once-existing sacrificial system of the Old Testament was capable.

38.—THE FORM OF THE MOHAMMEDAN TRADITION CONCERNING JOB.
Job xlii. 10.

℄ Respecting the patriarch Job, the Mohammedans have a tradition, evidently founded on the Bible narrative, but in several particulars curiously and fancifully amplified. They say that after Job's property and children had been all reft from him he was afflicted with a filthy disease, his body being full of worms, and so offensive, that as he lay on the dunghill none could bear to come near him: that his wife (whom some of them call *Rahmat*, the daughter of Ephraim, the son of Joseph, though others say she was *Makhir*, the daughter of Manasseh) attended him with great patience, supporting him by what she earned with her own labour; but that the devil, appearing to her one day, after reminding her of her past prosperity, promised, if she would worship him, to restore all they had lost. She asked Job's consent to close this bargain; but he was so angry at the proposal that he swore, if he recovered, to give his wife a hundred stripes. At length Job uttered this prayer, "Verily, evil hath afflicted me: but Thou (meaning the Lord) art the most merciful of those that show mercy." Immediately God sent Gabriel, who, taking the patriarch by the hand, raised him up; at the same time a fountain sprang up at his feet, at which, having drunk, the worms fell off his body, and washing therein he recovered his former health and beauty. God also restored unto him twice as much as he had lost; his wife also became young again, and in course of time bore him twenty-six sons. To satisfy his oath God directed Job to take a palm-branch having 100 leaves, and with this to strike his wife a blow, or 100 blows at once. To express the vast amount of Job's riches, after his restora-

38.—The Form of the Mohammedan Tradition concerning
Job.

tion, some of the Easterns say that he had two threshing-floors, one for wheat, the other for barley; and that God sent two clouds, which rained gold on the one threshing-floor and silver on the other, until they ran over.

39.—PRE-CHRISTIAN CROSSES.
Matt. xvi. 24.

℧ Our Lord referred to the cross, as a well-known symbol, before He consecrated it by suffering upon it. "It is not remarkable that this, perhaps simplest of all geometrical figures, should have attracted the notice of many diverse and ancient races, and even have been regarded as a sign of potent mystical meaning. This subject has been treated with a good deal of fantastic theory by S. Baring-Gould, M.A., more philosophically by Creuzer, and by various travellers and observers of ancient remains in many lands. Sir Robert Ker Porter mentions the hieroglyph of a cross, accompanied by cuneiform inscriptions, which he saw on a stone among the ruins of Susa. Prescott mentions its occurrence among the objects of worship in the idol temples of Anahuac, in Mexico. It was found on the temple of Serapis, at Alexandria, which fact was urged by the pagan priests to induce Theodosius not to destroy that building. It was probably a Nilometer, or, perhaps, the so-called 'Key of the Nile,' frequently held in the hand of Egyptian deities as the emblem of life, or the symbol of Venus, probably of Phallic significance. It is found also on Babylonian cylinders, on Phoenician and Etruscan remains, and among the Brahminical and Buddhist antiquities of India and China. It was also the sign of the Hammer of Thor, by which he smote the great serpent of the Scandinavian mythology. On rather slender evidence S. Baring-Gould attributes its use to the prehistoric lake-dwellers of Switzerland. It was also found, he asserts, combined with certain ichthyic representations, in a mosaic floor of pre-Christian date, near Pau, in France, in 1850. This example was probably post-Christian."

40.—SITUATION OF BABYLON.
Isa. xiii. 19.

℧ "Of all the seats of empire—of all the cities that the pride or power of man has built on the surface of the globe—Babylon was the greatest. Its greatness, as it was originated, so in large measure

was secured, by its natural position. Its founders took advantage of
the huge spur of tertiary rock which projects itself from the long
inclined plane of the Syrian desert into the alluvial basin of
Mesopotamia, thus furnishing a dry and solid platform on which a
flourishing city might rest, whilst it was defended on the south by
the vast morass or lake, if not estuary, extending in that remote
period from the Persian Gulf. On this vantage-ground it stood, exactly crossing the line of traffic between the Mediterranean coasts
and the Iranian mountains; just, also, on that point where the
Euphrates, sinking into a deeper bed, changes from a vast expanse
into a navigable river, not wider than the Thames, at London,
where, also, out of the deep rich alluvial clay it was easy to dig the
bricks, which from its earliest date, came floating down the river
from the springs in its upper course. Babylon was the greatest of
that class of cities which belong almost exclusively to the primeval
history of mankind; 'the cities,' as they are called by Hegel, 'of the
river-plains,' which have risen on the level banks of the mighty
streams of Egypt, Mesopotamia, India, and China, and thus stand
in the most striking contrast to the towns which belong to the second stage of human civilisation, clustering each on its Acropolis,
or its Seven Hills, and thus contracted and concentrated by the necessities of their local position as obviously as those older capitals
possessed from their situation an illimitable power of expansion."

41.—SENTIMENT CONCERNING THE BLOOD.
Gen. ix. 4.

℅ "The warm blood of men and of quadrupeds and birds seemed
to contain the very soul or life of the living earthly creature—to
be almost identical with its soul. The Book of Origins hardly
knows how to put this sufficiently strongly in the passages devoted
to it. Now when the life and the soul were held to be something
sacred, and the more tender feelings of certain nations took this
view very early, it would follow that the blood too must be considered a sacred thing, and be regarded quite differently from the rest
of the body. The sight of that which was held to be the soul itself,
carried the mind immediately to thoughts of God, placed directly
before it something full of mystery, and filled it with that immeas-
urably profound awe which overpowers man whenever he sees any
rent in the veil between him and the Divine. In accordance with
such feelings, blood could be scarcely touched, still less eaten, by

pious men; and ancient Jahveism impressed its immunity in every way as deeply as possible. Even the inviolability of human life received support from the sanctity of the blood. To taste the minutest portion of animal blood was something horrible; even the blood of such animals as were allowed for eating, but not for sacrifice, was to be poured 'like water' upon the ground, and covered over with earth."

42.—A Tradition accounting for Moses' Slowness of Speech.
Exodus iv. 10.

℃ The way in which the Jews account for the defective oratorical powers of Moses is ingenious. They say that when Moses was an infant in the court of Egypt, Pharaoh was one day carrying him in his arms, when the child suddenly laid hold of the king's beard, and plucked it very roughly. At this Pharaoh was very angry, and ordered the child to be killed. The Queen, however, interfered, representing to the King that the child was so young, he could not have known what he was doing, that, indeed, he could not distinguish a burning coal from a ruby. Pharaoh ordered the experiment to be tried, and when the ruby and the burning coal were placed before him, Moses took up the coal, and, childlike, placed it in his mouth, and burnt his tongue. This procured his pardon, but it caused the impediment in his speech in after years.

43.—The Disgrace of the Cross.
Gal. v. 11.

℃ "In the earliest ages of the Church the cross was the badge of infamy and sign of shame—the punishment of the basest of slaves and the vilest of malefactors. It was regarded with a loathing and abhorrence more intense than that in which the felon's gibbet is held to-day. Its very name was an abomination to Roman ears, and it was denounced by the prince of Roman orators as a most foul and brutal punishment, an infamous and unhappy tree. Hence this Christian emblem became the object of scoffing and derision by the persecuting heathen. An illustration of this is seen in the blasphemous caricature of the Crucifixion, found upon the walls of the palace of the Caesars, and attributed to the time of Septimus Severus. It represents a figure with an ass's head attached to a

cross, which another figure, standing near, salutes by kissing the
hand, or adores in the classical sense of the word. Beneath is a
rude scrawl, which has been interpreted thus: 'Alexomenos wor-
ships his god;' probably the sneer of some Roman legionary at a
Christian soldier of Caesar's household. Lucian also contemptuously speaks of our Lord as a 'crucified impostor.' "

44.—RECENT INFORMATION ABOUT THE RIVER JORDAN.
Gen. xiii. 11.

⟪ We are indebted to the Palestine Exploration Society for the
following complete account of the most interesting of Bible rivers:—
"The Jordan is formed by the junction of three streams—the
Hasbany, the Leddan, and the Banias; the first, issuing from a
large fountain near Hasbeya, on the western slopes of Anti-
Lebanon, at an altitude of 1,700 feet above the level of the sea,
runs down the mountain glen of Wady-et-Teim to the plain of El
Huleh, cutting for itself a deep chasm in the rock; the second
flows from the fountain at Tell-el-Kady, 701 feet above the sea;
and the third derives its supply of water from the springs which
well up at the foot of a mound in front of the great cavern at
Banias, at the base of Mount Hermon, and 1,140 feet above the
sea. The three streams run together at the lower end of the plain
El Huleh, and shortly afterwards the Jordan loses itself in a
morass, and spreads out into the lake El Huleh, the 'waters of
Merom' of the Bible: this lake is four and a quarter miles long,
two and three quarter miles wide, and 373 feet above the sea. For
two miles after leaving the lake the river runs with a sluggish current, but it then enters a narrow gorge, with high and somewhat
precipitous hills on either side, and for the next nine miles is a
foaming torrent descending nearly 900 feet to the level of the Sea
of Galilee, which lies 626 feet below the Mediterranean. The Sea
of Galilee is a pear-shaped sheet of water, the broad end being towards the north; the greatest width is six and three-quarter miles,
and the extreme length twelve and a quarter miles; the lake is almost surrounded by hills, from 1,000 to 1,500 feet high, that occasionally recede from the shore, giving place to small plains, one of
which is the plain of Gennesareth. Between the Sea of Galilee and
the Dead Sea, a distance of 66 miles, the Jordan valley, or, as it is
here called, the 'Ghor,' is from one to twelve miles wide; the valley is in some places exceedingly fertile, in others perfectly barren;

it is bounded on the west by the mountain system of Palestine, and towards the sun-rising by the edge of the great eastern plateau. The river descends with innumerable windings through a lower valley of its own, from 40 to 100 feet below the level of the Ghor, and along its margin there is a belt of tropical jungle, which is frequently alluded to in the Bible as the 'excellency' or 'pride' of Jordan, usually in connection with the lions that were wont to dwell in it. So tortuous is the course of the river, that though the two seas are only 66 miles apart, its actual length is about 200, and in this distance there is a fall of 666 feet. The Dead Sea, which receives the waters of the Jordan, is 1,292 feet below the Mediterranean, and is about 46 miles long, its greatest width being ten and a-half miles. On the east and west the lake is shut in by the barren hills which rise abruptly from its shores, but at its southern end there is a level plain—and then the ground rises to the ridge 787 feet above the sea, which separates the waters of the Dead Sea from those of the Red Sea. The shores of the Dead Sea are generally barren, but there are not wanting little oases, the luxuriant vegetation of which has frequently called forth the admiration of travellers."

45.—FAMINES IN THE REIGN OF CLAUDIUS.
Acts xi. 28.

❡ History records *four* famines in the reign of Claudius (A.D. 54–68): no one of them, however, was general to all the world, nor even to all the Roman Empire; and one of them was almost confined to Palestine, or, at least, was more severely felt there than in other parts. The first was at Rome, in the first and second years of Claudius, and arose from the difficulties of introducing adequate supplies of corn from abroad. These difficulties were chiefly local, and remedied by making a port at the mouth of the Tiber, and a convenient passage from it to the city. The second scarcity occurred in the ninth year of Claudius, and is mentioned by Eusebius, the sole authority, as afflicting Greece only, where a modius of wheat was sold for six drachms. The cost would be 160s. the quarter at the present value of silver. This, therefore, would be a truly famine price. The third dearth was at Rome in the eleventh year of Claudius. It seems to have been of the same nature with the first. The granaries had become exhausted, while the ships which might, under ordinary circumstances, have brought from foreign ports the produce of the last harvests, were

kept away by adverse winds and weather. The fourth dearth, but
the second in time, is that which afflicted Judaea towards the end
of the fourth year of Claudius. It is mentioned by Josephus, and in
terms which would alone suggest that this was the famine which
the sacred historian had in view.

46.—ZIPPORAH'S EXCLAMATION.
Exodus iv. 24–26.

⟮ When Moses turned back to Egypt to effect Israel's deliverance, but was overtaken on his way by a dreadful sickness, and it
seemed as though Jahveh required his life, Zipporah, his first wife,
seized a sharp stone, with it cut her son's foreskin off, threw this
before the feet of the father, her husband, and upbraided him as a
bloody bridegroom (*i.e.* as a husband whom she now saw she had
married under the grievous condition of shedding her child's
blood, unless she were to lose the husband himself). But just at
that very juncture Jahveh released Moses, and the wife, full of joy
for the restoration of her husband, broke out into the altered exclamation, "a bloody bridegroom for circumcision" (*i.e.* I see now
that the blood shall involve no one's death, but only circumcision).
More clearly than is done in this brief typical narrative, the original essence of circumcision according to its most ancient
significance, cannot be described. It is a rite which cannot be performed without loss of blood, and there is, no doubt, a possibility
that the patient may die of the wound; it is, therefore, essentially a
bloody sacrifice of one's own body, difficult to render, such as man
may regard with shuddering fear. But he who has offered up to his
God this flesh of his own body and this blood, and bears circumcision on his person as a permanent token of this hardest sacrifice,
becomes thereby for the first time a man well pleasing to his God,
and may even become the Saviour of his father. Thus, the tender
mother's horror at such an offering of her son's blood turns into
peace and joy.

47.—SENNACHERIB.
2 Kings xviii. 13.

⟮ According to the inscriptions on the slabs.of a palace near
Mosul this king's name was Sennachi-riba, and he was the son and
successor of Sargon, king of Assyria. Colonel Rawlinson has suc-

ceeded in reading the entire history of this king's wars with the Jews, and he finds it to agree in a remarkable manner with the Scripture record, even to the very items of the fine Hezekiah paid to Sennacherib, viz., "three hundred talents of silver and thirty talents of gold" (2 Kings xviii. 14). The Bible narrative proceeds (v. 16), "At that time did Hezekiah cut off the gold from the doors of the temple of the Lord, and from the pillars which Hezekiah, king of Judah, had overlaid, and gave it to the king of Assyria." Instead of this the Assyrian account states that Hezekiah also gave "the ornaments of the Temple, slaves, boys and girls, and men servants and maid servants for the use of the palace." It is a striking thing to find so close an agreement between records kept in different languages, and by people in bitter hostility to each other. The Assyrian slabs call Hezekiah, Khazakiahhoo; Jerusalem, Urselimma; and Judah, Yehoodah, words which are much better representations of the original Hebrew than our English rendering of them.

48.—CURIOUS IDEA CONCERNING THE LANGUAGE OF PARADISE.
Gen. iii. 1, etc.

⁋ There is a saying in the East that when our first parents were tempted in Eden and fell from their blissful estate, the serpent, wishing to beguile Eve, addressed her in Arabic, as the best instrument of persuasive eloquence. Eve spoke to her husband in Persian, the language of tenderness and affection; and the angel Gabriel, commissioned to expel them from Paradise, after vainly addressing them in various dialects, finally succeeded in frightening them away by the use of the Tartar-Turkish.

49.—MODE OF ORIENTAL SWIMMING.
Isa. xxv. 11.

⁋ The people of the East are fond of bathing, and many of them are expert swimmers. They all swim "hand over hand," alternately raising each arm out of the water, and thus never presenting the whole breast, but only one side to the stream. The American Indians, who are generally expert swimmers, uniformly practise the Oriental mode. Among the Assyrian sculptures which represent persons in the act of swimming, we have not discovered one that gives a different testimony. This curious fact will be found to illustrate and explain several passages of Scripture, such as Isa. xxv. 11. The ultimate lifting up of each arm and bringing it down with force, well expresses the repeated blows by which Moab was to "be trodden down as straw for the dunghill."

50.—THE PHANTOM KINGS OF ISAIAH.
Isa. xiv. 9–20.

℄ The scene described in the fourteenth chapter of Isaiah, when the phantom kings rise up from their thrones to welcome the dead king of Babylon, receives illustration from the description of Hades in the sixth book of the Izdhubar epic of ancient Babylonia, in which the descent of Istar into the underground world is narrated. Hades, "the land from which there is no return," as it is called in Accadian, is stated to be "a place of darkness," "where the dwellers long for light," where dust and mud are the food of the spirits, whose "chiefs are like birds with feathers, and light is never seen." Here in darkness "sit those wearing crowns, who from the days of old ruled the earth, to whom the gods Anu and Bel have given terrible names. Their food is made carrion; they drink stagnant water." Here sit "the chiefs and unconquered ones, the bards and great men, and the monsters of the deep of the great gods. It is the seat of Etana, the seat of Ner," and other famous hero-kings of the mythical past. The whole of the 14th chapter of Isaiah is filled with allusions to Babylonian beliefs. Thus the "Mount of the Assembly [of the gods] in the extremities of the north (v. 13) is Kharsak Kurra," "the mount of the East," the Accadian Olympus which was identified with the present Mount El-wand, and regarded as the cradle of mankind. On its peak the ark of the Chaldean Noah was supposed to have rested, and it was believed to support the vault and stars of heaven. Here dwelt the gods, and temples erected in its honour were to be found in most of the Babylonian towns.

51.—THE CAVE OF MACHPELAH.
Gen. xxiii. 19, 20.

℄ Dean Stanley's eloquent description of this sacred spot cannot be too well known. "The ancestral burial place is the one fixed element in the unstable life of a nomadic race, and this was what

Hebron furnished to the patriarchs. The one spot of earth which Abraham could call his own, the pledge which he left of the perpetuity of his interest in 'the land wherein he was a stranger,' was the sepulchre which he bought for four hundred shekels of silver from Ephron, the Hittite. It was a rock with a double cave ('Machpelah'), standing amidst a grove of olives or ilexes, on the slope of the table land where the first encampment had been made. The valley above which it stood probably occupied the same position with regard to the ancient town of Hebron that the sepulchral valley of Jehoshaphat did afterwards to Jerusalem. Round this venerable cave the reverence of successive ages and religions has now raised a series of edifices which, while they preserved its identity, conceal it entirely from view. But there it still remains. Within the Mussulman mosque, within the Christian church, within the massive stone enclosure probably built by the kings of Judah, is, beyond any reasonable question, the last resting-place of Abraham and Sarah, of Isaac and Rebekah; 'and there Jacob buried Leah,' and thither, with all the pomp of funeral state, his own embalmed body was brought from the palaces of Egypt. Of all the great patriarchal family Rachel alone is absent. All that has ever been seen of the interior of the mosque is the floor of the upper chamber, containing six chests, placed there, as usual in Mussulman sepulchres, to represent the tombs of the dead. But it is said that here, as in the analogous case of the tomb of Aaron on Mount Hor, the real cave exists beneath, divided by an artificial floor into two compartments, into the upper one of which only the chief minister of the mosque is admitted to pray in times of great calamity. The lower compartment, containing the actual graves, is entirely closed, and has never been seen by anyone within the range of memory or tradition."

In 1862, the Prince of Wales, with Dean Stanley, was permitted to see the tombs in the upper chamber, and after fully describing them the Dean adds: "It may well be supposed that to this—the sacred cave itself, in which one at least of the patriarchal family may possibly repose intact, the embalmed body of Jacob—our inquiries were throughout directed. One indication alone of the cavern beneath was visible. In the interior of the mosque, at the corner of the shrine of Abraham, was a small circular hole, about eight inches across, of which one foot above the pavement was built of strong masonry, but of which the lower part, as far as we could see and feel, was of the living rock. This cavity appeared to

open into a dark space beneath, and that space (which the guardians of the mosque believe to extend under the whole platform)
can hardly be anything else than the ancient cavern of Machpelah.
This was the only aperture which the guardians recognised. . . .
The original entrance to the cave, if it is now to be found at all,
must probably be on the southern face of the hill, between the
mosque and the gallery containing the shrine of Joseph, and entirely obstructed by the ancient Jewish wall, probably built across
it for this very purpose."

52.—CHEESES.
1 Sam. xvii. 18.

⁋ Three times, in the authorised version of the Bible, the word
cheese occurs, viz., Job x. 10, 1 Sam. xvii. 18, 2 Sam. xvii. 29. In
each of these texts, however, the word is used to translate a
different Hebrew term. It is difficult to decide how far these terms
correspond with our notions of cheese, for they express merely
different degrees of coagulation. Cheese is not, even in the present
day, common among the wandering Arabs; butter being much preferred by them. But they have a substance very probably corresponding with that mentioned in the books of Samuel, consisting
of coagulated buttermilk, which is dried until it becomes quite
hard, and is then ground. The Arabs eat this kind of cheese mixed
with butter.

53.—THE DEAD SEA.
Gen. xiv. 3.

⁋ M. Lartet has brought out a magnificent work, called *Exploration Géologique de la Mer Morte,* in which he gives the results of
his exploration of the Dead Sea, conducted ten years ago, under
the auspices of the late Duc de Luynes. M. Lartet shows that the
Valley of the Jordan, including the Dead Sea, runs along a
rectilineal fracture in Cretaceous and Eocene strata, the opposite
sides of the Dead Sea consisting of different kinds of rocks, and
thus suggesting the existence of a great fault. The present basin of
the sea, however, like the Jordan valley, has been largely scooped
out by subaerial denudation. M. Lartet believes that the drainage
of the country formed a great lake in the tertiary epoch by sinking
into a local hollow. The waters of the lake were, perhaps, fresh as

first, but became salt partly by evaporation, partly from brine-
springs, and partly from deposits of salt in the neighbourhood.
The Dead Sea, consequently, never formed part of an arm of the
sea extending northward from the Gulf of Akaba, as has frequently been maintained.

54.—Egypt a Waterless Land.
Deut. viii. 7–9.

ℂ In commending Canaan to the Jews Moses forcibly dwells on
the fact that it would prove to be a "land of brooks of water, of
fountains and depths that spring out of valleys and hills." This
would be especially attractive to the Israelites after their long experience of Egypt. On the great portion of Egypt rains never descend; it is simply a narrow valley of alluvial soil, closed in on the
east and west by perfectly barren mountains and sandy plains, and
watered once in the year by the flooding of the Nile, which is skilfully led by canals and ditches through the land. No springs appear to be found in it, because much of the country is a mere rec-
lamation from the sea by the deposits of mud periodically brought
down by the river. The only water that is drank is taken from the
river.

55.—The Measure of "Half an Acre."
1 Sam. xiv. 14.

ℂ "The standard measure of land throughout the Turkish empire
is called a *deunum,* and is the area which one pair of oxen can
plow in a single day; it is equal to a quarter of an acre, or a
square of forty *arshuns* (nearly one hundred feet). The expression
in the above text would be better rendered, within the space of
half a *deunum* of land."

56.—Whales in the Mediterranean.
Matt. xii. 40.

ℂ A large whale was lately stranded on the beach near Tyre, in
Syria, and the skeleton will most likely find its way to the cabinet
of the Syrian Protestant College at Beirût. This disposes effectually
of the question so often discussed with reference to the Book of
Jonah—*i.e.,* whether there be whales in the Mediterranean; though

the officers of the steamers that ply between Marseilles and Alexandria will tell the inquirer that whales are well known in that sea.

57.—SHIBBOLETH. SIBBOLETH.
Judges xii. 6.

¶ The peculiarities in the pronunciation of the common language of these Ephraimites and Gileadites did not concern this word Shibboleth alone, but the Ephraimites selected a term which they knew would test the physical peculiarity of utterance which characterised the Gileadites. So the Scotchman will test the Englishman by asking him to pronounce a word having the *ch* sound, such as *loch,* or *Auchtermuchty;* and the Englishman will test the Frenchman by requiring from him the *th* sound, as in *theatre.* There is a modern parallel of this inability of the Gileadites, which is well known to all the people in the Levant. The Greek language does not possess the *sh* sound, though it probably exists in all the cognate dialects. Whenever, therefore, a Greek learns an Oriental language, however proficient he may become in it, he is always betrayed by his substitution of *s* for *sh*. This is true even of those Greeks who have lived for generations upon the Asiatic coast, but chiefly use their own language.

58.—SEALING INSTEAD OF SIGNING ANCIENT LETTERS.
1 Kings xxi. 8.

¶ "State documents have the name and titles of the sovereign inscribed at the top, in a peculiar style, called the 'tourah,' or imperial cipher. They are usually sealed by the Minister of State. The seal is stamped in the following manner: Some ink is placed with the pen upon the end of the little finger, and rubbed on the face of the seal; the spot on the paper which is to be stamped is then wet with the tongue, and, resting against the index fingers of the left hand, the seal is firmly pressed upon it, leaving a clear impression upon the paper. When a man has no seal, he uses the end of his finger, and pressing it upon the paper, his name is then written by the side of his mark." The seal becomes, therefore, a very important thing, and a man will never part with it except in extraordinary circumstances. It is either carried in the bosom, fastened by a cord round his neck, or to his garment, or else on the finger in the form of a signet ring.

59.—BOOTHS FOR VINEYARD-KEEPERS.
Job xxvii. 18.

❦ "The watchman's hut, lodge, or booth, for the protection of the vineyards and melon and maize fields against thieves, herds, or wild beasts, is now called either *arishe* and *mantara,* if it is only slightly put together with branches of trees; or *chême,* if it is built up high in order that the watchmen may see a great distance. The *chême* is the more frequent; at harvest it stands in the midst of the threshing floors of a district, and it is constructed in the following manner:—

"Four poles are set up so as to form the corners of a square, the sides of which are about eight feet in length. Eight feet above the ground four cross pieces of wood are tightly bound to these with cords, on which planks, if they are to be had, are laid. Here is the watcher's bed, which consists of a litter. Six or seven feet above this, cross-beams are again bound to the four poles, on which boughs, or reeds, or a mat forms a roof, from which the *chême* has its name. (The word, in one of its forms, meaning 'to be stretched over anything after the manner of a roof.') Between the roof and the bed, three sides of the *chême* are hung round with a mat, or with reeds and straw bound together, in order both to keep off the cold night winds, and also to keep the thieves in ignorance as to the number of the watchers. A small ladder frequently leads to this bed chamber. The space between the ground and this chamber is closed only on the west side to keep off the hot afternoon sun, for through the day the watcher sits below with his dog, upon the ground. Here is also his place of reception, if any passers by visit him; for, like the village shepherd, the field watcher has the right of showing a humble hospitality to any acquaintance. When the fruits have been gathered in the *chême* is removed."

60.—THE TOMB OF JOSHUA.
Joshua xxiv. 30.

❦ Concerning this tomb, Lieut. Conder (who is connected with the Palestine Exploration Fund), says, "This is certainly the most striking monument in the country, and strongly recommends itself to the mind as an authentic site. That it is the sepulchre of a man of distinction is manifest from the great number of lamp niches which cover the walls of the porch: they are over 200, arranged in vertical rows." The tomb is a square chamber, with five excavations on three of its sides, the central one forming a passage leading into a second chamber beyond. Here is a single cavity, with a niche for a lamp, and here, there is good reason to believe, is the resting-place of the warrior chief of Israel.

61.—CALUMNIES AGAINST THE EARLY CHRISTIANS.
Acts xxviii. 22.

℺ Christianity had enemies on all sides. It offended men by presenting a higher standard of purity than their own. The secrecy attending some portions of the Christian worship aroused suspicions. Other societies, heretical or fantastic, which were popularly identified with it, brought the discredit of their practices upon the Christian Church. And we know with what virulence a certain party among the Jews attacked the Christian minister and the Christian system. Paul himself had bitterly suffered from their misrepresentations and violence. It is, however, instructive to notice with some precision what the charges were that were brought against the Christians.

The Agapae, and the more sacred Supper, furnished material for some of the more horrible charges. It was said that when they met, an infant was brought in covered with flour, and then stabbed to death by a new convert, who was thus initiated in the mysteries. The others then ate the flesh, and licked up the blood. This was the sacrifice by which they were bound together.

Another charge was that the members of a Christian Church met at night, and after a certain time the lights were put out, and dreadful scenes of immorality ensued.

Their holding aloof from all temples and altars brought on them the charge of Atheism, and it was actually declared that they worshipped their God under the mysterious form of a man with an ass's head.

There was an idea prevalent concerning them that they were worshippers of the sun, which seems to have arisen from the fact that they met on the day which was more and more generally known as the *Dies Solis,* and from their speaking of Christ as the true *light,* and of themselves as the *children of light.*

"Over and above all specific charges there was the dislike which
men felt to a society so utterly unlike their own. . . . They were
guilty of treason, because they would not sacrifice for the emperors, and looked for the advent of another kingdom. They were
ignorant, rude, and uncultivated, and yet they set themselves up
above the wisest sages. They led men to a dark fatalism by ascrib-
ing to God all their power to act. They showed a defiant obstinacy
in their resistance, even to death, to the commands of civil magistrates."

These were the chief of the calumnies with which the early
Christian Apologists found it necessary to deal, during the second
and third centuries of the Christian era.

62.—RAHAB SUPPOSED TO HAVE BEEN AN INNKEEPER.
Joshua ii. 1.

⁋ Some commentators, following Josephus, and the Chaldaean
interpreters, have endeavoured to make Rahab only a keeper of a
house of entertainment for travellers; translating thus:—"The
house of a woman an innkeeper." But in the face of the parallel
passages (*e.g.* Lev. xxi. 7; Jer. v. 7), this rendering cannot be
maintained: and it is a gloss in striking contrast with the simple
straightforwardness of the writer of this book of Joshua, and in-
consistent with the Apostolic phraseology (Heb. xi. 31; Jas. ii. 25).
Rahab had hitherto been, probably, but a common type of heathen
morality, but she was faithful to the dawning convictions of a
nobler creed, and hence is commended by Christ's Apostles for
that which was meritorious in her conduct.

63.—BEGGARS AT GATES.
Acts iii. 2.

⁋ The stationing of beggars, especially maimed beggars, at the
gate of the temple, was evidently suggested by the persuasion that
the feelings of those who were proceeding to, or had been engaged
in, an act of solemn worship, would be more inclined to charity
and benevolence than at ordinary times. It is in the same calculation that at the present day the gates of the great continental
churches, as well as the approaches to Mohammedan mosques, are
thronged with beggars at the hours of prayers. We know also that
the Pharisees and others in those days bestowed much alms in the

most public places, that their ostentatious charity might be "seen
of men"; and the perception of this weakness in a class of people
so wealthy had, doubtless, considerable influence in causing the
beggars of Jerusalem to resort in large numbers to places so public, and through which the Pharisees were so continually passing,
as the gates of the temple,—these people being more constant than
others in their attendance at the sacred courts.

64.—MINGLED PEOPLE.
Jer. xxv. 24.

℃ Some explanation of these people is obtained from the inscriptions of Sennacherib. The Hebrew word rendered "mingled people" is represented in Assyrian by *Urbi*. Now, in the inscription of
Sennacherib on Bellino's cylinder, line 13, the Urbi are conjoined
with the Arameans, who we know, from other inscriptions, were
nomad tribes, inhabiting the western bank of the Euphrates. The
Urbi, therefore, would seem to have been a similar class of people.
In Sennacherib's account of his campaign against Hezekiah he says
that the Jewish king had with him in Jerusalem some Urbi, who
served as soldiers. It would appear from this that the Urbi were
nomad Arabs, distinguished from the settled Arabs of the cities,
who hired themselves out as mercenaries to the neighbouring
princes, much as the Swiss did in the last century. Hence the word
might almost be rendered "confederates"; and this must plainly be
its meaning in Jer. xxv. 20, where it probably signifies the Arab
and Greek allies of the Egyptian king.

65.—THE IDOLATRY OF JEROBOAM.
1 Kings xii. 28, 29.

℃ It is necessary to discriminate all through the history of the
Israelites between the two forms of idolatry to which at different
eras they were prone. The one was the forsaking Jehovah for "the
gods of the nations," especially Baal and Ashtoreth, the Phoenician deities. Into this fearful sin Rehoboam fell (1 Kings xiv. 23),
where the word translated "groves" denotes the image (asherah)
of the goddess Ashtoreth. Compare what is said of Solomon's later
years, ch. xi. 33. It is not certain that Jeroboam was wholly clear
from this form of paganism (ch. xiv. 15); but his chief trans-

gression was in his adopting the second form of idolatry, *i.e.* the attempt to represent the true God under material forms. Dean Stanley even says of Jeroboam that "to keep the first commandment he broke the second," doing too much honour, perhaps, to the king's good intentions. It has also been suggested that Jeroboam, while adopting the Egyptian symbol, had also in mind the cherubim in the temple at Jerusalem, where the form of "an ox" was in part employed. Two hundred years after Jeroboam's time "the calves" were still the objects of adoration in Israel (Hos. xiii. 2, viii. 5, 6). "That of Dan was carried away by Tiglath-pileser" (2 Kings xv. 29); "that of Bethel ten years afterwards by Shalmaneser" (2 Kings xvii. 5, 6).

66.—EGYPTIAN BRICK-MAKING.
Exodus i. 13, 14.

℄ Making bricks appears to have been the principal occupation of the oppressed Israelites. The use of crude bricks was general in Egypt for dwelling-houses, tombs, and ordinary buildings, walls of towns, fortresses, and the sacred enclosures of temples. Stone was used for the temples themselves, and for quays and reservoirs. Small ancient temples, however, were sometimes built of crude bricks, which were merely baked in the sun, and never burnt, in early Pharaonic times. A great number of people were employed in this extensive manufacture. It was an occupation to which many prisoners of war were condemned, who, like the Israelites, worked for the king, brick-making being a government monopoly.

The process of brick-making is represented on the monuments at Thebes, and it is rendered doubly interesting from its exact correspondence with the record in Exodus (ch. v. 7–19). These pictures show the hardness of the work, the tales of bricks, the bringing of the straw (which was chopped up, and mixed with the clay, in order to render the bricks more compact, the straw serving much the same purpose that hair does in modern mortar), and the Egyptian taskmasters set over the foreign workmen. The Theban bricks of Thothmes III., who flourished in the 15th century B.C., not many generations after the Israelitish Exodus, measured 1-ft. by 0.75 and 0.55 in thickness, and weighed 37-lbs. 10-ozs. They were frequently stamped with a king's name while making, as the

Roman burnt bricks were with the name of a god, a place, a consul, a legion, a maker, or with some other mark.

67.—HAMAN'S PLAN FOR THE DESTRUCTION
OF THE JEWS.
Esther iii. 13.

❡ The consent given by Ahasuerus to the proposal of Haman to destroy all the Jews in the empire, though a most extraordinary proceeding, has been somewhat paralleled in modern times. During a war between the Russians and Turks in 1770, some of the Greeks, whose nation had long been under the Turkish yoke, sided with the Russians. This so enraged the Sultan that he conceived the horrible design of exterminating the whole nation; and no doubt the deed, so far as practicable, would have been perpetrated but for the timely advice of Hassan Pasha, who succeeded in gaining a general amnesty for the Greeks.

68.—LOCUSTS AND WILD HONEY.
Matt. iii. 4.

❡ Major-General Bisset, C.B., in his work entitled *Sport and War in Africa,* gives an interesting illustration of the use of these as food. "About the year 1830 some of the dispersed native tribes from the interior of Africa migrated into the Cape Colony to seek employment among the farmers. My father engaged one family, consisting of a man named Job and his two wives, with seven or eight children. Soon after their arrival a flight of locusts came from the interior, and night after night, whilst the locusts settled on the earth, the whole of this family, with great sandals of ox-hide tied on to their feet (very like Canadian snow-shoes), would walk about the whole night wherever the locusts were thickest. The next day the locusts would again take wing; but where this family had been walking about all night you saw acres and acres of ground covered with swarms of disabled locusts that could not fly away, and the natives would collect them and bring them home in baskets; they would then break off the wings, pinch off the tail end of the body, and pull off the head, and withdraw the inside of the locust; thus the body and legs alone remained, the inside of the body being covered with fat. This portion of the locusts was then spread open upon mats in the sun to dry, and when dry packed away in huts raised from the ground and built on purpose. These people received a very good ration of food, yet this family preferred the bread made from these locusts to any description of food. Their mode of manipulation was as follows:—A basketful of the dried locusts would be taken from the store, and one of the women would sit down on the ground by a flat stone, and with another round stone in her two hands would grind or reduce the locust to flour, and therewith make thick cakes, and bake them on the coals or in the ashes, and eat this locust-bread with wild honey. Honey was most abundant in the country at this time, and I have seen Job, after a day's hunting, carry home leather bags full, weighing more than I could lift from the ground. Hence I believe it was thus that John the Baptist 'lived upon locusts and wild honey' in the wilderness."

69.—PARCHED CORN.
Ruth ii. 14.

℄ Dr. Robinson thus describes the use of parched corn:—"In one field, as we approached Ruheibeh, nearly two hundred reapers and gleaners were at work, the latter being nearly as numerous as the former. A few were taking their refreshment, and offered us some of their parched corn. In the season of harvest, the grains of wheat not yet fully dry and hard are roasted in a pan or on an iron plate, and constitute a very palatable article of food. This is eaten along with bread, or instead of it. Indeed, the use of it is so common at this season among the labouring classes that this parched wheat is sold in the markets. The Arabs are said to prefer it to rice; but this we did not find to be the case."

Dr. Thomson says it is made thus:—"A quantity of the best ears, not too ripe, are plucked with the stalks attached. These are tied into small parcels, a blazing fire is kindled with dry grass and thorn bushes, and the corn-heads are held in it until the chaff is mostly burned off. The grain is thus sufficiently roasted to be eaten, and it is a favourite article all over the country. After it has been roasted it is rubbed out in the hand, and eaten as there is occasion."

Dr. Kitto describes a singular custom which still exists in the Western Islands of Scotland, and is called *gradden,* from the Irish word *grad,* signifying quick. "A woman, sitting down, takes a handful of corn, holding it by the stalks in the left hand, and then sets fire to the ears, which are presently in a flame. She has a stick in her right hand, which she manages very dexterously, beating off the grain at the very instant when the husk is quite burnt; and experience has taught the people this art to perfection. The corn may be so dressed, winnowed, ground, and baked within an hour after being reaped from the ground."

70.—THE WIDE DIFFUSION OF BAAL WORSHIP.
2 Kings xvii. 16.

℠ The Baal of the Phoenicians was the Apollo of the Greeks— that is, the sun personified as a man. Baal was worshipped by other nations, as the Carthaginians, Babylonians, and Assyrians. He is supposed by some to be the same as Moloch, to whom the Ammonites made their children pass through the fire. He was also called Bell, or Belus, and the images of Baal in different places were called Baalim.

The worship of Baal is believed to have prevailed throughout Scandinavia, and among the old Gauls and Celts. Traces of it are found in customs which, until very recently, lingered in Ireland, Wales, and among the Celtic population of the north of Scotland. Two days in the year are especially marked by fire solemnities— the 1st of May and the 31st of October. In some countries there are corresponding ceremonies on nearly the same days—that is, about the middle of the year and toward its close. The record is preserved of a custom which, so late as the beginning of this century, was common in the Highlands of Scotland. On the 1st of May, which was called Beltane Day, or the day of the fire of Baal, the boys of a town assembled on a moor, and, by digging a trench, formed a round table of the green sod. A fire was kindled near, where a custard was prepared of eggs and milk, and also a cake of oatmeal, which was toasted on a stone. After eating the custard, the cake was divided into equal portions, according to the number of persons present. One of the pieces was daubed with charcoal until perfectly black. All of them were then put into a bonnet, from which every person present blindfolded drew a piece, the last falling to him who held the bonnet. Whoever drew the black bit was the one marked out to be sacrificed to Baal, in order that he

might be propitious, and multiply the fruits of the earth, that there
might be enough for man and beast.

The writer who records this custom says, "There is little doubt
of these inhuman sacrifices having been once offered in this country as well as in the East, although they now omit the act of
sacrificing, and only compel the devoted person to leap three times
through the flames; with which the ceremonies of the festival are
closed. Beltane signifies the fire of Baal; Baal, or Ball, is the only
word in Gaelic for a globe. The festival was probably in honour of
the sun, whose return in his apparent annual course they celebrated on account of his having such a visible influence, by his genial warmth, on the productions of the earth."

71.—THE ATHENIAN ALTAR TO THE UNKNOWN GOD.
Acts xvii. 23.

ℂ The following traditions have gathered round Paul's reference
to this altar.

It is said that Dionysius, the Areopagite, was at Alexandria at
the time of Christ's crucifixion. In that city he witnessed the supernatural darkness which covered the earth at the expiry of the Son
of God, and knowing it was not caused by an eclipse, Dionysius
concluded that it was the act of some god whose name he was not
acquainted with; and on his return to Athens he erected the altar
in question to the God who had suddenly wrapped the world in
darkness.

According to another tradition, when the Athenians had lost a
certain battle there appeared a spectre in the city, who informed
them that he had inflicted the calamities upon them because,
though they worshipped other gods, and celebrated games in their
honour, there was no worship paid to him. The apparition
vanished without leaving its name. The Athenians, desirous of
doing honour to all gods, erected this altar, and on it placed the
celebrated inscription.

Another story affirms that the Athenians, on one occasion, being
seized with a burning distemper which would not allow them to
endure anything on their bodies, addressed themselves in vain to
all the gods whom they had been accustomed to revere; but as
they received no relief from their known deities they erected an
altar "to the unknown God," apprehending that some strange di-

vinity had smitten them. When they recovered, of course, they attributed their cure to the deity whom they had at last done their best to propitiate.

72.—Clause Missing in the Account of Cain and Abel.
Gen. iv. 8.

⁋ The literal translation of the Hebrew text of this verse is, "And Cain said to Abel his brother; and it came to pass," etc. It appears as if a clause were wanting. Such a clause is supplied in the Samaritan text, the Targums, the Septuagint, Syriac, Vulgate, and other versions; and there can be little doubt that it is genuine, and that the verse ought to run, "And Cain said to Abel his brother, *'Let us go out into the field.'* And it came to pass," etc.

73.—Jeshurun, as a Name for the People of Israel.
Deut. xxxii. 15.

⁋ In several passages of the Old Testament the people of Israel are called Jeshurun, as Deut. xxxiii. 5, 26, Isaiah xliv. 2, where, however, by mistake it is written *Jesurun*. The name, or rather epithet, has occasioned considerable perplexity among the commentators, both ancient and modern; and its precise meaning is not yet finally and satisfactorily settled. The best explanation given is that it is a term of endearment, wherein God is supposed to call Israel His Jeshurun, or His "good little people." The word literally means *supremely happy, dearly beloved*.

74.—The Book of Enoch.
Jude 14.

⁋ One of the most curious remains of early Christian literature that have come down to us is the Apocalypse, or Book, of Enoch. Owing to the quotation from it in the Epistle of Jude, the Book of Enoch occupied a prominent place in the Early Church, and patristic literature, from Justin and Irenaeus to Augustine and Jerome, is full of references to it. Tertullian (*De cultu fem.*, I. 3) declares that the book is genuine, and contains the veritable visions and prophecies of Enoch. The Greek version has long been lost, with the exception of some fragments preserved in Syncellus; and we owe our present knowledge of the work to the Ethiopic translation, three MSS. of which were brought to Europe by Bruce, in 1773. Other MSS. have since been obtained from Abyssinia, where the book is regarded as canonical, and Dillmann has published an excellent edition of the text. Translations of the book have been made by Archbishop Lawrence, in 1821; Dr. Hoffmann, in 1833–38; Prof. Gfrörer, in 1840; and Prof. Dillmann, in 1853. It is now clear that the book is a composite one, and that (at all events, in its Ethiopic form) it is made up of two separate works —one the Revelation of Enoch, and the other the Revelation of Jonah. Whether these two works were separated from one another in the Greek version is uncertain. The Revelation of Enoch is itself the product of different authors. The main bulk of the work, describing the visit of Enoch to Paradise, and the vision of the future history of the world which was revealed to him there, was written by a Jew, about 30 B.C. The rest of the work has been proved by Hilgenfeld to have been composed by a Christian, at the beginning of the second century. It is this part of the book which has been assigned by Ewald and others to the first century B.C., and regarded as evidence that the leading conceptions and terms of Christianity were already familiar to the Jewish people before the coming of Christ. The Messiah is called "the Son of Man," "the Son of Woman," "the Light of the Nations," and "the Hope of those who are troubled in their hearts." His pre-existence is asserted, as well as His redemption of the righteous and His future judgment of the world. While the blessed state of the "assembly" of believers and of the "elect" generally is described, the everlasting punishment which awaits all unbelievers is depicted in forcible language. But all this is really the work of a Christian, and so throws no light on the popular belief previous to the birth of our Lord. The passage quoted by Jude (xiv. 15) belongs to the original of Enoch, and occurs at the very beginning of the work. In the Ethiopic version it reads thus: "And behold He cometh with ten thousands of saints to execute judgment upon them, and will destroy the ungodly and make reckoning with all flesh for all that which the sinners and the ungodly have done and committed against Him." It was in consequence of this quotation that the Apostolic Constitutions (vi. 16) deny the authenticity and canonicity of the Epistle of Jude. The Book of Enoch, like the Book of

Noah, which has been amalgamated with it, is an interesting specimen of that apocalyptic literature, both Jewish and Christian,
which abounded from the second century B.C. to the second century A.D. Moral and religious lessons, suitable for the time, were
put into the mouths of bygone saints and prophets, who were
represented as describing under symbolic imagery the history of
the world from their own days down to those when the books
ascribed to them were really written. Besides the Book of Enoch,
another apocalyptic work, the Ascension of Isaiah, has also been
preserved to us in an Ethiopic dress. This is a work of no great
length which was composed by a Christian toward the middle of
the second century. A translation of it was published by Archbishop Lawrence.

75.—AGRIPPA AND BERNICE.
Acts xxv. 13.

℃ This king should be properly called Agrippa II. He was the son
of Herod-Agrippa, who died so miserably at Cesarea (Acts xii.
20–23). The first Herod-Agrippa was son of Aristobulus, and
grandson of Herod the Great. Agrippa II. was but seventeen years
of age at his father's death, and though the Emperor Claudius was
disposed to entrust to him all his father's kingdom, his friends dis-
suaded him from entrusting so large a kingdom to one so young.
Agrippa did, however, by grants from Claudius and Nero, obtain
eventually a considerable part of his father's territories, his dominions comprising a large district east of Jordan, with a portion of
Galilee.

Having been brought up at Rome, he was strongly attached to
the Romans, and, contrary to all his native inclinations as a Jew,
joined his forces with those of the Romans in the final siege and
destruction of Jerusalem.

Bernice was Agrippa's sister, and sister also of Drusilla, Felix's
wife (Acts xxiv. 24). She had been first married to her uncle
Herod, king of Chalcis, and on his death had become the wife of
Polemon, king of Pontus. She appears, however, to have left him,
and returned to her brother, with whom she lived in a way that
caused much public scandal.

These facts make it appear how much Agrippa would be called
to give up on becoming a Christian, and how certainly he would

resist too easy persuasions, and contemptuously intimate to the
Apostle that he was not to be so readily drawn into a confession.

76.—THE PALESTINIAN PLOUGH.
Isaiah xxviii. 24.

⁋ It consists of a long piece of wood, having one extremity fastened to the yoke, which rests on the necks of the oxen, and the
other attached to a shorter piece, obliquely transverse; one end of
the latter is set in the share, the other is held by the right hand of
the ploughman. The farmer usually makes his own ploughs, pur-
chasing the shares in the town. These shares resemble in form the
point of an arrow or spear, with a socket to receive the wooden
part, which is fastened to it with a peg or nail. It is evident that no
more can be done by such an instrument than scratch the surface
of the soil, and the ploughman had to go over the field in several
directions to effect his purpose, and then he did no more than
would now be accomplished by an ordinary harrow. The unusual
productiveness of the soil is proved in the fact that with such imperfect ploughing it did not soon become exhausted. The leaving
of the ground fallow during the Sabbatic and Jubilee years was
absolutely necessary for the renewal of its vitality. After the double
ploughing—the second time at right angles to the first—the sods
were broken down with a wooden harrow, and the seed sown
broadcast; these seeds being either covered with a harrow, or by
the treading over the field of a flock of sheep or goats.

77.—DAVID'S PERSONAL APPEARANCE.
1 Sam. xvi. 12.

⁋ It is not the habit of Scripture writers to give such elaborate
descriptions of features and dress as are characteristic of modern
writings, and the personal appearance of those introduced into
Bible narrative has to be gathered from slight and scattered hints.
In the case of David we are aided by knowing the peculiarities of
his race and tribe, and also by the contrasts in which he is set with
his elder brethren. He must have been of medium height, if not
actually short, contrasting unfavourably with the handsome Saul
and the gigantic Goliath. He had red or auburn hair; the word
translated *ruddy* meaning *red-haired*, being the same word as is

77.—David's Personal Appearance.

used for Esau (Gen. xxv. 25). Josephus, however, refers the term
to his tawny complexion. His bright eyes are especially noticed,
and as the terms "comely," "goodly," are applied to him, we may
suppose that he was remarkable for the grace both of his figure
and of his countenance, well made, and of great strength and agility. In swiftness and activity he could be compared to the wild ga-
zelle, with feet like hart's feet; and he says of himself, "A bow of
steel is broken by my arms." He probably carried a switch or
wand in his hand, such as would be necessary to repress his dogs,
he had his scrip or wallet round his neck, and a sling, which the
shepherds dexterously used to ward off beasts or birds of prey.

78.—CLAIMS OF RAS SUFSAFEH TO BE THE
MOUNT OF GOD.
Exodus xix. 2.

⁅ The identification of the actual peak which Moses ascended to
receive the Divine revelation cannot be regarded as finally settled.
The claims of Ras Sufsafeh have recently been set forth very
prominently. It is a high peak to the north-east of the great central
cluster of mountains overlooking the plain Er Rahah. In its favour
may be urged that it rises abruptly out of the plain, so that the
people could get near to it. Two extensive wadies, Wady-er-Râhah,
and Wady-esh-Sheikh, meet in front of it, giving abundant space
for the settlement of the Israelites. By these wadies, and valleys
running from them, the Israelites must have entered the Sinaitic
district. And they would bring them into the very centre of the
sublime mountainous region. While suggesting that a hill on the
opposite side of the wady now called *Sena* may possibly be the
true Sinai, Dean Stanley evidently favours the claims of Ras Sufsafeh. Dr. Durbin, who actually ascended this peak, observes: "No
one who has not seen them can conceive the ruggedness of these
vast piles of granite rocks, rent into chasms, rounded into smooth
summits, or splintered into countless peaks, all in the wildest confusion, as they appear to the eye of an observer from any of the
heights. But when we did arrive at the summit, . . . and cast our
eyes over the wide plain, we were more than repaid for our toil.
One glance was enough. We were satisfied that here, and here
only, could the wondrous displays of Sinai have been visible to the
assembled host of Israel; that here the Lord spoke with Moses;

that here was the mount that trembled and smoked in the presence
of its manifested Creator!"

Rival claims are set up in favour of Mount *Serbal,* in the north-
western section. This is a magnificent mountain, rising 6,342 feet,
and crowned with five peaks; but there is no plain in its vicinity
where the hosts of Israel could assemble to hear the voice of God.
The same objection was, until recently, regarded as fatal to the
older claims of *Jebel Musa,* which rises at the southern part of the
great central mass to the height of nearly 7,000 feet. Mr. Drew,
who visited the East in 1856–57, carefully examined the plains
lying south and east of Jebel Musa, and thinks he has vindicated
the rights of this mountain beyond dispute. "The plain, Wady-es-
Sebâyeh, widens and enlarges toward the south into a most
magnificent area for a much larger encampment than could be
placed in Er-Rahah; . . . at no point was the view of Jebel Mûsa
interrupted. It rose everywhere before us, through the three miles
over which Sebâyeh extends, as THE MOUNT. The wady meets all
the requirements of the scene of the encampment. It is well supplied with water, and is even now, with its gently sloping sides,
filled with vegetation."

Dean Stanley notices two points which are in favour of Ras Sufsafeh. "Moses is described as descending the mountain without
seeing the people; the shout strikes the ear of his companion before they ascertain the cause: the view bursts upon him suddenly
as he draws nigh to the camp, and he throws down the tables, and
dashes them in pieces 'beneath the mount.' Such a combination
might occur in the Wady-er-Râhah. Any one coming down from
one of the secluded basins of Ras Sufsafeh, through the oblique
gullies which flank it on the north and south, would hear the
sounds borne through the silence from the plain, but would not
see the plain itself till he emerged from the Wady-ed-Deir or the
Wady Leja; and when he did so he would be immediately under
the precipitous cliffs of Sufsafeh. Further, we are told that Moses
strewed the powder of the fragments of the idol on the 'waters' of
the 'brook that came down out of the mount.' This would be perfectly possible in the Wady-er-Râhah, into which issues the brook
of the Wady Leja, descending, it is true, from Mount St. Catherine, but still in sufficiently close connection with the Jebel Mûsa
to justify the expression, 'coming down out of the mount.' "

79.—THE PALM-TREE USED IN ARCHITECTURAL ORNAMENTATION.
1 Kings vi. 29.

℘ The earliest examples of the use of the palm-tree as a model in architecture may be seen in Egypt among the temples. The principal central building of Solomon's temple was adorned with golden bas-reliefs representing "palm-trees and chains." And in Ezekiel's vision of the temple, the pillars which supported the porch were carved in the form of palm-trees, and the walls and doors were adorned with the figure. It seems to have been the characteristic feature of Jewish ornamentation, just as the *acanthus* leaf was of the Grecian, and the vine and ivy leaves are of modern styles of architecture. Its use, however, was not confined to Palestine. Herodotus speaks of the hall of the temple of Sais, in Egypt, as being adorned with it; and it is found carved on the walls of the ancient palaces of Nineveh. The same decoration is met with in the East still. The Moslems avoid, even more than the Hebrews, any representations of living creatures; but the walls of their houses are elaborately painted with figures of fruits, flowers, and landscapes. "At the Dolma-Bakcheh palace of the Sultan, on the Bosphorus, every window of the building containing the women's apartments has a picture of a palm-tree painted externally upon the lattice which covers its entire surface."

80.—TRUE IDEA OF THE WORD ECCLESIA, OR CHURCH.
Acts ii. 47.

℘ "Although in the word 'ecclesia,' in its religious sense, the etymological meaning, 'of an assembly called forth by the herald,' is lost in the general idea of a 'congregation,' yet this original meaning gives a fitness to the consideration that Abraham, who was the first in the succession of the 'ecclesia,' or 'church,' was so by virtue of what is known in all subsequent history as his 'call.' The word itself, as applied to the summons which led the patriarch forth, rarely occurs in the sacred writers. But it gathers up in a short compass the chief meaning of his first appearance. In him was exemplified the fundamental truth of all religion, that God has not deserted the world; that His work is carried on by His chosen instruments; that good men are not only His creatures and His servants, but His friends."

81.—THE NAME EGYPT.
Gen. xii. 10.

℄ . . . The origin of the word Egypt has been a subject of some debate, but Brugsch seems to have hit on the right explanation. Αἴγυπτος is first found in the Odyssey, where it is used not of the country but of the Nile. Now the old Egyptian Empire, founded by Menes, had its centre and support at Memphis, a site, indeed, which Menes had recovered from the river, by means of a dyke, still existing under the name of *Koshéish*. The native name of Memphis was *Men-nofer,* "the good place," which appears in the Old Testament under the forms of Moph and Noph. It was consecrated to the god Ptah, and, consequently, received the sacred name of *Ha-ka-Ptah,* "the dwelling of Ptah." This name came to be extended to the country of which Memphis was the capital, and so in the form of Egyptus eventually passed into Europe. It must be observed, however, that Brugsch's derivation is not yet universally accepted, and Professor Goldschmidt, of Copenhagen, has proposed to see in Αἴγυπτος the Egyptian *Ukh-hap-t,* "the land of the good stream-sending spirit."

82.—MENE, TEKEL, UPHARSIN.
Dan. v. 25.

℄ "These mystic words were given, not in new signs or hieroglyphics, but in distinct Hebrew characters; and through their brief and broken utterance there ran a double, treble significance. *Mene,* the first word, twice recorded, carried with it the judgment that the days of the kingdom were *numbered* and *ended; Tekel* carried the doom that it was *weighed* and found *light; Peres,* the third, that it was *divided* and given to the *Persians* (Pharsin)—the first appearance in history of that famous name which now, for the first time, stepped into the older form of 'Elam,' and has never since been lost."—*Dean Stanley.*

83.—DEW OF HERMON.
Psalm cxxxiii. 3.

℄ Palestine is a land of mountains. Eminently conspicuous
among these rise the three peaks of Hermon on the north-east border, their snowy crowns, glittering in the sun, being visible from
almost any point in the promised land, the trusted landmark of
travellers in all the region between the Jordan and the sea. These
are the Hermons (not "Hermonites"), of which David, in the
sweet Forty-second Psalm, sings: "O my God, my soul is cast
down within me! Therefore will I remember Thee from the land
of Jordan and of the Hermons."

Palestine is also a land of dews. It is very dependent on them.
Destitute of rains for many months at a time, it relies for securing
crops on the heavy fall of dew which is nightly secured by its multitude of mountains. Hermon is no more conspicuous in the sight
than in the peculiar abundance of its dews. They become rain for
the thirsty land. "The dew on this mountain is proverbially excellent and abundant." "More copious dews," says Tristram, "we
never experienced than on Hermon. Everything was drenched with
it, and the tents were small protection. The under sides of our
mackintosh sheets were drenched in water, our guns were rusted,
dewdrops were hanging everywhere." Mr. Porter states: "One of
its hills is appropriately called 'Father of the Dew,' for the clouds
seem to cling with peculiar fondness round its wooded top."

84.—ISSACHAR LIKE A STRONG ASS.
Gen. xlix. 14, 15.

℄ Jacob's prophecy concerning this tribe is not intended to be so
strong a reproach as its terms may at first sight suggest to us.
Verse 14 should be read: "Issachar is a strong-boned ass, couching
down between the cattle-pens," or "sheepfolds." The characteristic
of the tribe is indicated by the habit of this particular animal,
which, according to its sluggish nature, willingly rests in the midst
of plenty, heedless of consequences, and ever readier to bear burdens than to resist oppression. The tribe of Issachar occupied the
fruitful plain of Esdraelon, where they found plenty of rich pas-
ture, but where they were also exposed to the inroads of desert
tribes and neighbouring nations, and "the prediction all points to

the habits of an indolent agricultural people, and to what is likely
to accompany such habits, an endurance of oppression in preference to a war of independence."

The territory assigned to Issachar was just such as to promise
domestic ease. Hilly towards the east and south, in the central part
lay that most fertile plain of Esdraelon almost proverbial for richness and beauty.

Kalisch says: "The descendants of Issachar were men of prudence and wise calculation. Having therefore gained abundant
wealth, and resolved to enjoy it, they pursued a domestic and foreign policy calculated to realise this end. Their shrewdness not
only enabled them safely to keep aloof from all external dangers,
and . . . peacefully to yield themselves to secure tranquillity, but
to win the esteem and deference of the fraternal tribes by useful
and valuable councils."

85.—ATTACK OF SABEANS AND CHALDEANS ON JOB'S PROPERTY.
Job i. 15.

⁋ Among the terrible calamities that in one day fell upon the patriarch of Uz, are mentioned the inroads of the Sabeans and the
Chaldeans; the former carrying off the oxen, and the latter the
camels. Desert life in those early times was very similar to that
which may be observed in our day. The weapons differ, but the
evil policy pursued in the far past by wandering hordes has been
perpetuated to the present. Theft of cattle and the slaughter of the
keepers are looked upon as the most manly and respectable occu-
pations a gentleman can engage in. In the romance of *Antar,* an
Arabian work, there is described a scene which was no doubt a
mere repetition of the foray which cost Job his oxen.

"They then departed," says the writer, "traversing the wilds, and
the wastes, and the plains, and the mountains, amounting in all to
250 famed warriors, 150 belonging to the Carad division, and 100
forming the party of Oorwah. The party proceeded till midnight,
when Antar, Oorwah, and fifty horsemen alighted, saying to his father and to his uncles, 'Do you go ahead with the women.' But he
and Oorwah mounted at daylight and gallopped over the plains till
they came to the pastures of the tribe of Fazarah. The sun was
just risen, and the cattle were grazing. Antar rushed upon them,
and drove away all the he and she camels, and the high-paced

horses that belonged to the tribes of Fazarah and Zeaad. And
when they had launched into the desert, 'Send on the plunder with
thirty horsemen,' said Antar to Oorwah, 'but do thou stay with
me, with these twenty men, that we may encounter the troops that
will come upon us.' Oorwah did so, and thirty went on with the
plunder, Antar and Oorwah slowly following with the twenty.

"As soon as the news of the seizure of their cattle reached the
tribe of Fazarah they all mounted, and hastened off in pursuit, to
the number of 500. They went on until they overtook Antar, who,
when he saw the horsemen and heard their shouts, turned upon
them and met them, and in less than an hour he had slain numbers of them. Oorwah and his people also slew those who were
destined to die that day, piercing their chest with the point of the
spear. Extinction and perdition fell on the tribe of Fazarah. Antar
smote off heads and skulls, and despatched the horsemen to the
mansions of annihilation."

86.—ABIMELECH'S PRESENT TO ABRAHAM.
Gen. xx. 16.

℃ This Philistine king of Gerar had taken Sarah into his harem.
Admonished by God in a dream, he restored her to Abraham, to
whom he gave a thousand pieces of silver, saying, "Behold he (or
it, the money) is to thee a covering of the eyes." This is declared
to have been intended as a reproof to Sarah, but the meaning of
Abimelech's expression is very obscure. The most simple explanation appears to be that his money was a charge to purchase veils
for Sarah and her attendants, who in tent life had not worn them,
that she might be known to be a married woman, exclusively
belonging to her husband.

87.—GLEANING CUSTOMS IN PALESTINE AND ENGLAND.
Ruth ii. 2.

℃ The law of Moses, and the usage founded on it, gave the poor
people of Israel the right of gleaning in the harvest fields. As the
owners of land were not required to pay what we call *poor's rates*,
or taxes for the support of the poor, they allowed very freely this
privilege of gleaning. It was, however, only too likely that the
poor would take undue advantage of this right, and subject the
harvesting operations to serious inconvenience, and therefore the

proprietor retained the power of nominating the persons who were to glean after his reapers. The poor had to apply to the proprietors for permission to glean in their fields. So we find that Ruth did not enter abruptly and commence gleaning where she chose, but asked permission of the overseer. Her expression, "After whom I shall find grace," shows she recognised the necessity of getting permission.

In this country there is a popular notion that the poor have a right to glean the fields after harvest; but the courts of law have finally decided against it. "A case, which has been regarded as settling the question, is reported in the law books. It was a solemn judgment in the Court of Common Pleas, that no such right could be claimed at common law. Mr. Justice Gould dissented, quoting the passages in the Levitical law which bore on the subject (Lev. xix. 9, 10, xxiii. 2; Deut. xxiv. 19), together with a recognition of the custom or privilege in the Private Enclosure Act of Basingstoke Parish. The other judges, however, were of opinion that it would be impolitic and dangerous to admit gleaning to be a right, and would, in fact, be prejudicial to the poor themselves, now provided for under various positive statutes. They also remarked that the custom of gleaning was various in different places, and was in many places restricted to particular kinds of corn, and could not, therefore, be set up as a universal common law right, that it would be opening a tempting door to fraud and idleness, and had never been specifically recognised by any judicial determination."

88.—HAZAEL'S EXCLAMATION.
2 Kings viii. 13.

℃ Canon Ryle offers the following explanation of these often quoted words: "The passage 2 Kings viii. 13 does not imply that Hazael's mind revolted from the idea of the crime he was to commit; the term 'dog' denoting *meanness* rather than *wickedness* (1 Sam. xvii. 43, xxiv. 14; 2 Sam. ix. 8; Job xxx. 1), and the text should rather run, 'What! such a dog as thy servant do such great things!' Hazael, accordingly, merely expresses wonder that so *mean* a person as himself should become king of Syria, and 'he seems, therefore, to afford a singularly inappropriate illustration of a novice in sin.' "

89.—LEGEND RESPECTING AARON'S GOLDEN CALF.
Exodus xxxii. 24.

⊄ The Mahometans say that the golden calf was not made by
Aaron himself, but by *Al Sameri,* one of the principal men
amongst the children of Israel. It was made of the rings and bracelets of gold, silver, and other materials, which the Israelites had
begged of the Egyptians. Aaron ordered Al Sameri to collect these
ornaments from the people, because they were carrying on a
wicked commerce with them, and to preserve them until Moses returned from the Mount. Al Sameri, understanding the founder's
art, put them all into a furnace, to melt them down into one mass,
and the mass came out in the form of a calf. The Israelites, being
so long accustomed to Egyptian idolatry, began to pay religious
worship to this image. Upon which, Al Sameri went further, and
taking some dust from the footsteps of the horse of the angel
Gabriel, who marched at the head of the people, threw it into the
mouth of the calf, which immediately began to low, and became
animated; for such was the virtue of that dust.

90.—INCENSE IN CONNECTION WITH THE SANCTUARY.
Exodus xxx. 7.

⊄ All over the ancient world the offering of perfumes formed a
recognised and indispensable part of religious worship. There is a
reference to this well-known fact in the inspired description of
idols, "Noses have they, but they smell not." Until very recently
the sweet sedge was strewn on the floors of some of the cathedrals
of England, particularly Norwich cathedral, and it exhaled, when
trodden, a delicious fragrance, which filled the whole building as
with incense. In Norway the churches are frequently decorated in
a similar manner with the fresh leaves of the pine and birch,
whose aromatic odour in the crowded congregation is very refreshing.

91.—ABOMINATION OF DESOLATION.
Matt. xxiv. 15.

⊄ Daniel first uses this term (Dan. ix. 27, xi. 31, xii. 11). His
prediction may be regarded as having its fulfilment when, under

the persecution of Antiochus Epiphanes, an idol was set up on the altar of God, apostate Israelites concurring in the sin. But the fact of our Lord's employing the term shows that it had some further reference. Our Lord declares that the fulfilment of Daniel's prophecy was to be the warning for his disciples to flee from the doomed city of Jerusalem. This would be simultaneous with the investment of that city by the Romans (Luke xxi. 20, 21); and therefore some have believed the investment, when Cestius Gallus first encamped around Jerusalem (A.D. 66), to be the "abomination of desolation" itself. But it is more likely that the abominable thing was something done by the Jews themselves. Now, *Josephus* mentions a profanation by the Zealots, who had got possession of the Temple, and to this, or some similar deed, we may suppose our Lord referred, as a warning sign to His disciples.

92.—THE DIFFICULTY OF HIDING THE INFANT MOSES.
Exodus ii. 2.

℃ We may be sure that Jochebed did not save the life of her child through those three anxious months without passing through many alarms, and mastering many difficulties. Oriental imagination has fabricated a story of miraculous escape, which may possibly have some foundation in old legends. They say that on one occasion his mother hid him in the oven from the officers of Pharaoh, who were searching for the Hebrew male children in order to put them to death. While in the oven, his sister, ignorant of the child's whereabouts, kindled the fire, and heated the oven for baking. Notwithstanding this, the child was afterwards taken out uninjured.

93.—THE MEANING OF THE TERMS,
BOZEZ AND SENEH.
1 Sam. xiv. 4.

℃ Between the camps lay the deep gorge of the Wady Suweinit, or Harith, here called "the passage of Michmash," which is described as running between two jagged points, or "teeth of the cliff," as the Hebrew idiom expressly calls them. One of these points or teeth was called *Bozez,* or the *shining,* probably from some such appearance in the chalky cliff; the other was called *Seneh,* or the *thorn,* probably from some solitary acacia bush on its top. Immediately above the garrison of the Philistines seems to

have been situated. It was up the sides of this ravine that Jonathan
and his armour-bearer made their adventurous approach.

94.—"Sealing the Servants of God
in their Foreheads."
Rev. vii. 3.

⁋ It appears to be common for the votaries of particular divinities to bear characteristic marks as indicative of their allegiance.
The secret society of the Thugs, in India, have a small mark tattooed upon the arm. Those who visit the Church of the Resurrection, at Jerusalem, during Easter, have a similar mark on their
left wrist; while the worshippers of Vishnoo and Shiva make a
stripe of red paint upon their heads on particular occasions, by
which they are distinguished from other men.

95.—Scribes as Letter-writers.
Ezra iv. 8.

⁋ Very few people in the East are able to write so as to conduct
their own correspondence. The office of scribe was a very practical
one even in the ancient palaces and courts, the scribe being the actual writer of all kinds of necessary documents, and keeping his
business to himself. A class of men exists at the present day all
over the East who secure a livelihood by writing petitions, letters,
and other documents for the illiterate. They seat themselves in
some public position, in front of a mosque or court of justice, having by their side a box which contains their writing materials, and
under them the rug or mat. The documents they write are similar
to one another, and formal in style: the gist of the matter is either
found at the close, after a profusion of compliments, or in a slanting line written upon the margin, which serves the purpose of a
postscript. This kind of scribes consists usually of old men, broken-
down school-masters, government clerks, or priests, and they can
obtain but a precarious living.

96.—"Sun, stand thou still."
Joshua x. 12.

⁋ The extract from the book of Hebrew odes, which is comprised in verses 12–15, needs only to be regarded as all other

recognised poetry is regarded, to dispose effectually of the so-called "astronomical difficulties" connected with the miracle. How, it is asked, are we to understand the sun "standing still, and hasting not to go down about a whole day;" or the sun and moon "staying until the people had avenged themselves on their enemies"? How, we may reply, do you understand the passage in Deborah's song of triumph,

> "*The* stars *in their courses* fought against Sisera"?

or David's description of his deliverance,

> "*The* hills melted like wax *at the presence of the Lord*"?

Place these extracts from Scripture poetry, or similar descriptive extracts from the writings of Milton or Dryden, side by side with that from the Book of Jasher, and what does fair and reasonable interpretation deduce from the glowing metaphors employed? Surely no more and no less than this, that in answer to the earnest prayer of the Israelitish leader the daylight was prolonged until victory had been secured. Doubtless a miracle was wrought, and by what means it is bootless to speculate, though we may compare it with the sign given to Hezekiah; but it presents itself as one of those Divine interpositions, so characteristic of Old Testament times, in which natural agencies were applied in a special manner by the Almighty on His servants' behalf.—*W. H. Groser.*

97.—JUSTIN MARTYR'S ACCOUNT OF OBSERVING THE LORD'S SUPPER.
1 Cor. xi. 20–34.

℄ In his account of the celebration of the Eucharist for the newly baptised, a portion of the service is described as follows:—"Then is presented to the brother who presides bread and a cup of water and mixed wine, and he, receiving them, sends up praise and glory to the Father of All, through the name of the Son and the Holy Spirit, and offers a thanksgiving at some length for that He has vouchsafed to us these blessings; and when he has finished the prayers and the thanksgiving all the people present respond by saying, 'Amen.' . . . And after the president has given thanks and the people responded, those who are called among us deacons give to each of those who are present to partake of the bread and wine and water over which thanks have been given, and carry them to those not present. And this meal is called with us *Eucharistia,* of which none is permitted to partake except one who believes that the things taught by us are true, and who has passed through the washing for remission of sins and new birth, and so lives as Christ commanded. For we receive these not as common bread or common drink, but as Jesus Christ our Saviour being incarnate by the Word of God possessed both flesh and blood for our salvation, so also we were taught that the food over which thanksgiving has been made by the utterance in prayer of the Word derived from Him is the flesh and blood of that incarnate Jesus. For the Apostles, in the memoirs which they wrote, which are called Gospels, transmitted to us that Jesus Christ thus charged them, that after taking bread and giving thanks, He said, 'Do this in remembrance of Me, for this is My body;' and that, in like manner, after taking the cup and giving thanks, He said, 'This is My blood,' and that He gave to partake to them alone."

Justin Martyr represents the sentiments and practice of the second half of the second century after Christ.

98.—MATTHEW'S GOSPEL WRITTEN IN HEBREW.
Matt. i. 1.

℄ While it is generally admitted that the three other Gospels were written by their authors in Greek, there has been much dispute concerning the language in which Matthew wrote his Gospel. Ellicott says that nearly all modern critics agree in recognising, not merely in isolated words and phrases, but in the general tone and diction of the first Gospel, the Hebraistic element. "The physiognomy of this first of our Gospels," to use the language of Da Costa, "is eminently Oriental." The language, though mainly simple and artless, not unfrequently rises to the rhythmical and even poetical, and is marked by a more frequently recurring parallelism of words or clauses than is to be found in the other Gospels: compare, for example, Matt. vii. 24–27, with Luke vi. 47–49.

99.—THE PAPYRUS OF THE JORDAN.
Matt. xi. 7.

℄ There is first a lateral trunk lying on the water and half submerged. This is sometimes as thick as a man's body, and from its lower side hang innumerable string-like roots, from three to five feet long, and of a deep purple colour. On the upper surface of the trunks the stems grow alternately in oblique rows: their thickness at the junction is often four inches, and their height fifteen feet, gracefully tapering until at the top is a little round knob, with long, thin, brown, wirelike hairs, eighteen inches long, which rise, and then recurving, hang about it in a thyrsus-shaped head. The stem, when dead, becomes dark brown in colour, and when dry it is extremely light; indeed, for its strength and texture, it is the lightest substance I know of.—*Mr. Macgregor* (Rob Roy).

100.—EASTERN RUNNERS.
2 Sam. xviii. 19–31.

¶ Men swift of foot were important personages in the days of the primitive nations. Races were instituted to encourage the natural rivalry that exists among men to excel in speed. It is to these that Paul refers when he says: "Wherefore, seeing we also are compassed about with so great a cloud of witnesses, let us lay aside every weight, and the sin which doth so easily beset us, and let us run with patience the race that is set before us, looking unto Jesus, the author and finisher of our faith" (Heb. xii. 1: see also 1 Cor. ix. 24; Phil. iii. 14; 2 Tim. iv. 7). The running of Cushi and Ahimaaz is told in 2 Sam. xviii. 19–31. Footmen ran before the chariots of august personages (2 Sam. xv. 1; 1 Kings i. 5; Jer. xii. 5). In Hezekiah's reign (2 Chron. xxx. 6, 10) we find an establishment of running postmen; and the same name (runners) is given in Esth. iii. 13, 15, viii. 14, to the Persian posts, though at that time they rode on mules and camels. Speed was an heroic virtue in those simple times.

101.—WOMEN AT EASTERN WELLS.
1 Sam. ix. 11.

¶ As in the long past ages, so at this day, water for domestic purposes in Syria is fetched by the young girls, or the women. Very often the fountains to which they resort are situated in the most romantic spots; and, as might be supposed from the presence of moisture, the vegetation around is luxuriant and manifold. To those spots the women, or the girls, go at least once in the day, "to draw water." They carry their pitchers on their heads if the bases of the pitchers are flat, on their shoulders when they taper away to a point. A traveller who passes the fountain and demands a draught is readily supplied, as is also any one who meets a girl as she is carrying her "water pot" home. In the latter case she will take down her pitcher and rest it on her arm while the traveller stoops to drink, touching the vessel with nothing but his lips. The fact that the women and girls have to fetch water is in no way regarded as a hardship or humiliation. It furnished them with a good excuse for a temporary escape from the house; and at the fountain they met with their neighbours, and could hear all the gossip of the town or village.

102.—JONAH'S GREAT FISH.
Jonah i. 17.

⁋ The word *ketos,* used in Matt. xii. 40, is not restricted in its meaning to a whale or a cetacean; "it may denote any sea-monster, either a whale or a shark, a seal, or a tunny of enormous size." Now, we find that the white shark exists in the waters of the Mediterranean, as well as in the Red Sea and the Indian Ocean, and often attains the length of thirty feet. Though it generally first bites its prey, it frequently swallows it entire. Cases are on record, sustained by the most undoubted authority, in which entire bodies were found in the stomach of this fish, such as a man, a man clad with armour, and even a horse! Moreover, naturalists have recorded that sharks have the habit of throwing up again whole and alive the prey they have swallowed.

103.—ANCIENT RUDDERS.
Acts xxvii. 40.

⁋ The original idea of a ship seems to have been taken from the shape and movement of aquatic birds. In imitation of their web feet, two oars or paddles were pushed out into the water, one on each side of the stern. The oar required to be strained, so as to produce resistance in the water, and thus bring the ship's head round; it would therefore have to be fastened tightly with some "rudder-bands." The modern and more easily managed single rudder has been adopted in imitation of the fishes, which guide their progress by the skilful motion of their tails. A steering paddle is, however, now sometimes found necessary in addition to the rudder.

104.—ALMUG TREE.
1 Kings x. 11, 12.

℺ This tree is also called *Algum* (2 Chron. ii. 8), and from it columns, balustrades, harps, and psalteries, were made by Solomon. It is usually supposed to be identical with the red sandalwood, *Pterocarpus santalinus,* of the East: it may, however, be the white sandal-wood, *Santalum album,* which is very fragrant, and of which costly utensils are still made in India.

105.—WINE BOTTLES MADE TO STAND FERMENTATION.
Matt. ix. 17.

℺ A well-known traveller in Syria tells us that there are several ways of making wine. Sometimes the grape-juice, after being trodden out, or pressed out in vats, is poured into large vessels, or into jars half buried in the earth in some cool place. A little lime is thrown in, which is supposed to control the process of fermentation, and to prevent its turning to vinegar. In the present day it appears that wine is not generally used until after its fermentation is completed. In many parts of the country skin bottles, similar to those mentioned by our Lord, are still used. They are chiefly made of goat skins, and are prepared in the following manner: "As soon as the animal is killed an opening is made in the skin large enough to introduce the lips, and a man begins to blow between the skin and the flesh, until the two are completely separated from each other throughout. The head and feet are then cut off, and the entire body of the animal is drawn out of its skin through the opening at the neck. The hair is sometimes partially removed, and the skin tanned. In Persia the skins are saturated with pitch. The opening at the neck is used for filling and emptying the vessel, while the four feet are tied or sewed up." When the grape-juice (new wine), which has yet to undergo the process of fermentation, is put in these skin bottles, care must be taken that they are either entirely new, or are proved able to stand the pressure. It is interesting to find that these skin bottles are still used throughout the East as far as Persia, in Northern Africa (some portions of which retain the ancient forms of life with singular completeness), and even in Spain.

106.—THE POMEGRANATE TREE.
1 Sam. xiv. 2.

⁋ No tree is more highly prized throughout the East than the pomegranate, whether for the beauty of its appearance, or for its fruit. It is the *Punica granatum* of botanists, and belongs to the natural family of plants called *Myrtaceae*. It is really more of a shrub than a tree, and bears a bright lustrous leaf. The wood is of yellow tint, and very fragile. There are two kinds of pomegranate trees, the one bearing delicious fruit, the other nothing but leaves and blossoms. The flowers have beautiful bright scarlet petals, encased in a bell-shaped calyx of a paler tint, stiff as leather, and regularly serrated round the border. The fruit is of the shape of an orange, of a flesh colour, with here and there rosy tints distributed over the surface; the rind is thick, and bright yellow on the inside. The pomegranate is filled with a great number of closely-packed kernels, chiefly consisting of a delicate juice, with small seeds in their centres. These kernels constitute the edible parts of the fruit. The juice is often manufactured into wine—the "spiced wine of the juice of my pomegranate," spoken of in Solomon's Song (ch. viii. 2). The pomegranate was extensively cultivated in Palestine in very ancient times, as is manifest from several passages of Scripture (*e.g.*, Num. xiii. 23; Deut. viii. 8). The pomegranate under which Saul tarried at Migron was probably a cluster or grove of these shrubs. The fondness of the Israelites for this fruit is shown by their using it for ornamental patterns in their most sacred art. Pomegranates were embroidered on the garments of the priests, and carved on the woodwork of the temple (Ex. xxviii. 33, 34; 1 Kings vii. 18, 20).

107.—THE NICOLAITANES.
Rev. ii. 6.

⁋ There is much difficulty in tracing this sect. Two explanations are given. The prevailing opinion among the Fathers was, that they were a sect founded by Nicolaus, the proselyte of Antioch, one of the seven deacons. Others think the actual founder was a

Corinthian named Nicolaus, who was noted for licentious practices. Archbishop Trench prefers a symbolical interpretation. Those
who held the doctrine of Balaam he thinks identical with those who
held the doctrine of the Nicolaitanes, and the term means "those
who, after the pattern of Balaam's sin, sought to introduce a
false freedom, the freedom of the flesh, into the Church of God."

108.—Woe unto you, Scribes and Pharisees.
Matt. xxiii. 13.

℀ The language of Christ in denouncing the hypocritical Scribes
and Pharisees has been deemed unnecessarily severe; but Jewish
literature gives quite as bad a picture of them. "Fear not *true*
Pharisees, but greatly fear *painted* Pharisees," said a Jewish ruler
to his wife when he was dying. "The supreme tribunal," said another, "will duly punish hypocrites who wrap their talliths around
them to appear—what they are not—true Pharisees." The Talmud
says there is the *"Shechemite"* Pharisee, who, like the young man
that bore the name (Gen. xxxiv. 19), obeys the law from interested motives: the *tumbling* Pharisee, who is so humble that he is
always stumbling, because he will not lift his feet from the
ground: the *bleeding* Pharisee, who is always hurting himself
against walls, because he is so modest as to be unable to walk with
his eyes open lest he should see a woman: the *mortar* Pharisee,
who covers his eyes over with a mortar lest he should behold a female: the *"tell me another duty and I will do it"* Pharisee: and the
timid Pharisee, who is actuated solely by fear.

109.—Assyrian Account of the
Invasion of Sennacherib.
2 Kings xviii. 13.

℀ This Assyrian monarch invaded Judah twice during the reign
of Hezekiah, the first campaign being highly successful (2 Kings
xviii. 13–16); the second overwhelmingly disastrous (2 Kings xix.
35). The first invasion took place about B.C. 702, and is recorded
in the annals of Assyria.

On an hexagonal clay prism, discovered at Nineveh in 1830, is
found, in cuneiform characters, an inscription giving a record of
several of the campaigns of Sennacherib. It is written in the first

person, and gives an account of the royal conquests. From among other details the following are selected as associated with the kingdom of Judah.

"And Hezekiah of Judah, who had not bowed at my feet, forty-six of his strong cities, his castles, and the smaller towns in their neighbourhood beyond number, with warlike engines I attacked and captured. 200,150 people, small and great, male and female, horses, mares, asses, camels, oxen, and sheep beyond number from the midst of them I carried off, and distributed them as spoil. He himself, like a bird in a cage, inside Jerusalem, his royal city, I shut up: siege-towers against him I constructed. The exit of the great gate of the city, to divide it he had given command. His cities which I plundered, from his kingdom I cut off, and to Mitinti, King of Ashdod; Padiah, King of Ekron; and Izmi-Bel, King of Gaza, I gave them. I diminished his kingdom. Beyond the former scale of their yearly gifts to my majesty I augmented, and I imposed them upon them. He himself, Hezekiah, the fearful splendour of my majesty had overwhelmed him; the workmen, soldiers, and builders, whom for the fortification of Jerusalem, his royal city, he had collected within it, now carried tribute, and with thirty talents of gold, eight hundred talents of silver; woven cloth scarlet, embroidered; precious stones of large size, couches of ivory, movable thrones of ivory, skins of buffaloes, teeth of buffaloes, dan wood, ku wood, a great treasure of every kind, and his daughters, and the male and female inmates of his palace, male slaves, and female slaves, unto Nineveh my royal city, after me he sent; and to pay tribute and do homage he sent his envoy."

110.—UNTYING KNOTS.
Daniel v. 12.

¶ When Belshazzar and his friends were disturbed by the handwriting on the wall, the queen advised the monarch to send for Daniel, whom she described as possessing, among other things, the spirit of *"untying knots"* (see margin); meaning, of course, that he had the power of explaining mysteries, and unravelling mental entanglements. Sir John Chardin, who visited Persia in the seventeenth century, relates that a patent given to himself by the Shah was addressed, among many other great officials, to the "superintendents who *unloose all manner of knots,* and who are under the ascendant of Mercury." In explanation, Sir John says, the Persians

MENE
MENE
TEKEL
UPHARSIN

110.—Untying Knots.

rank all penmen, books, and writings under Mercury, and hold that
all persons born under that planet are endued with a refined, pene-
trating, clear-sighted, and subtle wit. As the queen says that
Daniel possessed the "spirit of the holy gods," it is possible that
she may have referred him to the patronage of Mercury.

111.—BONES SCATTERED ON THE GROUND.
Psalm cxli. 7.

℘ It may not be easy to fix the exact meaning of the figure here
employed, but a passage in *Bruce's Travels* furnishes a possible explanation. He says, "At five o'clock we left Garigana, our journey
being still to the eastward and north, and at a quarter past six in
the evening arrived at the village of that name (Garigana), whose
inhabitants had all perished with hunger the year before; their
wretched bones being all unburied, and scattered upon the surface
of the ground where the village formerly stood. We encamped
among the bones of the dead; no space could be found free from
them." Among the Jews, to have no burial was considered a great
calamity; so also was it to have one's bones taken from their resting-place, and exposed to the day.

112.—LINEN DRESSES FOR THE PRIESTS.
Exodus xxxix. 27, 28.

℘ Every nation, recognising the prominent offices of its priesthood, imposes stringent regulations respecting the dress and general habits of its priests. In this particular the Mosaic ritual was
not less exacting than that of other countries. The high priest of
Egypt always wore a leopard-skin placed over his linen dress as his
official costume. The dress of the priests was exclusively of linen.
It is worthy of remark that the Egyptian and Jewish priests were
the only ones (except those of India) whose dresses were ordered
to be of linen. Those worn by the former were of the finest texture, and the long robe with full sleeves, which covered the body
and descended to the ankles, was perfectly transparent, and placed
over a short kilt of thicker quality reaching to the knees (Exod.
xxviii. 42). Some wore a long robe of linen extending from the
neck to the ankles, of the same thick substance, and some
officiated in the short kilt alone, the arms and legs being bare.
Some, again, had a long thin dress, like a loose shirt, with full

sleeves, reaching to the ankles, over which a wrapper of fine linen was bound, covering the lower part of the body, and falling in front below the knees; the hieraphoros, while bearing the sacred emblems, frequently wore a long full apron, tied in front with long bands, and a strap, also of linen, passed over the shoulder to support it; and some priests wore a long smock reaching from below the arms to the feet, and supported over the neck by straps. The head was frequently bare, sometimes covered with a wig, or a tight cap; but in all cases the head was closely shaved. They had a peculiar apparatus, it seems, for goffering their linen, one of which still exists in the Museum at Florence.

113.—Eastern Writing and Writing Materials.
Isaiah viii. 1; Ezek. ix. 3.

℟ The present customs of the Arabs may elucidate these passages, as well as other Scripture references to writing. "The Arabic, like the Hebrew, cannot be written with a quill, much less with a steel pen; nor can the Arabs employ the *stylus* of the Romans and Greeks. The pen is made of a small reed, about a quarter of an inch in thickness, and is generally of a dark brown colour, which is cut as we do a quill, with this difference, that instead of being sharp at the point it is broad and slanting, and is held sideways. The ink used is thick; it is made of gum, lamp-black, and water, and does not corrode like ours. The writing done with this ink is said to last for ever. A little roll of palm-threads, always kept in the inkstand, prevents its drying up. The inkstand is of brass, and occasionally of silver, while in some rare instances it is of gold. Its cover is of the same material, and it is firmly attached to a case holding pens, about six inches in length, which is stuck into the girdle, in a slanting position, so as to prevent the ink from running out, and to enable the writer to use it without removing it from his girdle. Merchants and scribes always wear such an inkstand in their belts, and it may be called the insignia of their office or trade. But when a man's occupation is stationary, confining him to a single spot, where he has a good deal of writing to do, if he be a judge, for instance, the governor of a large city, or an officer of state, he sits cross-legged in the corner of his divan, and has beside him a box, or a small chest, often handsomely carved or inlaid, in which he keeps his writing materials and documents, and upon which are set, in a small tray, a variety of little porcelain cups, with their covers, containing ink of various qualities, and black or golden sand, with a bundle of pens. In some parts of Egypt the inkstand yet consists of a small horn set up in a hole."

114.—ANOINTING THE BODY WITH OIL.
Luke vii. 46.

⁋ Van Lennep has collected some interesting references to this very ancient and familiar custom. "The heroes of Homer are described by him as restoring their weary limbs after a battle with frictions of oil. This was Alexander's practice. It was Pompey's daily habit also, as well as that of all the wealthy Romans. In the Scriptures it is alluded to as forming an habitual part of the toilet on special occasions; it was not, however, to be indulged in during periods of mourning. The head was anointed in connection with the daily recurring ablution.

"Egyptian monuments represent servants anointing guests on their arrival at their entertainer's house, and alabaster vases still exist which retain traces of the ointment they once contained. This was adopted from the Egyptians by the Jews, and the settlement of many of these people at Alexandria served to maintain Egyptian customs among them. This practice has disappeared in modern times, on account of the conquest of these lands by foreign nations. The hair is now anointed, but mostly by the women, since the men have the head shaved. The wrestlers, called by the Turks *Pekhliwans,* anoint themselves with oil before wrestling, as did the ancients preparatory to similar athletic exercises, in order to render their bodies more slippery under the grasp of their antagonists. The custom of anointing the body is still prevalent among some nations of Africa. The Abyssinian gentleman places a lump of butter every morning on the top of his head, and covers it with his bushy locks; as it melts it flows over his body; and the Hottentots so besmear their bodies with grease as to leave traces of it wherever they sit."

115.—THE INTRODUCTION OF IRON.
Gen. iv. 22.

⁋ Palaeontologists divide the history of the world roughly into the "Stone Age," when the chief weapons were made of stone, or flint; the "Bronze Age," during which the best weapons and instruments were made of mixed metals, called bronze; and the "Iron Age," during which iron and steel bear sway. Iron is undoubtedly a very ancient article, but there is no possibility of deciding when it was first discovered. There can be no doubt that it was used in ancient Egypt; but it is not preserved in any country beyond a certain time, because liable to destruction by rusting. The blue colour of swords and other weapons in the painted tombs of Thebes, shows that the Egyptians used iron, or steel, as well as bronze; and bronze appears to have been employed by the Romans and Etruscans long after iron implements and arms were common. Iron was known in the days of Job (xxviii. 2); the importance of the reference depends however on the date we assign to the Book of Job. Moses, in the passage heading this paragraph, mentions Tubal Cain as the instructor of every artificer in brass and iron. He also compares Egypt to the "iron furnace" (Deut. iv. 20). Og, King of Bashan, who probably lived about 1450 B.C., had a bedstead of iron (Deut. iii. 11). Homer shows that the quenching of iron to case-harden it was well known, for in his great poem he adopts it as a simile, and compares the hissing noise produced by piercing the eye of Polyphemus to the effects of plunging the heated metal in water (*Od.* ix. 391). On the Egyptian monuments we even see butchers sharpening their knives on a steel fastened to their apron; and weapons of that blue-coloured metal were represented in common use long before the Trojan War. In metallurgy the Egyptians possessed some secrets scarcely known to us; for they had the means of enabling copper to cut stone without hardening it by an alloy, and of giving to bronze blades the elasticity of steel with great hardness and sharpness of edge. For most of the above particulars we are indebted to a work by Sir Gardner Wilkinson.

116.—MANDRAKES.
Gen. xxx. 14.

⦅ From this passage, and the context, it appears that *mandrakes* were prized as articles of luxury. In Song Sol. vii. 13, they are referred to as giving a pleasant smell. But the root is anything but odoriferous according to European notions; indeed, most Westerns regard the smell as decidedly fetid. But a recent author, after quoting a number of authorities to show that mandrakes are

prized by the Arabs for this very odour which is so offensive to us,
says:—"It is well known that Orientals set an especial value on
strong-smelling things that to more delicate European senses are
unpleasing. The intoxicating qualities of the mandrake, far from
lessening its value, would rather add to it, for every one knows
with what relish the Orientals use all kinds of preparations to produce intoxication." The fruit of the mandrake is ripe at the wheat
harvest; it is yellow, of the size of a small egg, and filled with
seeds. The plant still grows near Jerusalem, and in various parts of
Syria. The botanical name is *Atropa mandragora;* and it is nearly
allied to the *Atropa belladonna,* or Deadly Nightshade. It is freely
eaten by the natives as wholesome, genial, and exhilarating; it is
believed to strengthen affection, and promote fecundity.

117.—PICTURES OF THE CRUCIFIXION.
Matt. xxvii. 35–37.

¶ The oldest extant representation of the Crucifixion is a miniature in a Syrian Evangelarium, of date A.D. 586, now in the
Laurentian Library at Florence. The treatment of the subject is exceedingly rude, bordering on the grotesque. The figure of our
Lord is crowned with a nimbus and clothed with a long purple
robe. The soldiers on the ground are casting lots for His garments,
and the sun and moon look down upon the scene. A companion
picture represents the ascension of Christ, and the effusion of the
Holy Spirit. "These are the oldest pictorial representations," says
Professor Piper, "of the earthly life of Jesus and of His exalta-
tion. . . . . At a somewhat later period," he continues, "they appear also in the West."

118.—DAVID'S MOTHER.
1 Chron. ii. 16; 2 Sam. xvii. 25, 27.

¶ The origin and name of his mother are wrapt in mystery. It
would almost seem as if she had been the wife or concubine of
Nahash, and then married to Jesse. This would agree with the fact
that her daughters, David's sisters, were older than the rest of the
family. Zeruiah and Abigail, though called in 1 Chron. ii. 16,
sisters of David, are not expressly called the daughters of Jesse;
and Abigail, in 2 Sam. xvii. 25, is called the daughter of Nahash.

119.—THE CAVE OF ADULLAM.
1 Sam. xxii. 1.

℄ One of the most satisfactory results of the labours of recent Palestine explorers is the identification of this cave. The traditional cave is an immense grotto known as Moghuret Khureitun, not far from Bethlehem, and quite close to Tekoa. Of this cave Drs. Thomson and Bonar give very elaborate descriptions. Later writers are inclined to place it at Deir Dubbân, about six miles north of Beit Jibrin (Eleutheropolis). M. Clermont Ganneau, however, was the first to discover what is probably the real site, under the existing name of Ayd-el-Mieh, which preserves all the essential letters of the Hebrew word. Lieutenant Conder, on behalf of the Palestine Exploration Society, has made a careful survey of the spot. He found the ruins of an ancient town, strongly situated on a height commanding the broad valley of Elah, which was the highway by which the Philistines invaded Judah. The "cave" is a series of caves, some of moderate size and some small, but quite capable of housing David's band of followers.

120.—BEARING THE SHOES.
Matt. iii. 11.

℄ The expression used by John the Baptist, when contrasting the glory of Christ with his own comparative insignificance, is given with a variation on the closing word. Matthew uses the word *bear,* Mark, Luke and John the word *unloose.* The phrase was probably proverbial, and, we can readily imagine, took some variety of form. Matthew's word has been thus explained: People of rank in Eastern lands had slaves to carry their sandals, which were often very costly articles, sometimes even made of gold. Those not wanted for immediate use were carried, in case of a journey being undertaken, by a slave, in a *sandalotheka,* or sandal-box; and the office of this slave John declared himself unworthy to perform for the Messiah.

121.—THE BIBLICAL LENTIL.
Gen. xxv. 34.

℄ The following account of this vegetable is taken from the *Gardener's Magazine:*—As regards the lentil mentioned in Holy Writ, proofs have been pretty numerous and plain that it is the same plant that is at the present day very extensively used in the East as meal and pulse, and sometimes as bread. The plant is known to botanists as *Ervum Lens*. The lentil is, perhaps, one of the most ancient of all plants, as it is mentioned early in Genesis, where we read that "Jacob gave Esau bread and pottage of lentils," and with which he purchased his birthright. It is again very conspicuously mentioned in that beautiful part of the Scriptures while speaking of King David fleeing from "his beloved son Absalom." The writer describes how "Shobi, the son of Nahash, brought beds and basons," and gave him for food "parched corn, beans, and lentils." Advancing through the historical books of Holy Writ, we find in Chronicles that during an extensive engagement between the Israelites and Philistines a "parcel of ground" full of lentils was captured by the Israelites. The passage here certainly reads "barley," but in the parallel passage in Samuel we read lentils; and the most recent travellers and experienced translators are satisfied that this "parcel of ground" was full of lentils. The question may arise, Why, in recording Esau selling his birthright for a "mess of pottage," the ancient writer uses the term "red porridge"? The best answer to this is to turn to Pliny, who is, perhaps, the most reliable authority on ancient gardening, and we find that he mentions two sorts of lentils, referring to one of them as "red," and this will explain Esau eating "that same red pottage." If that is not satisfactory, there is another surer authority to be found in Algiers and North Africa, where it is common to grow several species of lentils, one of which, on being boiled, yields a chocolate or reddish-coloured pottage. It must not be thought that the lentil is confined to North Africa and the East, because this is by no means the case, for it is in some parts of England and Wales cultivated as food for cattle. Like many of the vicias, it produces small flowers of pale purple and flat leguminous seed pods.

122.—CHERUB.
Ezek. x. 20–22.

⫶ Mr. Cheyne has suggested in the *Encyclopaedia Britannica* a new derivation of the word *cherub*. He connects it with the Assyrian *kurubu*, a synonym of *kurukku*, or *karakku*, the "circling" bird—*i.e.*, according to Dr. Delitzsch, the vulture. He endeavours to show (Ps. xviii. 10; 2 Sam. xxii. 11; and Deut. xxviii. 49) that the cherub was conceived of under the form of an eagle. At the same time, he does not exclude the connection of the word with the Assyrian *kirubu,* which M. Lenormant has found applied to the winged bull which guarded the entrance of the house in a talismanic inscription. The king of birds and the colossal steer might well, he thinks, have been denoted by a similar epithet. Ezekiel, writing by the side of the River Chebar, or Khabur, and, therefore, in the midst of Assyrian imagery, compares one of the four faces of the cherub to that of an ox (Ezek. i. 10). Sidikan, the modern Arban, was, it must be remembered, on the Khabur; and it was here that Layard found winged bulls, with cuneiform inscriptions commemorating the names of Assyrian governors of the place.

123.—NO REGULARLY LAID OUT FLOWER-GARDEN IN THE EAST.
Song Sol. v. 1.

℄ Many of our Western notions require to be modified when they are applied to the conditions and customs of the East. And it appears that the delightful associations we have with the tasteful, brilliant flower-garden cannot be applied to the Eastern garden, of which frequent mention is made in Scripture. Writing of the state of things actually observed by him, in the immovable East, Van Lennep says, "There is no such thing as a regularly laid out flower-garden. The vegetable patches are marked out with a line, but the flowers must take care of themselves. The rose shrubs grow along the garden walls, and other flowers and shrubs are at liberty to come up wherever they do not interfere with the production of useful plants. They have a domain of their own, however, the flower-pot, whether of burnt clay, or of plain boards roughly nailed together, or even a fragment of a water-jar, filled with earth for the purpose. These are arranged along the walls of the court, upon the balconies, under the trellis, upon the edge of the terraced roof, or even firmly set in mortar along the edge of a parapet. There flourish in the greatest luxuriance every variety of the carnation; there flaunts the double marigold, pride of the Turkish inhabitants everywhere; and there is the lovely green of the fragrant never-failing 'sweet basil,' the *habisk* of the Arabs, called by the Greeks *vasilico,* which gives its name to many a blushing maiden." There is no attempt to produce a large variety of garden plants and flowers. When they are not cultivated for the market, even the wealthiest classes are satisfied with a few favourite species, preferring the brightest colours, and those which exhale the most agreeable perfumes. The rose and carnation are favourites with all classes; and other fragrant flowers are highly valued, such as the narcissus, jasmine, tuberose, hyacinth, lilac, and violet. Aromatic plants are also cultivated, sprigs of which are carried about the person.

124.—LAND-MARKS.
Deut. xix. 14.

⁋ Eastern fields were not divided by hedge, or wall, or ditch; so there was much danger of confusing the separate properties of individuals. Farms in Europe are carefully marked off into fields, and the removal of hedges and fences cannot be effected without the knowledge of the parties concerned. The boundaries of parishes, however, often become uncertain, through the rearrangement of roads and multiplication of buildings; so that in many districts a yearly custom is retained of "beating the bounds." In the East advantage was taken, whenever possible, of natural divisions, such as river-beds, tributary stream lines, and edges of valleys; but in the open ground the separate properties were only marked by a deeper furrow, or large stones almost buried in the soil. The injunction not to remove a neighbour's landmarks was therefore of the utmost importance, as stealthy encroachments might easily be made by shifting these stones.

125.—PRAISE TO GOD FROM THE INFANTS.
Matt. xxi. 16.

⁋ The interest which our Lord took in little children, and His commendations of them, were in accord with the best thought of the Jewish people. The following sentences from the Talmud will indicate the tone of Jewish teaching respecting the children. "When God intended to give the law to the people, He asked them whom they would offer as their guarantees that they would keep it holy; and they said 'Abraham.' God said, 'Abraham has sinned— Isaac, Jacob, Moses himself, they all have sinned; I cannot accept them.' Then they said, 'May our children be our witness, and our

guarantees.' And God accepted them; even as it is written, 'From
the mouths of the wee babes has He founded His empire.'"

126.—Abraham the First Witness
to the Unity of God.
Gen. xv. 6.

℃ From the Book of Joshua we learn that the fathers of the Jewish race served idols when living beyond the Euphrates (Josh.
xxiv. 2, 14). Tradition declares Terah to have been a maker of
idols, and reports that Abraham was cast by Nimrod into a burning fiery furnace for refusing to worship him. What is certain is
that Abraham was the "first historical witness, at least for his own
race and country, to Theism, or Monotheism, to the unity of the
Lord and Ruler of all against the primeval idolatries, the *natural*
religion of the ancient world." The Koran gives the legend of the
conversion of Abraham. "When night overshadowed him, he saw a
star, and said, 'This is my Lord.' But when it set, he said, 'I like
not those that set.' And when he saw the moon rising, he said,
'This is my Lord.' But when the moon set, he answered, 'Verily, if
my Lord direct me not in the right way, I shall be as one of those
who err.' And when he saw the sun rising, he said, 'This is my
Lord. This is greater than the star or moon.' But when the sun
went down, he said, 'O, my people, I am clear of these things. I
turn my face to Him who hath made the heaven and the earth.'"

Another tradition gives an account of his presumed activities
against the idol worship. "The patriarch at first ridiculed the idols,
and thus endeavoured to induce his kindred to give up the worship
of them: failing in this, he entered the temples when the Chaldaeans were in the fields celebrating a great festival. He de-
molished all the images except the biggest, around the neck of
which he hung the axe with which the destruction had been
effected, thus making it appear that the greatest idol of the temple
had destroyed all the rest."

127.—The Greek Account of Sennacherib.
2 Kings xix. 35.

℃ Herodotus, the celebrated Greek historian, has given a curious
version of the destruction of Sennacherib's army, which runs as
follows: "Sethos, a priest of Vulcan (the god of fire), having suc-

ceeded to the throne of Egypt, treated the military of Egypt with
extreme contempt, as if he had no occasion for their services. . . .
The result was that, when Sennacherib, King of Arabia and Assyria, attacked Egypt with a mighty army, the warriors whom
Sethos had thus treated, refused to assist him. In this perplexity
the priest retired to the shrine of his god, before which he
lamented his danger and misfortunes. Here he sank into a profound sleep, and his deity promised him, in a dream, that if he
marched to meet the Assyrians he should suffer no injury, for he
would furnish him with assistance. The vision inspired him with
confidence; he put himself at the head of his adherents, and
marched to Pelusium, the entrance of Egypt. Not a soldier accompanied the party, which was entirely composed of tradesmen and
artisans. On their arrival at Pelusium, so immense a number of
mice infested the enemy's camp by night that their quivers and
bow-strings, together with the straps of their shields, were gnawed
to pieces. In the morning the Arabians (and Assyrians), finding
themselves without arms, fled in confusion, and lost great numbers
of their men. There is now to be seen, in the temple of Vulcan, a
marble statue of this king (Sethos), having a mouse in his hand,
and bearing this inscription:—'Whoever thou art, learn from my
fortune to reverence the gods.'"

128.—THE "SWIFT POSTS" OF ANCIENT TIMES.
Job ix. 25.

℄ Herodotus, the "Father of History," says, "The Persian messengers travel with a velocity which nothing human can equal. It
is accomplished in this manner: as many days as are required to
go from place to place, so many men and horses are regularly
placed along the road, allowing a man and horse for each day.
Neither snow, nor rain, nor heat, nor darkness are permitted to
obstruct their speed. The first messenger delivers his message to
the second, the second to the third, etc." Very often, however, the
same man who received the message from the king went post
along the whole route, changing his horse at every station.

Respecting the regularity and speed of the Roman posts, Gibbon, the historian, says: "The advantage of receiving the earliest
intelligence, and of conveying their orders with celerity, induced
the emperors to establish, throughout their extensive dominions,
the regular institution of posts. Houses were everywhere erected at

the distance of only five or six miles; each of them was constantly provided with forty horses, and by the help of these relays, it was easy to travel a hundred miles a day along the Roman roads."

The same historian also relates the following anecdote: "In the time of Theodosius, Cesarius, a magistrate of high rank, went post from Antioch to Constantinople. He began his journey at night, was in Cappadocia (165 miles from Antioch) the ensuing evening, and arrived at Constantinople the sixth day about noon. The whole distance was about 725 Roman miles, or 665 English miles."

This was remarkably good work for ancient times, though it does not greatly impress us who are accustomed to railways and telegraphs. Had Job been familiar with the high speed of modern travelling, he might still have compared the flight of his days to the swiftness of a post.

129.—COMMON SENTIMENT RESPECTING THE PUBLICANS.
Matt. v. 46.

⁋ Among the Jews, the publican class—including both those who farmed the taxes, and those who actually collected from the people—was regarded with unmingled detestation. They had a proverb, "Take not a wife out of a family where there is a publican, for they are all publicans." And it appears that the Gentiles did not think much better of this class. Xenophon said they were all robbers. Theocritus, being asked which was the worst kind of wild beast, replied, "On the mountains, bears and lions; in cities, publicans and pettifoggers." And another classical writer designates the life of a publican as "robbery beyond count, shameful greediness, a calling destitute of honour, a disgraceful traffic." The same kind of sentiment remains to the present day associated with the tax-collecting class, but it is usually no more than the unreasonable prejudice connected with the supposed hardship of *taxpaying*.

130.—THE EXCELLENCY OF CARMEL.
Isaiah xxxv. 2.

⁋ Van de Velde writes thus: "At every step the ancient glory of Carmel becomes more and more evident to me. What a memora-

ble morning in this wild flower-garden! The hawthorn, the jasmine, and many another tree and shrub, whose sweetly odorous
and elegant bunches of blossom are unknown to me by name, are
now in flower. The oak, the myrtle, and the laurel have tempered
their deep winter green with glittering leaflets of a lighter hue.
And what a variety of flowers are trodden by the traveller on his
way! There is not one I have seen in Galilee, or on the plains
along the coast, that I do not find here again on Carmel,—from
the crocuses on the rocky grounds to the fennel plants and narcis-
suses of the Leontes; from the intense red, white, and purple
anemones of the plains to the ferns that hide themselves in the
dark sepulchral caves. Yes! Carmel indeed is still Carmel: the
fruitful,—the graceful,—the fragrant,—the lovely mountain that it
was in the days of old."

131.—THE KENITE ORIGIN OF THE SACRED NAME.
Exodus iii. 14.

⁋ The Dutch scholar, Tiele, has endeavoured to show that the
name Yahveh (Jehovah) was borrowed by the Israelites from the
tribe of Kenites, and he supports his theory by the following arguments: (1) The Kenites were identical with the Midianites, and it
may readily be supposed that Moses learnt much during his long
stay among them; more especially in religious matters, since his
father-in-law, Jethro, was a priest. Then (2) secondly, Deborah in
her song represents Yahveh as coming from Edom—that is from
the southern desert, in which the Kenites lived. (3) Thirdly, it was
to the same desert that Elijah retired to commune with the Lord.
(4) Fourthly, the Rechabites of Kenite origin were zealous
worshippers of the Lord. And (5) lastly, Jael and Caleb belonged
to the Kenite stock, showing how close must have been the relationship between the Kenites and the Israelites. But none of these
arguments will bear close examination. It is more probable that
the Kenites learned the name of Yahveh from the Israelites than
that the converse was the case. The representation of God in
Deborah's song is plainly a poetical metaphor, and Elijah fled to
Horeb because it was in that region that the Law had been given.
The Rechabites had become an integral part of the Israelitish people long before we hear of Jonadab as zealous for the Lord, and
what is stated as the parentage of Jael and Caleb only proves how
intimate were the relations between the chosen people of God and

the Kenites. The origin of this intimacy may be found in the residence of Moses among the Midianites and his marriage with the
daughter of Jethro. It may be added that Ernest de Bunsen believes the Kenites and Rechabites to represent the "mixed" population that went out of Egypt at the Exodus, as well as "the stranger
in Israel" or "the stranger that is within your gates."

132.—HEROD'S JUDGMENT-HALL, OR PRAETORIUM.
Acts xxiii. 35.

⁋ The word *praetorium* is properly applied to the official residence
of provincial Roman Governors. In it they administered justice. In
connection with it, as with our old castles, there were prison-
chambers and guard-rooms, and in one of these Paul was lodged.
The term, however, came to be applied to any residence of a king
or prince, and indeed to any building having the character of a
palace. As this is particularly called "Herod's judgment-hall," it
seems probable that it was not the abode of Felix, but a palace,
built by Herod, which at the time was devoted to public uses, and
had become, in fact, the sessions house.

133.—RIDING OVER PROSTRATE BODIES.
Isaiah li. 23.

⁋ An Eastern custom, called the *Doseh,* still prevalent or but
recently extinct, explains the allusion made in this passage. Mr.
Lane, in his *Modern Egyptians,* says, "Here," in the park at Cairo,
"a number of *darweeshes* (dervishes) and others (I am sure there
were more than sixty, but I could not count their number), laid
themselves down upon the ground side by side, as close as possible
to each other, having their backs upwards, their legs extended, and
their arms placed together beneath their foreheads. They incessantly muttered the word '*Allah.*' About twelve or more *darweeshes,* mostly without their shoes, then ran over the backs of
their prostrate companions; some beating *bázes,* or little drums of
a hemispherical form, held in the left hand, and exclaiming
'*Allah!*' And then the Sheik approached; his horse hesitated for
several minutes to tread on the back of the first of the prostrate
men, but being pulled, and urged on behind, he at length stepped
upon them, and then, without apparent fear, ambled at a high
pace over them all, led by two persons who ran over the prostrate

men, one sometimes treading on the feet, and the other on the heads. The spectators immediately raised the cry of '*Allah, la, la, la, lah!*' Not one of the men thus trampled upon by the horse seemed to be hurt: but each, the moment the Sheik had passed over him, jumped up, and followed the Sheik."

The same ceremony was witnessed in Baalbec so late as 26th April, 1862. In this case fourteen devotees were selected for the ceremony, apparently much against their own will, and they were ridden over by two shereefs, or descendants of Mahomet.

134.—THE EVILS OF MIXED MARRIAGES.
1 Cor. vii. 10–17.

℃ Without some adequate impression of the debased moral condition of the pagan populations in the time of the Early Church, we shall not appreciate either the necessity for, or the wisdom of, Paul's advice concerning marriage. Tertullian describes both a Christian marriage, in which both parties are believing disciples, and a mixed marriage in which one member is a pagan. In the first case he speaks of the oneness of hope, prayer, practice, and pious service; no need of concealment, mutual avoidance, nor mutual vexation; distrust banished, a freeborn confidence, sympathy and comfort in each other, presiding over every part of their public and private existence.

In dealing with the serious evils to the woman which follow mixed marriage, especially when entered into after her conversion, he gives us a vivid picture of the social life of the early Christian age. "When the wife wishes to attend worship her husband makes an appointment for the baths. Instead of hymns she hears songs, and his songs are from the theatre, the tavern, and the night-cellar. Her fasts are hindered by his feasts. He is sure to object against nocturnal services, prison visits, the kiss of peace, and other customs. She will have a difficulty in persuading him that such private observances as crossing and exsufflation, are not magical rites."

Justin Martyr gives an illustrative case. "A woman married to a very wicked husband, herself as drunken and dissolute as the man, became a convert to the faith. Thoroughly reformed, she tried to persuade him by the precepts of the Gospel, and the terrors of eternal fire. Failing in her attempts, and revolted by the loathsome and unnatural compulsion to which her husband subjected her, she thought repudiation would be preferable to such a life. Her friends

prevailed on her to wait and hope for the best, but a journey to
Alexandria made her husband worse than before, and, driven to
despair, she sent him a divorce. Immediately he informed against
her as a Christian; a blow which she parried by presenting a petition for delay to the Emperor Marcus Aurelius, who granted her
request. Upon this her husband, thirsting for revenge, accused her
teacher in religious truth, and had the satisfaction of seeing three
lives sacrificed in succession to his vengeance."

135.—ALLELUIA.
Rev. xix. 1, 3, 6.

⁋ This is the liturgical form of the Hebrew word "Hallelujah." It
has been said that this term "neither Latin nor barbarian has ventured to translate from the sacred tongue into his own; in all lands
the mystic sound of the Hebrew is heard."

Some think that the Early Church transferred to the Christian
Paschal Feast the custom of singing psalms, accompanied with the
Hallelujah, at the older Jewish Paschal ceremonies; and in the
most ancient sacramentaries the Alleluia precedes and follows a
verse, just as in the Jewish usage it preceded and followed a
psalm.

"By the fourth century it seems to have been well known as the
Christian shout of joy or victory; for Sozomen tells of a voice
heard in the temple of Serapis at Alexandria, chanting Alleluia,
which was taken for a sign of its coming destruction by the Christians. The victory which the Christian Britons, under the guidance
of Germanus of Auxerre, with their loud shout of Alleluia, gained
over the pagan Picts and Scots (429), is another instance of the
use of Alleluia for encouragement and triumph."

136.—THE SITE OF GIBEAH OF SAUL.
Isaiah x. 29.

⁋ A great deal of uncertainty has always hung over the site of
Gibeah of Saul. In the first edition of *Biblical Researches,* Vol. II,
p. 114, Dr. Robinson regarded the modern village of Jeba lying
eastward of er-Ram as representing the biblical locality, at once
the Gibeah of Benjamin and of Saul. A little later, 1844, in the
first volume of the *Bibliotheca Sacra,* pp. 598–692, as the result
of further investigation, and partly from considerations brought

forward by a German critic and theologian, Gross, he modified
his position, so as to place Gibeah at a point bearing the name of
Tuleil-el-Ful, situated about two miles south of er-Ram, or Ramah;
but held to the view that Jeba must still be the spot of the biblical
Geba. In a recent note on this topic, published in the *Quarterly
Statement of the Palestine Exploration Fund,* Lieutenant Conder
holds that the names Geba, Gaba, Gabatha, Gibeah of Benjamin,
and Gibeah of Saul, all pertain to one place, Gibeah being the title
of the region of which Geba was the town, and brings out certain
incidental facts which go to show that Jeba, the point first selected
by Dr. Robinson, is the true site. For example, Tell el-Ful lies on
the main road, whereas the Levite turned aside from his route to
Gibeah of Benjamin (Judges xix. 13). This town, when taken by
Jonathan in the narrative, is connected with the rock Seneh (1 Sam.
xiv. 4), a word elsewhere translated "thorn," or "thorn-bush."
Josephus, also, speaking of Gabatha-Sauli, places it near the Valley
of Thorns, Ακανθών αὐλῶν—B. J. V. ii. 1; and even to-day a valley
lies just below Jeba, called Wadi Suweinet, "the valley of the little
thorn," or thorn-tree. In Gibeah of Benjamin the watchmen of
Saul were able to see the conflict going on at Michmash and to
hear the sound of battle (1 Sam. xiv. 5–16; whereas from Tell
el-Ful the field of Michmash is not visible and the two points lie
fully five miles apart. So also a cave large enough to accommodate
an ambush existed at Gibeah of Benjamin, or Geba. Nothing in
the way of a cavern occurs at Tell el-Ful; but a large cave is afforded by Jeba. This cave of Geba (Judges xx. 33) stands wrongly
as "the meadows of Gibeah" in our Authorised Version.

137.—CHEREM, EXCOMMUNICATION, AND ANATHEMA.
Lev. xxvii. 28, 29; John ix. 22, 34; 1 Cor. xvi. 22.

⁋ "Cherem" is a Hebrew term signifying the devotement of persons or property by a solemn vow to God: Such persons or property were regarded as put under a ban; they were wholly devoted,
given over, and there could be no redemption of them by a gift to
the sanctuary as in other cases. If persons, they must be slain, if
property it must be burnt, or given to the sanctuary. The word is
used in devoting idolaters, or the Canaanite cities to destruction. It
was permitted, as an act of piety to "devote" an enemy's city by
such a vow; the first city taken, as in the case of Jericho, being the

one wholly destroyed, offered that is to God as a kind of firstfruits of the war.

"Cherem" became afterwards one of the three degrees of excommunication in use among the Jews. The lightest form was called *Niddui;* this separated the man from all social intercourse for thirty days, and the period might, if necessary, be extended to sixty, and even ninety days. If the man remained impenitent, he incurred the second degree of punishment, called *Cherem.* This sentence was pronounced in a solemn assembly or court; no one was to eat with the person so sentenced, no association was to be had, no business was to be transacted with him; nor could he purchase anything but food. *Shammata* was the severest form of excommunication, in which the offender was solemnly devoted to destruction, as in the case of Achan. The term which Paul uses (1 Cor. xvi. 22), *Maranatha,* is similar in meaning to *Shammata,* "The Lord cometh."

"Anathema" is the Greek term representing the Hebrew *Cherem,* and indicates the excommunication practised in the Christian Church. The Early Christians exercised discipline on offending members in lesser and in greater forms. The greater is called *Anathema.* They regarded themselves as distinctly warranted in cutting off members from their body by our Lord's words (Matt. xviii. 17): and in using for such excision the term *Anathema,* they appealed to Paul's employment of the word, in Gal. i. 8. They regarded the *Anathema* as cutting a man off from the way of salvation; so that unless he received the grace of repentance he would certainly perish. The word is uniformly used in the Septuagint version as the equivalent of *Cherem;* and it seems reasonable to suppose that where it occurs in the New Testament Scriptures it is to be understood in the deeper sense—as relating to the spiritual condition—and not merely to exclusion from Church privileges.

138.—THE USE OF AMULETS.
Deut. vi. 8, 9; Acts xix. 19.

℄ The word "amulet" is best derived from the Arabic *hammalet,* a thing suspended: the idea of it is something hung upon the person which is supposed to have power to guard the wearer from unseen evils, demons, spectres, the evil eye, etc. The Egyptians carried this practice to a great extent. The scarabaeus, the hawk, the serpent, the hooded snake, an open eye, outspread wings, with or without formulae of prayer, are found in countless variety in all our museums, and seem to have been borne, some on the breast, some suspended by a chain round the neck. Moses, in this matter, as in so many others, did not attempt to destroy familiar ideas, but corrected them, directing the thoughts of the people to the living God by the papyrus scrolls, with texts written on them, which he enjoined should be worn on the person, and hung on the walls.

Through the whole history of Rabbinism, however, the tendency to the superstitious use of amulets was on the increase, and few Jews felt safe from evil spirits unless their bed was guarded by the *Mesusa*. "Mystic figures—the sacred tetragrammaton, the shield of David, the seal of Solomon—with cabalistic words A G L A (an acrostic formed from the initial letters of the Hebrew words for 'Thou art mighty for everlasting, O Lord'). Abracalan, and the like, shot up as a rank aftergrowth."

Superstitions such as these were checked by the first faith of the Early Christians, but with the decay of Church simplicity they crept in, and early traces of the use of such amulets can be found. "The followers of Basilides had their mystical Abraxas and Jaldabaoth, which they wrote on parchment, and used as a charm. Scarabei have been found, with inscriptions indicating Christian associations of a superstitious nature. The catacombs of Rome have yielded small objects of various kinds that were used apparently for the same purpose, a bronze fish with the word ΣΩΣΑΙΣ on it, a hand holding a tablet with ΖΠΟΕΣ, and medals. Jerome confesses that he had worn copies of the Gospels round the neck to guard himself against disease. "When the passion for relics set in they too were employed, and even Gregory the Great sent to Theodelinda two of these charms, one a cross containing a fragment of the true cross, the other a box containing a copy of the Gospels, each with Greek invocations, as a charm against the evil spirits that beset children."

The Christian Teachers strove against the growing superstition. The Council of Laodicea forbade the use of such "phylacteries" as they called them; Chrysostom denounces them in all their forms. And Augustine warns men against all such diabolical phylacteries.

De Foe tells of a charm used largely by the Londoners in the time of the great plague, formed of the letters of the word A B R A C A D A B R A set in various order. The belief in the living God of Love should deliver us altogether from the fears which have set men on seeking charms and amulets.

139.—THE ABANA AND PHARPAR RIVERS.
2 Kings v. 12.

⊄ The Abana, or as margin, Amana, has been identified with the modern *Barada*. It rises in the beautiful plain of Zebedâny, issuing from a little lake, and receiving in its course the waters of two or three fountains. Quitting this plain the Barady dashes over a cliff, thirty feet high, and runs through a magnificent ravine, past the ancient Abila, and is afterwards joined by the stream from 'Ain Fîjeh, one of the largest springs in Syria. Having emerged from the mountains into the plains of Damascus, the Barady flows through orchards and meadows till it enters the city, and passing through it, falls ultimately into the Bahret-el-Kibliyeh, or South Lake. At its rise the river is 3,343 feet above the sea, and 1,149 above Damascus, which is distant from the source about twenty-one or twenty-two miles. The extent of cultivated land it waters is estimated at 311 square miles.

Mr. Porter gives the following account of the stream which he identifies as the Pharpar:—

In a deep valley running far up into the heart of Hermon several small fountains burst forth, uniting into the Nahr-el-'Arny. This flows through a picturesque and rugged valley, entering the plain about five miles from its source, and winds a few miles farther till it reaches S'as'a. Here it is joined by another stream, the Nahr Beit-Jenn, which rising more to the south passes through a wild glen shaded by walnuts and poplars, and, augmented by another brook, a little below the village Beit-Jenn, crosses an undulating plain five or six miles to S'as'a. After the junction the river bears the name of the " 'Awaj," "curved;" and this is the ancient Pharpar. It does not approach very near to Damascus, but, flowing in its upper course through limestone strata, and afterwards through basalt, it waters the adjacent territory. S'as'a is about twenty-five miles from Damascus; and the greater part of the road is dreary and uninteresting. Some portions, however, of the course of the 'Awaj are picturesque, as it glides by meadows and cornfields fringed with poplars and willows. Its waters are diminished by canals constructed to irrigate neighbouring villages; and when it reaches a place called *Nejha*, the greater part of what remains is carried off by two canals. Below Nejha, therefore, its bed is often dry; but after the winter rains it continues to run with a deep and rapid stream into the lake *Heljány*. The district

through which the 'Awaj flows is called Wady-el-Ajam, extending
from the walls of Damascus along the base of Anti-Libanus, to the
borders of Jedûr beyond the 'Awaj. This district contains fifty-one
villages.

140.—The Shekinah as the Holy Ghost.
Exodus xl. 34.

ℂ The Jews understand by the term "Shekinah" that visible light
in the Tabernacle and Temple which indicated the presence of
God as the Holy Ghost. In the Targums, or ancient Jewish paraphrases of the Old Testament, are found the names of Jehovah, or
God; Memar, or the Word; and Shekinah, or the Holy Ghost. The
Rabbis assert that the Shekinah drove from the Holy of Holies the
prince of the air, and communicated a peculiar sanctity to the
place. They say that the Shekinah rests with the mild and humble,
but flies from the fierce and passionate. It resides with him whose
house is open to the stranger, and is found in the midst of two or
three persons who meet to study the law. They add that the
Shekinah has ten times changed its dwelling; and, at last, going on
the Mount of Olives, it continued there three years and a half, saying to the Israelites, "Return to me, my children, and I will return
to you." But seeing they would not be converted, it retired.

141.—Sentiments concerning Manual Labour.
Prov. xiv. 23.

ℂ The Greeks and Romans looked upon all mechanical work as
mean and vulgar, setting chief honour upon the military profession; but the Jews enacted that every boy should learn a trade, and
agreed with their Rabbi Juda, the wise, that "labour honours the
labourer." Up to the age of forty, Rabbi Johanan, son of Zakkai,
afterwards president of the Sanhedrim, was, like Mahomet, a merchant; Rabbis Juda and Menahem were bakers; Rabbi Eliezer,
supreme president of the schools of Alexandria, was a smith;
Rabbi Ismael, a needle maker; and Rabbi Joza Ben Chalaphta, a
tanner. The Rabbis are even said to have rejoiced in the phrase,
"Rabbi So-and-So, the shoemaker," or "the weaver," as the case
might be. But the Jews did not honour labour when it was not associated with learning.

142.—ANOTHER PARABLE OF THE WEDDING GARMENT.
Matt. xxii. 12.

℀ It is curious to find that the Jews have a parable very similar to that spoken by our Lord, though the comparison of them brings out, in a very forcible way, the infinite superiority of our Lord's teachings.

"Repent one day before death. There was a king who bade all his servants to a great repast, but did not indicate the hour. Some went home, and put on their best garments, and stood at the door of the palace. Others said, 'There is ample time; the king will let us know beforehand.' But the king summoned them suddenly, and those who came in their best garments were well received; but the foolish ones, who came in their slovenliness, were turned away in disgrace. Therefore repent to-day, lest to-morrow you may be summoned."

143.—A STRONG FIGURE DESCRIBING THE IDLE MAN.
Prov. xix. 24.

℀ This passage, as it stands in the English Version, lacks point. It would be better rendered thus: "A slothful man hideth (rather dippeth) his hand in the dish, and will not," etc. The explanation is simple: Arabs and other Orientals partake of milk and pottage in a very primitive style. A large wooden bowl is placed before them filled with milk or pottage, as the case may be; and five or six men surround it, each dipping in his hand instead of a spoon, and drinking the liquid out of his palm. They use their hands for spoons in taking milk and pottage, but not, it is said, in drinking water. With this explanation the passage gains force; it is impossible, surely, for laziness to go beyond this—the idle fellow dips his hand into the milk or pottage, but is too lazy to lift it to his mouth to feed himself.

144.—DESCRIPTION OF EBAL AND GERIZIM.
Joshua viii. 33.

℀ A few extracts from a report furnished by Colonel Wilson, of the Palestine Exploration Fund, will make the scene over which Joshua presided, and the transactions of the day, plain. He says:—

"On the 6th of March (1866) Lieut. Anderson and I arrived at Nablous (the ancient Shechem), with the view of carrying out some excavations on Mount Gerizim. Before, however, attempting to describe the results of our labours, it will be as well to give a general sketch of the locality. At Nablous the range of hills which traverses Palestine from north to south is pierced by a remarkable pass, running nearly east and west; on the north the pass is flanked by the range of Mount Ebal, rising at its highest point to 3,029 feet above the sea, or 1,200 feet above the level of the valley; on the south by the range of Mount Gerizim, rising to 2,898 feet. Between these two mountains the valley rises gently towards the east, to the water-parting between the Mediterranean and the Jordan, at which point there is a remarkable topographical feature which is not often met with—a recess on either side of the valley, forming a grand natural amphitheatre, probably the scene of the events described in Joshua viii. 30–35. . . . It is hardly too much to say of this natural amphitheatre that there is no place in Palestine so suitable for the assembly of an immense body of men within the limits to which a human voice could reach, where at the same time each individual would be able to see what was being done. The recesses in the two mountains are exactly opposite to each other, and the limestone strata, running up to the very summits in a succession of ledges, present the appearance of a regular succession of benches. A grander sight can scarcely be imagined than that which the reading of the Law must have presented; the Ark, borne by the Levites, on the gentle elevation which separates the waters of the Mediterranean from those of the Dead Sea, and 'all Israel, and their elders, and officers, and their judges, on this side and on that,' 'half of them over against Mount Gerizim, and half of them over against Mount Ebal,' covering the bare hillsides from head to foot. Two questions have been raised in connection with the reading of the Law; the possibility of hearing it read, and the possibility of assembling the twelve tribes on the ground at the same time. Of the first there can be no doubt; the valley has no peculiar acoustic properties, but the air in Palestine is so clear (homogeneous is a better word, for *clearness* of air does not assist the passage of sound), that the voice can be easily heard at a distance which would seem impossible in England; and as a case in point it may be mentioned that during the excavations on Mount Gerizim the Arab workmen were on more than one occasion heard conversing with men passing along the valley below. It is

not, however, necessary to suppose that every word of the Law
was heard by the spectators; the blessings and curses were, in all
probability, as familiar to the Israelites as the Litany or Ten Com-
mandments are to us, and the responses would be taken up as
soon as the voice of the reader of the Law ceased. With regard to
the second point, . . . there are few localities which afford so
large an amount of standing-room, on the same area, or give such
facilities for the assembly of a great multitude."

145.—SCORPIONS.
Deut. viii. 15.

℄ Palgrave, in his *Year's Journey through Central Arabia,* says
that on one occasion his rest was somewhat disturbed by a scorpion bite: not so serious an accident, indeed, as it sounds, considering the genus of the aggressor, but painful enough, though
soon passing off. "These desert scorpions are curious little creatures, about a fourth of an inch in length, and, apparently, all
claws and tail, of a deep reddish brown colour, and very active.
They abound throughout the sandy soil. In the day-time they
wisely keep out of the way, but at night come out to take the
cooler air. Their sting is exactly like the smart of a white-hot iron
point firmly pressed on the skin, and when I felt my forehead thus
assaulted I jumped up exceedingly quick, anticipating twenty-four
hours of suffering, the usual period allotted, at least in popular
credence, to the duration of scorpion torture; but I was agreeably
disappointed, for the pain did not last above an hour, was accompanied by a little swelling, and then went entirely off, hardly leaving any perceptible mark."

There are, however, different kinds of scorpions, and those mentioned by Palgrave must belong to the very smallest species. As
many as five different species have been counted in the region of
Sinai, some of which are also found in Lebanon. The scorpions in
the South of Europe are about an inch long, while in tropical regions they have been found as much as five inches in length.

The *Scorpio* is a genus of the class *Arachnida* (spider), order
Pulmonaria, section *Pedipalpi.* This genus is distinguished from
other groups of spiders by having the abdomen articulated and terminated by a curved spur: the *palpi* are large and the terminal
segment assumes the form of a lobster's claw, being in like manner
provided with pincers. The scorpion, properly so called, has six
eyes. These creatures lurk under stones and among ruins. They

run swiftly, curving the tail over the back: this they can turn in
any direction, and use for attack or defence, as it is provided with
a sting.

146.—HID TREASURE.
Matt. xiii. 44.

℀ In unsettled times it has been an almost universal custom to
bury treasures for security. In the last century, Baron du Tott, who
travelled in the East, found that the Tartars, though they received
large sums of money from the Dutch and Venetians in the way of
trade, never made much use of it among themselves, but, to make
it secure, buried most of it in the earth. All over the East there exists a superstitious belief that treasures are hidden in all old ruins,
and generally it is supposed that there is something magical about
the secret hoards, since no one can find a treasure without the use
of the proper enchantments. When Europeans first began to
explore the ruins of the Eastern world, the superstitious natives
could not believe that they had any motive other than the hope of
finding hidden treasures; and many a hapless explorer has suffered
every species of annoyance and interruption in his work on account of this prejudice. Even now the feeling has not died out,
though present travellers are free from the dangers that beset their
predecessors.

147.—ANOINTING THE SICK WITH OIL.
James v. 14.

℀ A very natural and simple explanation has been given to this
difficult and misused passage. Anointing the body with oil was the
sign of health. Those who were sick might not be anointed; nor
those passing through a time of mourning. The ancient customs in
relation to anointing may be illustrated by our customs in relation
to shaving the beard. The sick man will neither trouble himself,
nor be troubled, about shaving; but as soon as he begins to recover
he will return to his old and cleanly habits. So the ancients would
neglect daily anointing while under sickness, and their return to
their old ways was the sign of recovering health. When, therefore,
James enjoins the elders to anoint the sick man after prayer for his
restoration, he really says, "Pray for him in perfect faith, and
show that you have such strong faith by acting towards him as if
he were recovered. Whatsoever things ye ask when ye pray, be-

lieve that ye receive them, and ye shall have them. Anoint the sick
man as if he were restored to health again." The elders were to
"help him rise from the bed, wash, anoint his head and dress, and
rejoice with him in view of the healing mercies of God."

148.—"Could not bear up into the Wind."
Acts xxvii. 15.

℃ This expression literally translated would be, "Could not keep
her eyes to the wind:" and the allusion is to the figure of an *eye*
which is either painted or carved on each side of the bows of
many Oriental ships. So the ship resembled a great fish; "imagination gave life and sense to the craft, and it was supposed to peer
into the storm, and press forward to its goal." In ancient times
mariners were almost entirely dependent on their eyes—their look-
out—their observation of the coast-line, and the heavens, as they
had no compass, and very imperfect nautical instruments.

149.—Hindoo Version of a Virtuous Woman.
Prov. xxxi. 10–31.

℃ A picture in many respects similar to that given in the Book of
Proverbs, is found in the Code of Gentoo Laws, of Ancient India.

> *"A woman who always acts according to her husband's pleasure,*
> *And speaks no ill of any person,*
> *And who can herself do all such things as are proper for a*
>   *woman,*
> *And who is of good principles,*
> *And who bears a son,*
> *And who rises from sleep before her husband;*
> *Such a woman is found only by much, and many, religious works,*
> *And by a peculiarly happy destiny.*
> *A woman who is of good disposition,*
> *And who puts on her jewels and clothes with decorum;*
> *Whenever the husband is cheerful, the wife also is cheerful;*
> *And if the husband be sorrowful, the wife also is sorrowful;*
> *And whenever the husband undertakes a journey, the wife puts*
>   *on a careless dress and lays aside her jewels, and other*
>   *ornaments;*
> *And abuses no person;*
> *And will not expend a single dàm (about ¾d.) without her*
>   *husband's consent;*
> *And takes care of the household goods;*
> *And at the time of worship, performs her worship to the Deity in*
>   *a proper manner;*

And goes not out of the house;
And is not unchaste;
And makes no quarrels or disturbances;
And has no greedy passions;
And is always employed in some good work;
And pays a proper respect to all persons;
Such is a good woman."

150.—THE PRACTICE OF LIFTING UP
THE HANDS IN PRAYER.
1 Tim. ii. 8.

℄ This familiar Jewish attitude for praise and prayer (see Ps. lxiii. 4; cxxxiv. 2; Neh. viii. 6, etc.) naturally passed over to the Christian Church. Clemens of Alexandria, A.D. 192, is an early witness to the continued observance of the rite. After defining prayer to be "converse with God," he proceeds to say that therefore, as if reaching up to Him, we "raise the head and lift the hands towards heaven." Tertullian, his contemporary, "Worshipping with modesty and humility we the more commend our prayers to God, not even lifting up our hands too high, but with self-restraint and becomingly." Again, "We, Christians, looking upwards, with hands outspread, because free from guilt; with head bare, because we are not ashamed; lastly, without a remembrancer [of the names of the gods], because we pray from the heart." Origen, A.D. 230, says that among the many gestures of the body, we ought without doubt in prayer to prefer "the stretching forth of the hands, and the lifting up of the eyes;" and that when the devout man prays, he "stretches forth his soul towards God, beyond his hands, as it were, and his mind farther than his eyes." According to Eusebius, Constantine had himself represented on coins and in pictures "looking up to heaven, and stretching forth his hands like one praying."

151.—WHO WAS IN THE WORLD TO PUT
CAIN'S LIFE IN PERIL?
Gen. iv. 14.

℄ The general notion is that Adam was absolutely the first man that ever lived, and that all men have descended from the first pair who were placed in Paradise. The Bible assumes, though it nowhere directly teaches it, that all the *present* human inhabitants of the earth are the offspring of Adam and Eve; but it leaves us free

150.—The Practice of Lifting up the Hands in Prayer.

to form our own speculations concerning *Preadamites*. There may have been men long before Adam, and other races besides the Adamic might have existed, at least down to the time of the Flood. We are led to think that there must have been a family of men peopling the region not far from Eden at the time Abel was murdered, else Cain's fear, and God's precaution for his preservation, are alike inexplicable. Cain seems to have thought of some men who did not belong to his family, and those men he regarded as his enemies, who might be expected to kill every stranger that should intrude among them; but to prevent the worst in Cain's case, God set a mark upon him to protect him from the attacks of those among whom he might wander. All this fairly implies that there were people besides the small Adamite family then living at no great distance from the Edenians. To assume that Cain was afraid of some of his own kindred who had grown up and migrated to distant territories, is to assume an increase of Adam's family altogether unnatural.

A recent writer has attempted to explain the difficulty in a novel manner; it may be doubtful whether his view will bear critical examination, and it is given as a suggestion worthy of being thought over. He supposes that the two first chapters of Genesis record the creation of two distinct races, or rather the progenitors of two entirely distinct races. Those who were created first (Gen. i. 29), were never brought into covenant with the Creator, nor had they any law laid down for their observance. From them descended the race or tribes among whom Cain became an exile. But in Genesis ii. he thinks we have an account of the making of a totally distinct couple, the man being made from the dust of the ground, and then the woman from the rib of the new man. From this pair the present surviving race of man has descended. This may be as good a solution of the difficulty as any yet offered, it is by no means—and the writer knows this as well as any man—beyond the possibility of dispute.

152.—God no Respecter of Persons.
Acts x. 34, 35.

¶ It is very important that we should hold the right clue to guide us in understanding this saying. The question which recent events had solved in Peter's mind, was that of the admissibility of men of all nations into the Church of Christ. *In this sense only,* had he received any information as to the *acceptableness* of men of all nations before God. He saw that in every nation, men who seek after God, who receive His witness of Himself, without which He has left no man, and humbly follow His will as they know it—these have no *extraneous hindrance,* such as uncircumcision, placed in their way to Christ, but are capable of being admitted into God's Church, *though* Gentiles, and *as* Gentiles. That only such are spoken of, is agreeable to the nature of the case; for men who do not fear God, and work unrighteousness, are out of the question, not being likely to seek such admission. It is clearly unreasonable to suppose Peter to have meant that each heathen's natural light and moral purity would render him acceptable in the sight of God.

153.—"Be thou Removed."
Matt. xxi. 21.

❡ "Removing mountains" was among the Jews a common hyperbole for the conquest of stupendous difficulties. A great teacher was called by the Rabbis *gokêr hárîm,* or uprooter of mountains.

154.—Capital Punishments among the Jews.
Exodus xxi. 12.

❡ The death of condemned criminals was effected by "stoning," "burning," "slaying with the sword," and "strangling."

The "house of stoning," from which the culprit was thrown, was two stories high, "stoning" being synonymous with breaking the neck. It was the duty of the chief witness to precipitate the prisoner from the house with his own hands; if he fell on his breast, those on the spot turned him over on his back; if the fall had not instantaneously killed him, the second witness threw a stone upon his heart; if he still survived, the whole people hastened his death by casting stones upon him.

The punishments of "strangling" and "burning" were almost identical, notwithstanding the difference of name. In both cases the culprit was immersed to the waist in soft mud, and in the former case two men, by tightening a cord, wrapped in a soft cloth, round his neck, caused instantaneous suffocation. In the case of "burning," a lighted wick was thrust down the prisoner's throat as he opened his mouth for the last breath, the man being as nearly as

possible dead at the time. The corpse of the culprit, however executed, was first buried in a place specially appropriated to criminals. After a time, however, the bones were gathered up, and
transferred to the burial-place of his kin. The relatives then visited
the judges and the witnesses, as much as to say, "We bear no mal-
ice against you, for a righteous judgment have ye judged." There
was no confiscation of the prisoner's goods.

155.—SKILL OF JOSHUA'S PLAN OF CONQUEST.
Josh. v. 1, ix. 1.

℃ The strategy of the leader of "the host of the Lord" was, con-
sciously or unconsciously, of the highest order. Had the attack
been made upon the southern frontier, the invaders would have
found before them an ever-increasing mass of enemies, and the
successive mountain ranges of Hebron, of Jerusalem, and of
Ephraim. But when the Jordan was crossed near Jericho, that
frontier fortress captured, and the passes secured by the ambus-
cade that destroyed the city of Ai, Joshua was able to drive his
army, like a wedge, into the very heart of the hostile country, and
strike his blows right and left at the isolated divisions of the
enemy.

156.—PAYING MONEY BY WEIGHT.
Gen. xxiii. 16.

℃ Coined money was probably not introduced into Judaea until
the time of Cyrus, though some Jewish authorities doubt this. Before that time, gold and silver were paid by weight only. Hence we
are told that "Abraham *weighed* unto Ephraim the silver which he
had named in the audience of the sons of Heth, four hundred
shekels of silver, current with the merchant" (Gen. xxiii. 16). In 2
Kings v. 5, "six thousand *pieces* of gold" should be "six thousand
shekels." "Gold was carried in bars, from which portions were cut
when need arose, and the value was ascertained by weighing."

In China, money is weighed to this day. Even coin is weighed.
In Canton, if you give a shopman a half-crown, he always takes
out a small pair of scales and weighs it, and gives you change according to the weight. The small change all consists of coin broken
up into small bits, which are given by weight. In North China,
sycee is used. This is silver cast into lumps, called "shoes," which

are cut into pieces and weighed when the whole lump is not needed, just as the Jews used to do with their precious metals. The only coin used as such in China is the copper "cash."

Abraham's money was that "current with the merchant," probably for fineness. In Canton, every silver piece is examined by the "shroffs," or "compradors," and if good is stamped with the name of the shop. Every shop whose mark is on the silver is responsible for its fineness, or will change the money if you are dissatisfied with it.

157.—OPPRESSIONS AND EXTORTIONS
OF TAX-GATHERERS.
Luke iii. 13.

⁋ Present-day conditions of Eastern lands painfully illustrate the continuance of some of the most demoralising customs of the past. When the crop is reaped, and while the winnowing is actually going on upon the threshing-floor, the tax-gatherer stands by, and appropriates one-tenth as soon as the work is completed. The Mohammedan government adopts the oppressive system of the Romans, sells the tithes to the highest bidder, for a sum of money which he is ready enough to pay in advance. This purchaser, or farmer of the taxes, has then to make his profit on the transaction by forcing the most extravagant payments from the people, and in so doing he is armed with irresponsible authority. The tithe-gatherers go through the land, employing every device for the purpose of overreaching the cultivators of the soil, and obtaining from them more than their dues. The farmers are strictly ordered not to thresh their grain before the tax-gatherers are ready, which is the means of additional extortions. Crops, therefore, sometimes remain heaped upon the threshing-floors for many weeks, the distressed owners not daring to thresh and harvest them, and being compelled both to watch them by day and night, and to devise means to protect them from being wet with showers.

158.—A FIGURATIVE PROMISE OF ABUNDANT HARVEST.
Lev. xxvi. 5.

⁋ Wheat and barley are sown in Eastern lands in the autumn; the later crops in February. The barley crop is ready for cutting about the first of April; the wheat crop in the month of May, generally

towards the end of it. The harvest of the vineyards cannot be
gathered before the end of August; and the ploughing and sowing
for the following year cannot be done much before November.
When, therefore, it is promised that the harvesting and threshing
of the cereals shall reach from May to August, and the ingathering
of the vintage extend from August to November, it is plain that
extraordinary abundance and fruitfulness are intended.

159.—DIFFERENCES OF TEMPERATURE IN DAY AND NIGHT.
Gen. xxxi. 40.

℃ An Eastern traveller says: "Of my last days in the desert, I
could well say, as feelingly as Jacob, 'By day the heat consumed
me, and the cold by night.' With the setting sun a keen blast from
the north-west set in, which chilled us all to the bone, the wind
drifting the sand, like sleet, across the bleak, unsheltered plain, pil-
ing it up on the windward side of our tent's thin walls; at noon we
were in a burning soil and clime, and by night we had all the sensations of a northern winter."

160.—THE WORD "WOMAN."
Gen. ii. 22.

℃ In English, the qualification *wo*, placed before *man*, indicates
merely a difference of sex. In Latin, she is called the *mulier*, a
word derived from *mollior*—softer, more tender. In Hebrew, *ish*
signifies *man*, and the addition of a terminal vowel makes it *isha*
—a woman. In all three of these languages, the words used are
also applied to a *wife*. In Turkish, however, the name *karù*—
woman—is never applied to a wife; she is called, *ev*, which
signifies *house;* while the Armenians call her *ùndanik*, or the
keeper at home, a word which includes the children; they also call
the wife *gin, i.e.*, a woman.

161.—THE LOST TEN TRIBES.
Isaiah xi. 11.

℃ The history of the ten tribes, after their removal from Palestine
into Media, 721 B.C., by Shalmaneser, king of Assyria, is involved
in an obscurity which the assiduous efforts of scholars and

antiquarians have not been able to dispel. Media has since that period been overrun by so many devastating hordes; its political condition, its religious faith, its very language, have so many times been completely changed, each change implying the destruction of what preceded it, that the solution of this mystery is rendered quite improbable.

162.—THE LENGTH OF TIME THE EUROCLYDON LASTED.
Acts xxvii. 27.

℁ A storm lasting fourteen days must have been one of great violence. We need not, however, suppose that it continued throughout this period without intermission. Dr. Thomson says it is no uncommon thing to encounter similar storms at this day in the same part of the Mediterranean. "I have followed nearly the exact route of this disastrous voyage, and, as our noble steamer sailed in between Catzo and Candia—the Crete of the Acts—we were met by a tremendous wind, which tried the utmost power of her engines. Slowly and laboriously she ploughed her foaming furrow through the troubled sea, close under Crete, for twenty-four hours, and then ran into the harbour of Suda, which we found as quiet as a mill-pond; and, unlike Paul's Fair Havens, it would be quite commodious for the entire British navy to winter in. Here we remained a 'night and a day;' but, as the wind did not moderate, the captain became impatient, and sailed out in the very teeth of the gale. For a long time we made very little progress, and, as we ran under a certain island that was called Clauda, I could well understand that such a vessel as that 'ship of Alexandria' must have been exceedingly tossed with the tempest. However, by the aid of steam, we were carried in four, instead of fourteen days, to that 'certain island called Melita,' and into the glorious harbour of Valetta, instead of being wrecked at the entrance of St. Paul's Bay."

163.—THE USE OF MODERN GREEK IN EXPLAINING THE NEW TESTAMENT.
e.g. Acts i. 15; John xxi. 5.

℁ The language of the New Testament is a sort of medium between classic and modern Greek, and the latter often explains

terms upon which the former cannot throw any light. In Acts i.
15, for instance, there is a statement respecting "the number of
names" (*onomata*), *i.e.* the number of the disciples. Classical literature throws no light upon the expression; but it is constantly met
with among the moderns, who have even made of it a new word,
nomatoi, signifying men. So, likewise, the New Testament contains
many Orientalisms, which are more fully developed in the Romaic
or modern Greek; such, for instance, is the common mode of
addressing men as *paidia,* children, which we find in John xxi. 5.

164.—THE EGYPTIAN FIGURE OF JUSTICE.
Deut. i. 17.

❡ She was symbolised by a human form, without hands, to indicate that judges should accept no bribes; and not without hands
only, but sightless, to indicate that the judge is to know neither father nor mother, nor wife nor child, nor brother nor sister, nor
slave nor sovereign, nor friend nor foe, when he occupies the seat
of justice. He is not to be the client, but only to hear the cause;
and, uninfluenced by fear or favour, to decide the case upon its
merits.

165.—THE LEGEND CONCERNING THE DEATH OF ISAIAH.
Hebrews xi. 37.

❡ The expression "sawn asunder" is supposed to refer to the fate
of Isaiah, who perished during the wilful and idolatrous portion of
Manasseh's reign, when nearly ninety years old. Dean Stanley
says, "The story as given in the Talmud brings out an aspect of
Isaiah's mission not altogether alien to the authentic representations of it. It is the never-ending conflict between the letter
and the spirit. The king, as if entrenching himself behind the bul-
wark of the law, charges the prophet with heresy. Moses had said,
'No man shall see God's face and live.' Isaiah had said, 'I saw
the Lord.' Moses had said, 'The Lord is near.' Isaiah had said,
'Seek the Lord till ye find Him.' Moses had said, 'The number of
thy days will I perfect.' Isaiah had said, 'I will add to thy days
fifteen years.' With a true sense of the hopelessness of a controversy between two wholly uncongenial souls, the prophet is represented as returning no answer except by the name of God. The

hollow cedar tree, or carob tree, to which he escaped for refuge, closed upon him. They pursued him, and sawed the tree asunder with a wooden saw, till they came to his mouth. Then the blood flowed and he died."

166.—BEATING WITH RODS.
2 Cor. xi. 25.

⁋ This was a Roman punishment, inflicted by the civil authorities. It was usually executed by the *lictors,* who were in constant attendance on the principal magistrates, going before them as they went. The insignia of their office, as well as the dignity of the magistrate on whom they attended, consisted of a number of elm rods, bound with a thong into a bundle, which they carried on their shoulder. An axe was bound up in the bundle, and its head jutted forth from it. Within the city of Rome, however, the axe was omitted, out of respect to the Roman people. The bundle, in fact, comprised the apparatus of the lictor as executioner of the magistrates' sentence. The thong served him to bind the criminal, with the rods he inflicted beatings, and with the axe he beheaded.

167.—ANCIENT CISTERNS.
Jer. ii. 13.

⁋ These abound in Palestine, not only in connection with houses and cities, in which cases they are dug in the earth, and built round with solid masonry, but even in the most solitary part of the wilderness. The usual plan is to dig a tank in the ground, build round with stone-work, sometimes raising this several feet above the ground, and putting on it a roof. A flight of steps leads to the very bottom of the tank so that the water may be reached whatever its height in the cistern. Thomson says there are thousands of these ancient cisterns in Upper Galilee; and Van Lennep tells of a cistern in Northern Syria, close to the ruins of Gebel Simon, more than 100 feet in depth, and as many in width, hewn out of the solid rock, and accessible only through an opening at the top, which was covered with a large stone. These cisterns are very liable to crack and leak, especially those near the surface of the ground, and unscientifically constructed; and no more expressive figure of untrustworthiness could be found than a leaky tank, "a broken cistern that can hold no water."

168.—POINT OF A DIAMOND.
Jer. xvii. 1.

⁋ On this passage much light has been thrown by the cuneiform inscriptions. The prophet declares that "the sin of Judah is written with a pen of iron and with the point of a diamond. It is graven upon the table of their hearts." Now the word translated "table" is the very word used by the Assyrians to denote one of those clay tablets upon which their literature is engraved; and the "pen of iron" is the metal stylus employed for the purpose, a specimen of which was discovered at Konyunyik, by Mr. George Smith. Still more curious is the expression rendered "the point of a diamond." The first word of the expression literally signifies "a fingernail," and it is frequently met with in those Assyrian contract-tablets on which witnesses who were too poor to possess a seal impressed a nail-mark instead. From these nail-marks must have been derived the use of the word, to denote the point of a stylus made of some substance like a diamond.

169.—THE CUTTINGS AND WOUNDINGS
OF THE BAAL PRIESTS.
1 Kings xviii. 28.

⁋ Movers, following such ancient writers as Seneca, Lucian, Statius, and Apuleius, thus describes the processions of the strolling bands wandering about with the Syrian goddess:—"A discordant howling opens the scene. Then they fly wildly through one another, with the head sunk down to the ground, but turning round in circles so that the loose flowing hair drags through the mire; thereupon they first bite themselves on the arms, and at last cut themselves with two-edged swords which they are wont to carry. Then begins a new scene. One of them, who surpasses all the rest in frenzy, begins to prophesy with sighs and groans, openly accuses himself of his past sins, which he now wishes to punish by the mortifying of the flesh, takes the knotted whips, which the Galli are wont to bear, and lashes his back, and cuts himself with swords, until the blood trickles from his mangled body."

Van Lennep gives illustrations of the practices of the howling dervishes, which help in realising the Carmel scene.

"Our modern dervishes indulge in these cuttings only on special occasions, as, for instance, when a procession is organised, and proceeds to the suburbs of a town to pray for rain, or for deliverance from some public calamity: they then exhibit some of their fanatical performances, calling upon God, and cutting themselves with knives and swords, so that the blood runs, or piercing their almost naked bodies with wooden or iron spikes, from which they hang small mirrors. They sometimes become so exhausted with pain and loss of blood as to faint away, so that they have to be borne off." Sometimes those who are not dervishes are carried away by a similar impulse, and hope to render themselves acceptable to God by undergoing these voluntary tortures.

170.—MOSLEM TRADITION OF JONAH'S MISSION TO NINEVEH.
Jonah iii. 10.

℄ The events connected with Jonah's mission to Nineveh must have made a deep impression on the Oriental mind; and we cannot wonder that tradition and fable are found to exist side by side with the Bible narrative in this case, as in so many others, among such imaginative people as the inhabitants of Western Asia.

A Moslem tradition says that when Jonah first began to exhort the Ninevites to repentance, instead of attending to his warning they ill-treated him, so that he was obliged to leave the city, threatening them at his departure that they should be soon destroyed. When the time at which he had predicted the overthrow of the city drew near, the heavens became overcast with a black cloud, which shot forth fire, and filled the air with smoke. This cloud hung for a long time immediately over the city, and the Ninevites, in terrible consternation, fled to the fields, with their families and cattle, and there put on sackcloth, and humbled themselves before God, calling aloud for pardon, and repenting of their past wickedness. Whereupon God was pleased to forgive them, and the storm blew over.

171.—EASTERN USE OF PERFUMES.
Luke vii. 46.

℄ The Rev. Hugh Macmillan says:—"Perfumes were associated with almost every action and event in the life of the ancients. The free use of them was peculiarly delightful and refreshing to the Orientals. A bouquet of fragrant flowers was carried in the hand;

or rooms were fumigated with the odorous vapours of burning
resins; or the body was anointed with oil mixed with the aromatic
qualities of some plant extracted by boiling; or scents were worn
about the person in gold or silver boxes, or in alabaster vials, in
which the delicious aroma was best preserved. Beds, garments,
hair, and articles of furniture were perfumed with myrrh, aloes,
and cinnamon; and so indispensable were perfumes considered to
the feminine toilet, that the Talmud directs the apportioning of
one-tenth part of a bride's dowry for their purchase. When enter-
tainments were given, the rooms were fumigated; and it was customary for a servant to attend every guest as he seated himself,
and to anoint his head, sprinkle his person with rose-water, or
apply incense to his face and beard; and so entirely was the use of
perfumes on such occasions in accordance with the customs of the
people, that the Saviour reproached Simon for the omission of this
mark of attention, leaving it to be performed by a woman."

<h2 style="text-align:center">172.—HUSKS FOR SWINE.</h2>
Luke xv. 16.

℃ The husks (a mistranslation) of the kharûb tree are fleshy
pods somewhat like those of the honey-locust tree, from six to ten
inches long and one broad, lined inside with a gelatinous substance, not wholly unpleasant to the taste when thoroughly ripe. I
have seen large orchards of this kharûb in Cyprus, where it is still
the food which the swine do eat. In Syria, where we have no
swine, or next to none, the pods are ground up, and a species of
molasses expressed, which is much used in making certain kinds of
sweetmeats. The tree is an evergreen, which casts a most delightful
and refreshing shade to the weary traveller. In this country they
do not yield large crops, but in Cyprus, Asia Minor, and the
Grecian Islands, you will see full-grown trees bending under half a
ton of green pods. The kharûb is often called St. John's bread, and
also locust tree, from a mistaken idea about the food of the
Baptist in the wilderness. It is the *Ceratonia siliqua* of Linnaeus.

<h2 style="text-align:center">173.—THE DIFFERENT TASTE OF WATER
FROM DIFFERENT SPRINGS.</h2>
2 Sam. xxiii. 15, 16.

℃ Eastern people are great connoisseurs in the taste of water.
They drink very little else, except coffee without sugar, so they

learn to distinguish the peculiar quality of water from different
springs. Van Lennep tells us that "there are in Constantinople
shops in which nothing but water is sold, the price of a glass varying in accordance with the reputation of the spring whence it is
brought. A steamer regularly plies between the capital and the island of Marmora, seventy-five miles off, in order to supply the
Sultan's seraglio with the water of a celebrated spring. The actual
excellence of the water from the "well of Bethlehem" may partly
account for David's longing to drink of it; but there were probably
also home yearnings in his heart.

174.—A Vanishing Cloud.
Job vii. 9.

⊄ Bonar writes: "More than once we had noticed in our early
mornings, dull masses of cloud in the sky. As the sun got up and
gathered strength these all vanished. They did not drift away, or
pass to a different region of the heavens, but they vanished on the
spot, such was the absorbing power of the desert sun. Clouds that
would have brought a whole day's rain in our climate simply disappeared."

175.—The Migration of the Turtle Dove.
Song Sol. ii. 11, 12.

⊄ The return of this bird to Palestine in the spring is, as Dr. Tristram says, one of the most marked epochs in the ornithological
calendar (*see* Jer. viii. 7; Song Sol. ii. 11, 12). The dove here especially alluded to is the *Turtus Auritus*. "Search the glades and
valleys, even by sultry Jordan, at the end of March, and not a turtle dove is to be seen. Return in the second week in April, and
clouds of doves are feeding on the clovers of the plains. They
stock every tree and thicket. At every step they flutter up from the
herbage in front; they perch on every tree and bush; they
overspread the whole face of the land. So universal, so simultaneous, so conspicuous their migration, that the prophet might well
place the turtle dove at the head of those birds which 'observe the
time of their coming.'"

176.—GABBATHA.
John xix. 13.

⁋ A Chaldee word; the Hebrew word, *gav,* meaning "back," and Gabbatha would be an elevated ridge or hill. St. John, in his Gospel (xix. 13), says that the place to which Pilate brought Jesus was called *Lithostroton,* or pavement, and in Hebrew, Gabbatha. Josephus relates that there was such a pavement in the Temple. He also calls it *Lithostroton.* Some have supposed, but without much reason, that this was a portable pavement, such as it is known that the Roman generals carried about with them; but St. John calls it a place. It is probable that, as in other cases, there were two names, perfectly independent of each other, one familiar to the Jewish, and the other to the Greek-speaking population. Thus Gabbatha is not an interpretation of *Lithostroton,* any more than could Bethesda—"house of mercy"—be translated into Greek by any word signifying "five porches," and yet there might well be a Greek word (*pentestoai*) in use for this same reservoir.

177.—THE FORCE OF PAUL'S PLEADING WITH FELIX.
Acts xxiv. 25.

⁋ Antonius Felix was originally a slave, and brother to one Pallas, who had great influence over both the Emperors Claudius and Nero. He obtained his freedom from the Emperor Claudius, and was appointed (A.D. 51) Roman procurator of Judaea; Josephus says, on the banishment of Ventidius Cumanus. He was a man of some ability, but of bad character. He was sensual, mean, covetous, and cruel. He did good service in clearing the country of banditti; but under his tyrannical rule thousands of the Jews were stung to rebellion. His life, public and private, was one continued scene of tyranny, cruelty, and profligacy. Paul's reasoning concerning the claims of "righteousness and soberness," and his assurance of "judgment to come," might well stir such a guilty soul to some trembling. Felix was removed from office A.D. 60, and recalled to Rome, where he would have been punished for his many crimes, but for the intercessions of his brother Pallas.

178.—THE FESTIVAL OF HANNUKAH, OR DEDICATION.
John x. 22.

℄ In Jewish houses this is (on Christmas Eve) celebrated by the
display of antique candelabra, in which three lights will be allowed
to burn for about half an hour. The festival has nothing to do with
the anniversary commemorated by the Christian Church, but it has
some interest in its own way. In 169 B.C. Jerusalem was invaded
by Antiochus Epiphanes, who sacked the Temple, and erected in
its precincts a statue of Olympic Zeus. Then came the successful
revolt of the Maccabees. When they entered the Holy City, they
found the Sanctuary in ruins. "The heroes wept like children; they
rent their garments, and strewed ashes upon their heads." They set
about restoring the Temple, and on the 25th of Kislev, three years
after its pollution, they accomplished the task. The Feast of Dedication (Hannukah) was then held for eight days. The lamps of the
holy candlestick, figured so often on the Roman synagogues, in the
Catacombs, and on the Arch of Titus, were lighted, and the houses
of Jerusalem were illuminated. The miracle of the widow's cruse
was repeated, and one night's oil lasted (according to the tradition) for eight. On the yearly recurrence of the festival nowadays,
the family assemble, and the pretty ceremony of lighting the lamps
is gone through. One is burnt on the first night, two on the second,
and so on to the eighth; and the children join in a simple Hebrew
hymn. The feast does not involve any cessation from labour.

179.—THE CHANGE IN THE HEBREW LANGUAGE
MADE DURING THE BABYLONISH CAPTIVITY.
Nehemiah viii. 8.

℄ From the necessity of explaining the Hebrew Scriptures, it is
plain that the language of the people had materially changed during the residence in Babylonia. The original people of Babylonia
were Cushites (Gen. x. 8–10); this is proved by many inscriptions
of older date than the Assyrian kingdom, which are in an
Ethiopian (Cushite) dialect. During the supremacy of Nineveh, all
inscriptions cease in Babylonia; when they reappear 1,000 years
later, they are found in a Shemitish dialect, evidently owing to the
influence of Nineveh, which was occupied by a Shemitish race.
This language is called the Chaldee, and in it the later books of

the Bible were written. Gesenius finds traces of this dialect, more
or less evident and abundant, in the following Biblical books:—1
and 2 Chronicles, Ezra, Nehemiah, Esther, Jonah, Haggai, Zechariah, Malachi, Daniel, Ecclesiastes, Canticles, and some of the
Psalms. There is evidence in the New Testament that this Chaldee
dialect was the common spoken dialect of the Jewish people up to
the taking of Jerusalem by Titus, A.D. 74, when their dispersion in many lands led to the exchanging of it for the dialects
of the Gentiles.

Such expressions as Talitha Cumi; Abba; Ephphatha; Eli, Eli,
lama Sabachthani, belonging to this dialect, are retained in the
Gospels, and when our Lord quoted Isa. lxi. 1, in His visit to the
synagogue at Nazareth, He must have read it in the Chaldee version, since we find His words are neither those of the Hebrew
original nor of the Greek Septuagint translation. For several centuries after the Babylonish captivity, it was the regular custom in
the synagogues to read first out of the Hebrew Scriptures, and
then give the interpretation in the Chaldee dialect; in later times
the Chaldee Targums, or paraphrases, were used.

180.—THE HEBREW MARRIAGE CONTRACT.
Heb. xiii. 4.

℈ The ceremonies observed at marriages among the Orientals are
well known to Bible-readers, but the form of the Hebrew marriage
contract is not so familiar. It runs as follows:—"On such a day,
of such a month, in such a year, and on the banks of such a river
(generally signed in the open air, and on the bank of some river,
where convenient) N., son of N., said to N., daughter of N., Be
thou my wife according to the rites of Moses and the Israelites.
And, with the help of God, I will honour thee, maintain, clothe
thee, and feed thee, according to the custom of other husbands of
our nation; who honour, maintain, clothe, and feed their wives, as
they ought to do. I give thee for a portion, and for the price of thy
virginity, 200 zuzims (about 50 shekels, or a little over six pounds
English money) of silver, which is due to thee according to the
law. Besides which, I engage to provide thee with clothes and convenient food, as also to discharge that conjugal duty which is due
to thee, according to the customs of all nations.

"And the said N. has consented to become his spouse. More-

over, the said bridegroom has promised, by way of augmentation
of dowry, that besides the principal sum, he will give ———. And
what the said bride has brought with her is estimated at the value
of ———, which the said bridegroom acknowledges to have received, and to charge himself with, and has made us the declaration following:—'I accept and receive under my care and keeping
all that is above mentioned, as well for dowry as on any other account; and oblige myself and my heirs, under the security of all
my goods, whether movable or not, present or to come, even to
the cloak that I wear upon my shoulders, to give a true and faithful account to my said spouse, of all that she has brought to me as
a dowry, or on any other account, during my life, or at my death.
All which I promise to put in execution, according to the form
and tenor of the mutual contracts of marriage in use among the
children of Israel, and according to the rules of our Rabbins of
pious memory.' In testimony of which we have signed these presents, etc."

181.—MODE OF CONCEALING DAVID'S FLIGHT.
1 Sam. xix. 13–17.

⁋ Tradition represents that, for days together, a band of armed
men encircled the whole town in which David's house stood, waiting for him to come out. Michal, with quick-wittedness, planned
to secure his escape, and to provide him time to get safely away.
David, like Saul at Damascus, was let down from the house-win-
dow, probably outside the town-wall. It was reported that he was
sick in bed, and to keep up the idea Michal put the statue of the
household genius on the bed (as this belonged to the women's
apartment, it would not be missed), she covered the head with a
goat's-hair net, so say, to keep the flies from teasing the sick man,
but really to hide the appearance of the image. This device answered for some time, until Saul demanded David's removal, sick
or well. The Septuagint represents Michal's device as that of putting the liver of a recently-killed goat into the bed to imitate, with
its pulsations, the breathing of a sick man.

182.—THE FISH A SYMBOL OF CHRIST.
Luke v. 1–11; Matt. xiii. 47–49.

⁋ Our Lord only used the symbol of the fish in relation to His
disciples; and it is curious to find that those disciples by it

represented their Lord. The fish is a symbol of almost universal
occurrence in the painting and sculpture of the primitive church.
It is supposed that the reason for its adoption lies in the fact that
the Greek word for fish, ICHTHUS, contains the initials of the following sentence:—

I-esous CH-ristos TH-eou   U-ios   S-oter.
"Jesus   Christ   of God (the) Son, Saviour."

"At so early a period as the middle of the second century, and
under the continual dangers of persecution, the use of such a symbol for the person of the Lord was perfectly natural, as it would
attract no notice from the outer world; and in the same manner,
with even more obvious reasons, the form of the cross was frequently disguised up to the time of Constantine."

We may perhaps assume that whenever the fish was recognised
as the symbol of our Lord it was in consequence of the above
acrostic meaning having been discovered; and, if this was the case,
it must have been recognised from the very earliest days of Christianity. Clement of Alexandria numbers the fish among the Christian symbols, but does not state its special significance. Tertullian
says, "The fish is Christ, as *Ichthus;*" showing clearly that he had
the acrostic in mind. He adds that they who are born of Christ are
in their turn "smaller fishes." Augustine says, "If you join the first
letters of the five Greek words, Iesous, Christos, Theou, Uios,
Soter, you will have Ichthus, a fish, in which word Christ is myste-
riously designated."

There is only one ancient inscription known, however, in which
this word appears as an acrostic; this slab was found in the year
1839, beneath the surface, in an ancient cemetery, near Autun,
and the inscription was first published by Cardinal Pitra. It probably belongs to the fourth or fifth century.

183.—SHEEPMASTERS' FEASTS.
1 Sam. xxv. 36.

⁋ Great numbers of sheep were kept on the downs of the south
country of Judah, and there were owners of immense flocks, like
Nabal, whose sheep, through the year, were scattered abroad in
the district, under the care of the shepherds. Those shepherds were
responsible for the flock, and required to attend to their food,
their safety, their night shelter, and their increase. But, once in the

year, all the flocks were brought back to the master's farm for shearing; and in connection with such a meeting of the shepherds, it was customary to hold a great feast of rejoicing and reunion; a kind of harvest-home. It is singular to find David asking a share of the abundance of food characteristic of such a time; but it should be understood that he had some claim, beyond mere charity, because his followers had defended the shepherds from the attacks of Arabs, and secured the safety of their flocks in the wild country where they had fed.

184.—LOCUSTS AS AN ARTICLE OF FOOD.
Matt. iii. 4.

℺ Writing with a most extensive and prolonged acquaintance with Eastern habits and customs, Van Lennep dispels all doubt as to the nature of John the Baptist's food. He says:—

"The full-grown locust is extensively eaten by the poorer classes throughout Africa, Arabia and Persia, particularly by the Bedouin of the desert. When the locusts come down upon the face of the earth, crowds of people go forth and collect vast numbers of them in bags, even loading horses and cattle with the booty. They are roasted and eaten as butter upon loaves of bread, resembling shrimps in taste, or they are boiled in water with a little salt, dried in the sun, and, being deprived of their wings and legs, are packed in bags for use. They are beaten to a powder, which is mixed with flour and water, made into little cakes, and used as a substitute for bread when flour is scarce. Dried locusts are generally exposed for sale in the markets of Medina, Bagdad, and even Damascus."

By Mosaic law the Hebrews were allowed to eat the locust.—Lev. xi. 22.

185.—THE TEMPLE OF BEL IN BABYLON.
Ezra v. 14.

℺ Dean Stanley gives the following account of this remarkable building:—"The most prodigious and unique building of all was the Temple of Bel—which may well have seemed to the Israelites the completion of that proud tower 'whose top was to reach to heaven.' It was the central point of all; it gave its name to the whole place—Bab-el or Bab-bel, 'the gate of God or Bel,' which, by the quaint humour of primitive times, had been turned to the Hebrew word 'Babel,' or 'confusion.' " (Gen. xi. 9.)

It was the most remarkable of all those artificial mountains or beacons, which, towering over the plains of Mesopotamia, "guide the traveller's eye like giant pillars." It rose like the great pyramid, square upon square, and was believed to have reached the height of 600 feet. (This however may have been the winding rather than the perpendicular height.) Its base was a square of 200 yards. No other edifice consecrated to worship, not Carnac in Egyptian Thebes, nor Byzantine St. Sophia, nor Gothic Clugny, nor St. Peter's of Rome, have reached the grandeur of this primeval sanctuary, casting its shadow far and wide over city and plain. Hither, as to the most sacred and impregnable fortress, were believed to have been transported the huge brazen laver, the precious brazen pillars, and all the lesser vessels of the Temple of Jerusalem, together doubtless with all the other like sacred spoils which Babylonian conquest had swept from Egypt, Tyre, Damascus, or Nineveh. And when from the silver shrine at the summit of this building, the whole mass of mingled verdure and habitation for miles and miles was overlooked, what was wanting in grace or proportion must have been compensated by the extraordinary richness of colour. . . . The several stages of the temple itself were black, orange, crimson, gold, deep yellow, brilliant blue, and silver.

186.—AN OLD TRADITION CONCERNING THE ARK.
1 Peter iii. 20.

⁋ We are not told in Scripture how long Noah's Ark was in building; an Eastern tradition, however, asserts that Noah was two years in building it, and that it was framed of Indian plane tree wood; that it was divided into three stories, of which the lowest was allotted to beasts, the middle one to men and women, and the uppermost to birds. They further say that the men were separated from the women, during the whole time of the flood, by the body of Adam, which Noah had taken on board.

This last part of the tradition was also held by some of the Eastern Christians, who evidently regarded the ark as a monastic establishment.

187.—THE SHAPE OF THE ARK.
Gen. vi. 15.

℄ Very little can be known on this matter. The word used, *tebah,* may mean a chest or a boat: and we may more easily conceive of it as a chest, divided into nests or compartments, in three tiers or stories, and having a range of windows above to admit air and light. The windows, however, appear to have been arranged so that the inhabitants should not see what was happening around them. Taking 21 inches as the length of the cubit, the ark would be 525 feet in length, 87 feet 6 inches in breadth, and 52 feet 6 inches in height; comparing this with the *Great Eastern* ship an idea of size may be gained. That vessel is 680 feet long, 83 broad, and 58 deep.

The ark was never intended for sailing, all that was required of it was that it should *float,* and contain the largest possible amount of storage. It would, of course, drift; but its movements were altogether out of the control of those who were within it. It had neither mast, sail, nor rudder, and was in fact nothing more than a floating box. "The figure which is commonly given of it by painters, there can be no doubt is wrong."

A curious proof of the suitability of the ark for the purpose for which it was intended was given by a Dutch merchant, Peter Jansen, the Mennonite, who, in the year 1604, had a ship built at Hoorn of the same proportions (though not of the same size) as Noah's ark. It was 120 feet long, 20 broad, and 12 deep. This vessel, unsuitable as it was for quick voyages, was found remarkably well adapted for freightage. It was calculated that it would hold a third more lading than other vessels without requiring more hands to work it. A similar experiment is also said to have been made in Denmark, where, according to *Reyher,* several vessels called "fleuten" or floats were built after the model of the ark.

188.—THE LIZARD AND CHAMELEON.
Lev. xi. 30.

℄ In Western Asia there are still found a great variety of small lizards, most of them of a dark colour, but some variegated, and one species of a bright orange. They are graceful in form and movement, and perfectly innocuous. The species most probably re-

ferred to in the above passage is the only one of any considerable
size found in the country: it is about as large as a common rat,
and of a bright green colour. This kind appears to be venomous,
for it is said that its bite has sometimes proved fatal to dogs. It is,
however, very difficult to fix the exact species. Some think the
Lacerta stellio is meant, a lizard so named from the bundles of
star-like spines upon the body. Others prefer to identify it with the
Ptyodactulus gecko, or fan-foot lizard, from the toes of which a
poisonous matter exudes, raising pustules on the skin which it
touches. Lizards are especially plentiful in ruined buildings.

The *Chameleon* is about half the size of the common rat. "It is
a species of tree lizard, extremely homely and uncouth, presenting
the appearance of an animal formed of bones alone, with a thin
skin covering them. The five toes of its feet are united, so as to
form but two, resembling a thumb and forefinger. It uses its bony
tail as a prehensile instrument, by twisting it round a branch. Its
protruding eyeballs are covered with a thin skin, having a small
opening in the centre in front of the pupils; this moves to and fro,
as the vision is attracted to different objects, and the two eyes
being usually turned in independent directions, give the creature a
most singular appearance. Its motions are slow to an extreme, and
as it creeps along its entire body gradually assumes the colour of
the branch, or leaves of the tree on which it rests, becoming grey,
green, yellow, reddish purple, or black, as the case may be, and
thus rendering it invisible alike to its enemies and to its prey.
When a fly or any other insect comes within the chameleon's reach
he turns toward it one of his goggle-eyes, and suddenly and unerr-
ingly darts out upon it his long and slender tongue, whose extremity is furnished with a glutinous matter, and which can be
protruded to a distance of twice the animal's length, being formed
on the principle of the spy-glass. So sudden and rapid is the act of
thus seizing and despatching its prey, that the ancients believed
this creature lived on air."

The chameleon, in common with other lizards, is never eaten.

189.—CREATION'S VOICE OF PRAISE.
Job xxxviii. 7.

℄ There was a beautiful tradition among the Jews, which Lan-
cisius quotes from Philo. It is to this effect. When God had
created the world, He asked the angels what they thought of this

work of His hands. One of them replied that it was so vast and so perfect that only one thing was wanting to it—namely, that there should be created a clear, mighty, and harmonious voice, which should fill all the quarters of the world incessantly with its sweet sound, thus day and night to offer thanksgiving to its Maker for His incomparable blessings. . . . Thus our thanksgiving should not be an exercise of devotion practised now and then. It should be incessant—the voice of a love which is ever living and fresh in our hearts.

190.—EATING TOGETHER AT EASTERN MEALS.
Mark xiv. 20.

⊄ The Eastern table is like a large dish, standing on four feet; when not in use it is set upright, and made to rest against the wall. In putting it in order for a meal, a large cloth is first spread upon the floor, to receive the falling crumbs; the table is then set in the middle of the room, or near a sofa, where some of the guests sit while eating, the rest taking their places cross-legged upon the floor. The reclining posture at meals seems formerly to have been generally adopted in Western Asia. The present custom must have been introduced by some nomadic tribe, probably the Arabs or the Turks, to whose tent life it is eminently adapted. A long and narrow cloth is arranged all round the table, which the company spread upon their knees, and use as a napkin in common; at other times each guest is provided with a napkin, a corner of which he tucks into his bosom, or under his chin, and spreads the rest upon his knees. The meal is served in single dishes, set, each in turn, in the centre of the table, *all eating together,* from the same dish, as in our Saviour's day. It is common, even now, for the host at the table to dip a piece of bread in the gravy, or choose out some dainty morsel, and give it to one of the guests. On great occasions, or when special honour is sought to be shown to a guest, as many as thirty or forty dishes may be successively brought upon the table.

191.—THE THREE RANGES OF SINAITIC MOUNTAINS.
Exodus xix. 1, 2.

⊄ Dean Stanley gives the most complete account of this sacred district of Sinai. He writes:—"The mountains, flanked by the

190.—Eating Together at Eastern Meals.

sandstone formations—being themselves the granitic kernel of the whole region—are divided into two, or perhaps three groups, each with a central summit. These are (1) the north-western cluster, which rises above Wâdy Feirân, and of which the most remarkable mountain—being in some respects also the most remarkable in the whole peninsula—is Mount Serbâl; (2) the eastern and central cluster, of which the highest point is Mount St. Catherine; and (3) the south-eastern cluster, which forms, as it were, the outskirts of the central mass, the highest point of which is Um Shaumer, the most elevated summit of the whole range. Of these points Mount St. Catherine, with most of its adjacent peaks, has been ascended by many travellers; Mount Serbâl by a very few, of whom only four have recorded their ascent; Um Shaumer has been ascended by none but Buckhardt, and by him not quite to the summit.

"The colours of the range are very remarkable. Red, with dark green, are the predominant hues. These colours, especially in the neighbourhood of Serbâl, are diversified by the long streaks of purple which run over them from top to bottom.

"Another feature, less peculiar, but still rigidly characteristic, is the infinite complication of jagged peaks and varied ridges. When seen from a distance, as from the hills between Sinai and 'Akaba, this presents as fine an outline of mountain scenery as can be conceived, but the beauty and distinctness of a nearer view is lost in its multiplied and intricate confusion. This is the characteristic described by Sir Frederick Henniker, with a slight exaggeration of expression, when he says that the view from Jebel Mûsa, is as if 'Arabia Petraea were an ocean of lava, which, whilst its waves were running mountains high, had suddenly stood still.' "

192.—JOSHUA'S COMMAND TO THE SUN
TO STAND STILL.
Joshua x. 12.

℃ A careful examination of this passage will convince the candid reader that no miracle whatever is asserted, and that an ordinary phenomenon is narrated in an elevated poetical style. Some explanation of Joshua's words is plainly necessary from every point of view, seeing that it is the earth that moves, not the sun; and it could serve no purpose to Joshua that both sun and moon should be held in the sky at the same time. If Joshua had the light of the sun he would not need also the aid of the moon. The language is poetical and figurative, representing simply the desire of Joshua for the prolongation of light, so that the full fruits of victory might be reaped. The connection of the storm with the day's battle should be carefully noticed. The storm-clouds, filling the sky, threatened to bring on the darkness of night early and suddenly. The removal of these would prolong the sunshine and light of day, and when the sun set permit the full, clear moonshine to continue light enough for the pursuers to complete their work.

Of the different explanations that have been offered of precisely what occurred, the following is a *résumé:*—

The defeated Amorites were *going down* a steep rugged path, in wild confusion, amid all the horrors of a tropical storm. The warriors of Israel, when they reached the top of the pass, saw their foes flying down the road below them; but they also saw the advancing tempest threatening to blot out the light and stop the pursuit. These black clouds, blotting out the light of the sun, would bring the day to a premature close, and give their foes the opportunity of escape. Nothing could be more natural than the sudden prayer of Joshua, recorded for us in poetic terms, that the darkening clouds might be dispersed, and the light be prolonged.

Efforts have been made to explain the so-called miracle as an optical one; some suggesting an extraordinary refraction of the sunlight; others a parhelion; yet others, continuous lightning, lasting through the night.

After the introduction of the Copernican theory, those who still upheld the view that an astronomical miracle was wrought modified their hypothesis, so far as concerns the means by which the prolongation was effected. They taught that the motion of the earth on its own axis was temporarily suspended. Rev. E. Greswell suggests, that "the relations of mean and actual nocti-diurnal time, disturbed, of course, by the miracle in the days of Joshua, were again adjusted in the days of Hezekiah."

Kepler says, "They will not understand that the only thing which Joshua prayed for was that the mountains might not intercept the sun from him."

Bishop Wordsworth writes, "The result, therefore, at which we arrive is this: that, by the working of God, listening to the prayer of Joshua, the *light* of the *sun* was miraculously continued to Israel, *in a particular place,* and the *moon's light* was stayed from *rising,* while it was *night* to those who were beyond the sphere of the operation of the miracle."

Professor Young has offered an ingenious illustration of this narrative. "Light is not merely an emanation of luminous particles, any more than sound is an emanation of sonorous particles from a sonorous body; in each case a *medium* of conveyance is necessary; and the vehicle of light is the luminiferous ether. Suppose, now, a void had been introduced above the scene of Joshua's operations; then, if the vibrations essential to light in the lower region had not been suffered to cease, the light would have been continued to be supplied without any abatement of intensity."

193.—WOODEN WATER-JARS.
John iv. 28.

¶ The water-carriers used jars of stone or earthenware, and skins of animals, but there were also wooden jars, of which an Eastern traveller gives the following description:—

"We were riding on a plateau, when a mounted villager whom we met stopped us, and insisted on selling us a wooden jar. He asked us two piastres, or fourpence, English money, and we got it for threepence. These jars are used for carrying water on a horse while travelling, and they keep it very cool, as it is constantly, though slowly, oozing through the pores of the wood; care, however, must be used, lest they remain empty, in which case they are sure to crack and become useless. We long made use of ours, and found we could not do without it. It is manufactured from the common pitch-pine of the country, and is cut with an axe and jackknife. In the villages, it takes the place of earthen jars, and the nomadic tribes use no other. Labour must be cheap indeed where such an article can be made for so paltry a sum."

194.—THE ORIGINAL INHABITANTS OF CANAAN.
Gen. xii. 6.

¶ The oldest inhabitants of Canaan were probably Cushites, from Egypt; but, before the time of Abraham, these had been expelled by the Hittites, and other Shemites, who spoke what is now called the Phoenician dialect. Abraham, when he arrived in the Land of Promise, found the population consisting, at least in very large measure, of tribes with which he would have close affinities of blood and language. (The careful reader will observe the race distinctions between the aboriginal tribes, the Rephaim, Zanzummim,

Emim, Anakim, and the conquering peoples, Hittite, Hivite, etc.)
This seems, at first sight, utterly at variance with the common conception of Abraham as a solitary wandering stranger, in the midst
of strangers. And yet the evidence would appear to bear it out.
For, in the first place, we have not the least hint in the Biblical
narrative that points to any difference of language, such as we
often have when the Jews came into contact with nations whose
speech was really unintelligible to them; as, for instance, the Egyptians (Ps. lxxxi. 5, cxiv. 1), the Assyrians (Isa. xxxvi. 11), and the
Chaldees (Jer. v. 15). On the contrary, we find Abraham negotiat-
ing with the children of Heth; Isaac making a treaty with
Abimelech, king of Gerar; Jacob and his sons "communing" with
the people of Shechem, without the slightest reference to the need
of any interpreter between them. Again, the names of persons and
places in the early days, when Abraham first visited the land, we
find to have been such as admit at once of explanation from the
Hebrew or the Phoenician language. "Melchizedek" is "the King of
Righteousness;" "Abimelech," "the father of the king;" "Kirjath-
sepher," "the City of the Book," and so on. A suggestion has indeed been made that these are only Hebrew translations of the
original forms; but this is sufficiently disproved by the analogy of
similar cases, where we find no such translation to have taken
place. It is, indeed, most unlikely that if the nations of Canaan had
spoken a dialect essentially different from that of the Hebrews, the
latter should have ever understood sufficiently the meaning of the
proper names in use among their neighbours, to have translated
them into names of corresponding signification among themselves.

195.—THE BOOK OF JASHER.
Joshua x. 13.

¶ This work is otherwise mentioned only in 2 Sam. i. 18; and all
knowledge of its character and contents must be inferred from
these two extracts. Both of these have a poetical character; the one
being a national song of triumph, the other a national elegy. "Both
passages are unquestionably rhythmical in structure and poetical
in diction." The word *Jasher,* or more correctly *Jashar,* is most
probably an appellation of the theocracy, that is, of the people of
Israel considered as the covenant people, and it has much the
same force as the word *Jeshurun* (Deut. xxxii. 15). Ewald thinks
the book illustrated "by historical songs, how an upright man in
Israel, a Joshua, or a Jonathan should live; what glorious victories

he could achieve; what glory he would gain." The collection was compiled by degrees. It must be carefully distinguished from the collection of psalms, and should be regarded as a book of heroic poems, recording the greater national deeds and national events. No separate book, entitled the *Book of Jasher,* was extant among the Jews after the Christian era. Bishop Lowth imagined that it was a collection of national songs, so called, because the book probably commenced with the words *á: yâshir, then sang,* etc. In all nations there has been a constant disposition to preserve the record of great national deeds in heroic song; and, though not a literary people, it may reasonably be supposed that the Israelites followed the common impulse. The existence of Moses' song, and Deborah's, suffice to prove that such poems were composed on great occasions.

"There are extant, under the title of the *Book of Jasher,* two Rabbinical works, one a moral treatise, written in A.D. 1394, by R. Shabbatai Carmuz Levita, of which a copy, in MSS., exists in the Vatican Library; the other, by R. Tham, treats of the laws of the Jews in eighteen chapters, and was printed in Italy in 1544, and at Cracow in 1586. An anonymous work, printed at Venice and Prague in 1625, and said to have made its first appearance at Naples, was believed by some Jews to be the record alluded to in Joshua. It contains the historical narratives of the Pentateuch, Joshua, and Judges, with many fabulous additions. R. Jacob translated it into German, and printed his version at Frankfort-on-the-Maine, in 1674. It is said, in the preface to the first edition, to have been discovered at the destruction of Jerusalem, by *Sidrus,* one of the officers of Titus, who, while searching a house for the purpose of plunder, found in a secret chamber a vessel containing the books of the Law, the Prophets, and Hagiographa, with many others, which a venerable man was reading. Sidrus took the old man under his protection, and built for him a house at Seville, where the books were safely deposited. The book in question is probably the production of a Spanish Jew of the thirteenth century."

196.—EASTERN ABLUTIONS.
John xiii. 14.

¶ "I never understood the full meaning of those words of our Lord about being washed," says Statham, "until I beheld the better sort of East Indian natives return home after performing their customary ablutions. Thus as they return to their habitations barefoot, they necessarily contract, in their progress, some portion of dirt on their feet; and this is universally the case, however nigh their dwellings may be to the water side. When, therefore, they return, the first thing they do is to mount a low stool, and pour a small vessel of water over their feet to cleanse them from the soil they may have contracted in their journey homeward. If they are of the higher order of society, a servant performs it for them, and then they are clean every whit."

197.—Early Christian Accounts
of Simon the Sorcerer.
Acts viii. 20.

¶ The Scripture record gives us but a brief account of Simon, merely stating that he "bewitched the people of Samaria with his sorceries." No particulars are given of the arts he practised, or of the means by which he led the people astray. Clement of Rome, however, A.D. 91–100, and Anastasius, A.D. 398, give some details of his deeds and power; these we may regard rather as the tradition that grew up around his name, than as fairly representing the facts of his life. They are interesting as aiding us to realise the prevailing thought in the early Christian Church.

They say that when, and to whom he pleased, Simon could make himself invisible; he created a man out of the air; he passed through rocks and mountains, as if nothing stood in his way; he threw himself from a precipice without sustaining any injury; he flung himself into a fire, but escaped unhurt. Bolts and chains were powerless to detain him; he animated statues, so that they appeared to the beholders as men and women; he made the furniture and table of a house change places at will, without a visible mover; he metamorphosed his visage into that of another person; he could transform himself into a sheep, a goat, or a serpent; he walked the streets attended with multitudes of strange figures, which he affirmed to be the souls of the departed; he made trees and branches of trees spring up whenever he pleased; he set up and deposed kings at will; and he caused a sickle to go into a field of corn, which, unassisted, would cut down twice as much as the most industrious reaper.

Clement, in answer to the obvious query, why Simon wanted the gift of the Holy Ghost, when he was already possessed of so extraordinary powers, says that he complained, because in his sorceries he was compelled to perform tedious ceremonies, and employ incantations, while the Apostles seemed to perform their miracles spontaneously, and without effort.

198.—TWO WORDS FOR "REPENTANCE" IN THE BIBLE.
Matt. xxvii. 3.

⁋ Chillingworth remarks, "It is worth observing, that when the Scripture speaks of that kind of repentance which is only sorrow for something done, and wishing it undone, it constantly useth the word, *metaméleia,* to which forgiveness is nowhere promised. So it is written of Judas, the son of perdition, *metamelêtheìs 'apétrepse,* he repented, and went and hanged himself; and so constantly in other places. But that repentance to which remission of sins and salvation is promised, is perpetually expressed by the word, *metánoia,* which signifieth a thorough change of the heart and soul, of the life and actions."

199.—THE BOOK OF LIFE.
Rev. xx. 15.

⁋ In the Jewish public registers, all that were born of a particular tribe were entered on the list of their respective families under that tribe. This was the *Book of Life,* and when any of these died, his name might be considered as blotted out of the list. "In China, the names of the persons who have been tried on criminal processes are written in two distinct books, which are called the book of life and the book of death; those who have been acquitted, or who have not been capitally convicted, are written in the former; those who have been found guilty, in the latter. These two books are presented to the emperor by his ministers, and he, as sovereign, has a right to erase any name from either: to place the living among the dead, that he may die; or the dead, that is, the person condemned to death, among the living, that he may be preserved. Thus he blots out of the book of life or the book of death, according to his sovereign pleasure, on the representation of his ministers or the intercession of friends."—B.T.

200.—Story of Judgment on Neglected Hospitality.
Job xxxi. 31, 32.

℟ The Arabs pride themselves on the exercise of their hospitality. Stories of judgments by which the want of hospitality has been visited form an important element of the popular traditions of the Arabs. *Wetzstein* relates the following as a specimen:—"In the spring of 1860, as I came out of the forest of Gôlan, I saw the water of Râm lying before us, that beautiful round crater in which a brook that runs both summer and winter forms a clear but fishless lake, the outflow of which underground is recognised as the fountain of the Jordan, which breaks forth below in the valley out of the crater Tell-el-Kadi; and I remarked to my companion, the physician Regeb, the unusual form of the crater, when my Bedouins, full of astonishment, turned upon me with the question: 'What have you Franks heard of the origin of this lake?' On being asked what they knew about it, they related how that, many centuries ago, a flourishing village stood here, the fields of which were the plain lying between the water, and the village of *Megdel Shems*. One evening a poor traveller came while the men were sitting together in the open place in the middle of the village, and begged for a supper and a resting-place for the night, which they refused him. When he assured them that he had eaten nothing since the day before, an old woman, amidst general laughter, reached out a *gelle* (a cake of dried cow-dung, which is used for fuel), and drove him out of the village. Thereupon the man went to the village of *Nimra* (still standing south of the lake), where he related his misfortune, and was taken in by them. The next morning, when the inhabitants of Nimra woke, they found a lake where the neighbouring village had stood."

201.—Tradition concerning the Patriarch Job.
Job xlii. 17.

℟ At the end of the Greek and Arabic copies of the Book of Job and also of the Vulgate, is found the following account of the patriarch, said to have been taken from the Syriac. "Job dwelt in the Ausitis, on the confines of Idumaea and Arabia; his name at first was Jobah. He married an Arabian woman, by whom he had a son called Ermon. He himself was son of Zerah, of the posterity of Esau, and a native of Bozrah; so that he was the fifth from Abraham. He reigned in Edom, and the kings before and after him reigned in this order:—Balak, the son of Beor, in the city of Dinhabah; after him, Job (otherwise called Jobah). Job was succeeded by Husham, prince of Teman. After him reigned Hadad, the son of Bedad, who defeated the Midianites in the fields of Moab. The name of his city was *Arith*. Job's friends who came to visit him were, Eliphaz, of the posterity of Esau, and king of Teman; Bildad, the king of the Shuhites; and Zophar, king of the Naamathites.

It should be distinctly understood that this tradition is simply interesting and curious, its trustworthiness cannot be affirmed, as the real origin of Job is shrouded in impenetrable mystery, and his personality depends on the date that must be fixed for the composition of the book that goes by his name.

202.—The Site of Carchemish.
2 Chron. xxxv. 20.

℘ While waiting at Aleppo, on account of the plague, Mr. George Smith, the learned Eastern scholar and archaeologist, explored the banks of the Euphrates northward from Bales (the Assyrian Balikh), and at Yarabolus, a village on the western side of the river between Tiber and Dasharar, discovered the ruins of the ancient capital of the Hittites, Carchemish. The ruins of the city are on an extensive scale, and the discovery of them bids fair to rival in importance that of Nineveh itself. The architectural remains, as might have been expected, show a combination of Egyptian and Assyrian art; and the inscriptions in the Hamathite character which Mr. Smith found upon the spot prove that this mode of writing originally came from the Hittites. Carchemish commanded one of the best fords across the Euphrates, lying midway between the northern ford of Samosata and the southern ford of Thapsacus or Tiphsah ("the passage" from *pha'sakh*, 1 Kings iv. 24); and the possession of it was accordingly much coveted by the Assyrian kings. The modern name Yarabolus is clearly a corruption of Hierapolis, the name by which Carchemish went in classical times.

203.—Eloah, Elohim.
Gen. i. 1.

⁋ The names by which the Supreme Being is called in the Old Testament, and especially in Genesis, are chiefly two, *Elohim,* and *Jehovah,* the first is usually rendered "God," the second "the Lord." The name "Elohim" is derived either from the Arabic *Alaha,* to fear, reverence, worship; or more probably from the Hebrew *Alah,* to be strong, to be mighty. It is the simple generic name of God—"The Mighty." It does not occur in the singular in the earlier books of Scripture, except in the abbreviated form of *El.* The plural is probably a plural of excellence and majesty. Max Müller, however, gives further information concerning the use of this name for God. The name by which the Deity is known throughout the patriarchal or introductory age of the Jewish Church is *Elohim.* In this name has been discovered a trace of the conciliatory, comprehensive mission of Abraham, the first prophet of the true religion. Elohim is a plural noun, though followed by a verb in the singular. When "Eloah" (God) was first used in the plural, it could only have signified, like any other plurals, "many Eloahs," and such a plural could only have been formed after the various names of God had become the names of independent deities, that is, during a polytheistic stage. The transition from this into the monotheistic stage could be effected only in two ways; either by denying altogether the existence of the Elohim, and changing them into devils—as was done in Persia—or by taking a higher view, and looking upon them as so many names invented with the honest purpose of expressing the various aspects of the Deity, though in time diverted from their original intention. This is the view that we may presume to have been taken by Abraham.

204.—Easy Procuring of False Witnesses.
1 Kings xxi. 13.

⁋ An Eastern missionary, illustrating the different way in which a Christian and a Moslem is treated in a Turkish court of justice, says:—"In all matters which affect a Moslem, the testimony of a Christian or a Jew is inadmissible. The consequence is that false witnesses are in such demand that Moslems, ready to swear to anything required of them, are always found at the door of the

Mehkemeh (justice-room). It is a regular profession, and brings a good income. For there is, in fact, no punishment either for perjury, or for bribing judge or witnesses."

Such false witnesses were easily obtained at the trial of our Lord before the Sanhedrim.

205.—THE LOST LANGUAGE OF PISIDIA AND LYCAONIA.
Acts xiv. 11.

℃ The following extract is taken from Van Lennep's *Travels in Asia Minor*. Speaking of one of his companions on board a ship, he says, "The Greek gentleman from *Isbarta* is a druggist there, and visits Constantinople on business. He seems to have paid some attention to antiques, and showed me a fine cornelian, beautifully cut on one side in the form of a beetle, and bearing on the other the figure of a man, who appeared to be jumping the rope. He also mentioned having had in his possession a small stone, with an inscription in Greek characters, but in a language apparently now lost. It ran as follows:—

ΘΩΒΑΡΡΑΒΟ
ΥΛΑΚΛΣΑΚΙΣ
ΑΒΡΑΣΑΣΕ
ΩΑΩΗ

and on the other side—

NALH
EXEXE

"Isbarta is an ancient Pisidia, and there is no doubt that the aboriginal inhabitants long preserved their own language, as was still the case in Lycaonia in the time of the Apostles. Their language was reduced to writing by the adoption of the Greek alphabet, with additions required for sounds peculiar to it. Inscriptions found in Caria, Lycia, Pisidia, and generally in the south-western portions of the Peninsula, probably belong to the same language, now lost. It would be interesting to ascertain whether any remains of that language can be found among the villages of the mountainous regions which have so long defied the successive dynasties that have conquered the rest of the country, but left them much of their independence. Or it may be that some of the now wandering tribes still preserve those ancient languages; for it is certain that

they speak dialects which bear no resemblance to the Greek or the
Turkish."

206.—STONE RECENTLY FOUND AT GEBAL.
Ezekiel xxvii. 9.

¶ This Gebal is seated on an eminence near the Mediterranean,
north of Beirût.

The Comte de Vogüé has lately made a communication to the
Académie des Inscriptions et Belles-Lettres concerning a stone or
stele lately exhumed at Djebeïl, the Biblical Gebal, and the Byblos
of the Greeks and Romans. The stone was found near a spot indicated by M. Renan as likely to contain ruins of the celebrated
temple of the goddess of Byblos, M. Renan being guided partly by
the local topography and partly by the negative results of the
trenches dug in 1860 by the French *Mission de Phoenicie*. The
size of the stone is $1\frac{13}{100}$ metres high by $\frac{56}{100}$ metre wide and
from $\frac{23}{100}$ to $\frac{26}{100}$ of a metre thick, and De Vogüé deduces some
remarkable conclusions from these dimensions which we have not
space to epitomise even. At the top is the Egyptian disc with
wings, slightly varying from its ordinary form as occurring in
Egypt. Below is a figure of the goddess, who is to the life, if we
may use that expression, an Egyptian Isis-Hathor, with the costume, position, and insignia; the closely fitting robe, the arrangement of the hair, the head-ornament consisting of a solar disc and
two horns, and her right hand raised as if in benediction, while the
left grasps the long papyrus-stalk sceptre. Before (to the right) the
goddess stands the king, offering a libation, his dress much
resembling the Persian and somewhat the Assyrian. Below is an inscription in Phoenician, in fifteen lines, of which the lower right-
hand corner is broken away and about one-third of the rest quite
indistinct, some being quite illegible. In linguistic characteristics it
has some Hebraisms that have not appeared hitherto on any other
Phoenician inscriptions together with some new forms of the relative pronoun (or, rather, demonstrative used as a relative, like the
English *that*). The king's name De Vogüé transliterates as "Yehawmelek;" which is just like the Hebrew Jehiel, substituting
melek for *el,* and with just such a variation as would be if
Mehujael were written Mehijael in Hebrew, of which there are
some parallels. The vocalisation, as Urimelek in place of Ari-

melek, is preferred, as Lenormant has discovered the name thus
vocalised on a prism enumerating kings conquered by Sennacherib, which, with very little doubt, is the same king here mentioned—the grandfather of Yehawmelek, the only opposing circumstance being the Persian costume represented on the stele,
which would put this man a little later. Many of the words on the
stone remind us of the description of the details of Solomon's
Temple. The inscription, however, is full of details that are of interest to the Hebraist and the mythologist, and would better be left
to be studied as a whole by those who desire it. The style of the
characters is much like that of those on the sarcophagus of Esh-
munazar; as are also the borrowed style of sculpture and ornamentation—both Egyptian. The stone bears marks of having had further ornaments in metal fastened upon it, the nail-holes of which
are still distinct. The translation of the inscription is as follows, the
brackets enclosing not only obliterated, but doubtful places:—

"I am Yehawmelek, King of Gebal, son of Yahdibaal, son of
the son of Urimelek, King of Gebal, a dynasty which the lady
Baalath-Gebal has established over Gebal. I am invoking my lady
Baalath-Gebal. . . . and I am offering to my lady Baalath-Gebal
this altar of brass which is in this [court] and this sculptured gate
which is over against the entrance, and the . . . of gold, which is
in the midst of the stone which is upon that sculptured gate, and
this portico with its columns, the [architrave] which is upon them
(*i.e.* upon the columns) and its roof which I have caused to be
constructed, I, Yehawmelek, King of Gebal, for my lady Baalath-
Gebal; because when I invoked my lady Baalath-Gebal, she heard
my prayer, and made for me delight. May Baalath-Gebal bless the
bow of Yehawmelek, King of Gebal. May she preserve his life;
may she prolong his days and his years over Gebal in a reign of
righteousness; and may the lady Baalath-Gebal give him . . . for
the . . . dynasty this sculptured gate, the work of this building
[which I have dedicated] to my lady Baalath-Gebal, . . . and
may the lady Baalath-Gebal the . . . to him and exalt (?) his
seed."

The inscription probably belongs to the fifth, sixth, or seventh
centuries before Christ—hardly earlier. The name Yehawmelek is
probably "May the king [Moloch or Baal] preserve his life." The
sculpture over the inscription is interesting as giving the earliest
representation of this goddess. The same general shape, except the
Egyptian features of the face, are preserved in the later Graeco-
Roman sculptures.

207.—ALLUSIONS TO THE QUICK BLOSSOMING
OF THE ALMOND TREE.
Jeremiah i. 11, 12.

℃ The almond tree was evidently well known in Palestine in very ancient times; Jacob sent almonds to the governor of Egypt (Gen. xliii. 11); and Solomon would not have used the simile recorded in Eccles. xii. 5, if the allusion had not been familiar to every one. The tree is light and graceful, with a small, delicate leaf, and is very extensively grown, being planted both in gardens and along the hedges of vineyards.

It is the first of trees to blossom, and hence the Romans applied to it the epithets "vigilant" and "watchful." Its blossoms, which are white and plentiful, burst forth in January, even before the leaf-buds appear. At that season the almond trees seem, at a distance, like numerous hoary heads scattered over the fields and along the valleys. Almonds are of two kinds, soft-shelled and hard-shelled; a variety of the latter being the "bitter-almonds."

The early flowering of the almond will explain the somewhat obscure text placed as the heading of this paragraph. "The word of the Lord came unto me, saying, Jeremiah, what seest thou? And I said, I see the rod of an almond tree (that is, in the original, I see a *shâkêd*). Then said the Lord unto me, Thou hast well seen, for I will *hasten* (*shôkêd*) my word to perform it."

Another, and perhaps a better, explanation is the following:— *Sheked* (read without the points), in Hebrew, is a verb, signifying "to be awake," "nimble," etc. It is also an adjective, with the meaning, "watchful." Hence it is applied as a noun to the almond tree. Jeremiah says, "I see a *sheked*," that is an almond-tree; and the Lord replies, "I *sheked*," that is, I am "watchful" over my word to bring it to pass. Such a play upon words is very common in the Hebrew Bible.

208.—TERRITORY OF ISRAEL AT THE DEATH
OF SOLOMON.
1 Kings iv. 24, 25.

℃ The extent of territory occupied by the twelve tribes at the death of Solomon is calculated by Kiepert at 12,810 English square miles, excluding the Philistine territory. Of this area Israel occupied about 9,375, and Judah, 3,435 square miles. Hence it appears that the whole area of Palestine was nearly equal to that

207.—Allusions to the Quick Blossoming of the Almond
Tree.

of the kingdom of Holland, or that of the six northern counties of
England (13,136 square miles). The kingdom of Judah was rather
less than Northumberland, Durham, and Westmoreland (3,683
square miles); the kingdom of Israel was very nearly as large as
Yorkshire, Lancashire, and Cumberland (9,453 square miles).

209.—Passages from the Laws of Menu
to compare with Psalm xv.

℄ In the Psalm is found a brief but comprehensive description of
the practically good man, who unites the worship of Jehovah with
a life of rectitude. Several of the items mentioned find an echo in
a passage of the Laws of Menu, the ancient lawgiver of the Hindoos, whose works have been translated into English by Sir
William Jones.

The passage to which reference is here made runs thus:—

> *"Let a man continually take pleasure in truth, in justice,*
> *In laudable practices, and in purity:*
> *Let him chastise those whom he may chastise in a legal mode:*
> *Let him keep in subjection his speech, his arm, and his appetite:*
>
> *Wealth and pleasure repugnant to law let him shun;*
> *And even lawful acts, which may cause future pain,*
> *Or be offensive to mankind:*
>
> *Let him not have nimble hands, restless feet, or voluble eyes:*
> *Let him not be crooked in his way:*
> *Let him not be flippant in his speech, nor intelligent in doing*
>   *mischief:*
>
> *Let him walk in the path of good men:*
> *The path in which his forefathers walked:*
> *While he moves in that path he can give no offence."*

210.—Begging Children showing the Decay
and Curse of Egypt.
Psalm cix. 10.

℄ A recent traveller vividly describes the demoralisation of the
present children of Egypt, and so illustrates the curse which the
Psalmist would draw down on his enemies.

"The Egyptian children are all beggars, insolent or cringing as
the case may be; a single one is humble and persistent; a pack of
them are clamorous and threatening. It is said that the first duty of

the parent after the birth of a child is to whisper in his right ear the *adán,* or call to prayer. I doubt if he hears it, for the first word he seems to know, certainly the first one he can pronounce, all along the Nile is, 'backsheesh.' Begging is a birthright; it is the in-grained inheritance. I never saw a baby, old enough to articulate anything, who would not hold out his dirty little hand and say 'Ba'sees.' And this habit of begging is somewhat different from the Italian mendicancy taught by ages of dependence upon monas-teries, and often the result of absolute want. It is the Oriental desire for a gift, and is as strong in the men as it is in the children. It is a national demoralisation, a desire of getting something for nothing, the laziness of waiting on Providence often, and some-times it may be traced to the very ancient custom of gift-giving, which in the Orient amounts to a mere exchange. But, all the same, the habit has become one of cringing dependence. And if the Egyptian child is father of the man, you may expect no new change in the nation (except from external influences) in the next thousand years than the last thousand has brought."

211.—A LODGE IN A GARDEN OF CUCUMBERS.
Isaiah i. 8.

❡ The *cottage* and the *lodge* in this verse refer to essentially the same kind of erection. Both the vineyards and melon gardens require to be watched to keep off the attacks of thieves, as well as the foxes, jackals, and hares. In some convenient spot a small wooden booth is erected, consisting of four upright poles driven into the ground, and rising to the height of some eight or ten feet. Two or three feet from the ground the poles support a platform, which constitutes the floor of the booth; and here the watchman sits day and night. Above his head is a rude roof of leafy boughs, to serve as a shelter from the sun by day, and the heavy dew at night. Travellers say it would be difficult to conceive of anything having a more lonely appearance than one of these "lodges."

Dr. Thomson says, however, that the "true point of the compari-son will not appear until the crop is over, and the lodge forsaken by the keeper. Then the poles fall down, or lean everyway, and those green boughs with which it is shaded will have been scat-tered by the wind, leaving only a ragged, sprawling wreck—a most

affecting type of utter desolation—'as Sodom and like unto
Gomorrah.'"

212.—OIL, AS NOW EXTRACTED FROM THE PALM-TREE.
Isaiah xli. 19.

℄ Among the Jews the oil used was chiefly taken from the "olive-
tree;" and that tree is probably referred to by Isaiah in the above
passage as the "oil-tree." We may well suppose, however, that
some of the oil was extracted from the *palm*-tree; and the following
description of this process, as now carried on in Africa, will aid us
in realising the oil manufacture of bygone times:—The River
Bonny supplies the largest quantity of palm-oil that is brought
from any river in Western Africa. The trade with the natives is
carried on by barter, the oil being paid for mostly in Birmingham
and Manchester manufactures—glass and agate beads of various
forms, sizes, and finish, being some of the recognised articles of
exchange. The fruits from which the oil is obtained are borne in
dense heads or spadices, sometimes measuring two feet long and
two or more feet in circumference, the fruits themselves being
each about an inch or an inch and a half long, and an inch in diameter. The seeds are inclosed in a very hard bony shell, which is
again covered with a softish pulpy substance, outwardly, when
ripe, of a bright orange or yellow colour. It is from this outer,
fleshy portion of the fruit, that the best oil is obtained. On the
West African coast one of the most important branches of manufacture is that of palm-oil. When sufficiently ripe the fruits are
gathered, chiefly by men. They are boiled by women, in large
earthenware pots, after which they are crushed in mortars. They
are then placed in large clay vats filled with water, and women are
employed to tread out the oil, which immediately comes to the
surface, when it is collected and again boiled to throw off the
water, after which it is placed in barrels or casks for exportation.
Good palm-oil is of a bright orange or deep yellow colour, about
the consistency of butter, and when fresh it has an agreeable smell,
somewhat resembling violets. It is now most extensively used in
the manufacture of soap and candles, and also for greasing the
axles of railway carriage wheels. The two first uses, however, are
what the plants are mostly prized for. In Africa the solid oil is
used for culinary purposes, often in place of butter, and the hard
seeds are made into various ornamental articles.

213.—THE REASON FOR KEEPING DOVES IN THE EAST.
Isaiah lx. 8.

⊄ This passage is explained by the fact that, in some Eastern lands, towers or houses are erected for the sole use of pigeons, which take possession of them in enormous numbers. The buildings are not erected for the benefit of the birds, but for the sake of their droppings, which are highly prized as a *manure*. The towers are pierced with "windows," or apertures, and are internally honeycombed for the convenience of the pigeons. The large flocks that resort to those buildings, fully illustrate the prophet's allusion. The income of a single pigeon house often amounts to £70 per annum. Perhaps the difficult text, 2 Kings vi. 25, may be explained by reference to this manure. It cannot be that the people bought the dung for food; for it could not nourish them. It was probably wanted for manure, to force the growth of vegetables within the city walls, the only supply which the people of Samaria then had to depend upon. When it is remembered that a pint of this manure cost five pieces of silver, we may form some faint conception of the rigour of the famine.

214.—MOHAMMEDAN REPRESENTATION OF EZEKIEL'S VISION OF THE VALLEY OF DRY BONES.
Ezek. xxxvii. 1–10.

⊄ Either the Mohammedans, or else the Rabbis, from whom the Moslem writers borrowed many of their fables, have strangely corrupted the account of this vision. They say that some of the children of Israel left home, either to escape a pestilence or to avoid serving in a religious war. But, as they fled, God struck them dead in a certain valley. About eight days or so after, the prophet Ezekiel, happening to pass that way, wept as he looked upon their bones; whereupon God said to him, "Call to them, O Ezekiel, and I will restore them to life." And accordingly, on the prophet's call, they all arose, and lived for several years after; but they retained the colour and odour of dead bodies as long as they lived: the clothes they wore became black as pitch, and these qualities they transmitted to their posterity.

Set against such a story, the refined Biblical records present the most marked contrasts.

215.—AHASUERUS.
Esther i. 1.

℩ Rawlinson says, "The name Ahasuerus is undoubtedly the proper Hebrew equivalent for the Persian word which the Greeks represented by Xerxes, . . . and we are at once struck with the strong resemblance which his character bears to that assigned by the classical writers to the celebrated son of Darius. Proud, self-willed, amorous, careless of contravening Persian customs; reckless of human life, yet not actually bloodthirsty; impetuous, facile, changeable, the Ahasuerus of Esther corresponds in all respects to the Greek portraiture of Xerxes, which is not the mere picture of an Oriental despot, but has various peculiarities which distinguish it even from the other Persian kings."

216.—EASTERN HOUSEHOLDS.
Exodus i. 1.

℩ Our Western ideas of family life are unsuitable to represent Eastern households and families, and some knowledge of the essential differences between the two kinds of family is necessary in order to explain many Scriptural allusions. "In the West, when a son is married, he usually leaves the parental roof, and, if he do not set up in business on his own separate account, his relation to his father is regulated on the same principles as obtain in the case of a partnership. In the East, on the contrary, the sons bring their wives to the parental home, where a particular room is allotted to each, while the housekeeping remains one. The sons continue to assist their father, and live in complete subordination to him; and they bring home their gains to a common purse, which is controlled by the father alone, and furnishes alike the supplies required by the whole household. We thus frequently meet with families which consist of fifty, and even seventy-five members, all living under one roof, and having all things common.

"This accounts for the indefiniteness of the Turkish census, which enumerates the *houses* or *households* alone, but does not particularly inquire into the number of persons of which each is composed."

217.—OUTSIDE STAIRCASES.
Matt. xxiv. 17.

⁋ Our Lord assumes the existence of some kind of outside stairs when he gives this counsel, "Let him that is on the house-top not come down to take anything out of his house." He is to take the nearest and shortest way of escaping into the country; but he could only avoid the necessity of descending through the house by the existence of some kind of outside steps. Trench says that commonly there was a flight of steps on the outside of the house, as well as, or sometimes instead of, an internal communication of the same kind. "Such every traveller in those parts of southern Spain which bear a permanent impress of Eastern habits will have seen." Thomson says, "The stairway is often outside of the house, but *within the exterior court.* It would not be either agreeable or safe to have the stairs land outside the enclosure altogether, and it is rarely done, except in mountain villages, and where roofs are but little used. The stairs not infrequently end in the *lewan,* but more commonly in some lower part of the court. The urgency of the flight recommended by our Lord is enhanced by the fact that the stairs do lead down into the court, or *lewan.* He, in effect, says, 'Though you must pass by the very door of your room, do not enter; escape for your life, without a moment's delay.'" Van Lennep says, "The staircase, of stone or wood, which leads to the flat roof, is usually upon the outside of the house, and starts from the central court. Tame pigeons or doves are fond of building their nests in the 'secret places' (Song Sol. ii. 14), underneath these stairs."

218.—SOLOMON'S POOLS OF WATER.
Eccles. ii. 6.

⁋ The "pools of Solomon" were very likely constructed as much for pleasure as for utility. The Orientals love to look upon water, whether running or still. In the houses of the wealthy there are generally found tanks for the gratification of this taste, some of them only a foot or two in diameter. This tank is set in the court, just in front of the principal room; a fountain at the rim is ever running, and frequently a jet plays in the centre of the basin, cooling the atmosphere, and also making liquid music for the ear.

In sight of the fountain the guests are placed, when such happen
to be visiting the house. To secure a plentiful supply of water for
these fountains, the Orientals often now go to great expense, as
Solomon seems to have done.

219.—ONLY ALLUSION TO JEWISH HISTORY ON THE EGYPTIAN MONUMENTS.
1 Kings xiv. 25, 26.

℄ Dean Stanley gives an account of the inscription recording the
invasion of Shishak from an Egyptian point of view:—"On the
southern side of the temple of Karnac at Thebes, is a small temple, built by Rameses III. Of this, one corner was sculptured inside
and outside by the king, called in the Egyptian language *Seson-
chosis,* in the Hebrew *Shishak,* in the LXX. *Susakim,* perhaps by
Herodotus *Sasychis.* He copied almost exactly the figures already
carved on the other parts of the temple, so that their forms and attitudes are mostly conventional. But in one of the processions thus
represented there is to be found the only direct allusion to Jewish
history on the Egyptian monuments. On one side stands the King
himself, on a colossal scale, holding in his hand a train of captives.
Meeting him is the God Amon, also leading a train of lesser captives by strings, which he holds in his hand, and which are fastened round their necks. On eleven are inscribed the names of
their cities, and of these the third from Amon's hand was believed
by Champollion to bear the name of *King of Judah.* This
identification, which for many years attracted traveller after traveller to gaze on the only likeness of any Jewish king that had survived to our time, has been of late much disputed. It is now, perhaps, only permitted to dwell on the Jewish physiognomy of the
whole series of captives, and on the contrast, so striking from the
inverse intensity of interest with which we regard them, between
the diminutive figures and mean countenances of the captives from
Palestine, and the gigantic God and gigantic conqueror from
Egypt."

220.—TARES (*Lolium temulentum*).
Matt. xiii. 24–30.

℄ In winnowing wheat it was found necessary to pass it through
sieves of different sizes in order to remove the small stones, lumps

of earth, and foreign seeds, which were too heavy for the wind to
carry away. Of the seeds found among the corn grains, the most
troublesome are those of the Tares, a weed commonly known as
Darud. Its kernels are somewhat smaller than those of wheat, and
they must be cleaned away, as if allowed to remain in any quantity among the wheat, they mar the quality of the flour, make it
taste bitter, and even produce dizziness and nausea after eating.
Usually, women and children sit round a pile of wheat, and pa-
tiently pick out the tares one by one. At the first growing the
wheat and the tare look alike, but the difference begins to be apparent as the ear begins to form, and when both are ripe there is
no difficulty at all in distinguishing the one from the other. The
tares are not pulled up from among the wheat, unless they are
found in too great an abundance. Compare the mode of treating
the charlick, or the poppy, that grows in English cornfields: these
are usually allowed to flower, which they do earlier than the wheat
among which they grow; they can then be readily observed, and
removed before they have time to seed. Neither of these plants,
however, has, even in its earlier growth, any likeness to the wheat,
such as may be remarked in the case of the tares.

221.—ALPHA AND OMEGA.
Rev. i. 8.

⁋ It would be both more correct and more expressive to render
this sentence, "I am *the* Alpha and the Omega." Alpha (A) is
the first letter of the Greek alphabet, and Omega (ω) is the last
letter. In the early Church these two letters came to be frequently
used as symbols of Christ. Sometimes the compound symbol took
this form,

the letters being suspended from the upper arms of the St.
Andrews' cross. Another form was the following,

The letters are found in many other arrangements besides these, and very many works of Christian antiquity were adorned with them. They were also worn on rings and seals, frequently in the form of a monogram. Shortly after the death of Constantine (A.D. 337) the letters were stamped on the current coins of the Roman Empire.

The use of the symbol in the primitive church amounted to a quotation of Rev. xxii. 13, and was regarded as a confession of faith in Christ's own assertion of His Infinite and Divine nature. The Arians, who denied the divinity of Christ avoided the employment of the symbol, but after the outbreak of that heresy its use became almost universal among the orthodox.

It is worthy of remark that Alpha is once used by an ancient writer in the same sense as our A 1.

222.—INFLUENCE OF THE CAPTIVITY UPON THE JEWS.
Ezek. xxxvi. 24–28.

❡ The chief effects of the Captivity upon the Jewish people may be thus summarized. 1. The old tendency to idolatry was finally eradicated. From the time of the return to the present day, the Jews have been a purely monotheistic people. Their evil tendency has been to formality and ceremonialism rather than to idolatry. 2. There had sprung up a deep reverence for the letter of the Law, and for their great Lawgiver, Moses. This developed into the Rabbinical system, accumulating traditions, and overloading Mosaism with petty and wearisome regulations. 3. The love of agriculture had declined, and had given place to a taste for commerce and trade. This explains the preference so many felt for their Chaldaean homes, and accounts for the subsequent scattering of the Jews throughout the cities of the Roman Empire. 4. The vernacular language had undergone a change, the old Hebrew giving place to the Chaldee. The language spoken in the time of our Lord, had been further affected by the temporary conquest of Syria, and is known as Syro-Chaldaic.

223.—FULFILMENT OF PROPHETICAL JUDGMENTS ON EGYPT.
Isaiah xix.

℃ Dr. A. Thomson, recording the impressions of a personal visit to Egypt, says: "Looking down from the Pyramids upon Egypt, it is impossible not to be struck with its unique position in the religious history of the world. From the earliest times down through that long series of ages in which a divine revelation was being given to the world through the medium of the chosen people, Egypt stands forth in history as the chief antagonistic and unchanging enemy of the church of God. We except the period when Jacob and his family found a sunny refuge in Goshen; but how few generations elapsed before their house of refuge became their house of bondage, and Israel in the brick-kilns became the most cruelly oppressed and down-trodden of slaves! Egypt, in consequence, became the vast theatre on which the more awful attributes of God were manifested, just as Palestine became the selected scene in which the wonders of His grace should be revealed. Those ten plagues in which the whole nation was punished, and shame put upon their false divinities through the very form of the miraculous judgment, awfully culminating in the death of every first-born in the land, and in the destruction of the proud Pharaoh and his armed charioteers in the Red Sea, were unapproached in their terrific scale of retribution in any of the older nations of the world; and yet this long line of ever darkening and deepening judgments taught the guilty people and their rulers no lesson of repentance. All through the centuries of the Jewish church and the period of the prophetic revelation, Egypt appears either as the tempter or as the persecutor of Israel, dividing the guilt, in this respect, with the Babylonian and Assyrian monarchies to the east of the sacred land.

"No burden, therefore, reads more darkly in the books of the prophets than that of Egypt. There is a minuteness of detail, a graphic picturing and intensity of colouring, an adaptation to the characteristic customs of the people and to the characteristic features of Egyptian scenery, in such elaborate predictions as those in the 19th chapter of Isaiah, and in certain passages of Ezekiel, that cannot be exceeded. These were spoken and placed on record when Egypt was still in the meridian of her power, and contending with the great monarchies on the banks of the Euphrates and the Tigris for the supremacy of the nations. And yet they were all fulfilled. With Gibbon and Volney as involuntary witness, and modern Egypt looked down upon by us from the Pyramids, we behold events corresponding not only to every line, but to every letter of the inspired oracles. The harmony is startling. When we read in those prophets that Egypt should 'become the basest of nations,' that 'there should no more be a prince of the land of Egypt,' that the country should become 'destitute of that whereof it was full,' and when we place side by side with these oracles the facts that during the long ages of the Mameluke supremacy her rulers were imported strangers and slaves, that for two thousand years no native prince has ever sat upon her throne, but its sovereignty has often been sold to the highest bidder, that the papyrus and the flax, and the manufacture of fine linen, which were once her glory, have now vanished, and the land which was once, with Sicily, the granary of the Roman Empire, is scarcely able to supply bread to its own inhabitants, it would be madness to call such things as these accidental coincidences."

224.—APPEARANCE OF THE NILE OR SHIHOR.
Gen. xli. 1.

℃ "The eastern sky was red with the early dawn: we were on the broad waters of the Nile—or rather, its Rosetta branch. The first thing which struck me was its size. Greater than the Rhine, Rhone, or Danube, one perceives what a sea-like stream it must have appeared to Greeks and Italians, who had seen nothing larger than the narrow and precarious torrents of their own mountains and valleys. As the light broke, its colour gradually revealed itself, —brown like the Tiber, only of a darker and richer hue—no strong current, only a slow, vast, volume of water, mild and beneficent as his statue in the Vatican, steadily flowing on between its two, almost uniform, banks, which rise above it much like the banks of a canal, though in some places with terraces or strips of earth, marking the successive stages of the flood.

"These banks form the horizon on either side, and therefore you can have no notion of the country beyond; but they are varied by a succession of Eastern scenes. Villages of mud rise like ant-hills, with human beings creeping about,—like ants, except in numbers and activity. Mostly they are distinguished by the minaret of a

well-built mosque, or the white oven-like dome of a sheykh's
tomb; mostly, also, screened by a grove of palms, sometimes inter-
mixed with feathery tamarisks, and the thick foliage of the carob-
tree or the sycamore. Verdure, where it is visible, is light green,
but the face of the bank is usually brown. Along the top of the
banks, more like scenes in a magic lantern, and as if cut out
against the sky, groups of Arabs, with their two or three asses, a
camel, or a buffalo."—*Sinai and Palestine.*

225.—EYES PLUCKED OUT BY BIRDS.
Prov. xxx. 17.

℗ It is said by naturalists, that ravens, in attacking their prey, always aim at the eyes, and after blinding the animal, and thus rendering it mad with terror, confusion, and pain, leisurely proceed
with the work of destruction. Other fierce birds, such as hawks, act
on the same plan; and it is asserted that, in Persia and Asia Minor,
falcons were formerly trained to attack men in the same way. It is
matter of doubt, however, if *ravens* ever attacked living men. The
passage above may mean that those who rebel against their parents
shall die in battle, and become the prey of ravens and eagles, some
of them being devoured by the one class of birds, and some by the
other; or it may express the popular belief of the age in which the
proverb was made, that those who rebelled against their parents
would meet with some signal and terrible punishment.

226.—RED CORAL.
Ezek. xxvii. 16.

℗ In this passage "coral" is mentioned as a valuable commodity
in merchandise, in which Syria traded with Tyre; the word occurs
in connection with emeralds, purple, broidered work, fine linen,
and agate. The coral is a well known marine substance, not valued
now as if it were a precious stone, but probably in the time of Job
regarded as of value sufficient to be reckoned with gems. It was
not rare. It is now found in abundance in the Red Sea, and probably was in ancient times obtained there. Shaw says:—"In rowing
gently over it (the Port Tor), while the surface of the sea was
calm, such a diversity of Madrepores, Fucuses, and other marine
vegetables, presented themselves to the eye, that we could not for-

bear taking them, as Pliny had done before us, for a forest under water. The branched Madrepores particularly contributed very much to authorize the comparison; for we passed over several that were eight or ten feet high, growing sometimes pyramidical, like the cypress, and at other times having their branches more open and diffused, like the oak; not to speak of others which, like the creeping plants, spread themselves over the bottom of the sea."

Coral is a hard, cretaceous, marine substance, arising from the deposit of calcareous matter by a minute polypous animal, in order to form a cell, or polypidom, into whose hollows the tenant can wholly or partially retire. They abound in the Red Sea, but are also found in the Mediterranean. It is of different colours, white, black, red. The red kind was anciently, as at present, the most valued, and was worked into various ornaments. The Hebrew word translated *coral* in our Bibles is *ramoth*. There is, however, another word, *peninim*, which may be either coral or pearls.

227.—BATS.
Isaiah ii. 20.

℄ The Hebrews called the "bat," the "night bird," from its well-known habit of flying after sunset. It was one of the "birds," or rather "creatures of the wing," that the Israelites were forbidden to eat. Many travellers have noticed the immense number of bats that infest the caves in the East. Mr. Layard says that, on one occasion, when visiting a cave, those reptiles compelled him to retreat. The bats spend the whole winter in a state of torpor. When the hybernating season arrives, they crowd into caves and other sheltered places, where they suspend themselves head downwards, hanging by their hind claws to roof and sides, to every little crag or ledge, and even to each other. In this condition they continue until the following summer, when, on fine evenings, they issue forth to catch the flying insects on which they feed.

228.—PROBABILITY OF THE EXISTENCE OF A LIBRARY AT JERUSALEM DURING THE MONARCHY.
Prov. xxv. 1.

℄ Recent Assyrian discoveries, revealing as they do the existence of well-organized libraries and a highly-developed literature in both Babylonia and Assyria from an early date, have given us the right to conclude that the Jewish monarchy also was not so illiterate as is currently supposed. Libraries like those of Assyria existed in the great cities of Phoenicia, as we know from Josephus and the Phoenician writers to whom he alludes; and it is more than probable that a similar library was also to be found in Jerusalem itself. At all events we may infer from Proverbs xxv. 1, that in the reign of Hezekiah there was the same royal patronage of letters in Judah as there was at Nineveh; and the copying and re-editing of old Babylonian texts, which formed a chief part of the work performed by the scribes of Assurbani-pal, finds its parallel in the care bestowed upon "the proverbs of Solomon, which the men of Hezekiah, king of Judah, copied out." Shebna, "the scribe," and Joah, the son of Asaph, "the recorder" or "remembrancer," are among the most important personages of Hezekiah's court, and we may compare with them the *tur-sipri* or "chief-librarian" of Assyria, who seems to have occupied an equally prominent place. Arguing from the analogy of Assyria, the Jewish library would have been public and attached to the royal palace, and in it would have been deposited those "chronicles of the kings" of Israel and Judah to which reference is so often made in the historical books of the Old Testament.

229.—THE NEED FOR WASHING AT MEALS.
2 Kings iii. 11.

⁋ "Everything, in the East, being cooked soft, a whole lamb, a chicken, or a turkey, is torn in pieces with the hands, and passed round to the company, who eat it, holding it in their fingers. It may well be supposed that washing does not come amiss after such labours. The servants, therefore, having a towel thrown upon the left shoulder, come forward to every member of the company, and presenting the *ileyen* (basin) with the left hand, while they drop upon the right knee, offer the scented soap it bears upon its little cup, and pour tepid or scented water from an *ibrik* (pitcher) which they carry in the right hand. The soiled water passes out of sight through the perforated cover of the basin. These utensils are ordinarily of whitened copper, but they are sometimes made of solid silver, and even gold."

230.—BARNABAS' ESTIMATE OF PAUL.
Acts xi. 25, 26.

⁋ Dr. Porter points out that the fact of Barnabas going to Tarsus
to seek Paul is very suggestive. There was a great spirit of enquiry
at Antioch, and the need for a man who was an eloquent speaker,
a sound arguer, and a devout, earnest believer. Barnabas thought
of Paul, and decided that he was the very man. When Paul went
to Jerusalem, after his conversion, the body of the disciples were
afraid of him. They distrusted his sincerity. "But Barnabas had a
deeper insight into character. He appears to have perceived at
once, not only the glorious transformation effected in the man, but
the vast importance of such a convert to the Christian cause. He
felt that he was adapted to just such a sphere as was opened for
labour among the learned and polished people of Antioch. His accomplished scholarship, his logical acumen, his profound knowledge of human nature, his zeal, his courage, and the prestige of his
name, were calculated to make a deep impression. At Antioch the
new sect was increased and organized on a broad and liberal basis.
Paul's great work, as the Apostle of the Gentiles, now commenced
in real earnest; and we find that, at the very outset, he cast aside
all Jewish prejudice, all feelings of race and nationality, and boldly
propagated a religion whose doctrines, rites, and moral precepts
were suited, as they were intended, for all mankind. This religion
became so clearly and sharply defined under the wise teaching and
superintendence of Paul, that it could no longer be confounded
with Judaism. It now, for the first time, forced itself upon the
stage of the world's history as a distinct faith, and its votaries received the distinctive name of 'Christian.'"

231.—LEVELLING MOUNTAINS TO MAKE A HIGHWAY.
Isaiah xl. 3, 4.

⁋ This passage, of which the force may not at once strike the
reader, is well illustrated by a description which Diodorus Siculus
gives of a march of Semiramis, Queen of Persia. "In marching towards Ecbatana she came to a mountain called Zarkeum, which,
extending many furlongs, and being full of craggy precipices and
deep hollows, could not be passed without taking a long and circuitous route. Being desirous, therefore, of leaving an immortal

monument of herself, as well as to make a shorter way, she ordered the precipices to be cut down, and the hollow places to be
filled up with earth; and, at a great expense, she made a plain
open road, which to this day is called the road of Semiramis. Afterwards she made a progress through Persia and all her other dominions in Asia, and wherever she came she ordered the mountains and craggy rocks to be cut down, and at a vast expense made
the ways level and plain. On the other hand, in low or champaign
places she raised mounds."

Something similar to this may possibly have been known to the
prophet, and from it his imagery appears to be borrowed.

232.—THREE KINDS OF OATHS OR SWEARING.
Gen. xiv. 22.

⟪ In early times we find no scruples about the employment of the
oath. As then humanity had to become accustomed to a mutual
reverence for truth and fidelity, it was natural that its use should
be frequent and its signs forcible. We may distinguish three kinds:
—1. The simple kind, when a private individual would confirm
something in a sacred manner by his own spontaneous action. He
would call on the name of his God, and the Semitic nations raised
the right hand, as if in a challenge, to heaven. (This Abraham did
in the case referred to in the above passage.) Along with the name
of God, the person swearing would at the same time designate his
other attributes, his power and greatness, or whatever else of the
essence of this God appeared to him at the moment of swearing of
special significance. One of the shortest and finest of the assevera-
tive phrases is that of the last King of Judah: "As Jahveh lives,
who has created for us this soul!" (Jer. xxxviii. 16). There is a peculiar Hebrew word, which means "to bind oneself by seven
(things)." According to this the person swearing deemed it necessary to call upon seven things as witnesses of his declaration, or as
enduring monuments of the truth. It might be seven men whom he
invoked, or seven gods, or else he might touch seven sacred objects, or take seven steps to a sacred stone. (This last was customary amongst the ancient Indians in concluding treaties.) Sometimes seven sacrificial animals were presented (Gen. xxi. 27–31).
2. The oath became an adjuration, when it was used to compel another to confess the truth, or observe a command. Then the pun-

ishments imprecated from heaven would undoubtedly be always expressed in the strongest language. In the patriarchal times, the person who desired to bind another to the strictest truth used to make the latter lay his hand under his own hip; on that part of the body out of which, according to ancient ideas, posterity proceeded. Thus he would refer the latter to the whole of posterity at once, and to its revenge should he break his promise. 3. When the oath was employed in making contracts or alliances, each of the two contracting parties made the other utter aloud the words of the contract which concerned him, these mutual promises being accompanied by similar oaths and imprecations.

233.—TRADITIONAL WORDS OF CHRIST.
John vi. 63.

⁋ The Gospels must not be supposed to record all the utterances of our Lord Jesus Christ; many are altogether lost; some, we may well suppose, have been preserved by tradition.

For instance, in the Codex Bezae, an ancient and valuable manuscript of a portion of the New Testament, supposed to belong to the sixth century, and preserved in the University Library at Cambridge, there is a remarkable addition to Luke vi. 5. It is as follows:—"On the same day, seeing one working on the Sabbath, he said to him, 'O man, if indeed thou knowest what thou doest, thou art blessed; but if thou knowest not, thou art accursed, and a transgressor of the law.'" "The story," says a recent writer, "is too striking, too intrinsically probable, to be at once rejected as unauthentic. Nothing could more clearly illustrate the spirit of our Lord's teaching, as it was understood, for instance, by St. Paul. For the meaning of the story obviously is—If thy work be of faith, then thou art acting rightly: if not of faith, it is sin."— (Compare 1 Cor. viii.; Rom. xiv. 14, 23.)

Other sayings ascribed to Christ are shorter, some of them may be given:—"Show yourselves tried among money-changers." "He who is near me is near the fire (probably of purification, or of persecution); he who is far from me is far from the kingdom." "Keep the flesh pure, and the seal unspotted." "For those that were sick I was sick, and for those that hunger I suffered hunger, and for those that thirst I suffered thirst." "In whatsoever I find you in this will I also judge you." "Never be joyful, except when ye shall look on your brother in love."

A very old tradition relates that "Jesus, the son of Mary, said, 'He who longs to be rich is like a man who drinks sea-water: the more he drinks the more thirsty he becomes, and never leaves off drinking until he perishes.'"

234.—SPRINKLING THE BLOOD.
Lev. iv. 6, etc.

℧ Ewald thus explains the various ceremonies of sprinkling—"It was in the sprinkling of the blood, the proper sacrament of sacrifice, that the distinction between the guilt-offering and the expiatory-offering in the narrow sense, came most clearly to the front; and it is easy to understand why it would reveal itself most plainly here. As it was right that the blood of an expiatory-offering for public transgressions should be made far more conspicuous to eyes and sense, so it was sprinkled on an elevated place, or even on one which was extraordinarily sacred. The way, too, in which this was done was marked by three stages. If the atonement was made for an ordinary man, or for a prince, the priest sprinkled the blood against the high towering horns of the outer altar, and poured the remainder, as usual, out at its base; if it was made for the community, or for the high priest, some of the blood was seven times sprinkled against the veil of the Holy of Holies, then some more against the horns of the inner altar, and only what was then left was poured out as usual at the base of the outer altar. The third and highest stage of expiation was adopted on the yearly day of atonement. On the other hand, in the case of the guilt-offering, no reason existed for adopting any unusual mode of sprinkling the blood. It was sprinkled, just as in other cases, round the sides and foot of the outer altar. As soon as this most sacred ceremony of the sprinkling was completed, then, according to the ancient belief, the impurity and guilt were already shaken off from the object to which they had clung."

235.—TALKING WITH THE EYES AND HANDS.
Prov. vi. 13.

℧ This passage is part of the description of a naughty person; but the custom referred to in it was not confined to people of that class.—(See, for instance, Psalm cxxiii. 2.)

Every nation makes more or less use of the hands as vehicles of
thought, but the Orientals appear to have been very proficient in
the art. Some of the most important orders are given by the motions of the hands. In the Seraglio of the Grand Turk this method
of communication appears to have been carried to a high pitch of
perfection. Master Robert Withers, whose narrative appeared in
"Purchas's Pilgrims," about 200 years ago, says, "In the Seraglio
there are many dumb men, both old and young, who have liberty
to go in and out, with leave of the Caper Agha. And this is worthy
of observation, that in the seraglio, both the king and others can
reason and discourse of anything as well and as distinctly, by nods
and signs, as they can by words—a thing well befitting the gravity
of the better sort of Turks, who care not for much babbling. The
same is also used among the sultanas, and other of the king's
women; for with them likewise there are divers dumb women,
both old and young. And this hath been an ancient custom in the
Seraglio; wherefore they get as many mutes as they can possibly
find, and chiefly for this one reason, that they hold it a thing not
befitting the Grand Signior, neither stands it with his greatness, to
speak to any about him familiarly; but he may, in that manner,
more tractably and domestically jest and sport with the mutes than
with others that are about him."

236.—A Battlement for the Flat Roofs.
Deut. xxii. 8.

℧ This is a very wise and humane command, showing how thoroughly considerate and practical the Mosaic legislation was. It
ought to be still enforced by law wherever the roofs are flat, and
resorted to for business, relaxation, or for sleeping. In Syrian cities
flat roofs are a great comfort. The ordinary houses have no other
place where the inmates can either see the sun, "smell the air," dry
their clothes, set out their flower-pots, or do numberless other
things essential to their health and comfort. This is particularly
true within the city walls; but even in villages the roof is very useful. There the farmer suns his wheat from the mill, and the flour
when brought home, and dries his figs, raisins, etc. A Syrian missionary illustrates the dangers of falling from them, if they are not
properly guarded by parapet, fence, or battlement. "The roofs of
these houses afford such a delightful promenade, and the prospect
is so beautiful, that I can scarcely keep away from them, day or
night. So absorbed was I just now in gazing about, that, if it had

not been for the parapet, I should have walked quite off, and then
have found myself on the ground with a broken limb or neck, I
suppose. As it was, I made a desperate stumble, and was excessively frightened."

237.—EARLY TRADITION CONNECTED WITH
JAMES'S DEATH.
Acts xii. 2.

℣ Clement of Alexandria narrates that the man who accused
James before the judges became so affected by the martyr's con-
stancy, that he too immediately embraced Christianity; and, along
with James, was condemned to be beheaded. As they went to execution, the new convert asked forgiveness of the Apostle, who de-
liberated a little with himself as to whether he should treat him as
a brother or not; but, after a short pause, he embraced him, and
said, "Peace be with you;" after which their heads were struck off.

238.—ATONEMENT-DAY AMONG MODERN JEWS.
Lev. xvi.

℣ On the previous day the most pious go to the synagogue about
two o'clock, and remain there until four. Having returned and
breakfasted, the ceremony of *keparoth,* or atoning sacrifices, takes
place. The sacrifice consists of a cock for a male, and a hen for a
female. . . . The ceremony is performed by the head of the family; for himself first, and then for his household. After repeating a
cabalistic prayer composed for the occasion, he takes the cock in
his hand. . . . He then moves the atonement round his head, saying, "This is my atonement; this is my ransom. This cock goeth to
death; but may I be gathered, and enter into a long and happy life,
and into peace." All this is repeated three times. Having done so
for himself, he does in like manner for the members of the family,
introducing the alterations that are to be made for the other persons. As soon as the prescribed order is performed, they lay their
hands on the atonement, as was usual with the sacrifices, and immediately after it is given to the *shochet* to be slaughtered. The
synagogue is lighted up with numerous candles, and the evening
service commenced, which brings in the great festival of *Yom
Kippur,* or day of atonement. This service consists chiefly of taking of vows, and is continued for three hours. "The following

morning, *i.e.,* the morning of the day of atonement, the service
commences about six o'clock, and continues all day until the evening." "At sunset a trumpet is blown, as a signal that the duties of
the day are over; the whole closing with the words, 'Next year we
shall be in Jerusalem!' " Every Jew who has the least feeling of Judaism, attends the synagogue on the day of atonement. . . .
Leather shoes, or anything made of calf's skin, are not allowed to
be worn on this day, in sad remembrance, we are told, of the
golden calf worshipped by their forefathers. Consequently, the
majority wear cloth boots or shoes; whilst those who are not so
provided go with only stockings on their feet. Neither are they allowed to adorn themselves with any gold ornaments, in remembrance of the materials of which the golden calf was made.

239.—TURTLE DOVES.
Song Sol. ii. 12.

℘ In Asia Minor, in the month of May, these birds may still be
seen fluttering about. They spend the whole summer in the northern portions of the Peninsula, where they breed, and then, in the
autumn, they disappear. They are seen feeding in the grain-fields,
drinking at every spring and fountain, and on the edge of every
stream, and collecting in large numbers in the thickest trees during
the heat of the day. They seem to spend their nights mostly upon
the rocks. Though they destroy much grain and fruit, they are
general favourites, and are destroyed only for food. They breed
about the month of July, and are shot as soon as fully fledged. The
flight of the turtle has a very peculiar sound, which we might call
silvery; it is certainly unlike that of any other of the feathered
tribe. When it flutters overhead, its outspread tail presents a semi-
circle of black set in white. Its cooing is often heard in every
direction—among the trees, on the wall fences, upon the ground,
and on the rocks, and they are frequently seen sitting side by side
upon a branch, or fluttering in pairs.

240.—ART REPRESENTATION OF THE
GARDEN OF GETHSEMANE.
Matt. xxvi. 36.

℘ During the first four centuries and a half, at least, the subject
of our Lord's passion seems to have been approached, but not en-

tered upon—as by representations of the betrayal, the scene before Pilate, etc. The Garden of Gethsemane is one of the earliest of these approaches to actual delineation of our Lord's sufferings. The Manuscript Gospel of St. Augustine, very possibly made use of by the Bishop himself, contains a most interesting picture of the betrayal in the garden, which is represented not only by trees but by a curious serpentine representation of the brook Kedron, bursting out of a rock like the Barada at Ain Fifi, or the Jordan at Tell-el-Khady. This subject is carved on the casket of the Brescian library, dating from the fifth or sixth century.

241.—DEATH OF HEROD.
Acts xii. 21.

℄ Josephus gives some details respecting the tragic death of Herod, which are worthy of note. It appears that the king put on a dress of peculiarly brilliant texture for this special occasion, and that when he appeared in the theatre the beams of the rising sun were so splendidly reflected from the silver garment as to give him the appearance of a supernatural being; the spectators were struck with awe and admiration, and cried out, "It is the voice of a god." Herod is said to have reproved his courtiers in these words when death was near: "Behold your god is now condemned to die."

242.—EASTERN BEDDING CUPBOARDS.
2 Kings xi. 2.

℄ The cupboards are a very important part of the Eastern house; for, as the people have neither chests, bureaus, nor wardrobes, everything has to go into the cupboard, which is permanently built into the wall.

Besides the smaller cupboards, the fourth side of the room, where there is no sofa or divan, is occupied by two larger cupboards, where the bedding of the family is stowed during the day. For the night this bedding is spread upon the floor of the room. It consists of wool mattresses, cotton pillows with coloured and embroidered pillow-cases, and yorghans, or cotton wadded coverlets, with the sheet stitched on every time it is put on clean. Each room is occupied during the day, and becomes a bedroom at night. In wealthy families each member has his or her own room, and only meals are taken in common; but with the poorer people a single room is made to suffice for the whole family.

243.—THE TREE OF LIFE.
Gen. iii. 24.

⁋ The tree called *arbor vitae* (Tree of Life) is doubtless familiar
to many of our readers. It is found sculptured on ancient Egyptian
tombs, as a symbol of belief in another existence beyond the
grave. The curious point about it is that it should receive this
name in preference to any other tree. Some have supposed that
this is due to the fact that while an evergreen it loses its fresh
colour, assuming a much darker shade in winter and renewing its
bright green hue in spring.

In an old, rare book called "Adam's Repentance," is the following legend concerning it:—Seth, the third son of Adam, went to
the gate of Paradise at the request of his dying father, and there
received from the angel in charge three seeds of the tree of life,
which he put in the mouth of Adam, when he buried him. From
these grew three saplings, from which were taken the wood for
Moses' rod and that by which the waters of Marah in the desert
were sweetened. The temple of David was also built of the wood
of these trees, and the bench on which the heathen Sibyls sat when
they prophesied the coming of Christ. Moses' rod was planted in
Canaan and also became a tree, from which the cross of Christ,
the new tree of life, was made, and the eternal life, lost in Adam,
is regained.

This legend is fully portrayed in a picture on the altar of a
church in Leyden.

It is, perhaps, founded on a simpler story told by Sozomen, the
ecclesiastical historian, that at Hermopolis, in Egypt, stood the tree
Persis, the fruit, leaves, and bark whereof possessed wonderful
healing qualities. When the Virgin Mary, on her flight to Egypt
with the infant Jesus, rested under this tree, it bowed its whole
length in humble reverence to Jesus as the true Lord of life and
health.

In the Middle Ages it was said that whosoever would eat of the
wood of this tree of life would be preserved from weakness and
decrepitude, and would be rendered invincible as Achilles. It was
also said that to eat of its foliage would cause one to forget all
hunger and care. This is probably true, but the tree would not

then be one of life but one of death. The active principle in the leaves in poisonous, and is not now used as medicine except by the Homoeopathists, under the name Thuja.

244.—JERUSALEM CALLED THE HOLY CITY.
Isaiah xlviii. 2.

⁋ In many passages of the Old Testament (Neh. xi. 1, 18; Isaiah xlviii. 2; Dan. ix. 24), as well as in a few passages of the New (Matt. iv. 5; xxvii. 53; Rev. xxi. 2), Jerusalem is called emphatically "the Holy City." This designation, at first a mere epithet, eventually became a proper name, and *Je-ha-Kodesh* seems, in some cases, to have superseded the more general name of Jerusalem. In other instances the two designations ran together: on some of the Hebrew shekels the inscription was *"Jerusalem Kedoshah,"* or *"Ha Kedoshah."* It is worthy of remark that this name was not confined to the Jews; other nations, especially the Arabs, regularly gave the city the same honourable title; and to this day, Mohammedans though they are, the only name they have for Jerusalem is *El Koods,* or *The Holy;* and this name they appear to bestow on no other city.

245.—RED POTTAGE.
Gen. xxv. 29–34.

⁋ *Edom,* a word signifying *red,* was the name given to Esau because of the sale of his birthright to Jacob for a mess of red lentile pottage. Through Esau, the word Edom was afterwards applied to the district inhabited by himself and his descendants. This Edom was situated along the south-eastern border of Palestine, between the Dead Sea and the Gulf of Akabah. It included the valley of the Arabah and the region about Mount Seir, and seems to have extended southwards and eastwards, without any very clearly defined boundary, as the descendants of Esau or Edom increased. It was through this district of northern Arabia that Palgrave passed on his way to the exploration of the central table land of the great Arabian peninsula; and it was while traversing this country that a circumstance occurred, between which and the Bible story of the red pottage there is a very remarkable coincidence. Palgrave relates it in the following words:—"The day passes on.

About noon our host naturally enough supposes us hungry, and accordingly a new dish is brought in; it looks much like a bowl full of coarse red paste, or bran mixed with ochre. This is samp, a main article of subsistence to the Bedouins of northern Arabia. Throughout this part of the desert grows a small herbaceous and tufted plant, with juicy stalks, and a little ovate, yellow-tinted leaf; the flowers are of a brighter yellow, with many stamens and pistils. When the blossoms fall off, there remains in place of each a four-leaved capsule, about the size of an ordinary pea; and this, when ripe, opens to show a mass of minute reddish seeds, resembling grit in feel and appearance, but farinaceous in substance. The capsules are gathered, the seed separated from them, and kept, like a stock of flour, for the ensuing year. These seeds, when wanted for use, are coarsely ground in a handmill, then mixed with water, and boiled into the substance which we now had before us. Its taste and quality were pretty well hit off by Salem, who described it as 'not so good as wheat, and rather better than barley-meal.'"

246.—GENERAL INVITATIONS TO EASTERN BANQUETS.
Prov. ix. 2–4.

℘ Although this passage is allegorical, yet it is founded on a well-known custom. Invitations to feasts and banquets were, no doubt, often of a particular and exclusive kind; but in many other instances they were general, and addressed in public to rich and poor, friends and strangers. The banquet prepared by Wisdom was of this latter description; and the manner of giving the invitation is worthy of notice. There was, until recently, a custom in Egypt which, as described by Hasselquist, very aptly illustrates this passage. This traveller, when in Egypt, saw a number of women going about the streets in a very singular, but no doubt ancient manner, inviting people to a public banquet. There were ten or twelve of them, covered with black veils, such as were then customary in the country. Four eunuchs preceded them, and after them followed several Moors with walking-staves. As they passed along they all united in making a great noise. The traveller was told that the sound was intended to express the joy of the party, though he could not recognise the element of joy in the sounds they uttered. The sounds were singular, shrill, and quavering, and in this way the public were invited to the banquet.

It appears that Wisdom also made her invitation by females, for she sent forth her maidens; the invitation was made in public, and apparently in a shrill voice, for "she crieth" (by her maidens) "upon the high places of the city."

In New Testament times it would seem that men-servants were sent on these social errands.

247.—ALABASTER VASES.
Matt. xxvi. 7.

¶ Alabaster, a calcareous spar, appears to have been a favourite material for the manufacture of elegant vases, both for use and ornament, from the most remote ages. The following account of this substance is given by Pliny, in his "Natural History:"

"This stone is hollowed out into vessels for holding unguents, it having the reputation of preserving them from corruption better than anything else. In a calcined state it is a good ingredient for plaisters. It is found in the vicinity of Thebes, in Egypt; and of Damascus, in Syria; that of Damascus being whiter than the others. The most esteemed kind, however, is that of Carmania, the next being the produce of India, and then those of Syria and Asia. The worst in quality is that of Cappadocia, it being utterly destitute of lustre. That which is of a honey colour is the most esteemed, covered with spots curling in whirls, and not transparent. 'Alabastrites' is considered defective when it is of a white or horn colour, or approaching to glass in appearance."

At *Alabastron,* in Egypt, there was a manufactory of small pots and vessels for holding perfumes, which were made from a stone found in the neighbouring mountains. The Greeks gave to these vessels the name of the city from which they came, calling them *alabastrons.* This name was eventually extended to the stone of which they were formed; and at length the term *alabastra* was applied without distinction to all perfume vessels, of whatever materials they consisted. Thus Theocritus speaks of golden *alabastra.*

248.—THE ARK OF BULRUSHES.
Exodus ii. 3.

¶ The Hebrew word *goma,* translated bulrush, is derived from the verb *to imbibe, to soak up water.* The stalk is of a vivid green, of a triangular form, and tapering towards the top. It terminates in a tuft or crown of small grassy filaments, each about a foot long. This singular vegetable was used for a variety of purposes, the principal of which was the structure of boats and the manufacture of a writing material. Papyrus boats are frequently noticed by ancient writers. Plutarch describes Isis going in search of the body of Osiris, "through the fenny country in a bark made of the papyrus;" Pliny mentions the "ships made of the papyrus, and the equipments of the Nile;" and Lucan the poet has, "the Memphian boat is made of the thirsty papyrus." Theophrastus also, when describing the papyrus, says, "they make boats and ships of it." The bodies of such boats were composed of rushes, which were bound together with the papyrus; and the mode of rendering them impervious to water is satisfactorily pointed out by the coating of pitch with which they were covered—the Hebrew word being precisely the same as that used for pitch by the Arabs to the present day—"daubed it with *slime*," *i.e.*, with bitumen; the *bitumen* cemented the rushes together, the pitch served to keep out the water. There seems to be considerable similarity between the ark or boat in which Moses was deposited, and the curious vessels which are at the present day employed in crossing the Tigris. They are perfectly circular in shape, and are made with the leaves of the date-palm, forming a kind of basket-work, which is rendered impervious to the water by being thickly coated with bitumen.

249.—MEALS PREPARED ON THE SEA-SHORE.
John xxi. 9.

❡ According to Plutarch, it was a customary thing among the Greeks to take a meal by the sea-shore. This was done for the sake of the scenery, the fresh sea breeze, and for the fresh fish so easily obtained there. It appears also that the Arabs, Syrians, and all other tribes dwelling upon the Mediterranean coast of Palestine, were, and are, in the habit of doing the same; and it is a regular custom with the fishermen there to go ashore at meal times, or when they are hungry, and cook some of the fish they have caught for their own immediate use.

250.—THE BOOK OF ENOCH.
Jude 14, 15.

❡ In one respect, at least, this passage is of singular interest. It is a direct quotation, to all appearance, from an apocryphal work, known as the "Book of Enoch." Some account of this book may be given. It was well known in the second century of our era, and was either referred to or quoted from by Justin Martyr, Irenaeus, Anatolinus, Clement of Alexandria, Origen, and Tertullian. But though so extensively read in the early church, the Book was lost for fourteen or fifteen centuries afterwards, only fragments being found in any part of the learned world. In the last century, however, Bruce, the great African traveller, brought home one or two complete manuscript copies, written in Ethiopia, from Abyssinia. The manuscripts were deposited at Paris, and at Oxford, and several translations have been published. The book is in every respect a curiosity; and it appears to have been written somewhat in imitation of the Book of Daniel. That there is a very close resemblance between Jude 14, 15, and the Book of Enoch, ii., will be seen by comparing the following translation:—"Behold He comes with ten thousands of His saints, to execute judgment upon them, and destroy the wicked, and reprove all the carnal for everything which the sinful and ungodly have done, and committed against Him."

There is no reason whatever for supposing that the work, as it at present exists, is the work of Enoch the patriarch. It contains much that is curious, a little that is edifying, and a great deal that is paltry. Still, as a venerable relic of a world that has disappeared, it is worthy of some respect.

251.—A FAMILIAR SPIRIT.
Lev. xx. 27.

℔ The name of the sacred serpent, according to Bryant, was in the ancient language of Canaan, variously pronounced Aub, Ab, Oub, Ob, Oph, Op, Eph, Ev; all referable to the original ארב, or אב; which, being derived from אב, (inflare) was perhaps applied to the serpent from his peculiarity of *inflation* when irritated. The verse above should read, "in whom there is an 'OB."

The word ארב is translated by the Septuagint, *ventriloquist,* implying that the possessor of the 'Ob spoke from his stomach, where he pretended that the spirit presided. This "speaking from the belly" is the Greek notion of *inflation,* adopted by the Septuagint in accommodation to the received opinions respecting the Pythian priestess.

It is a curious coincidence that, as the Witch of Endor is called *Oub,* and the African sorceress *Obi,* from the serpent-deity *Oub;*

so the old English name of a witch, *hag,* bears apparent relationship to the word *hak,* the ancient British name of a species of snake.

The Assyrian inscriptions appear to afford another and a different explanation of the term *'Ob.* In Accadian, where magic plays a large part, *ubi* meant "the summoning of a spirit." This the Assyrians borrowed, under the form of *ubutu,* or *abutu,* the feminine representative of the Hebrew *'Ob.*

252.—CUSTOMS OF PETITIONING KINGS, ETC., IN THE STREETS.
2 Kings vi. 26.

⚌ The scene described in this passage might easily have taken place in China to-day. The walls of Chinese fortified cities are some fifteen feet broad, protected on the exterior by battlements with embrasures, while on the inside the houses are built against them, and at the gates stone steps lead down to the streets of the city. The woman might have come from one of the houses abutting against the wall, or she might have come up the steps: this however is forbidden in time of peace, and probably would be prevented in time of war.

It is very difficult to get access to high officers in China, unless a vast number of underlings, doorkeepers, clerks, and secretaries receive heavy rewards. When, however, any one, especially a helpless woman, has a very great grievance, custom allows her to stop the sedan-chair of the great man in the street, and present her petition. The king might have been thus stopped, while going his round of inspection on the walls.

253.—ETERNAL LIFE.
Matt. xxv. 46.

⚌ It requires to be understood that the term *eternal* has no exclusive reference to duration. It is to be treated as expressive of the character, quality, and value of a thing; and value is reckoned among men partly by the length of time a thing will last. Properly "Eternal life" is to be regarded as something distinct from, and opposed to, what is natural, earthly, carnal. It is out of the reach of all terms that are merely indicative of time. It does not mean everlasting, as if what it refers to could be measured by hours, or years, or centuries, and so, by being drawn out without limit, become, or be characterised as, eternal on that ground. It stands for what is divine, spiritual, Godlike, and may be applied to what is possessed and enjoyed now—the life of God in the soul of man, which is "eternal life" because of its distinctive quality and nature. It is that, at this moment, wherever it exists, as much as it can ever be—as much as it will be myriads of ages hence, and when time itself shall be no more. The word Eternal is also properly applied to God (Deut. xxxiii. 27; Rom. i. 20), but it is a most miserable limitation of its meaning in this relation, to suppose that it merely means, "the God who will last for ever."

254.—ECCENTRIC BOUNDARIES OF THE TRIBES.
Joshua xv.–xix.

℃ Thomson, in "The Land and the Book," writes: "The reason why the boundaries of the different tribes were so eccentric originally, and are now so difficult to follow, was that the 'lots' were not meted out according to geographical lines; but lands of certain cities lying more or less contiguous were assigned to each tribe. These cities were the capitals of small principalities or districts, just as Tibnin, and Hunin, and Bint-Jebail are now. The territory of one might extend far to the east of the city, that of the next to the west. It is now absolutely impossible to draw lines around the separate 'lots' with any degree of certainty. Their general positions with relation to each other, however, can be ascertained with sufficient exactness for all important purposes in the study of Biblical geography."

255.—"GOD ACCEPTETH NO MAN'S PERSON."
Gal. ii. 6.

℀ The idea here desired to be conveyed is evidently that God takes no account of the mere appearance, or outside, of a man; He looks through these to the heart, and judges what the man really is in principles and disposition. The force of the contrast, however, is more vividly brought out by observing the origin of the word *person*. It comes from the Latin word *persona,* a face or mask; and is evidently made from *per-sono,* to sound through; conveying the idea of the sound of the voice coming through the open space left for the mouth in the masks of the actors in the ancient plays; and suggests at once the word, *impersonate, i.e.,* to take a character not our own. Thus we get the idea conveyed in the passage above, that God looks behind the mask which we may assume, and at what is underneath, knowing and judging our real characters while others judge only by our outside appearance.

256.—NO PAPER-REEDS NOW IN EGYPT.
Isaiah xix. 7.

℀ The tourist in Egypt, looking for Bible illustrations, is likely to be disappointed when he finds no "bulrushes" or "reeds" answering to those spoken of in the history of the infant Moses. No sign of flag, reed, or other aquatic plant appears, either along the Nile or elsewhere. Yet there must have been such plants in former times: the monuments depict them in great variety—the *lotus* being the principal; and the rolls of papyrus found in the tombs testify to the existence of such plants, the papyrus having been made from the bark of the paper-reed. The *disappearance* of these plants was specifically predicted by the Scripture writers. The Prophet Isaiah says, "The reeds and flags shall wither; the paper-reeds by the brooks, by the mouth of the brooks, and everything sown by the brooks shall wither, be driven away, and be no more."

But the question arises, *Why* do not aquatic plants now grow in Egypt? The physical conditions now existing in this country are the same which have always prevailed. The divine fiat does not now resist natural laws for the fulfilment of prophecy. Aquatic plants,—which, as Herodotus testifies, were extremely valuable,—were reared, in the time of Egypt's prosperity, by artificial means

255.—"God Accepteth no Man's Person."

involving the preparation of reservoirs and "brooks." By means of
"ponds" and "sluices," too, the fish were multiplied. The prediction of Isaiah therefore relates to the destruction of these nice arrangements of artificial life, on which depended the country's high
prosperity. It is quite consistent with the civilisation of the time
that the bathing-place of Pharaoh's daughter should be a cultivated
garden bordering the Nile, where seclusion could be had.

257.—THE TRANSLATION "BREECHES."
Gen. iii. 7.

℄ Our readers are aware that an edition of the Scriptures in
which the word in our present English version translated *aprons*
was translated *breeches,* has long been known as the "Breeches
Bible." This was printed in 1560: but the word was in fact used by
both Chaucer and John Wickliffe more than a century before.

John Wickliffe's translation was completed in 1380, and it was
extensively circulated. 170 manuscripts of the Wycliffite versions
still exist. In this work, Gen. iii. 7, is thus rendered, "And the
eizen of both ben openyd and whanne thei knowen hein silf to be
naked thei soweden togidre leeuis of a fig tree and maden hem
brechis."

In Chaucer's "Persones Tale" may be found the following passage, "And anon the eyen of hem bothe opened en and whan that
they knewe that they were naked, they sowede of fige leves in
maner of *breches* to hiden here membris."

Caxton's version, printed by Wynkyn de Worde in 1527 (thirty-
three years before the Breeches Bible), renders the passage, Gen.
iii. 7; "They toke figge leaves and sowed them togyder for to cover
their membres, in manner of *breches.*"

Breeches is probably taken from the word *Brecan* to break, and
is referred to that part of the body which is broken, or bent in sitting down. Hence it means the middle. The rebellious sea, says
Robert of Gloucester of King Cnut, "wax an hey (high) and watte
hys *brych* all aboute;" *i.e.,* rose as high as his middle. By a usual
custom the name of the part is transferred to the garment, and
breeches were and are aprons, as well as trousers. Hence the apron
of a gun which covers the breeching has been itself called by the
name. To *breech* is also to put on, or cover with clothes; (thus we
say of a little boy that he will shortly be breeched); and perhaps

this wider meaning attached to it in those days, when, as Cowper
says of clothes:—

> *"Save their own painted skins our sires had none,*
>   *As yet* black breeches *were not."*

258.—TRIBULATION, ITS LATIN DERIVATION.
Rom. v. 3.

℄ Our word "tribulation" is derived from the Lat. *tribulum*—a
corn drag, consisting of a heavy piece of wood, armed underneath
with pieces of iron or sharp flints, and drawn over the corn by a
yoke of oxen,—either the driver or a heavy weight being placed
upon it,—for the purpose of separating the grain from the husk
and cutting the straw. As the tribulum was used for separating
beans, &c., from the pods enclosing them, it had to be adapted in
its *construction* and *weight* to the kind of pods, &c., over which it
was passed; so that, in any case, it might break the husks without
crushing the seeds. Thus a divinely appointed *tribulation,* God's
tribulum, is intended to separate the evil without injury to the
good. Wherefore "we glory in tribulation also."—Romans v. 3.

259.—THE VINEYARD WATCHMAN.
Job xxvii. 18.

℄ In Turkey now the police service of the vineyards is done by
officers called Bekjis, or watchmen, one individual being entrusted
with the charge of a certain district. They generally select as their
place of observation an elevated spot, a hillock, upon which they
erect a frame, or booth, which we have minutely described in another paragraph. From this frame they have a general view of the
ground committed to their charge; and their practised eye immediately discovers any intruder, whether man or beast. This task is
easy enough in the day-time; but in the night the hares, foxes, and
jackals creep out of their hiding places, and the Bekji has to patrol
and frighten by his movements the enemies which darkness hides
from him. These Bekjis are usually very active in their district,
keep the city authorities acquainted with all that is going on, and
are much relied on when anything occurs requiring the inter-
ference of the law. They are paid by a tax levied upon the land-
lords; but they have private entrances into every vineyard, know

where the best fruit is to be had, and make a good profit out of
the game which lies within their district.

260.—THE SWEET INFLUENCES OF PLEIADES.
Job xxxviii. 31.

CANST THOU BIND THE SWEET INFLUENCES OF PLEIADES?

¶ In these words there lies hidden a fundamental physical truth
which has been concealed from mankind for thousands of years,
and has only been brought to light in quite recent times. By the
Greeks this cluster of stars was called Pleiades, from *pleein,* to sail,
because it indicated the time when the sailor might hope to under-
take a voyage in safety; it was also called Vergiliae from *ver,* the
spring, because it ushered in the mild vernal weather favourable
for farming and pastoral employments. Job therefore would understand the question as meaning "canst thou hinder or retard the
spring." The discovery of modern science has laid open the true
depth of the divine question. The Chaldean word translated in the
Authorised Version Pleiades is *chima,* meaning literally a hinge,
pivot, or axle which turns round and moves other bodies with it.
The attention of astronomers had for years been directed to the
question of the sun's stationary or movable condition, and it is
now received as an ascertained truth that the sun has itself a central point around which its system revolves. This central point has
been ascertained by M. Madler, of Dorpat, after many intricate
calculations and laborious observations, to be Alcyone, the
brightest star of the Pleiades group, and that it is the centre or
axle of our solar system. So great is the force exerted by this star
that though at a distance thirty-four millions of times greater than
that from our earth to the sun, it draws our system round it at the
rate of 422,000 miles a day in an orbit which it will take many
thousands of years to complete.

261.—HIRE PAID IN A SHARE OF THE PRODUCE.
Gen. xxx. 32.

¶ The mode in which Jacob arranged for payment of his services
may be illustrated by the following extract from the Gentoo laws,
the very ancient code of India.

"If a person," says the ancient law-giver, "without receiving

wages, or subsistence or clothes, attends *ten* milch cows, he shall
select for his own use the milk of that cow which ever produces
most; if he attend to more cows, he shall take milk, after the same
rate, in lieu of wages. If he attend to one hundred cows for the
space of one year, without any arrangement for wages, he shall
take to himself one heifer of three years old," and the milk of all
the cows every eighth day. "If he attend two hundred cows," he is
to get the milk of one day, etc., and also a cow and her calf. "Cattle," the law goes on to say, "shall be delivered over to the
cowherd in the morning; the cowherd shall tend them the whole
day with grass and water, and in the evening shall redeliver them
to the master, in the same manner as they were entrusted to him:
if by the fault of the cowherd any of the cattle be lost or stolen,
that cowherd shall make it good. If the cattle suffer,—by thieves,
tigers, pits, rocks, etc., if the cowherd cries out, no fault lies on
him, the loss shall fall on the owner. When employed night and
day, if any by his fault be hurt, he shall make it good. When a
cowherd hath led cattle to a distant place to feed, if any die of
some distemper, notwithstanding the cowherd applied the proper
remedy, the cowherd shall carry the head, the tail, the forefeet, or
some such convincing proof taken from that animal's body, to the
owner of the cattle; having done this, he shall be no further an-
swerable; if he neglect to act thus, he shall make good the loss."

These extracts will serve in some measure to illustrate several
other passages of Scripture. *E.g.*, David rescued the lamb from the
lion and bear (1 Sam. xvii. 34). The prophet Amos, who was a
herdsman refers to the shepherd, taking "out of the mouth of the
lion two legs, or a piece of an ear." What could this be for, except
to carry convincing proof to his master? The cowherd's milk instead of wages, will remind the reader of Paul's question, "Who
feedeth the flock, and eateth not of the milk of the flock?" (1 Cor.
ix. 7.)

262.—"GRAVEN ON THE PALMS."
Isaiah xlix. 16.

❡ It was the practice among the Hebrews and other Eastern nations, to trace upon the palm of the hands the outlines of any object of affection or admiration. By this means the traveller always
had before him a visible memorial of the city or place he had
visited. The sketch, although necessarily imperfect, was never-

theless indelible, as it was produced by puncturing the skin with a
sharp instrument, and introducing into the punctures a peculiar
die, very much in the same manner in which a sailor prints on his
arm the figure of an anchor or the initials of his own name. From
the indestructible nature of the sketch the process might be called
a species of engraving, and by reason of its permanent character it
served constantly to refresh the memory regarding various particulars associated with the place so delineated. In this custom the oriental metaphor expressing attachment seems to originate: "It is
written on my palms," and likewise the answer which Jehovah
gives to Zion's complaint that the Lord had forgotten her, "Behold, I have graven thee upon the palms of My hands: thy walls
are continually before Me."

263.—SEALING A COVENANT WITH A GIFT OF SEVEN SHEEP.
Gen. xxi. 28.

℄ This passage narrates a curious ceremony. There was a dispute
between Abimelech and Abraham respecting the well at Beersheba, and Abraham gave Abimelech, in addition to other presents, seven ewe lambs as a witness for him that he had digged this
well, and the dispute was closed by a mutual oath. A passage occurs in Bruce's travels that beautifully illustrates this custom, and
shows the wonderful persistency of Eastern manners. Bruce, while
in Abyssinia, wished to go from one place to another, and the
Sheikh had assured him that the journey might be undertaken with
safety. "But," said I, "suppose your people meet us in the desert,
how shall we fare in that case? Should we fight?" "I have told you,
Sheikh, already," says he, "cursed be the man that lifts his hand
against you, or even does not defend and befriend you to his own
loss, even were it Ibrahim, my own son." Then, after some conver-
sation, the old man muttered something to his sons in a dialect
Bruce did not understand, and in a little time the whole hut was
filled with people, the priests and monks of their religion, and the
heads of families. "The great people joined hands, and uttered a
kind of prayer—really the oath—about two minutes long, by
which they declared themselves and their children accursed if ever
they lifted their hands against me in the field, in the desert, or on
the river; or, in case that I or mine should fly to them for refuge,
if they did not protect us at the risk of their lives, their families,

and their fortunes, or, as they emphatically expressed it, 'to the death of the last male child among them.' Medicines and advice given on my part, faith and promises pledged on theirs; two bushels of wheat, and *seven sheep* were carried down to my boat."

264.—PHRYGIAN, ETC., LEGENDS OF THE FLOOD.
Gen. vi. 17.

ℭ The traditions of many nations preserve the recollection of the Flood. They may be found in the Chaldaean and Phoenician mythology, among the Persian, Indian, Chinese, and American nations. The Greeks had their tradition of Deucalion and Pyrrha. Among the Phrygians was a legend of a King Annakos, or Nannakos, in Iconium, who lived to the age of 400 years, foretold the Flood, and in prospect of the destruction awaiting them, wept and prayed for his people. As late as the time of Septimius Severus, a medal was struck at Apamea commemorating this event. On it is the representation of a square vessel floating on the water, and through an opening in it two persons, a man and a woman, are visible. On the top a bird is perched, while another is flying towards it carrying a branch between its feet. In front of the vessel the same pair stand as though they had just landed on dry ground. On some specimens the letters NΩ, or NΩE, have been found.

265.—GARDENS CONNECTED WITH EASTERN HOUSES.
Isaiah lviii. 11.

ℭ Describing the houses, etc., of Tocat, in Asia Minor, Van Lennep says: "The outside of the houses is far from attractive, being plain, uniform mud-walls, pierced at most with a few small and high windows; but when you go in at the gate, you find a paved court, a piazza, and doors and windows opening upon it, or upon the garden in the rear.

"Almost every house has more or less of a garden adjoining. There is neither system, nor regular laying out. Trees are scattered about with little or no plan, and patches for vegetables are laid out as most convenient, onions and cabbages being the universal favourites. But the ornament most prized in a garden, one which all seek to possess if they can possibly afford it, is the marble tank —square, oblong, or octagonal—with a spout in the centre *always out of order.* They would not give up that spout in the centre for a good deal, although it does not play once in a generation; but they sit there and think how fine it would be to see it work, and it is almost the same as if they *did* see it. These tanks are often very tastefully cut and ornamented. The ground around them is always well smoothed, and fine grass is sown upon it, and kept fresh by frequent sprinkling. A vine is generally made to shade the spot by growing upon a trellis overhead. It is the height of Oriental luxury to spread a carpet on the grass, sit cross-legged upon it, and draw the narguile, or sip a cup of coffee. Many take their meals here all the summer. Company gathers here and spends the cooler hours of the day, and even part of the night; and music—the native guitar, tambourine, or drum—is called to enhance the general enjoyment. Children romp here, and women gossip; and, on a hot summer's afternoon, women, boys, and girls, all jump in and cool themselves in the chilly tank."

266.—CENTRAL POSITION OF PALESTINE.
Ezek. v. 5.

❡ All the routes—both by land and water—which connected the three parts of the ancient world passed through Palestine. The commerce between Asia on the one, and Europe and Africa on the other hand, had its centre in the great mercantile cities of Phoenicia and Philistia. Towards the south the Araba led to the Gulf of Elath, and the Shephelah to that of Hero-opolis, while toward the East the ordinary caravan road led to the neighbouring Euphrates, to the Persian Gulf, and thence to the important countries of Southern Asia. Even the highways which connected Asia and Africa touched Palestine. A much-frequented commercial route led from Egypt to Gaza, and from Damascus over the plain of Jezreel to the Phoenician coast.

267.—EGYPTIAN FINE LINEN.
Gen. xli. 42.

❡ It is generally supposed that the "fine linen" of Scripture must have been very coarse in comparison with that now produced from our looms. There is, however, no sufficient ground for such a supposition. Sir Gardener Wilkinson says: "The fine texture of the

Egyptian linen is fully proved by its transparency, as represented in the paintings (where the lines of the body are often seen through the drapery), and by the statements of ancient writers, sacred (see Gen. xli. 42; 2 Chron. i. 16) as well as profane; and by the wonderful texture of a piece found near Memphis, part of which is in my possession. In general quality it is equal to the finest now made; and, for the evenness of the threads, without knot or break, it is far superior to any modern manufacture. It has in the inch 540 threads, or 270 double threads in the warp, and 110 in the woof. Pliny mentions four kinds of linen particularly noted in Egypt, the Tanitic, the Pelusiac, the Butiric, and the Tentyritic; and the same fineness of texture was extended to the nets of Egypt, which were so delicate that they could pass through a man's ring; and a single person could carry a sufficient number of them to surround a whole wood. The transparent fineness of the linen dresses of men and women in the Egyptian paintings recalls the remark of Seneca on 'Sericas vestes,' so thin that a woman dressed in one of them appeared as if naked."

268.—A DIFFICULT VERSE.
Jer. xlvi. 15.

⁋ Among Dr. Kennicott's manuscript notes preserved in the Bodleian Library is one on the reading of Jer. xlvi. 15, which reads in English: "Why are thy valiant men swept away? They stood not because the Lord did drive them." The Hebrew is confused in its numbers, and literally reads: "Why *is* thy valiant *men* swept away? *He* stood not because the Lord did drive him." The first clause reads in Hebrew: מדוע נסחף אביריך. But forty-eight manuscripts read אבידך, in the singular, which makes it grammatically consistent, but not very intelligible: "Why is thy mighty man swept away?" Here comes in light from the Septuagint, which translates the first clause very differently: "Why has Apis, thy chosen bull, fled?" This implies a different division of the letters, as follows: מדוע נס חף אבירך, in which הף is taken for Apis, as the first guttural is so often dropped in Greek (*cf.* Apries and Hophra). The Carpentras Aramaic inscription calls Apis חפי, and the termination *is* of Apis does not belong to the stem. The Hebrew אביד can properly be translated bull (Ps. xxii. 12); and "chosen" is a gloss, perhaps taken from a valiant reading בהיר, and נס is the regular Hebrew word for "fled." With this division the Hebrew would be translated: "Why has thy bull Apis fled?" We have, then, in this passage a case of irony directed against Egyptian idolatry, like that over the Moabite Chemosh, Jer. xlviii. 46.

269.—Sitting Upon Heaps of Stones.
Gen. xxxi. 46.

⁋ From Niebuhr's travels it appears that sitting upon heaps of loose stones was a custom in Arabia even so late as the last century. He says that when he was in Yemen, in South-Eastern Arabia, he was admitted to an interview with the *Imam* of that region. "I had gone from my lodgings indisposed; and by standing so long (in the royal presence) found myself so faint that I was obliged to ask permission to quit the room. I found near the door some of the principal officers of the court, who were sitting, in a scattered manner, in the shade upon stones, by the side of the wall. Among them was the nakih (the general, or rather master, of the horse), Gheir Allah, with whom I had some acquaintance before. He immediately resigned his place to me, and applied himself to draw together (other) stones into a heap, in order to build himself a new seat."

270.—Marriage and Marriage Feast.
Matt. xxii. 2.

⁋ "Made a marriage for his son" of the A. V. would be more correctly rendered by "Made a marriage-feast for his son." The same correction is to be applied to verses 4, 9, and also ch. xxv. 10. The use of the plural $\gamma\acute{\alpha}\mu o\upsilon\varsigma$ is "marriage-feast," in distinction from "a marriage" or "marriage" of the singular number. Yet the other verses show that the evangelist attached the meaning of "marriage-feast" to the singular number, as is done in the LXX.—Gen. xxix. 22; Tobit viii. 19.

271.—The Chief of Asia.
Acts xix. 31.

⁋ When Paul was at Ephesus, contending with the silversmith, Demetrius, and the party he raised, it is said that "certain of the chief of Asia" advised him not to trust himself in the theatre,

where the excited and unruly mob had assembled. But this term
"chief of Asia" gives no idea of the particular persons referred to.
The Greek word used is "Asiarchs"—men who had charge of the
public games and the religious spectacles, which were important
features of social life in those countries and times. These officers
were chosen annually by their several cities, the election being subject to the approval of the pro-consul. It appears that they must
have been men of means, as they were expected to provide public
spectacles at their own expense. Probably the name continued to
attach itself to the individual even after the close of his tenure of
office. Some of these gentlemen, according to the narrative, were
Paul's friends, and they strongly urged him to keep out of the
reach of the tumultuous mob, whose violent character they could
so well estimate; and thus, very likely, they were the means of sav-
ing the Apostle's life.

272.—COMPARISON OF TEACHINGS
OF BUDDHISM AND SCRIPTURE.
Matt. v.–vii.

⁋ Some of the Buddhist parables, such as those of the mustard
seed or of the sower, remind us forcibly of the Gospels, and it is
curious to find an injunction to those who are "of a pious mind"
to keep the Sabbath, or, as it is termed, "to observe Uposatha on
the 14th, 15th, and 8th days of the lunar fortnight; and Pâtih-
ârika," or Lent, "should also be duly observed." The eight com-
mandments of Buddhism are the following: (1) One should not
destroy life. (2) One should not take what is not given. (3) One
should not tell lies. (4) One should not become a drinker of intoxicating liquors. (5) One should refrain from unlawful sexual intercourse. (6) One should not eat unseasonable food at nights. (7)
One should not wear garlands or use perfumes. (8) One should
sleep on a mat spread on the ground. To these may be added the
command to a man to "maintain his father and mother in a just
manner, and to practise a just trade. The householder observing
this with diligence reaches the self-shining gods." It is curious that
this is the only commandment with promise. The precepts laid
down in the "Buddhist Beatitudes" are especially interesting. A
deva asks: "Many angels and men have held various things blessings, when they were yearning for happiness. Do thou declare to

us the chief good." To this Buddha replies: "Not to serve the
foolish, but to serve the wise; to honour those worthy of honour:
this is the greatest blessing. To dwell in a pleasant land, good
works done in a former birth, right desires in the heart: this is the
greatest blessing. Much insight and education, self-control, and
pleasant speech, and whatever word be well spoken: this is the
greatest blessing. To support father and mother, to cherish wife
and child, to follow a peaceful calling: this is the greatest blessing.
To bestow alms and live righteously, to give help to kindred, deeds
which cannot be blamed: this is the greatest blessing. To abhor
and cease from sin, abstinence from strong drink, not to be weary
in well-doing: this is the greatest blessing. Reverence and low-
liness, contentment and gratitude, the hearing of the Law at due
seasons: this is the greatest blessing. To be long-suffering and
meek, to associate with the tranquil, religious folk at due seasons:
this is the greatest blessing. Self-restraint and purity, the knowledge of the noble truths, the realisation of Nirvâna: this is the
greatest blessing. Beneath the stroke of life's changes, the mind
that shaketh not, without grief or passion, and secure: this is the
greatest blessing. On every side are invincible those who do acts
like these, on every side they walk in safety, and theirs is the
greatest blessing."

273.—THE EGYPTIAN CITY CALLED ON.
Gen. xli. 45.

⁋ On is the same as *Heliopolis*, an Egyptian city which stood on
the verge of the desert, about four and a half miles east of the
apex of the Delta. Its site is still marked by the massive walls that
surrounded it, and by a granite obelisk erected about 3,900 years
ago. The Egyptian name of Heliopolis was EI-N-EE, "the abode of
the Sun." For this the Hebrew *On*, or *Aôn* (Aven in Ezek. xxx.
17), was regarded as an equivalent. It was translated *Beth
Shemesh*, the house of the Sun, in Jer. xliii. 13. The large and
lofty crude brick walls of Heliopolis enclosed an irregular area
3,750 feet by 2,870, having the houses of the people on the north
side covering a space of 575,000 square feet, to the south of
which stood the temple of the Sun. This occupied a large portion
of a separate enclosure, and a long avenue of sphinxes led to the
door; the remains of some of these sphinxes may still be traced.

Abdallatif, an Eastern traveller, in the year A.D. 1200 saw many colossal sphinxes, partly prostrate, partly standing. He also saw the gates or propylaea of the temple covered with inscriptions; he describes two immense obelisks whose summits were covered with massive brass, around which were others one half or one third the size of the first, placed in so thick a mass that they could scarcely be counted, most of them thrown down.

"Heliopolis had its priesthood, a numerous and learned body, celebrated before other Egyptians for their historical and antiquarian lore; it long continued the university of the Egyptians, the chief seat of their science; the priests dwelt, as a holy community, in a spacious structure appropriated to their use.

"The site is now marked by low mounds; . . . . its area is at present a ploughed field, a garden of herbs; and the solitary obelisk which still rises in the midst of it is the sole remnant of the former splendours of the place." This obelisk is from 60 to 70 feet high, of a block of red granite. It bears hieroglyphic inscriptions, and, being formed in the shape of a cross, has attracted the special notice of Christian antiquaries.

274.—CARE IN MAKING COPIES OF THE SCRIPTURES.
Psalm xviii. 30.

❡ The expression used in this verse, "the word of the Lord is tried," may be applied to the extreme care with which every word, letter, and mark of the older Scriptures were preserved. One unacquainted with historic fact is invariably surprised at the first sight of one of the old Bibles produced with a pen. We spent a rare hour in examining that famous Samaritan Pentateuch, kept with such care at Shechem. Nobody can conceive how beautifully regular are the characters, how finished are all the lines, and the letters clear to the end. The minuteness with which one manuscript is a fac-simile reproduction of the other is simply a marvel. So fearful of making any mistake were all those professional copyists, of permitting any inaccuracy, or introducing any alteration whatever, that they counted the words and the letters, the points and the accents, chapter by chapter, through the entire volume. And if in their standards, as often happened, even one of the square Hebrew characters was smaller or larger in size than the others in the word where it occurred, they conscientiously repeated it as they found it.

275.—THE NATURAL ENEMY OF THE LOCUST.
Exodus x. 4.

℃ It appears that, in the economy of nature, every creature that might multiply to a perilous destructiveness, is kept within limits by the operations of some natural enemy; and Van Lennep gives a description of the bird whose attacks keep in check the destructive locust.

"Farther on, we saw for the first time the great enemy of the locust, which has of late years made his appearance in Asia Minor simultaneously with the devastating flights of locusts with which some portions of the country have lately been visited. This bird is of the size and shape of the common blackbird (Merula) of the country, but its body is of a light pink, while the wings and tail are black. It is called 'Merle rouge' by the European inhabitants of the country. We subsequently sought in vain for these birds, and even offered rewards to the little boys who would bring us their eggs, but to no purpose. They go in flocks, and their habits seem to resemble those of the starling, of which there are several species in this country. There appears to be no doubt that this bird is the great enemy of the locust, for we had been assured, from different quarters, that the havoc they made among those destructive insects is truly astonishing. The Government have recognised the fact by strictly forbidding their being killed; and the natives generally attribute to their agency the timely disappearance of the great swarms of locusts which last year threatened to devour everything in the western part of the country. It is also said that the bird never occurs where there are no locusts; but we looked in vain for the insects where we saw the birds."

276.—JAPANESE ARKS.
Joshua iii. 6.

℃ . . . . The Japanese ark-shrines described by Mr. W. Simpson, in the "Transactions" of the Society of Biblical Archaeology are called *Termo-Sama,* or "Heaven's Lord," and *Mi-Koshi,* or "precious seat." They are miniatures of a Japanese temple, with a

square cella, overhanging roof, folding doors, and wooden fence.
Like the temples, too, they are built of wood and bronze. The
shrines which belong to the Buddhists have an image within them;
those used in the service of Shintoism, the state religion, merely
contain the three symbols of the mirror, the sword, and the jewel.
The latter is said to represent cloth or hemp, one of the offerings
of the primitive age. The mirror symbolises the sun; and a legend
recounts how the first was made by a mythic blacksmith, with iron
from the mines of Heaven. The arks are borne upon men's shoulders by means of staves, just as was the Israelite ark of the covenant.

277.—A SOCRATIC PARALLEL
TO CHRISTIAN TEACHING.
Rom. i. 20.

℄ Socrates, having been told that Aristodemus the Little neither
sacrificed to the gods, nor prayed to them, but ridiculed those who
did so, said to him, "Tell me, Aristodemus, do you admire any
men for their genius?" "I do," replied he. "In Epic poetry I most
admire Homer, in dithyrambic Melanippides, in tragedy Sopho-
cles, in statuary Polycletus, in painting Zeuxis." "Those who form
images without sense or motion, and those who form animals en-
dowed with sense and vital energy, which class of works," said
Socrates, "appears to you the more worthy of admiration?"
"Those," replied Aristodemus, "who form animals, by Jupiter! for
they are not produced by chance, but by understanding." Aristodemus further admitted that things having an evident adaptation
to a given end were the productions of intelligence. On this admission Socrates proceeds: "Does not He then who made men at first
appear to you to have given them, for some useful purpose, those
parts by which they perceive different objects, the eyes to see what
is to be seen, the ears to hear what is to be heard? What would be
the use of smells, if no nostrils had been assigned us? What perception had there been of sweet and sour, if a tongue had not
been formed to have a sense of them? Does it not seem to you a
work of forethought to guard so tender a member as the eye with
lids like doors, to open and shut as required; to screen it with
eyelashes from the action of the wind; and to shelter it from the
annoyance of perspiration by the coping of the eye-brows; to fit

the ear for receiving all kinds of sounds without obstruction; to
adapt the front teeth of animals for cutting, and the back ones for
grinding the food; can you doubt whether such a disposition of
things is the result of chance or intelligence?" "No, indeed," replied
the sceptic, "but to one who looks at those matters in this light they
appear like the work of some wise maker who studied the welfare
of animals." "And do you think," said Socrates, "that you yourself
have any portion of intelligence? And can you suppose that nothing intelligent exists anywhere else? When you know that you have
in your body but a small portion of the vast earth, and but a small
portion of the vast quantity of existing water, do you imagine that
by some extraordinary good luck, you have seized for yourself
alone all existing intelligence, and that this assemblage of vast bodies, countless in number, is maintained in order by something void
of reason?" "By Jupiter!" replied Aristodemus, "I can hardly suppose that there is any ruling intelligence among that assemblage of
bodies, for I do not see the directors, as I see the agents of things
done about me." "Nor do you," replied Socrates, "see your own
soul which directs your body; so that by like reasoning, you may
say that you yourself do nothing by understanding, but everything
by chance."

The whole dialogue is too long to be given here. These extracts
may suffice to show how the reasoning of Socrates was in harmony
with the principles laid down so much more fully and clearly by
the great Apostle. Natural Theology is now somewhat despised,
but, when wisely stated, its great principles cannot be refuted.

278.—AQUEDUCTS DISCOVERED IN
THE KEDRON VALLEY.
2 Chron. xxxii. 3, 4.

⁋ From the reports of the Palestine Exploration Society we take
the following, which may serve to illustrate the water-works which
Hezekiah undertook. The most curious discovery, however, made
in the Kedron Valley, was a system of rock-hewn aqueducts.
"Down the valley of the Kedron, and south of Siloam, there is the
well of Job or Joab (Bîr Eyûb), about which there are many curious traditions which connect it in many ways with the ancient
temple. It has been examined, but to my mind there is yet a mystery concealed there. It is a well 100ft. deep, without appearance

of connection with any surface drains, and yet after heavy rains it fills up and overflows in a voluminous stream. South of this well, about 500 yards, there is a place called the Well of the Steps, by the Arabs, about which they had a tradition that there were steps leading up to the well of Joab. I had the ground opened, and at 12ft. below the surface came upon a large stone which suddenly rolled away, revealing a staircase cut in the solid rock leading to a rock-cut chamber and aqueduct running north and south. It was filled up with silt or fine clay. We cleared it out to the north about 100ft., and found it to be a great aqueduct 6ft. high, and from 3ft. 6in. to 4ft. broad. When the winter rains came on, a stream burst through the silt and, completely filling the passage, found its way up the steps and rolled down the valley in an abundant stream, joining that of the well from Joab. In April the stream abated, and in May we were able to commence again; and, working day and night, we may expect to reach the city in six months. We are working with English barrows in the Aqueduct, much to the delight of the Arab workmen, who take a childish pleasure in using these new toys. We clean out at present about 15 cubic yards in twenty-four hours. Looking at this aqueduct in a sanitary point of view, we might suppose it built for carrying off the sewage of the city; and from a military point of view, for carrying secretly off any superabundant water to the nearest crevice in the rock; possibly it may have been used for both purposes.

"This aqueduct is cut through the hard *mezzeh* limestone to the west of the Kedron, and is from 70 to 90ft. below the rock surface and 50ft. below the present level of the floor of the Kedron Valley. By following it up it was hoped that most important discoveries would result; it was even supposed by some that it was the drain from the Temple by which was carried away the offal of the sacrifices. But these anticipations were disappointed. After tracing it for nearly 2,000ft. in the direction of the city, it suddenly stopped."

279.—THE PLAGUE OF LICE.
Exodus viii. 16.

℄ The Egyptians were of cleanly habits, and this infliction must have been to them an extreme annoyance. They were careful to keep all infested with them out of their temples. Their priests were

clad in linen garments, and every precaution was adopted to keep
themselves free from such vermin. Bryant says, "The Egyptians
affected great external purity; and were very nice both in their persons and clothing; bathing and making ablutions continually. Uncommon care was taken not to harbour any vermin. They were
particularly solicitous on this head, thinking it would be a great
profanation of the temple which they entered, if any animalculae
of this sort were concealed in their garments. The priests, says
Herodotus, are shaved, both as to their heads and bodies, every
third day, to prevent any *louse* or any other detestable creature
being found upon them when they are performing their duty to
the gods. The same is mentioned by another author, who adds,
that all woollen was considered as foul, and from a perishable animal; but flax is the product of the immortal earth, affords a delicate and pure covering, and is not liable to harbour insects. We
may hence see what an abhorrence the Egyptians showed towards
this sort of vermin, and what care was taken by the priests to
guard against them. The judgments, therefore, inflicted by the
hands of Moses were adapted to their prejudices. It was, consequently, not only most noisome to the people in general, but was
no small odium to the most sacred order in Egypt, that they were
overrun with these filthy and detestable vermin."

280.—FLAX.
Exodus ix. 31.

⁋ The expression used in this verse indicates that the seventh
plague was sent about the beginning of the month of March. The
Hebrew word for the flax plant is *pishtah.* Flax (*Linum usitatissimum*) belongs to the natural order *Linaceae,* or flax family,
under which two genera are ranked, namely flax (*Linum*), and
flax-seed (*Radiola*). Four British species are ranked under the former, and one under the latter. These are perennial flax (*L.
perenne*), narrow-leaved flax (*L. angustifolium*), common flax (*L.
usitatissimum*), purging flax (*L. catharticum*), and thyme-leaved
flax-seed (*Radiola millegrana*). Like the cotton-plant flax it may be
traced to India, whence, at a very early period, it was carried to
Syria and Egypt. It then spread westward, until, about the time of
the Roman conquest, it appears to have been introduced into
Britain.

281.—COALS OF JUNIPER.
Psalm cxx. 4.

℀ Burckhardt found the Bedaîoin of Sinai burning the roots of the juniper (desert broom, rithm, retem, or genista) into coal; and says that they make the best charcoal, and throw out the most intense heat. It has been suggested, with probability, that these were the coals on which Elijah's cake was baked, when he was supplied in his desert journey, the same desert shrub affording him alike shade and fuel.

282.—BETHABARA.
John i. 28.

℀ Lieut. Conder, connected with the Palestine Exploration Society, has found a ford not marked on any map, now called Mukhadet Abára, at such a distance from Cana in Galilee, and of such a character, as apparently to answer all the requirements. Some confusion arises from this place being also called Bethany, not of course the familiar Bethany of Lazarus and his sisters.

283.—TERAPHIM.
Judges xviii. 14.

℀ Ewald, the great German Biblical scholar, has collected all the information that it may be possible to obtain concerning the primitive Teraphim, or family divinities. "An image of this sort did not consist of a single object, but of several distinct parts, at any rate when the owner cared to have one of the more fully adorned and perfect specimens. The essential kernel of it, made either out of stone or wood, always attempted to exhibit the image of a god in human form, even life size; but already in the earliest times this by itself was readily regarded as too plain. It generally received, therefore, a coating of gold or silver, either over the whole body or only particular portions; and hence the caustic speech of the stricter worshipper of Jahveh, who detested all worship of images, and delighted in mocking at the product of the chisel and the ladle which formed the two constituent elements of such idols. It may, however, be understood that, where the noble metals were plenti-

ful enough, the idols might be cast entire of them. Up to this
point, then, a family god, without regard to its special form, was
prepared just like the image of any other god; it was something
added to this which formed the specific distinction of the primitive
family god of the Israelites. In order to understand what this was,
it is of the utmost consequence that we should remember that
these domestic deities were employed from the earliest times to
furnish oracles, so that the word *Teraphim* is absolutely identical
with oracular divinity. For this purpose the first addition to the
image was an *Ephod*, *i.e.*, a magnificent robe put over the shoulders, having on its breast a casket containing the lots employed in
determining the oracle. In the second place a kind of mask was
placed over the head of the image, in which the priest who was
seeking the oracle probably had to perceive by sundry tokens
whether the god was willing or not to give an oracle at all at that
particular time. These masks alone made the image properly complete, and from them the divinities received their name of *Teraphim* (meaning, a nodding countenance or living mask). At the
same time we can understand from this how the Teraphim can be
sometimes described as of a similar size to that of a man, sometimes as smaller, and therefore capable of easy concealment under
the saddle of a camel, for the principal element consisted of the
two proper oracular constituents, especially in the case of a household divinity which had been preserved for a long period, and was
regarded with great affection. Somewhat like this were the forms
of the family gods, dating, as we cannot doubt, from the most ancient days of the nation; and if we consider the extraordinary te-
nacity with which everything of a domestic character held its
ground with little alteration in spite of the opposition of the fundamental principles of Jahveism it will not surprise us to find
many continuing for centuries to seek for protection and counsel
from these family gods, only finding in them now an image of Jahveh himself."

284.—THE BULRUSH.
Exodus ii. 3.

℄ "The bulrush is one of the sedge family of plants (*Cypera-
ceae*). Several kinds are noted for the uses to which they are put.
The edible cypress (*C. esculentus*) is much cultivated in France.
Its roots are sweet and agreeable to the taste. In Holland one spe-

cies (*C. arenaria*) is planted on the dykes, whose soil it binds together by its intertwisting roots. But the most celebrated species is
the true paper-reed (*C. papyrus*), the Sacred Byblus (*Byblus
hieraticus*) of Strabo. The cellular tissue of this plant was carefully
divided, and when in a moist state, it was pieced together, and
made into a long roll. This when dried was used for writing on.
Hence our word paper. The Hebrew word *gōme*, which is employed in the above passage, points to the absorbing power of the
plant, and so does the Greek translation *biblos*, from which our
word Bible is derived. This and allied species yielded material also
for making boats, ropes, sandals, baskets, and even articles of
clothing.

"Upwards of 2,000 species are included in the *Cyperaceae*. The
papyrus of the Nile has a triangular stem, grows to the height of
above six feet, and is noted for its gracefulness and beauty. It is
now very rare in Egypt, if indeed it is to be found at all. Sir
G. Wilkinson affirms that it is unknown. It is to be met with in Sicily,
on the banks of the Anapus."

285.—THE SCENE OF ELIJAH'S REVELATION.
1 Kings xix. 8, 9.

¶ Bonar's description enables us vividly to picture the surroundings of the prophet in this the most solemn hour of his life. He
says: "One or two chapels I passed at different halting places.
Then came the hollow or basin more than half way up the
hill, in the midst of which stands the old cypress, called Elijah's
tree; hard by which there is a well or circular pond, containing a little water. The chapel of that prophet is also shown
here. It is out of this mountain wady that the rugged top of Jebel-
Moûsa rises like a cone out of the hollow of some vast crater. . . . . We saw the 'great and terrible wilderness' around
us. . . . . No green spot, no tree, no flower, no rill, no lake, but
dark brown ridges, red peaks, like pyramids of solid fire. No
rounded hillocks, or soft mountain curves such as one sees even in
the ruggedest of home scenes, but monstrous and misshapen cliffs,
rising tier above tier, and surmounted here and there by some
spire-like summits, serrated for miles into rugged grandeur, and
grooved from head to foot by the winter torrents that had swept
down like bursting water spouts, tearing their naked loins, and cut-

ting into the very veins and sinews of the fiery rock; a land of
darkness, as darkness itself, and of the shadow of death; without
any order, and where the light is as darkness."

286.—THE CAVE OF ADULLAM.
1 Sam. xxii. 1.

℃ This has been traced traditionally at a place called Khureitun,
where is a great cave which has been explored by Captain Warren
and Lieut. Conder. Later writers are inclined to place it at Deir
Dubbân, about six miles north of Beit Jibrin (Eleutheropolis).
M. Clermont Ganneau, however, was the first to discover the site of
Adullam and the existing name of Ayd el Mieh, which preserves
all the essential letters of the Hebrew. Lieut. Conder has now
made a careful survey of the spot. He finds the ruins of an ancient
town (Genesis xxxviii. 1, 12, 20), strongly situated (Joshua xii.
15, and 2 Chron. xi. 7) on the height commanding the broad valley of Elah, which was the highway by which the Philistines invaded Judah (1 Sam. xvii. 17), and where David killed Goliath.
Roads connect it with Hebron, Bethlehem, and Tell es Safiyeh—
the probable sight of Gath. There are terraces of the hill for cultivation, scarped rock for fortification, tombs, wells, and aqueducts.
The "Cave" is a series of caves, some of moderate size and some
small, but quite capable of housing David's band of followers. If
this site be adopted, it will be seen that some of the most picturesque events of David's life are collected into a small area, bringing out most clearly the nature of the incidents recorded, such as
the swiftness with which he avenged the foray of the Philistines in
Kilah; the strong places which he held barring the valley to the
enemy on the one hand, and protecting himself from Saul on the
other.

287.—A PROVERB CONCERNING THE SOW.
2 Peter ii. 22.

℃ "There is no regeneration for the sow in any amount of
washing by water; the ablution over, away she wends again to her
wallowing in the mire. Like the canine race (dishonourably characterised in the same true proverb), the porcine is of ill account in
holy writ. As the flesh of the swine is formally prohibited as

'unclean' in Leviticus, so in Isaiah the offering of swine's blood is, by implication, denounced as almost inconceivably abominable; and the 'eating swine's flesh, and the abomination, and the mouse,' are with execration connected together (Is. lxvi. 3, 17). Of the Mahometans we are assured that nothing in the creed or practice of Christians does so much to envenom the hatred of Mahometans against them, as the fact of their eating pork. Besides its being an offence to their religion, their aversion to the flesh of the 'unclean beast' resembles an instinctive antipathy, such as 'the idea of uncleanness, when once it thoroughly sinks into the feelings, seems always to excite in those whose personal habits are scrupulously cleanly.' "

288.—FORTY STRIPES SAVE ONE.
2 Cor. xi. 24.

℃ To explain this singular custom of inflicting "forty stripes save one" a few words from Moses may be quoted. "And it shall be, if the wicked man (brought to the judges for trial) be worthy to be beaten, that the judge shall cause him to lie down and to be beaten before his face, according to his fault, by a certain number. Forty stripes he may give him, and not exceed; lest, if he should exceed, and beat him above these with many stripes, then thy brother shall seem vile unto thee" (Deut. xxv. 2, 3). On this subject, as on most others, the Jews refined, and affected great concern. And lest they should accidently inflict more than forty stripes, they resolved to stop short at thirty-nine. And to insure exactitude both ways they invented a scourge of thirteen thongs, and with this instrument the culprit was struck three times. By this ingenious method the law's demands were met, and the prisoner was secured against excessive punishment. This fully explains the nature and details of Paul's punishment.

289.—BUTTER, OR CURDLED MILK.
Judges iv. 19.

℃ In Arab tents are usually seen skin bags or "bottles" suspended from the posts of the tent, whose mouths are sometimes kept open by three sticks placed in triangular position, which are used as churns for making butter, or in the manufacture of sweet curds,

white cheese, and curdled milk, or *leben.* "This last preparation of
milk is greatly esteemed by all Orientals, and doubtless dates back
to a high antiquity. It is believed by the Arabs to have been
divinely revealed to Abraham, who handed the knowledge of it to
the world through his posterity; while others assert that when
Hagar, with her child, was sent away by Abraham and was
perishing with thirst in the wilderness, an angel brought her a
refreshing draught of this "Oriental nectar," which has ever since
been held in the highest estimation by all true Ishmaelites. *Leben,*
however, seems to be well known and fully appreciated throughout Tartary, and among the aboriginal tribes who dwell in the
neighbourhood of the Caucasus. It is always kept ready for use in
the tent of the Arab, a large dish of it, usually made of camel's
milk, being often set near the entrance of the tent, where all who
are thirsty may bend the head and drink. *Leben* is called in the
Hebrew Scriptures *Khemah,* which our English version wrongly
translates *butter,* and sometimes *milk*. The following passages are
admitted to contain references to this beverage:—Gen. xviii. 8;
Jud. v. 25; 2 Sam. xvii. 29; Job xx. 17, xxix. 6; Isa. vii. 22.

290.—THE ARAB TENT.
Gen. iv. 20.

℄ From a recent traveller in the East we gain the following minute description of the Arab tent. In the form and construction of
it there seems to have been very little difference in the different
countries. The trim, neat tents now familiar to us on garden lawns
will not worthily represent the tent of actual nomad life.

"The Turkmans of Asia Minor live under the same kind of tent
as is used to this day by their kinsmen in Tartary. It is circular,
about twelve feet in diameter, and is constructed by driving firmly
into the ground, in a circle, a number of long elastic branches,
split in two, which are bent towards the centre, and there fastened
together. Large pieces of felt are then spread upon this framework, in such a manner as to shed the rain. The tent has thus the
shape of half a sphere, of little more than a man's height. A similar tent is represented in the sculptures of Nineveh. The form and
materials of the Arab tent are also doubtless of the greatest antiquity. It is made of goat's hair cloth, always black, or of a dark
brown, about three-fourths of a yard wide, manufactured by the
women of the household, and cut in long strips, which are stitched

together at the edges until the desired width is obtained. This tent-cloth possesses the double advantage of being waterproof, and of absorbing the sun's rays, and it is thus actually cooler than the white tent of the more civilised traveller. The strips of the cloth run in the direction of the tent's length, for it is in shape a parallelogram, with the door or entrance at one of the long sides. It is supported by wooden posts, called pillars, varying in number, so that sometimes there are as many as twenty-four; the usual number, however, is nine, set up in three rows across the width of the tent. At intervals along the border of the tent-cloth are fastened ropes, which are attached to the tent-pins by their loops. These pins are wooden stakes or pegs, sometimes called 'nails,' about three feet in length, with a notch at the thicker end. They are driven firmly into the ground, being 'set in a sure place' by means of a wooden mallet or hammer (Eccl. xii. 11; Isa. xxii. 23). In setting up a tent, the edge of the cloth is stretched by pulling each 'cord' in turn, passing a stake into its loop, and driving it into the ground. This requires the co-operation of several persons, and is generally done by the women and children. The tent-cloth is thus raised to a considerable height above the ground, and the space is enclosed all around, except the entrance, by curtains of hair-cloth, or reed matting, the latter allowing a free circulation of air. The interior is divided into two equal parts by a curtain hung upon the three central pillars. In Mesopotamia, the left hand is occupied by the male members of the household, the entrance being in front and next to the partition curtain, while the right hand is the harem, or women's apartment. In Arabia, however, the men's apartment is on the *right* side, and the women's on the left."

291.—BALDNESS BETWEEN THE EYES.
Deut. xiv. 1.

℃ Orientals admire eyebrows that meet over the nose, presenting the appearance of a bow; and where nature has denied them this ornament, they imitate it by artificial paint. This is removed in case of mourning, and the hair growing there naturally is plucked, in order to disfigure the face. This is done now, and it appears that it was also done in ancient times; for Moses forbade the Hebrews to "make any baldness between their eyes for the dead."

292.—EGYPTIAN WATERS TURNED TO BLOOD.
Exod. vii. 17.

℃ The hateful character of this plague in the view of the Egyptians may be realised by a reference to the Egyptian mythology. Osiris and his spouse Isis were both born of Nutpe, who answers to the goddess Rhea of the Greeks and Latins, the daughter of Heaven and Earth. To Nutpe were also born Typhon and Nephthys his wife—two who are ever in direct antagonism to the good deities, Osiris and Isis. Typhon was the representative of the evil principle—the source of all cruelty, oppression, violence, murder and physical misery. Blood was ever associated with him. To touch it was pollution. In this plague they saw the triumph, as they would think, of the hated Typhon; and the waters which they had regarded as the spouse of their benevolent divinity, herself adored, no longer offered them nourishment, but thrust on their notice wherever they found them the loathed presence of the head of all evil. They turned away in disgust from everything which reminded them of Typhon. In their efforts to propitiate this abhorred deity, they offered the so-called Typhonic victims, which were chosen from their resemblance to blood, as red oxen, and even red-haired strangers, or Typhonic men. Throughout the whole land of Egypt the people, by means of this plague, were made to feel that contempt had been poured on the idols in which they trusted.

293.—THE HEBREW WORD NABI, OR PROPHET.
Exod. vii. 1.

℃ "The Hebrew word for a prophet is *Nabi*, which comes from a word that signifies to boil up, to boil forth as a fountain, and hence to pour forth words as those do who speak with fervour of mind, or under a Divine inspiration. The word, therefore, properly describes one who speaks under a peculiar fervour, animation, or inspiration of mind, produced by a Divine influence, or else one who speaks, whether in foretelling future events, or in denouncing the judgments of God, when the mind is full, and when the excited and agitated spirit of the prophet pours forth the commissioned words, as water is driven from the fountain. The very name, therefore, strongly manifests the constraining power from

above by which the prophets were moved, and through which they
spake."

294.—NAZARETH.
Luke ii. 39.

⌐ It is interesting to know something of the situation of this
place, and of the scenery surrounding it, which must have exerted
a very important influence on Jesus during the time of his boy-
hood and youth. One of the most effective descriptions is given by
Renan. "Nazareth was a small town in a hollow, opening broadly
at the summit of the group of mountains which close the plain of
Esdraelon on the north. The population is now from three to four
thousand, and it can never have varied much. The cold there is
sharp in winter, and the climate very healthy. The town, like all
the small Jewish towns at this period, was a heap of huts built
without style, and would exhibit that harsh and poor aspect which
villages in Semitic countries now present. The houses, it seems, did
not differ much from those cubes of stone, without exterior or interior elegance, which still cover the richest parts of the Lebanon,
and which, surrounded with vines and fig-trees, are still very
agreeable.

"The horizon from the town is limited; but, if we ascend a little
the plateau, swept by a perpetual breeze, which overlooks the
highest houses, the prospect is splendid. On the west are seen the
fine outlines of Carmel, terminated by an abrupt point, which
seems to plunge into the sea. Before us is spread out the double
summit which towers above Megiddo; the mountains of the country of Shechem, with their holy places of the patriarchal age; the
hills of Gilboa, the small picturesque group to which are attached
the graceful or terrible recollections of Shunem and of Endor; and
Tabor, with its beautiful rounded form, which antiquity compared
to a bosom. Through a depression between the mountains of
Shunem and Tabor, are seen the valley of the Jordan and the high
plains of Peroea, which form a continuous line from the eastern
side. On the north, the mountains of Safed, in inclining towards
the sea, conceal St. Jean d'Acre, but permit the Gulf of Khäifa to
be distinguished. Such was the horizon of Jesus. This enchanted
circle, cradle of the kingdom of God, was for years His world.
Even in His later life He departed but little beyond the familiar

limits of His childhood. For yonder, northwards, a glimpse is caught, almost on the flank of Hermon, of Cesarea Philippi, His furthest point of advance into the Gentile world; and here, southwards, the more sombre aspect of these Samaritan hills foreshadows the dreariness of Judaea beyond, parched as by a scorching wind of desolation and death."

The kind of impression made on the devout mind by a visit to this spot is well illustrated by the words of Tischendorff. "A few months before, I had stood upon the loftiest pyramid, with the desert, the Nile, and Cairo at my feet. I had since stood upon Sinai, the majestic mountain of the Lord, and had thence petitioned heaven itself, like a bosom friend. From the minaret at the summit of the Mount of Olives, I had viewed at once the Holy City, with Bethlehem's heights, and the mountains of Samaria, the wonderful Sea of Sodom, and the mountains of Moab; yet to-day (on the height crowning Nazareth) I felt as a child who had yet seen nothing but his own home, and knew nothing of the world. I looked towards Tabor in the east; the lesser Hermon and Gilboa peered upwards in its vicinity, and guided me to the mountains of Samaria in the south. Then I looked towards the west, and beheld the forelands of Carmel, and in the blue distance Carmel itself. Amid all these mountain heights the broad plains of Esdraelon reposed before me, as if encircled by eternal walls. But beyond Carmel, to its left as well as to its right, lay, like a festal day in glittering beauty, the mirror of the Mediterranean. In the north a second extensive plain spread forth, with Cana, the little town of the marriage, and the 'Horns of Hattin,' where the army of Saladin trampled under foot all the conquests of the Crusaders. In the north-east, lastly, shone down, like a divine eye, behind desert groups of mountains, the summit of the great Hermon, enveloped in its eternal snows; and, withdrawing my gaze from those distant scenes, I looked down upon Nazareth, which clung, like a darling child, to the hill above which I stood.

"What were the feelings of my soul during this survey? The admiration and devotion then felt have no words to express them; but a psalm of the inspired David was rushing to the lips, to resound to the depths of the unfathomable ocean, and to ascend to the snowy summit of Hermon. What may this watch-tower have been to our Saviour? A symbol of His kingdom upon earth—of the Gospel of redemption, as it embraced heaven, earth, and seas with the arms of maternal affection; as it compressed together both the past and the future, in the one great hour upon Golgotha. The snow of Hermon looks like the grey head of Time—like the past; the sea, pregnant with mystery, like the future. Between both reposes the present, this dew-drop, reflecting infinitely rich images from the rays of the morning sun."

295.—Tradition concerning Isaiah's Death and Burial.
Heb. xi. 37.

℃ Kitto says:—"That Isaiah was sawn asunder, as the Jews allege, we should have been inclined to doubt, on the ground that there does not appear to have been any such mode of inflicting the punishment of death among this Jewish people. But St. Paul, in the Epistle to the Hebrews" (our readers are aware that the authorship of the Epistle to the Hebrews is doubtful), "counts being 'sawn asunder' among the deaths to which the ancient saints had been subjected: and as Isaiah is the only one to whom this death has been ascribed, it seems likely that the traditional memory of the fact existed in the time of the Apostle, who thus gives to it his inspired sanction. It is, therefore, a point which we shall not question, although it cannot positively be affirmed as a fact, any more than the statement that this dreadful death was inflicted by a *wooden saw* in order to increase the torture and protract the agony.

"We are further told that the corpse of this chief of prophets was buried hard by Jerusalem, under the Fuller's Oak, near the Fountain of Siloam, whence it was, in a later age, removed to Paneas near the sources of the Jordan, and that it was eventually transferred, in A.D. 404, to Constantinople. But in all this there is nothing on which we can rely."

296.—The Plague of Pharisaism.
Matt. xxiii. 5.

℃ The Talmud, a Jewish work consisting of traditions, proverbs, laws, philosophy, religion, etc., "inveighs even more bitterly and caustically than the New Testament against what it calls the 'Plague of Pharisaism,' 'the dyed ones,' 'who do evil deeds like Zimri, and require a goodly reward like Phinehas;'" "they preach

beautifully but do not act beautifully." Parodying their exaggerated logical arrangements, their scrupulous divisions and sub-
divisions, the Talmud distinguishes seven classes of Pharisees.
These are—1. Those who do the will of God from earthly motives; 2. They who make small steps, or say, just wait awhile for
me; I have just one more good work to perform; 3. They who
knock their heads against walls in avoiding the sight of a woman;
4. Saints in office; 5. They who implore you to mention some
more duties which they might perform; 6. They who are pious because they *fear* God; 7. The real Pharisee is he who "does the will
of his Father in Heaven *because he loves Him.*"

297.—ABRAHAM'S PURPOSE IN GOING TO EGYPT.
Gen. xii. 10.

℧ According to Josephus, Abraham was a man of learning, and
travelled both for his own instruction, and for the purpose of im-
parting his own knowledge to those who were willing to receive it.
His special inquiries related to the being and nature of God, he
himself being a monotheist, and a champion of that doctrine. "He
went down to Egypt, not only to escape the famine, but also to
learn any wisdom the Egyptian priests might be able to teach—to
know what they said concerning the gods; designing either to
follow them, if they had better notions than he, or to convert
them into a better way, if his own notions proved the truest. For
whereas the Egyptians were formerly addicted to different customs, and despised one another's sacred and accustomed rites, and
were very angry with one another on that account, Abraham conferred with each party of them, and confuting the reasonings they
made use of, every one for his own practices, demonstrated that
such reasonings were vain, and void of truth; whereupon he was
admired by them in those conferences as a very wise man, and one
of great sagacity, when he discoursed on any subject he undertook;
and this not only in understanding it, but in persuading other men
also to assent to him. He communicated to them arithmetic, and
delivered to them the science of astronomy; for, before Abraham
came into Egypt, they were unacquainted with those parts of
learning, for that science came from the Chaldaeans into Egypt,
and from thence to the Greeks also."

298.—HINDERERS OF THE REBUILDING
OF JERUSALEM.
Neh. iv. 1.

⁋ According to the Bible account, the Gentile tribes who occupied Samaria, and were afterwards known under the general name of Samaritans, endeavoured to hinder the workmen employed at rebuilding the walls. The Rabbis give a very curious account of these events. They say that the people, to the number of 180,000, at one time, beset Jerusalem, when Ezra and Nehemiah collected 300 priests, and went forth to excommunicate their enemies according to the greater excommunication—that is, utter separation from the Church as the enemies of all goodness. The priests were accompanied by 300 boys, each carrying a copy of the law in one hand, and a trumpet in the other. The boys sounded the trumpets while the priests excommunicated their adversaries. They pronounced a curse upon whoever should eat bread with them, a curse as heavy as that denounced for eating swine's flesh. They then besought God to deprive them of all part in the future resurrection, and to grant that they might never become proselytes. This was equal to asking that the Samaritans, and their descendants to the latest time might be excluded from salvation. The terrible curse, say the Rabbis, so terrified the Gentiles that they precipitately fled.

299.—TRAFFIC IN CITY GATES.
2 Kings vii. 1.

⁋ A custom, similar to that indicated in this passage, prevails in most Eastern cities. We take testimonies respecting the matter from two men, whose names are well known in connection with Oriental customs, etc.—

Mr. Layard says:—"Frequently in the gates of cities, as at Mosul, the recesses by the gates are used as shops for the sale of wheat and barley, bread and grocery."

Mr. Morier says:—"In our rides we usually went out of the town" (Teheran, in Persia) "at the gate leading to the village of Shah Abdul Azum, where a market was held every morning, particularly of mules, asses, and camels. At about sunrise the owners of the animals assemble and exhibit them for sale. But, besides,

here were sellers of all sorts of goods in temporary shops and
tents; and this, perhaps, will explain the custom alluded to in 2
Kings vii. of the sale of barley and flour in the gate of Samaria."

300.—THE EAGLE STIRRING UP HER NEST.
Deut. xxxii. 11, 12.

⁋ The long sojourn of Moses in the wild districts of Sinai must
have rendered him familiar with the habits of some of the larger
birds of prey. A person accustomed to observe accurately the
habits of animals, reports having seen an eagle in one of the deep
gorges of the Himalayas, thus teaching its young to fly. While with
his glass he watched several young ones on a ledge of rock at a
great height, the parent bird swept gently past the young, one of
which ventured to follow, but seemed as if unequal to the flight.
As it gently sunk down with extended wings, one of the parent
birds glided underneath it, and bore it aloft again. "It is not necessary," says a recent traveller, writing in view of a deep chasm in
the Lebanon range, "to press every poetical figure into strict
prosaic accuracy. The notion, however, appears to have been prevalent among the ancients, that the eagle did actually take up her
yet timid young, and carry them forth to teach them how, and em-
bolden them to try their own pinions. To this idea Moses seems to
refer in Exod. xix. 4. The fact is not impossible: the eagle is
strong enough to do it, but I am not aware that such a thing has
ever been witnessed. I, myself, however, have seen the old eagle
fly round and round the nest, and back and forth past it, while the
young ones fluttered and shivered on the edge, as if eager but
afraid to launch forth from the giddy precipice. And no wonder,
for the nest 'is on high,' and a fall from thence would end their
flight for ever."

301.—TOWERS IN THE EAST.
Judges ix. 51.

⁋ A writer familiar with Indian life gives the following illustration of the above passage. "When once entering an Indian city
which was surrounded by high walls, and only approached through
its massive stone gateway, I was struck by seeing a stronghold or

fortress in its midst, which rose up like a rocky mountain, having on its heights a tower, while around its base were walls with battlements, and a deep moat beneath.

"I was told that in times when one petty *Najali* or chief had been making constant incursions against another, it had been the custom to have a stronghold within the cities that there might yet be a place of refuge if the enemy succeeded in taking the gates; and here in times of danger the aged and helpless men, women, and children were conveyed, and also the cattle and other valuables."

302.—EATING IN THE MORNING.
Eccles. x. 16.

℘ Dr. Turner, the Polynesian missionary, says:—"It is considered unmanly in Samoa to eat early in the morning. It is even the language of abuse to hint that a person does so. It is like comparing him to a pig, which is fed the first thing in the morning."

303.—TRANSLATION OF THE MOABITE STONE
OF KING MESHA.
2 Kings iii. 4.

℘ This inscribed stone was first seen at Dibân (ancient Dibon) by the Rev. F. A. Klein, in August, 1868. He only took a sketch of it. Since then a copy of the inscription has been taken, and the following is the most recent translation, issued by M. Clermont Ganneau, published by the Count de Vogüé, June 1870:—

"I am Mesa, son of Chamosgad, King of Moab, the Dibonite. | My father reigned thirty years, and I have reigned after my father. | And I had built this sanctuary for Chamos in Qarha [sanctuary of salvation], for he has saved me from all aggressors and has made me look upon all my enemies with contempt. |

"Omri was King of Israel, and oppressed Moab during many days, and Chamos was irritated at his aggressions. | And his son succeeded him, and he said, he also, 'I will oppress Moab,' | In my days, I said 'I will . . . him. . . . and I will visit him and his house.' | And Israel was ruined, ruined for ever. Omri gained possession of the land of Medeba. | And he dwelt there. . . . [Ahab] his son lived forty years, and Chamos made him [perish] in my time. |

"Then I built Baal Meon and constructed Qiriathaïm. |

"And the men of Gad dwelt in the country of [Ataro]th from ancient times, and the King of Israel had built the city of Ataroth. | I attacked the city and I took it, | and I killed all the people of the city, as a spectacle to Chamos and to Moab, | and I carried away from there the . . . and I brought it to the ground before the face of Chamos at Qerioth, | and I brought there the men of Saron (or of Chofen) and the men of Maharouth (?).

"And Chamos said to me, 'Go; take Nebah from Israel.' | I went by night, and I fought against the city from the dawn to midday, | and I took it: and I killed all, seven thousand [men, and I carried away with me] the women and the young girls; for to Astar Chamos belongs the consecration of women; | and I brought from there the vessels of Jehovah, and I dragged them on the ground before the face of Chamos. |

"And the King of Israel had built Yahas, and resided there during his war with me. | And Chamos drove him from before my face: I took from Moab two hundred men in all; I made them go up to Yahas, and I took it to annex it to Dibon. |

"It is I who have built Qarha, the Wall of the Forests and the Wall of the Hill. | I have built its gates, and I have built its towers. | I have built the palace of the king, and have constructed the prisons of the . . . in the midst of the city. |

"And there were no wells in the interior of the city in Qarha: and I said to all the people, 'Make you every man a well in his house,' | and I dug cisterns for Qarha for . . . of Israel. |

"It is I who have built Aroer, and made the road of Arnon. |

"It is I who have built Beth Bamoth, which was destroyed. | It is I who have built Bosor which (is powerful) . . . Dibon of the military chiefs, for all Dibon was submissive. | And I have filled . . . with the cities which I have added to the land (of Moab). |

"And it is I who have built . . . Beth Diblathain, and Beth Baal Meon, and I have raised there the . . . the land. | And Horonaim, he resided there with . . . | And Chamos said to me, 'Go down and fight against Horonaim.' | . . . Chamos, in my day . . . the year . . ."

304.—THE ANCHOR AS A SYMBOL.
Heb. vi. 19.

℄ The anchor, in one form or another, was known among the most ancient navigators of whom we have any record; and very early, as was natural, it became a symbol of Hope. The Jews were not a maritime people, and they probably borrowed both the anchor and the symbolic use of it from their Gentile contemporaries. From the text quoted above it appears that the anchor, as a symbol of Hope, was well-known in the Apostolic Church. The early Christians engraved it on rings, sculptured it on monuments, and on the walls of cemeteries and catacombs. Sometimes the symbol was associated with the *fish,* which was regarded as a symbol of Christ Himself. The anchor still holds its place as a sign of Hope, and will do so probably to the end of time.

305.—COSTUME OF AN EASTERN BRIDE.
Jer. ii. 32.

℄ Describing present day Oriental customs, Van Lennep says: "The costume of the bride is deemed a matter of the highest importance, since much may depend upon the effect produced by the first sight of her which her husband is supposed to obtain. She sometimes wears the very bridal suit which her mother wore before her, and, in some instances, that of her mother-in-law; but usually a new outlay is made for the occasion at the expense of the bridegroom. The friends of the bride's family take this opportunity to show their goodwill by sending presents which, with the rest of the trousseau, are exhibited in a room set apart for the purpose during the week preceding the wedding. Orientals are celebrated for their love of display and magnificence, and some of the costumes prepared for such occasions are rich and gorgeous beyond expression. The following description of a bridal *entary,* or wedding robe, was given us by an Oriental tailor, who had often seen, as well as assisted in making, such a dress. It should measure six yards from the shoulders to the end of the train, and the long sleeves must sweep the floor. One of the finest he described was of rose-coloured silk; it was spread out upon a carpeted floor, while seven women skilled in embroidery worked upon one side of the

long breadths, and seven upon the other side, under the direction
of an embroiderer in chief of their own sex, who designed the pattern, and appointed to each one her work. The first layers of
embroidering with gold-thread had already been wrought by men,
and the women were now putting on the finishing touches by sew-
ing on golden spangles and pearls. The sum paid to the directress
alone, for superintending the needlework on this single robe was
five hundred dollars, while her charge for the work done by her
subordinates was two thousand five hundred dollars. In speaking
of it, she said, in a deprecating tone, 'Ten years ago I used to
make such dresses for the sultan's slaves, and now he has grown so
economical that I make them only for his wives.' The entire cost
of this robe, materials and all, was estimated at ten thousand dollars. Indeed these garments are often priceless, for they are
embroidered with diamonds and other precious stones, in clusters
or bouquets, the buttons from the throat to the waist and sleeves
consisting of diamond 'solitaires!' These are worn, not by princely
and royal personages alone, but also by the wives and daughters of
grandees and bankers in Constantinople, Cairo, Damascus, and all
the chief cities of the empire."

306.—JOSEPHUS' ACCOUNT OF AGRIPPA I.
Acts xii. 1.

❡ Josephus records an incident in the life of Agrippa I, who was
grandson of Herod the Great, which in some respects parallels the
account given in Mark vi. of the feast of Herod Antipas. Agrippa
was high in favour of the Roman Emperor Caius, and when
at Rome he made a splendid feast, to which he invited the Emperor. Caesar was delighted with the magnificence of the banquet,
and as the time went by became merry and open-hearted; and
pressed Agrippa to put it in his power to bestow upon him some
signal mark of his favour, promising that anything he might ask
should be done, provided it was within the compass of his ability.
The use Agrippa made of his advantage redounds greatly to his
credit. Caius was just at this time insisting upon having his own
statue erected in the Temple at Jerusalem, and the Jews were just
upon the point of open insurrection. So Agrippa, instead of asking
for larger dominions, or higher dignity, besought the Emperor to

refrain from forcing his statue into the Temple. His request was granted, and for the time being, much bloodshed was prevented.

307.—JEWELLERY OF EASTERN WOMEN.
Isaiah iii. 20, 21.

⁋ Van Lennep writes:—"It is customary for young ladies who have reached the marriageable age to wear, on special occasions all the jewels they are to receive as their dowry; and I have in mind a fine young girl of fifteen, who upon such an occasion, presented the appearance of a restless stream of gold pouring from the head down to the feet. She wore a head-dress consisting of a fez covered with gold coins, and fringed with tassels of pearls; from her neck were hung chains of gold coins to the value of £500 sterling, reaching below her waist in front. A string of the largest of these was fastened upon each shoulder, and descending diagonally across the breast and back, met on the other side and extended to the knees. Her fingers were covered with rings, diamonds, and precious stones; her jacket, of purple velvet, was richly embroidered with gold cord, and gold coins were braided into each narrow tress of her long flowing hair; her *entary,* or robe, was of red silk woven with gold thread, and the full trousers, peering out at the open sides, were of red silk. The slippers, too, were embroidered with gold thread. There certainly was a good deal of jingle when she walked; she was a fair illustration of what Orientals pride themselves in excelling in, *i.e.* Saltanat, a splendid show."

308.—RELIGION AMONG THE GENTILES
ILLUSTRATED BY THE PERSIAN FAITH.
Rom. ii. 14, 15.

⁋ Paul affirms that the case of the Gentiles was by no means so desperate as his prejudiced countrymen had unwarrantably assumed. In the most abandoned and corrupt religions there are certain features, often distorted indeed, that still show their kinship to Christianity.

One of the very oldest and purest religions in the world is that of *Zoroaster,* or *Zurthost,* the ancient prophet of Persia, who is said to have flourished about 600 B.C. His followers were called, in later times, by the Mohammedans, who were their bitter persecutors, *Guebres,* or Ghebers (dogs, or infidels); they, however, call themselves *Behendies,* or, followers of the true faith. Europeans know them as the so-called *Fire-worshippers,* though they say they do *not* worship it. They are still found in Persia, and in Western India, being called Parsees in the latter country. The Indian followers of Zoroaster are descendants of a body which migrated from Persia at the time of the Mohammedan invasion, to escape the horrors of persecution. They still retain their ancient religion, though tainted with Hindoo superstitions. Since 1852, however, some reforms have been effected.

The following quotation from a Parsee catechism will both illustrate the words of Paul, and show what kind of doctrines these interesting people believe. The sacred book of the Parsees is called the Zendavesta.

"*Question.* Whom do we of the Zarthosti (Zoroastrian) community believe in?

"*Answer.* We believe in only one God, and do not believe in any besides Him.

"*Quest.* Who is that one God?

"*Ans.* The God who created the heavens, the earth, the angels, the stars, the sun, the moon, the fire, the water, or all the four elements, and all things of the two worlds; that God we believe in. Him we worship; Him we invoke; Him we adore.

"*Quest.* Do we not believe in any other God?

"*Ans.* Whoever believes in any other God but this, is an infidel, and shall suffer the punishment of hell.

"*Quest.* What is the form of our God?

"*Ans.* Our God has neither face nor form, colour nor shape, nor fixed place. There is no other like Him. He is Himself singly such a glory that we cannot praise or describe Him, nor our mind comprehend Him.

"*Quest.* What is our religion?

"*Ans.* Our religion is 'worship of God.'

"*Quest.* Whence did we receive our religion?

"*Ans.* God's true prophet—the true Zurthost (Zoroaster) Asphantamân Anoshirwân—brought the religion to us from God.

"*Quest.* What religion has our prophet brought us from God?

"*Ans.* The disciples of our prophet have recorded in several books that religion. Resting our faith upon these few books, we

now remain devoted to our good Mazdiashna religion. We consider these books as heavenly books, because God sent the tidings
of these books to us through the holy Zurthost.

"*Quest*. What commands has God sent us through His prophet,
the exalted Zurthost?

"*Ans*. To know God as One; to know the prophet, the exalted
Zurthost, as the true prophet; to believe the religion and the
Avesta brought by him as true beyond all manner of doubt; to believe in the goodness of God; not to disobey any of the commands
of the Mazdiashna religion; to avoid evil deeds; to exert for good
deeds; to pray five times in the day; to believe in the reckoning
and justice on the fourth morning after death; to hope for heaven
and to fear hell; to consider doubtless the day of general destruction and resurrection; to remember always that God has done
what He willed, and shall do what He wills; to face some luminous
object while worshiping God."

309.—ELIJAH'S MANTLE THROWN ON ELISHA.
1 Kings xix. 19.

⁋ "This ceremony has always been considered by Eastern people
an indispensable part of the consecration of the sacred office. It is
in this way that the Brahmins are still invested with the priestly
character, a yellow mantle being thrown across their shoulders,
which is buckled round the waist with a sacred ribbon; and it is in
this way too that the Persian sooffees are appointed. The master,
in the anticipation of death, selecting one of his favourite pupils,
bequeaths his antiquated garment to the youth, who by that act is
publicly recognised as his successor, and looked upon as inheriting,
along with the mantle, the virtues and powers of his venerable
precursor. The Suffavean dynasty, who long occupied the throne
of Persia, owed the origin of their family to the reputation which
the founder of it enjoyed for sanctity. That person, who was universally regarded as a holy man, was succeeded by his grandson,
Juncyd, who took up his mantle after the death of his grandsire,
and a crowd of disciples flocked to him as the heir of the talents
and qualifications of his deceased relative. It was evidently owing
to the prevalence of the same Asiatic sentiments among the
Israelites, that the succession to the prophetic office was determined by the descent of his master's cloak of camel's hair cloth afterwards upon Elisha, and so well was the action understood, as

conveying to the servant the spirit and authority of the master,
that he was universally acknowledged as the successor of that eminent prophet, and the leading champion in his age of the cause of
God."

310.—ANCIENT KEYS.
Isaiah xxii. 22.

⁋ Keys and locks in Palestine are very frequently now, and were
doubtless in old time, large, and both of them made of wood. But
the handle is sometimes of brass or silver, ornamented with filigree
work. Ancient keys are described as crooked, bent into the shape
of a sickle, and, like it, borne on the shoulder. If there is a bunch
to be carried, they hang down, some before, others behind. A single key is suspended by a handkerchief tied to the ring, it is then
placed on the shoulder, while the handkerchief is in front. And there
is a kind of proverbial expression in use to designate a man's consequence when it is said that he carries the key. Hence we see how a
key in Scripture is a symbol of authority, and a bestowal of keys is
equivalent to the entrusting any one with a weighty charge. There
is a somewhat similar custom among ourselves, certain officers of
state receiving on appointment a golden key.

311.—LOCUSTS USED FOR FOOD.
Matthew iii. 4.

⁋ As a rule, where locusts are mentioned, whether in the Bible or
in other books, they are referred to as an object of unqualified
dread, harbingers of famine, turning the fruitful fields to a wilderness. In the text above quoted, however, the locust, instead of
being the devourer, is itself eaten; and even at the present time, in
some parts of Arabia, the arrival of locusts is regarded as a sort of
harvest home. A traveller in Central Arabia, Mr. Palgrave, gives
the following interesting account of an invasion of locusts. "On a
sloping bank at a short distance in front we discerned certain large
black patches, in strong contrast with the white glister of the soil
around; and at the same time our attention was attracted by a
strange whizzing, like that of a flight of hornets, close along the
ground, while our dromedaries capered and started as though
struck with sudden insanity. The cause of all this was a vast swarm

of locusts, here alighted in their northerly wanderings; their camp
extended far and wide, and we had already disturbed their out-
posts. These insects are wont to settle on the ground after sunset,
and there, half stupefied by the night chill, they await the morning
rays, which warm them once more into life and movement. This
time our dromedaries did the work of the sun, and it would be
hard to say which of the two were most frightened, they or the locusts. But if the beasts were frightened, not so their masters. I really thought they would have gone mad for joy. Locusts are here
an article of food, nay, a dainty, and a good swarm of them is
begged of heaven in Arabia no less fervently than it would be
deprecated in India or Syria. This difference of sentiment is
grounded on several reasons; a main reason lies in the diversity of
the insects themselves. The locust of Inner Arabia is very unlike
whatever of the same genus I have seen elsewhere. Those of the
north (parts of Arabia and Syria) are small, of a pale green
colour, and resemble not a little our own ordinary grasshoppers.
They are never, to my knowledge, eaten by the Bedouins or vil-
lagers of Syria, Mesopotamia, and Irak, nor do I believe them eat-
able under any circumstances, extreme hunger perhaps alone ex-
cepted. The locust of Arabia is, on the contrary, a reddish-brown
insect, twice or three times the size of its northern homonym,
resembling a large prawn in appearance, and as long as a man's
little finger, which it also equals in thickness. This locust, when
boiled or fried, is said to be delicious, and boiled or fried accordingly they are to an incredible extent. However, I could never persuade myself to taste them, whatever invitations the inhabitants of
the land, smacking their lips over entomological 'delicatesses'
could make me to join them. Barakat (Palgrave's companion)
ventured on one for a trial; he pronounced it oily and disgusting,
nor added a second to the first. The swarm now before us was a
thorough god-send for our Arabs (guides), on no account to be
neglected. Thirst, weariness, all was forgotten, and down the riders
leaped from their starting camels; this one spread out a cloth, that
one a saddle-bag, a third his shirt, over the unlucky creatures destined for to-morrow's meal."

312.—JANNES AND JAMBRES.
2 Tim. iii. 8.

℄ According to very ancient traditions, Jannes and Jambres, who
withstood Moses before Pharaoh, were two sons of Balaam. They

were called, it is said, from Upper Egypt to confront and defeat, if possible, the leader of the Israelites. When those magicians met Moses, and witnessed some display of his miraculous power, they jeeringly said, "Thou bringest straw into Egypt, where abundance of corn grew," a proverb very similar to our own which speaks of "carrying coals to Newcastle." By this sneer the magicians wished to show Moses that his miracle-working power was an article of which Egypt did not stand in need, since her own wise men were possessed of it in abundance. The Orientals believe that Jannes and Jambres wrought no real miracle, but merely met those of Moses by the products of jugglery.

313.—PAUL A MASTER TENT-MAKER.
Acts xviii. 3.

℧ Professor Plumptre has given some suggestions respecting the character of Paul's business, and business relationships, which deserve serious attention. "The tone of the above passage surely implies that Paul did not work under Aquila and Priscilla as a labourer, but with them as a partner. To make and fashion, for tents and other like uses, the rough sail-cloth of goat's hair, which was the staple manufacture of Cilicia, and perpetuated the memory of its origin in the Latin *Cilicium* (sackcloth), was naturally the occupation of St. Paul, and Aquila came from a country which presented like conditions with Cilicia, and was therefore probably conspicuous for the same industry. But Aquila and Priscilla appear as holding a position and possessing a culture above that of the class of craftsmen. Apollos, the eloquent Jew of Alexandria, submits himself to their teaching (Acts xviii. 20). All the churches of the Gentiles owed them thanks (Rom. xvi. 4). They had a church in their house at Rome, *i.e.,* either they were wealthy enough to have a house which served as the meeting place for the Christians in their neighbourhood, or those whom they employed were numerous enough to form a congregation. With such as these St. Paul worked on a footing of equality, contributing, we may well believe, in some small measure at least, capital as well as labour. In other towns, where no such special opportunities presented themselves as at Corinth, we may think of him as practising the same occupation by himself, taking a shop, as at Rome he for two years occupied a hired house with his companions, working with his own hands and exposing his wares for sale

there, or in the public market-place. This seems a far more probable picture of his life than that he should voluntarily have taken
his place among the workmen, slaves, or others, of a heathen
master or of any unbelieving Jew. His habit of fixing his quarters
for many months in the same city, as at Thessalonica, Corinth,
Ephesus, made this, of course, a perfectly feasible arrangement."

314.—RISING WHILE IT IS YET NIGHT.
Prov. xxxi. 15.

℃ It might be thought that this only meant that the good wife
rose early in the morning, before it was light, to prepare the family breakfast. But the following curious account will show that
possibly there is more literalness in the words of King Lemuel
than might have been supposed. G. Octavius Wray, in his journal
in Palestine (1863), relates the following: "Our quarters for the
night are a family dwelling-house, consisting of one chamber thirty
feet square, with dome roof of solid masonry; on one side of the
room is a raised floor of ten feet in breadth, with a wood fire
under an insufficient chimney. Besides this, and the closed door,
there is no other opening. The inner boundary of the daïs is a wall
of clay, six feet high, with hollow places filled with wheat and
barley—the family granary. On the floor of the daïs sleep the
grandfather, or patriarch, and his family of children and grand-
children, male and female, some eight of them, under a vast blan-
ket. That this custom is ancient is shown by the lazy man in the
parable, 'My children are with me in bed; I cannot rise and give
thee' (Luke xi. 7). The lower part of the house contains our four
horses, the syce, and an unknown number of cows, goats, and
barn-door fowls. The first cockcrow approaches, and within three
minutes of midnight by my watch the cock flaps his wings, crows
lustily, and rouses the family, who come and crouch round the
fire, except the old woman, or Surah, the princess of the tribe,
whose privilege it is now, as it was when Abraham entertained the
angels, to make the cakes. She takes from a recess in the wall her
kneading-trough and meal, and kneads the dough at the head of
the bed; next, puts it into a large flat basket, together with a small
earthenware lamp, placing the cover of the basket over all. She
thus stalks forth into the darkness, with the light streaming
through the wicker-work of her basket, to get the cakes baked at

the village oven. Presently she returns; the family eat, drink water,
talk, and then to bed again, none of them having offered to assist
the old woman in her labours from beginning to end."

315.—CHRIST'S TEACHING ABOUT FORETHOUGHT.
Matt. vi. 34.

❡ S. Cox says:—"*Forethought* is no more forbidden than
thought. A wise man, a man with 'discourse of reason,' *i.e.*, a man
in whom reason is not dumb and inert, must 'look before and
after.' There would be no unity in his life, no continuous development and activity, no linking on of month to month and year to
year, if he did not look forward and scheme for the future as well
as for the present. What Christ forbids is so looking onward to to-
morrow as to cloud to-day, so anticipating the future as to darken
the present. And this is the very point at which we commonly
fail. . . . It is our needless fears, our groundless anxieties, which
undo us. Now it is from this pernicious habit of 'borrowing trouble
from the future,' as though we had not enough of it in the present, that Christ would save us. 'Trust in God for the future.' He
says; 'do your duty to-day, and leave to-morrow with Him. And
let this Trust be your tranquil haven, your harbour of refuge,
whenever the waves of care run high.'"

316.—DIVERS WASHINGS.
Heb. ix. 10.

❡ The religious rites of the Mosaic ceremonial must have involved the use of enormous quantities of water; and it has always
been found difficult to explain how the water necessary for ablutions could have been obtained during the forty years' wandering
in the wilderness. It is just possible that, as the following facts will
suggest, their ablutions were performed during the journey by
other means than that of water. An old traveller relates that the
Arabs, "if they cannot come by any water, then they must *wipe*
(themselves) as clean as they can, till water may conveniently be
had; or else it suffices to take Abdees (purification) upon a stone,
which I call an imaginary Abdees;" *i.e.*, to smooth their hands over
a stone two or three times, and rub them one with the other, as if
they were washing with water—the like Abdees sufficeth when any
are sickly, so that water might endanger their life—and after they

have so wiped, it is *guise, i.e.,* lawful, "for them to do as they would had their purification been really done by water."

In a Mohammedan treatise on prayer it is said, "In case water is not to be had, that defect may be supplied by earth, a stone, or any other product of the earth." It has been asserted that sand was frequently used for the same purpose, and even poured over the hands like water. It is possible that thus, or in some similar way, the Israelites in the desert purified themselves when water was scarce. It has also been suggested that it might have been for a similar purpose that Naaman the Syrian took two mules' load of earth back with him from Palestine. He might have taken Jordan water, but that would not last. The earth, however, would serve the same purpose for many years (2 Kings v. 17).

317.—HISTORY OF ANNAS, THE HIGH PRIEST.
John xviii. 13.

¶ The name Annas appears to be a contracted form of *Ananias, i.e., Hananiah.* He was the son of Seth, and in the year 7 A.D. he was appointed to the office of High Priest by Quirinus, then governor of Syria. But in the beginning of the reign of Tiberius, 14 A.D., he was removed by Valerius Gratus, the procurator of Judaea, and was succeeded by Ismael, the son of Phabi. Soon after, Eleazar, the son of Annas, became High Priest, and, a year later, Simon, the son of Camithus; and then, in another year, Joseph Caiaphas, Annas' son-in-law, was appointed, and held the dignity till 36 or 37 A.D. Annas continued to bear the title of High Priest, and it is not easy to adjust the particular relation in which he and Caiaphas stood one to the other. Some have imagined that Annas was *Sagan,* or deputy, to Caiaphas; others, that Annas was still president of the Sanhedrim during the high priesthood of Caiaphas. But perhaps the respect and power he evidently retained were owing to his age, and to his being father-in-law to the High Priest. He lived to advanced years; and five of his sons enjoyed the same pontifical dignity with himself.

318.—EXPENSES OF EASTERN COURTS.
Eccles. v. 11.

¶ Eastern courts, more so perhaps than Western, have always been noted for the immense number of perfectly useless people kept about them, and consequently also for the quantities of provisions consumed. Thus "Solomon's provision for one day was thirty measures (a measure equals from 80 to 100 gallons English) of fine flour, and threescore measures of meal, ten fat oxen, and twenty-one oxen out of the pastures, and an hundred sheep, besides harts, and roebucks, and fallow-deer, and fatted fowl" (1 Kings iv. 22, 23). An ancient traveller gives the quantities consumed in the Turkish Court early in the past century. He remarks, "One may judge of the numbers who live in this palace by the prodigious quantity of provisions consumed in it yearly, which some of the cooks assured me amounted to more than 30,000 oxen, 20,000 calves, 60,000 sheep, 16,000 lambs, 10,000 kids, 100,000 turkeys, geese, and goslings, 200,000 fowls and chickens, 100,000 pigeons, without reckoning wild fowl or fish, of the last of which he (the cook) only named 130,000 *Calcan bats,* or turbots."

319.—Fastening as a Nail in a Sure Place.
Isaiah xxii. 23.

℩ An old writer says that "They do not drive with a hammer the nails that are put into the Eastern walls: the walls are too hard, being of brick; or if they are of clay, they are too mouldering; but they fix them in the brick-work as they are building. They are large nails with square heads like dice, well made, the ends bent, so as to make them like cramp-irons. They commonly place them at the windows and doors in order to hang upon them, when they like, veils and curtains."

This account gives the highest conception of security, as the nail cannot leave its place without the destruction of the wall, into which it is built.

320.—Oil out of the Rock.
Deut. xxxii. 13.

℩ Two explanations of this figurative expression have been suggested. The olive-tree appears to prefer a chalky marl soil, abounding in flints. It delights to insinuate its roots into the clefts of the rocks and crevices of this flinty marl. It may, however, also be observed, that in ancient times the olives were ground to a pulp in huge stone basins, by rolling a heavy stone wheel over them,

and the oil was then expressed in stone presses established near by.
Frequently these presses with their floors, gutters, troughs, and cisterns, were all hewn out of the solid rock, and thus it literally
"poured out rivers of oil," as Job describes it in his parable.

321.—DIVINE HONOURS PAID TO THE NILE.
Exodus vii. 14–18.

℃ The sacred character attached to this most wonderful of all
rivers made the miracle of changing it into a blood-like appearance peculiarly impressive. The river-god was unable to defend his
own waters against the uplifted power of Jehovah. In earliest times
the devotions paid to the water of their river were given by the
Egyptians to Osiris, the sun-god, who was believed to send the
waters to our earth. M. Chabas thus translates a hymn to Osiris,
probably bearing date about B.C. 1700. "From him descend the
waters of the heavenly Nile, from him proceeds the wind. The air
we breathe is also in his nostrils for his own contentment and the
gladdening of his heart; he purifies the realms of space, which
taste of his felicity, because the stars that move therein obey him
in the height of heaven." In time the Nile itself came to take the
place of the sun-god in the superstitious creed of Egypt. Hardwick
says: "The Egyptian mind is seen descending more and more entirely from the worship of the heavenly bodies to the contem-
plation of the marvellous agencies at work in its immediate neighbourhood. In earlier times Osiris was enthroned upon the sun; but
now the Nile itself is substituted for that glorious luminary. Then
the spouse of the great sun-god was the mother and nurse of universal vegetation; now she is the single land of Egypt fructified
and gladdened by the Nile. Then Osiris was a nature-god, a verbal
representative of forces, active in the varied processes of nature;
now he has been moulded into the great civilising hero of
Mizraim, binding men together in a fixed society, teaching agriculture, and subduing nations, not by force alone, but by the charms
of eloquence and music. Then his death was the suspension of all
vital power without the least distinction of locality; now it coin-
cides precisely with that season of the year in Egypt when decay
and barrenness are everywhere ascendant through the valley of the
Nile. The reason of this gradual localising of the story—this confusion, one might call it, of the sun with the Egyptian river—is
hardly to be sought in the prevailing fancy that the Nile and sun

were wont to meet together at the western horizon, and after
plunging down into the under-world, came forth again together
from the caverns of the east. An explanation, simple in itself, and
serving also to account for other kindred stories, is suggested by
the fact that the Egyptian had been gradually tempted to associate
every genial fertilising power in nature with the annual overflow
of his great river.

322.—ALOES.
Psalm xlv. 8.

℃ The Hebrew word translated *aloes* refers to a tree wholly
different from that which supplies the *aloe* of commerce. The one
yields a fragrant perfume, the other a bitter drastic medicine.
Modern botanists have found in the *Aquilaria agallocha,* an Indian
plant, a resemblance so close to the aloe of Scripture as to leave
little doubt to its identity. The aromatic power of the aloe wood
has led to its being greatly esteemed in India, where it is held sacred, and cut down amid religious ceremonies.

323.—AIN JIDY, OR ENGEDI.
1 Sam. xxiii. 29.

℃ Lieut. Conder reports as follows: The spring of 'Ain Jidy comes
out from beneath a rock on a little plateau 500 feet above
the Dead Sea, and 1,200 feet below the top of the cliffs. Its temperature at the spring head on a cool cloudy day we found to be
83° Fahr., unpleasantly warm to the taste, though the water is
clear and sweet. I was not previously aware that it was a thermal
spring. The stream flows in a long cascade over the steep face of
the cliff, and is lost in channels for irrigation beneath. Its course is
marked with tall rushes and low bushes, and the gigantic leaves of
the 'Osher, the yellow berries of the Solanum, or apple of Sodom,
and the flat cedar-like tops of the thorny Dardára, make a thicket
round the spring. The bulbuls and hopping thrushes delight in this
cover, and on the cliffs above, the black grackles, with their golden
wings and melodious note, may be seen soaring. Beneath the
spring on every side are ruined garden walls and terraces, and a
large terraced mound or tell, perhaps the site of the ancient town.
An aqueduct leads from the spring to Wady el Areijeh, where are

other smaller water channels, relics of some well-watered garden of perhaps Crusading times. The tombs found by Dr. Tristram we did not see, but what seemed to me of most interest was a rude, square, solid platform, about 10–15 feet wide, and 3 feet high, consisting of unhewn blocks, and having very much the appearance of what might not unnaturally be expected to exist in such a spot—namely, an ancient altar, dating back, perhaps, to Jewish times.

There is a ruined mill, apparently modern, at the spring, and a building resembling a small tower, beneath the gorge of Wady el Areijeh, but beyond what is mentioned above, we saw no indications of antiquity. Not a single palm exists this side of the Dead Sea, and the shore presents alternately masses of boulders and broken stones, or fine shingle, very tiring to walk upon. The whole extent is utterly barren until the cane-brake and marshy ground near the northern springs and Ras Feshkhah are reached.

324.—ADOPTED CHILDREN.
Genesis xv. 3.

℃ *Forbes,* in his *Oriental Memoirs,* says:—It is still the custom in India, especially among the Mohammedans, that in default of children, and sometimes where there are lineal descendants, the master of the family adopts a slave, frequently a Haffshee Abyssinian, of the darkest hue, for his heir; he educates him agreeably to his wishes, and marries him to one of his daughters. As the reward of superior merit, or to suit the caprice of an arbitrary despot, this honour is also conferred on a slave recently purchased or already grown up in the family, and to him he bequeaths his wealth, in preference to his nephews, or any collateral branches. This is a custom of great antiquity in the East, and prevalent among the most refined and civilised nations.

325.—EASTERN WRITERS.
Psalm xlv. 1.

℃ When recently travelling in Palestine, the only one thing which our redoubtable dragoman, Mohammed Achmed, openly acknowledged that he could not do was to write even so much as his own name. He *sealed* each contract he was obliged to make with us in a dauby sort of way, plunging a somewhat ostentatious finger-ring he wore directly into the ordinary ink, and then impressing it with an unsatisfactory blot upon the paper. He gave us to understand that few Egyptians, at least, cultivated the art; for it was not deemed any more humiliating to be ignorant of it than of music. Indeed, a man of means would supply any necessity of this kind pretty much in the same way. If he wanted writing done, he would employ an amanuensis; and if he wanted music done, he would hire a player. He was not expected to have such accomplishments.

In Palestine and all through the East the people sit or squat on cushions, and tables are low. Inkstands or inkhorns are generally of brass, a bulb at one end holding the black mixture, and the long handle being hollow to receive the pens. These last are mere pieces of slender reed, whittled rudely down to a point, no split, no spring whatever to them. The ink is thick and ropy, being made out of lampblack mixed with beef's gall. Professional amanuenses carry these horns with them, wearing them thrust through their girdles.

It is to the quickness of preparation, which such an apparatus would assume, that the Psalmist refers, when in the 45th Psalm he says, "My tongue is the pen of a ready writer." Never did an expression seem more out of place than this, however. Nothing is ever "ready" in Oriental countries. The exasperating coolness of delay, with which everything is done, or rather not done, provokes one of our expeditious habit and mood of mind almost beyond endurance. We needed to have letters written for us, and we received them—more for curiosity, perhaps, than anything else.

Then one of the missionaries would explain to us. The scribe would make arrangements with as much deliberation as if he were going to sign a treaty. Out came the inkhorn, then a reed was selected, then the paper must be folded just so, he laid it on his hand, spreading it out over his left palm, using no other support, except the end of a single finger underneath each letter as he painfully formed it.

326.—HORNS OF IRON.
2 Chron. xviii. 10.

ℭ Bruce, in describing the head-dress of the governors of Abyssinia, says,—"A large broad fillet was bound upon their forehead,

and hid behind their head. In the middle of this was a horn, or
conical piece of silver gilt, about four inches long, much in the
shape of our common candle extinguishers. This is called *Kiru*,
and is only worn in reviews or parades after victory." Such, possibly, were horns of iron which Zedekiah made for himself, when he
presumed in the name of Jehovah to flatter his prince with the
promise of victory.

327.—EASTERN CISTERNS.
Jer. ii. 13.

ℂ In a land like Palestine, where water is plentiful to excess in
winter, and exceedingly scarce during summer, cisterns are the
most appropriate contrivances for securing a perennial supply.
From the ancient times, long in fact before the settlements of the
Israelites were there, the land abounded with cisterns, though, of
course, many more were required to supply the dense population
that flourished there in Israel's palmiest days. Not only are cisterns
found in every town and village, but in even the most solitary
spots in the wilderness. In many cases they consist of large tanks,
more or less sunk in the earth, and walled round the sides with
masonry, the walls frequently rising above the ground, and termi-
nating in a roof. A door in one side of the structure leads to a
flight of steps reaching to the very bottom of the tank. By means
of the steps the water is always accessible, however low it may become. Some of the Eastern cisterns are very large. One in Northern Syria, near the ruins of Gebel Simon, is more than 100 feet in
depth, and the same width. This enormous cavern is hewn out of
the solid rock. There is one under the Temple platform in
Jerusalem far more extensive even than the one above mentioned,
though not so deep. This also is cut out of the native rock, portions being left here and there, as rude pillars to support the roof.
One of the most ancient forms assumed by cisterns was that of a
circular shaft, some 15 feet in diameter, carried slanting down into
the solid rock at an angle of about 45 degrees with the horizon.
These were frequently tunnelled to the slanting depth of 100 feet
or 150 feet, the whole distance being traversed by a flight of steps.
At Constantinople there are two large ancient cisterns called the
"thousand and one pillars," from the number of stone supports

which bear up the roof. One of the cisterns is still used for water-ing the city.

The "cisterns that would hold no water," are such as are dug in porous rock or soil, and never properly cemented. Such could only disappoint the unhappy men who were foolish enough to trust in them for their summer supply of water.

328.—STONE PILLAR WORSHIP.
Isaiah lvii. 6.

⫷ Martin, in his very curious account of the Western Islands of Scotland in 1703, describes repeatedly numerous pillar stones, which were then objects of respect in the several localities; and in one instance he states, that an image, which was held in veneration in one of the islands was swathed in linen. Speaking of the island of Eriska, to the north of Barra, Martin says,—"There is a stone set up to the south of St. Columbus' Church, about eight feet high, and two broad. It is called by the natives *the bowing stone;* for when the inhabitants had the first sight of the Church, they set up this stone, and then bowed, and then said the Lord's Prayer.

329.—TWO KINDS OF GOVERNORS IN ROMAN PROVINCES.
Acts xiii. 7.

⫷ The term translated *deputy* in this passage should be *pro-con-sul,* and Conybeare and Howson have collected information which proves its precise appropriateness. "In the reign of Augustus, and of each of his successors from Tiberius to Nero, the provinces of the Roman Empire were divided into two classes. On the one side we have those which were supposed to be under the Senate and people. The governor is appointed by lot, as in the times of the old republic. He carries with him the lictors and fasces, the insignia of a consul, but he is destitute of military power. His office must be resigned at the expiration of a year. He is styled *pro-consul.* On the other side are the provinces of Caesar, those in which the em-peror took the responsibility of preserving public order by military occupation. In these cases the governor may be styled *pro-praetor;* but he is more properly *legatus,* the representative or commissioner of the emperor. He goes out from Italy with all the pomp of a military commander, and he does not return till the emperor recalls him. And to complete the symmetry and consistency of the system, the subordinate districts of these imperial provinces are regulated by the emperor's *Procurator,* or *High Steward.* The New Testament, in the strictest conformity with the historical authorities of the period, gives us examples of both kinds of provincial administration. We are told by Strabo and by Dio Cassius, that "Asia" and "Achaia" were assigned to the Senate; and the title, which in each case is given to the governor in the Acts of the Apostles is *pro-consul.* The same authorities inform us that Syria was an imperial province, and no such title as *pro-consul* is assigned by the sacred writers to "Cyrenius, governor of Syria," or to Pilate, Festus, and Felix, the procurators of Judaea, which was a dependency of the great and unsettled province of Syria.

Dio Cassius informs us that Cyprus was retained by the emperor for himself. If we stop here, we naturally ask the question, and some have asked the question rather hastily, how it comes to pass that St. Luke speaks of Sergius Paulus by the style of *pro-consul?* But any hesitation concerning the strict accuracy of the sacred historian's language, is immediately set at rest by the very next sentence of the secular historian, in which he informs us that Augustus restored Cyprus to the Senate in exchange for another district of the empire, a statement which he again repeats in a later passage of his work. It is evident, then, that the governor's style and title from this time forward would be *pro-consul,* exactly as the Evangelist has recorded it.

330.—CASTING HIS FLOWER AS THE OLIVE.
Job xv. 33.

¶ "The olive is the most prodigal of all fruit-bearing trees in flowers. It literally bends under the load of them. But then not one in a hundred comes to maturity. The tree casts them off by millions, as if they were of no more value than flakes of snow, which they closely resemble. So it will be with those who put their trust in vanity. Cast off, they melt away, and no one takes the trouble to ask after such empty useless things, just as the olive seems to throw off in contempt the myriads of flowers that signify nothing, and turns all her fatness to those which will mature into fruit."

331.—JEWISH SYNAGOGUE BUILDINGS.
Matt. xii. 9.

℃ Capt. Wilson gives the following description as the result of his discoveries in connection with the Palestine Exploration Society: —The buildings are always rectangular, having the longest dimensions in a nearly north and south direction, and the interiors are divided into five aisles by four rows of columns, except in the small synagogue at Kefr Birim, where there have been only two rows of columns and three aisles. The masonry of the walls is well built and solid, of native limestone; the stones are set without mortar, the faces finely dressed, and traces of plaster are found inside.

One special peculiarity in these synagogues is that the entrances, usually three in number, face the south in every case except at Irbid, where the form of the ground necessitated a different construction, and where the entrance, as in the case of the Temple, faced the east. Thus the worshipper in every case had to turn his back on Jerusalem whenever he entered the synagogue, a practice entirely opposed to the general custom of other Oriental religions. The columns supporting the roof have, at Tel Hum (the probable site of Capernaum) and Kerazeh (Chorazin), Corinthian capitals; at Irbid both Corinthian and Ionic; and at El Jish, Kefr Birim, Meiron, Um el Amud, and also at Irbid, a peculiar description of capital, which seems of pure Jewish growth. The arrangement of the columns is the same in all. The inter-columnar distances are very small; but whether this arose from any want of constructive skill, or an attempt to assimilate the buildings to something of the same kind in the Temple at Jerusalem, is difficult to say. There is one striking peculiarity to be noticed: the two corner columns at the northern end invariably have their two exterior faces square, and the two interior faces formed by half-engaged columns.

Very interesting are the few remains left of sculptured objects. At Nebartein is an inscription in Hebrew, and a representation of the seven-branched candlestick, similar to, but of rougher workmanship than, the well-known one on the Arch of Titus at Rome, and identical with one found in the Catacombs at Rome. At Kefr Birim are what appear to be representations of the Paschal Lamb, the Vine of Judah, and a vase, perhaps the Pot of Manna. At Tel Hum the Pot of Manna appears again, and something like a reed, which may possibly be Aaron's Rod. These objects have also been photographed and are among our series. They show that among the ancient Jews, as among modern Mohammedans, the law forbidding the representation of living objects was not strictly enforced.

332.—The Site of Capernaum.

Matt. iv. 13.

¶ The site of Capernaum has been identified either with Tel Hum or with Khan Minyeh. Captain Wilson has come to the conclusion that the true site is to be found at the former. The chief arguments in favour of this view are, 1st, the name, Capernaum being merely the village (Caphar) of Nahum, while the word Tel is the name given by the Arabs to any mound of ruins; 2nd, the greater importance and extent of the ruins found at Tel Hum compared with those found at Khan Minyeh; 3rd, Captain Wilson identifies the Round Fountain of Capharnaum, mentioned by Josephus, with a spring at Et Tabigah; 4th, he examined a large synagogue at Tel Hum, built of white limestone brought from a distance. The architectural details show that the building is probably of later date than the time of our Lord; but we may well believe that this building must have stood on the site, if it is not indeed a restoration, of the White Synagogue of Capernaum, mentioned by Josephus, in which our Lord taught. On the other hand, the excavations at Khan Minyeh produced only masonry and pottery of comparatively modern date. The chief argument in favour of the latter site is the discovery by Dr. Tristram, in the spring Et Tin, of a fish found also in the Nile, the *coracinus*. This is stated by Josephus as having been a peculiarity of the Round Fountain at Capharnaum. The fish has not been found in the spring at Et Tabigah, but it may in the course of eighteen centuries have become extinct.

333.—Moslem Form of Prayers.

Matt. vi. 7.

¶ From a Syrian missionary we obtain the following description of Moslem prayer habits:—First the cloak, or the Persian rug, is spread on the ground towards the south, no matter in how public a place the call to prayer may find them. Then the man raises his

open hands till the thumbs touch the ears, exclaiming aloud,
Allah-hù-Akbar—God is great. After uttering mentally a few short
petitions, the hands are brought down, and folded together near
the girdle, while he recites the first chapter of the Koran, and
two or three other brief passages from the same book. Then he
bends forward, rests his hands upon his knees, and repeats three
times a formula of praise to "God most great." Then, standing
erect, he cries *Allah-hù-Akbar*, as at the beginning. He drops upon
his knees, and bends forward until his nose and forehead touch the
ground, directly between his expanded hands. This he repeats
three times, muttering all the while the same short formulas of
prayer and praise. The next move brings him to his knees, and
then, settling back upon his heels, he will mumble over various
small petitions, with sundry grunts and exclamations, according to
taste and habit. This is the proper course of one regular Rek'àh,
which may, at will, be repeated two or three times.

334.—THE HORNET.
Josh. xxiv. 12.

¶ The Hornet, Heb. *tzireah,* is the *Vespa crabro* of entomolo-
gists, one of the Vespidae, or wasp family of insects. It is much
larger than the common wasp, is of a dark brown colour, very
active and fierce. Its sting is very severe, and is often deadly.
It still abounds in Palestine. The arms with which they annoy are
two darts, finer than a hair, furnished on the outer side at the end
with several barbs not visible to the naked eye, and each moving
in the groove of a strong and often curved sheath, frequently
mistaken for the sting, which, when the darts enter the flesh, usually injects a drop of subtle venom, furnished from a peculiar vessel in which it is secreted, into the wound.

335.—LUKE THE BELOVED PHYSICIAN.
Col. iv. 14.

¶ *Francis Jacox* thus writes about him:—"Luke, the beloved physician." The name and the fame are immortal. Luke and Demas
are with the Apostle when he writes from his prison in Rome to
the saints and faithful brethren at Colosse. When he writes a little
later—a very little later—from the same city, and in the same
bonds, to Timothy, his own son in the faith, Demas has forsaken

him, having loved this present world; but Luke is with him—*only*
Luke is with him.

In the long-tried and unswerving fidelity of this, "the ablest and
most accomplished of all his friends," Paul the aged, a prisoner in
Rome, would find no little solace in the midst of his many trials.
We have only to read the words, "the beloved physician," in order
to learn the place the Evangelist occupied in the affections of St.
Paul. By the loving and tender exercise of that skill which, as a
physician, he possessed, he may have greatly conduced to the comfort of his often afflicted friend; and by his bold, unselfish, and
devoted faithfulness, even to the end, he contributed to cheer and
brighten the last trying months which were spent on earth by the
great Apostle.

336.—BUILDING WITH UNTEMPERED MORTAR.
Ezek. xiii. 10, 11.

℄ *Kitto* gained an illustration of this passage by watching the
building of a new house in a Median village. The men were building it with *cob walls,* as that term is known in Devonshire and
Cornwall. It is a wall made of beaten earth rammed into moulds
or boxes, to give the parts the requisite shape and consistence, and
so deposited, by the withdrawal of the mould, layer by layer, upon
the wall, each layer drying in its place as the work proceeds. The
blocks are usually of considerable size, and are of various quality
and strength, as well as cost, according to the materials employed,
and the time expended upon them. The simplest are merely of
earth, or of earth compacted with straw. This is the kind which
the prophet had in view, and which is used in Devon, and in Morocco as well as in the East. It cannot stand against heavy rains;
and therefore, unless the climate be very dry, it requires to be faced
or coated with a *tempered mortar* of lime or sand, as a fence
against the weather. Without this, the body of the wall is liable to
the contingencies described by the prophet.

337.—APOCRYPHAL ACCOUNT OF OUR LORD'S
TRIAL BEFORE PILATE.
Matt. xxvii. 2.

℄ There is no intimation given in either of our four Gospels that
any one spoke in favour of Christ, either at His trial before the

Sanhedrim or before Pilate. In the early Church, however, there
were received traditions to the effect that several of our Lord's
friends did defend Him. In the "Gospel of Nicodemus," an
apocryphal book of the early Church, there is an extensive record
of the trial before Pilate. A few of the more interesting passages
from this we now transcribe.

After many accusations had been made before Pilate, and some
of the Victim's friends had given rebutting evidence, Nicodemus
rose and said, "I spake to the elders of the Jews, and the Scribes,
and Priests, and Levites, and all the multitude of the Jews in their
assembly, 'What is it ye would do to this man? He is a Man who
has wrought many useful and glorious miracles, such as no man
on earth ever wrought before, nor will ever work. Let Him go,
and do Him no harm, ... because the very miracles for which
ye accuse Him are from God, and He is not worthy of death.'"

The Jews then said to Nicodemus, "Art thou become His disciple, making speeches in His favour? . . . . Mayst thou receive His
doctrine for truth, and have thy lot with (this) Christ!"

Nicodemus replied, "Amen; I will receive His doctrine and my
lot with Him, as ye have said."

Another Jew rose up and said, "I lay for thirty-eight years by
the sheep-pool at Jerusalem, labouring under a great infirmity, and
waiting for a cure which should be wrought by the coming of an
angel, who at a certain time troubled the water. . . . And when
Jesus saw me languishing there He said to me, 'Wilt thou be made
whole?' And I answered, 'Sir, I have no man, when the water is
troubled, to put me into the pool.' And He said to me, 'Rise, take
up thy bed and walk.' And I was immediately made whole."

Others of those who had been healed gave their testimony. And
a certain woman, named Veronica (Matt. ix. 20, etc.), said, "I
was afflicted with an issue of blood twelve years, and I touched the
hem of His garment, and presently the issue of my blood
stopped."

(Eusebius, the ecclesiastical historian, asserts that this Veronica
erected a statue in honour of Christ, as well as to show her gratitude for the miracle by which she had been restored to health.)

338.—HOREB, SINAI.
Exodus iii. 1.

⁋ The precise reference of these two names is very difficult to
trace. Dr. Robinson and other writers urge that Sinai is used in

the Scripture for a particular range of mountains, and Horeb as
the name of one of them. Dr. Bonar holds that Horeb is the name
of a region in which Sinai stands. Dean Stanley has, however, indicated the more probable import of the terms. He says, "It appears to me that the special use of these terms depends on a distinction of usage rather than of place. 1. In Exodus, Leviticus,
Numbers, and Judges, *Sinai* is always used for the scene of the
giving of the Law. *Horeb* being only used twice—for the scene of
the Burning Bush, and of the Striking of the Rock (Exod. iii. 1,
xvii. 6, are doubtful; Exod. xxxiii. 6 is ambiguous). 2. In Deu-
teronomy *Horeb* is substituted for *Sinai,* the former being always
used, the latter never, for the Mountain of the Law. 3. In the
psalms the two are used indifferently for the Mountain of the Law.
4. In 1 Kings xix. 8, it is impossible to determine to what part, if
to any special part, *Horeb* is applied."

339.—RUSHING TO THE HOUSETOPS.
Isaiah xxii. 1.

℄ Dr. Thomson forcibly illustrates the reference of this passage,
which is full of difficulty to those having only Western notions and
associations. "From v. 2 we might suppose that the people had
gone to the roofs to eat, drink, clap hands, and sing, as the Arabs
at this day delight to do in the mild summer evenings. But from
vv. 4, 5, it is plain that it was a time of trouble, and of treading
down, and of perplexity, which naturally suggests the idea that the
inhabitants had rushed to the tops of the houses to get a sight of
those chariots and horsemen of Elam and Kir, with whom their
choice valleys were full, and who were thundering against the
gates of the city. And as Oriental houses generally have no windows looking outward into the streets, or, if there are any, they
are closely latticed, there is no place but the roofs from whence
one can obtain a view of what is going on without. Hence when
anything extraordinary occurs in the streets, all classes rush to the
roof, and look over the battlements. The inhabitants of Jerusalem,
at the time of the Persian invasion, were probably seized with
frenzy and madness, as they were long after, at the siege of Titus.
According to Josephus, some revelled in drunken feasts, and kept
the city in alarm by their stirs and tumults; some were engaged in
plunder and murder, when the slain were not dead in battle; some
wept bitterly, like Isaiah, and refused to be comforted 'because of

the spoiling of the daughter of my people;' in a word, it was a day of universal and utter confusion. Nobody could sit still, but all hurried to the housetops, either to join in untimely riots of fanaticism or drunken despair, or to watch with fear and trembling the dreadful assaults upon their walls and gates."

340.—THE ALTAR OF ED.
Joshua xxii. 10–34.

⸿ Mentioned only once in the Bible, this altar erected by the two and a half tribes on their return to Western Palestine as a "witness" that they too were co-heirs with their brethren on the other side of the river, had dropped entirely out of all hope of recovery. The place has now been found by Lieut. Conder, its name still existing on the high peak of Kurn Surtabeh, in the valley of the Jordan.

341.—THE HORNED BULL AS AN IMAGE OF DEITY.
Exodus xxxii. 4.

⸿ "A prejudice in favour of the image of the *horned bull* existed from the days of the Hyksos, or Shepherd Kings of Egypt among certain sections of the Jewish nation; and though it was suppressed by triumphant Mosaism, at certain periods it regained the ascendancy with unexpected obstinacy. This image never denoted domestic protecting deities, but the guardian divinity of the whole realm and people, and it was undoubtedly, like all other images borrowed from animals, originally nothing but a symbol for weapons and standards. In history it appears in the earliest annals of Israel as the token of the former supremacy of Joseph in Egypt, and therefore also of his tribe, and would of itself have been innocent had not the people imagined that they had found in it an image of Jehovah Himself. Strictly suppressed, therefore, by Moses, it nevertheless rose easily to the surface again—in the first instance in the tribe of Joseph, at times when the remembrance of the former alliance with the mighty and fair Egypt was revived—and it finally became dominant in the kingdom of the ten tribes with all the greater facility as the origin of this kingdom caused it to incline more closely to Egypt."

342.—THE SITUATION OF GERAR.
Gen. xx. 1, 2.

℃ Lieut. Conder reports as follows:—Perhaps the most interesting question in this part of the country is that of the site of Gerar. This ancient town, the dwelling-place of Abraham and Isaac, is indicated as being between Kadesh (on the east) and Shur (on the west). In later times we find that Asa, having defeated the Ethiopians near Mareshah (2 Chron. xiv. 13), drove them back on the road to Egypt as far as Gerar. To Eusebius Gerar was known as being twenty-five Roman miles from Eleutheropolis, or from Beit Jibrin. Dr. Robinson was here, as usual, the first to hear of the existence of the name, and Mr. Rowland, travelling from Gaza to Khalasa, came upon a broad valley called Jorf el Jerár (the banks of Gerar), which he identifies with the valley of Gerar in which Abraham lived. To Vandevelde the ruin of Umm el Jerár was pointed out as situated near Tell el Jema, but he does not appear to have visited the spot.

Even Murray's new map is defective in this part of the country, and the run of the valleys is incorrectly shown. The great Wady Ghuzzeh runs from Beersheba to the sea some six miles south of Gaza. At about the same distance from the city, rather towards the east, on the north bank of Wady Ghuzzeh, and in the position with regard to Tell el Jema indicated by Vandevelde, we found the site of Umm Jerrár, which is thirty English miles in a straight line from Beit Jibrin. The Jorf el Jerrár must be applied to the precipitous earthy banks of this great valley, the bed of which is here about 200 yards wide. The word Jorf is applied throughout Palestine to similar mud cliffs. If we attach any value to the indications of the Onomasticon, which seem to me to be generally very correct, we cannot put Gerar farther south. The valley is wide enough to explain how the Patriarch is said to pitch his camp in it, and at the time we visited the spot a large encampment of the Terabin Arabs was settled on the north bank. One great question remains, that of the wells of Abraham. We could neither find nor hear of any wells in the neighbourhood, or indeed any nearer than Beersheba. The springs, too, marked on the maps are equally fabulous. The Arabs, who are extremely numerous, supply themselves with water by digging in the bed of the valley, when they come upon it. These excavations, or small ponds, are known as *Hafireh*. The valley has evidently been entirely formed by water-action of

considerable violence, and it receives the drainage of an immense
area, as its head is close to Hebron, whence it runs by Beersheba
to the sea, a distance of over sixty miles. It is, indeed, the longest
watercourse in Palestine. When I was last at Hebron, a stream
three feet deep and some ten to fifteen feet broad was rushing
along its upper course. On reaching the plain the water sinks into
the soil and supplies the living wells of Beersheba as well as the
Arab Hafireh lower down its course. We are accustomed to consider Abraham's wells to have been very important and durable
works, partly because the stone-work of the wells at Beersheba is
generally attributed to the Patriarch. The Arabic inscription which
we discovered in the principal well at Beersheba shows this to be a
fallacy, and I think we have evidence that Abraham's wells at
Gerar were not very important works in the fact that, though
made in a friendly country, they had become filled up in the time
of Isaac, who was obliged to re-dig them. It would seem to me,
therefore, that the Arab Hafireh sufficiently fulfil the requirements
for the site of Gerar as far as water supply is concerned.

343.—STORING HARVESTS AGAINST FAMINE YEARS.
Gen. xli. 34–36.

℃ Mr. Scarlett Campbell has contributed some information concerning the mastery of famine conditions in Bohemia, in the years
1770–71, which may illustrate the plan which Joseph recommended to the King of Egypt. In those years the Bohemian
harvests totally failed, and over a million of human beings died of
hunger. In order to prevent such a catastrophe in future, a law
was made obliging every commune to keep a large store of corn,
each landowner being obliged to contribute a certain quantity; in
times of scarcity he could borrow corn from the public granary,
but had to pay it back after the ensuing harvest. This system was
kept in force till within a few years ago, but owing to the introduction of roads and railways, it is no longer necessary.

344.—THE INGREDIENTS AND USE
OF THE HOLY INCENSE.
Exodus xxx. 34–36.

℃ STACTE, Heb. *nataph*, to drop or distil; either a distillation
from the myrrh-tree, or the *storax*, a sweet smelling, resinous gum,
which distils of its own accord. ONYCHA, the crustaceous covering

of certain shell-fish, which was used as an ingredient in perfumes. GALBANUM, the resin of a thorny umbelliferous shrub-like fennel, which is said to be efficacious in fumigations for driving away serpents. FRANKINCENSE, Heb. *lebonah*, from *laban*, to be white, the whitest being the purest. It was obtained by incisions in the shrub, called *amyris*, or *juniperus thurifera*. This mixture was to be pounded into very small particles, and deposited as a very holy thing in the tabernacle, before the ark of the testimony, so that there might be a store of it always in readiness.

According to Rabbinical tradition, a priest or Levite, one of the fifteen prefects of the temple, was retained, whose special duty it was to prepare this precious compound; and a part of the temple was given up to him for his use as a laboratory, called, from this circumstance, "the House of Abtines." So precious and holy was this incense considered that it was forbidden to make a similar perfume for private use on pain of death.

Various ideas have been formed as to the significance and use of incense. Some suppose that it was employed to conceal or neutralise the noxious effluvia caused by the number of beasts slaughtered every day in the sanctuary. Some attach a mystical import to it, and regard it as a symbol of the breath of the world arising in praise to the Creator; the four ingredients of it representing the four elements. Some think it merely corresponded to the perfume so lavishly employed about the person and appointments of an Oriental monarch. It is, however, most in accordance with Scripture references to regard it as the symbol of prayer. It was offered at the time when the people were in the posture and act of devotion; and their prayers were supposed to be presented to God by the priest, and to ascend to Him in the smoke and odour of that fragrant offering. Dr. George Wilson notices "that this symbolical mode of supplication had this one advantage over spoken or written prayer, that it appealed to those who were both blind and deaf —a class that are usually shut out from social worship by their affliction: the hallowed impressions shut out by one avenue were admitted to the mind and heart by another."

345.—A CROWN OF LIFE
FOR FAITHFUL SMYRNAEANS.
Rev. ii. 10.

℄ Like other cities, Smyrna had its favourite tutelary deity and worship. It was Dionysius, the god of wine, who represented the

productive, overflowing, and intoxicating power of nature, which
carries man away from his usual quiet and sober mode of living.
Wine is the most natural and appropriate symbol of that power,
and is therefore called "the fruit of Dionysius;" and he is called
the god of wine, the inventor and teacher of its cultivation, the
giver of joy, and the disperser of grief and sorrow. The story of
the violent death and subsequent resurrection of this god was particularly celebrated by the people of Smyrna, and there may be a
reference to this in the figure chosen to represent Christ. "These
things saith the first and the last, which was dead, and is alive
again." The priests who presided annually at the celebration of the
resurrection of Dionysius were persons of distinction, and at the
end of their year of office they were presented with a crown. To
this it would seem that reference is made in the promise, "And I
will give thee a crown of life." A contrast is drawn between Christ
and the crown He gives to His servants, and Dionysius and the
perishable crown bestowed upon his priests by the authorities of
Smyrna. The Smyrnaeans had a superstitious regard for chance
phrases as material for augury, and this mode of addressing the
Church would therefore be all the more forcible.

346.—Fishing in the Lake of Galilee.
Matt. xiii. 47, 48.

⟪ The Sea of Galilee in Christ's time, so far from being, as is
often imagined, a retired rural region, was the centre of a large
and thriving population. Six cities of considerable size were
crowded along the western bank of this inland lake; the commerce
from the East to the great maritime ports of Tyre and Sidon
passed along its upper shore; warm mineral springs on the southern shore made Tiberias a famous watering-place for the wealthy
Romans. One of the chief avocations of the peasant population
was fishing. This was pursued in fishing-boats or smacks, skiffs
generally, somewhat resembling our modern yawl in size and
shape, and altogether by nets. Fishing with line and hook was almost if not altogether unknown. To comprehend the accounts of
fishing in the life of Christ, and the references to it in His teaching, we must conceive, not of a dainty fisherman with pole and
reel, going out to whip the mountain stream in sport, but of a
group of sturdy workmen, casting the net, and working all day
long, and sometimes all the night, in a toil which required less of
rare dexterity than of patience and persistence. Take Christ's para-

ble of the drag-net, in Matthew, chapter xiii. This net, or seine, is
one of little depth but great length. One side is kept close to the
bottom by weights; the other is buoyed up by corks or bladders, so
that it stands upright in the water like a wall. Having been spread,
the fishermen draw it at both ends to the shore, inclosing in it
every fish not small enough to escape through its meshes.

347.—STRABO'S ACCOUNT OF THE TROGLODYTAE, OR CAVE-DWELLERS.
Gen. xiv. 6.

ℭ The *Horites,* mentioned in this passage, got their name from
their dwelling in caves. "The mode of life among the Troglodytae
is nomadic. Each tribe is governed by tyrants. Their wives and
children are common, except those of the tyrants. . . . The
women carefully paint themselves with antimony. They wear
about their necks shells, as a protection against fascination by
witchcraft. In their quarrels, which are for pastures, they first push
away each other with their hands, they then use stones, or, if
wounds are inflicted, arrows and daggers. The women put an end
to these disputes by going into the midst of the combatants, and
using prayers and entreaties. Their food consists of flesh and bones
pounded together, wrapped up in skins and then baked, or
prepared after many other methods by the cooks, who are called
Acatharti, or impure. In this way they eat not only the flesh, but
the bones and skins also. They use, as an ointment for the body, a
mixture of blood and milk; the drink of the people in general is
an infusion of the *paliurus* (buckthorn); that of the tyrants is mead,
the honey being expressed from some kind of flower. Their winter
sets in when the Etesian winds begin to blow, for they have rain,
and the remaining season is summer. They go naked, or wear
skins only, and carry clubs. . . . Some of them are circumcised
like the Egyptians. The Ethiopian Megabari have their clubs
armed with iron knobs. They use spears and shields which are covered with raw hides. The other Ethiopians use bows and lances.
Some of the Troglodytae, when they bury their dead, bind the
body from the neck to the legs with twigs of the buckthorn; they
then immediately throw stones over the body, at the same time
laughing and rejoicing, until they have covered the face. They then
place over it a ram's horn, and go away. They travel by night. The

male cattle have bells fastened to them, in order to drive away wild beasts with the sound. They use torches also and arrows in repelling them. They watch during the night, on account of their flocks, and sing some peculiar song around their fires."

The excavated dwellings of the *Horites,* who belonged to the class of the Troglodytae, are still found in hundreds in the sandstone cliffs and mountains of Edom, and especially in Petra.

348.—SOLOMON'S PORCH.
Acts iii. 11.

℀ This porch or cloister was on the eastern side of "the court of the Gentiles," the wall of which was built, Josephus tells us, of immense white stones, each of which was twenty cubits long, and six cubits high (Mark xiii. 1). The porch consisted of two rows of pillars, each one piece of polished white marble, which supported a roof of cedar curiously engraven. It was called Solomon's, not because it was the same that was built by Solomon, but because, being erected on the artificial terrace built by him, and constructed on the same plan, it retained its original name. It was in this porch, or in the court in front, that the traffic of the money-changers and the sale of oxen and doves were carried on; and it was here also that our Lord was surrounded by the unbelieving Jews when they threatened to take His life (John x. 23).

349.—ANCIENT ENGINES OF WAR.
2 Chron. xxvi. 15.

℀ It may be asked, were these engines of Uzziah's time properly "inventions?" The word used does not signify "invented;" but there is nothing unreasonable in supposing that these were the creation of the military skill of the period.

"Such engines for throwing stones and darts, once invented, continued to be used in the siege and defence of cities down to the time of the invention of artillery. The engines for throwing stones are known in military history by the name of *ballistae,* and those for casting darts, of *catapultae.* They varied in power, like our cannon. Some of the *ballistae* used in sieges threw stones of three hundred, some of a hundred, some of fifty pounds weight, while those employed in the battlefield cast still smaller weights. The darts projected from the *catapultae* varied in like manner from small beams to large arrows, and their range exceeded a quarter of a mile, or 450 yards. All these instruments were constructed upon the principle of the sling, the bow, or the spring, the last being an elastic bar bent back by a screw, or a cable of sinews, with a trigger to set it free, and contrived either to impel darts by its stroke, or to cast stones from a kind of spoon formed towards the summit of its spring."—*Kitto.*

350.—EASTERN FEASTS GIVEN TO THE POOR.
Matt. xxii. 9.

ℭ Roberts thus illustrates the Oriental custom referred to by our Lord—"It is common in the East for a rich man to give a feast to the poor, the maimed, and the blind, as it is in England for a nobleman to entertain men of his own degree. Does he wish to gain some temporal or spiritual blessing? he orders his head servant to prepare a feast for one or two hundred poor guests. Messengers are then despatched into the streets and lanes to inform the indigent that on such a day rice and curry will be given to all who are there at the appointed time. Long before the hour the visitors may be seen bending their steps towards the house of the Raja. There goes the old man who is scarcely able to move his palsied limbs, while he talks to himself about better days; and there the despised widow moves with a hesitating step. There the *sanyasi* or *pandarum* boldly brushes along, and scowls upon all who offer the least impediment to his progress. There objects, suffering under every possible disease of our nature, congregate together, without a single kindred association, excepting the one which occupies their expectations. The food is ready, the guests sit in rows on the grass (Luke ix. 14), and the servants begin to hand out the portions in order. Such is the hunger of some, that they cannot stay to allow the mess to cool, and they suffer the natural consequences of their impatience; others, upon whom disease or age has made a fatal inroad, can scarcely taste the provision. Some of high caste, while eating, growl at those of lower grades for having presumed to come near them; and others, on account of the high blood which flows in their veins, are allowed to take home their own portion. What a motley scene is that; and what a strange contrariety in their talk! Some are bawling out for more food, though they are already gorged to the full; others are talking about another feast, which is to be given in such a village; and a few who have gained a sight of the host are loudly applauding his princely generosity. He is delighted to hear their flattery; all that they utter falls sweetly on his ears, and is grateful to his feelings; for the higher the tone, the greater is his relish. He has gained his object; *taramum,* that is 'charity,' has been cultivated; he has himself been exhilarated with adulation; he has got a 'name in the street' (Job xviii. 17), and the gods have been propitiated."

351.—THE COUNTRY OF MOAB.
Ruth i. 2.

℄ It is singular that Elimelech, when pressed by famine, did not seek relief, as the patriarchs had done, by sojourning in Egypt. If, however, this famine occurred in the days of Eli, the constant war between Israel and Philistia would sufficiently account for his not turning toward Egypt. The Philistines would be sure to close the roads through their country.

Moab offered the most attractive prospect to Elimelech, who very probably had large flocks and herds. The name "Moab" stands in the Bible for three districts on the east of the Dead Sea. One of these is called expressly "The *Field* of Moab;" and this is the technical phrase used throughout the Book of Ruth. Another district is called "The *Land* of Moab," and the third is known as "The Dry,"—*i.e.* the dry canton—"of Moab." The district called "The *Field* of Moab," or Moab Proper, has the precipices which border the Dead Sea on its western limit, a semicircular sweep of hills on the east, behind which lies the Arabian desert. On the north it is defended by the tremendous chasm down which the river Arnon foams; while on the south the two ranges between which it lies run together, meet, and shut it in. It was a high table-land, dotted with cities, on which the grass grew sweet and strong; and it has been in all ages, as it is even now, a favourite haunt of pastoral tribes.

352.—A FIGURE OF DIVINE DELIVERANCE.
2 Sam. xxii. 7–16.

℄ The Rev. J. J. S. Perowne explains the above verses thus: "The deliverance is now pictured as a magnificent theophany. God comes to rescue His servant as He came of old to Sinai, and all nature is moved at His coming. Similar descriptions of the Divine

manifestation, and of the effects produced by it, occur Psalm
lxviii. 7–8; lxxvii. 14–20; Exodus xix.; Judges v. 4; Amos ix. 5;
Micah i. 3; Hab. iii.; but the image is nowhere so fully carried out
as here. David's deliverance was, of course, not really accompanied by such convulsions of nature, by earthquake, and fire, and
tempest, but his deliverance, or rather his manifold deliverances
gathered into one as he thinks of them, appear to him as a marvellous proof of the Divine Power, as verily effected by the immediate presence and finger of God, as if He had come down in visible form to accomplish them. The image is carefully sustained
throughout. First, we have the earthquake, and then, as preluding
the storm, and as herald of God's wrath, the blaze of the lightning
(verses 8, 9). Next, the thick gathering of clouds, which seem to
touch and envelop the earth; the wind and the darkness which
shrouds Jehovah riding on the cherubim (10, 11). Lastly, the full
outburst of the storm, the clouds parting before the presence and
glory of Jehovah, and pouring upon the earth the burden with
which they were heavy—the thunder, and the lightning, and the
hail—the weapons of Jehovah by which, on the one hand, He dis-
comfits His enemies, and, on the other, lays bare the depths of the
sea and the very foundations of the world, that He may save His
servant who trusts in Him."

353.—TRADITIONS CONCERNING THE
PROPHET JEREMIAH.
Jer. i. 1.

℃ Very little is known with any certainty respecting the prophet
Jeremiah, and, as we have noticed in some other cases, legend has
attempted to supply the place of authentic history. The following
stories, though evidently fabulous, are interesting, as indicating the
respect in which the memory of the prophet was held:—

It is said that he appeared on one occasion to Judas Mac-
cabaeus. This happened more than four hundred years after the
prophet's death. Judas and Onias, the high priest, were then in
difficulties, as the Graeco-Syrian general had repulsed their army.
In this position of affairs, and just when the Jews needed to be
inspirited, Jeremiah appeared to the two leaders—a "man with
gray hairs, and exceedingly glorious, who was of a wonderful and
excellent majesty. He presented Judas with a sword of gold, saying, 'Take this holy sword, a gift from God, with which thou shalt
wound the adversaries.'"

353.—Traditions concerning the Prophet Jeremiah.

Another legend says that Jeremiah, when in Egypt, foretold to the priests that their idols would be overthrown by an earthquake, at the time that the Saviour of the world should be born, and be lying in a manger. From that time the Egyptians are said to have had a virgin represented with a child lying in a manger, to which they paid Divine honours. This is too evidently a tradition fashioned by the early Christian Church to confirm its cherished beliefs.

It is further stated that Alexander the Great visited Jeremiah's tomb, and being informed of the predictions of the prophet concerning his own person and conquests, ordered his body to be removed to Alexandria, where he erected a magnificent monument over him.

The most interesting story, however, respecting this prophet is found in 2 Maccabees i., ii. It is well known that the holy and celestial fire miraculously kindled upon the altar in the days of Moses (Lev. ix. 24), and rekindled in the same manner in Solomon's days (2 Chron. vii. 1, 2), was extinguished at the Captivity, and, so far as can be gathered, was never subsequently relit. The second book of Maccabees, however, says that Jeremiah took the sacred fire just before the deportation of the Jews, and hid it in a cistern. When the Jews returned to Jerusalem, seventy years later, and sought for the fire, they found nothing but muddy water in the cistern. Here was a difficulty. The sacrifice was already on the altar, and the people were waiting for the signal of its acceptance. Nehemiah ordered the priests to bring out the thick water from the cistern and sprinkle it over the wood and the sacrifice. At the moment this was done the sun was hid behind a cloud, but shortly after he shone out with his usual brilliancy, and immediately the wood took fire, and the sacrifice was consumed.

The same record also states that Jeremiah, previous to leaving Judaea, took the tabernacle, and the Ark of the Covenant, and the Altar of Incense, and carried them to Mount Nebo, where he hid them in a cave. Those articles remain there until this day, and will never be discovered until God collects the people of Israel together.

354.—WHO WERE THE MAGI?
Matt. ii. 1.

⁋ From Canon Farrar's *Life of Christ* we take the following paragraph:—

"The name 'Magi,' by which they are called in the Greek of St.

Matthew, is perfectly vague. It meant originally a sect of Median
and Persian scholars; it was subsequently applied (as in Acts xiii.
6) to pretended astrologers, or Oriental soothsayers. Such characters were well known to antiquity, under the name of Chaldeans,
and their visits were by no means unfamiliar even to western nations. Diogenes Laertius reports to us a story of Aristotle's, that a
Syrian *mage* had predicted to Socrates that he would die a violent
death; and Seneca informs us that magi, *qui forte Athenis erant,*
had visited the tomb of Plato, and had there offered incense to
him as a divine being. There is nothing but a mass of confused
and contradictory traditions to throw any light either on their
rank, their country, their number, or their names. The tradition
which makes them kings was probably founded on the prophecy
of Isaiah (lx. 3). The fancy that they were Arabians may have
arisen from the fact that myrrh and frankincense are Arabian
products, joined to the passage in Ps. lxxii. 10.

"There was a double tradition as to their number. Augustine and
Chrysostom say that there were twelve, but the common belief,
arising perhaps from the triple gifts, is that they were three in
number. The venerable Bede even gives their names, their country,
and their personal appearance. Melchior was an old man with
white hair and long beard; Caspar, a ruddy and beardless youth;
Balthasar, swarthy and in the prime of life. We are further informed by tradition that Melchior was a descendant of Shem,
Caspar of Ham, and Balthasar of Japheth. Thus they are made
representatives of the three periods of life, and the three divisions
of the globe; and, valueless as such fictions may be for direct historical purposes, they have been rendered interesting by their
influences on the most splendid productions of religious art. The
skulls of these three kings, each circled with its crown of jewelled
gold, are still exhibited among the relics in the cathedral at
Bologna."

355.—FEASTS UNDER THE VINE AND FIG-TREE.
Zech. iii. 10.

℄ The Orientals are, and were, fond of what we should call pic-
nics, or feasts in the open air, under the trees by the way-side, by
the banks of rivers and streams, or in any other suitable spots.
And the sense of the above passage from the prophet Zechariah
seems to be this:—In your time of plenty and prosperity, having

enough and to spare, as you sit at your meals by the way-side, or under your vines and fig-trees, you shall heartily invite the passers by to stop and partake of refreshment with you.

Dr. Chandler, in his account of travels in Asia Minor, relates that at Philadelphia some families who sat under the trees by a rill of water, actually invited him and his friends to stop and partake of their meal with them.

356.—THE COLOUR OF THE RED SEA.
Exodus xiv. 2.

℞ A question that has puzzled scholars found a solution some time since in the observation of an American submarine diver. Smith's Bible Dictionary discusses learnedly the name of the Red Sea. The dictionary surmises that the name was derived from the red western mountains, red coral zoophytes, &c., and appears to give little weight to the real and natural reason which came under the diver's notice. On one occasion he observed, while under the sea, that the curious wavering shadows, which cross the lustrous golden floor like Frauenhofer's lines on the spectrum, began to change and lose themselves. A purple glory of intermingled colours darkened the violet curtains of the sea-chambers, reddening all glints and tinges with an angry fire. Instead of that lustrous, golden firmament, the thallasphere darkened to crimson and opal. The walls grew purple, the floor as red as blood; the deep itself was purpled with the venous hue of deoxidised life-currents.

The view on the surface was even more magnificent. The sea at first assumed the light-tawny or yellowish-red of sherry wine. Anon this wine-colour grew indistinct with richer radiance; as far as the eye could see, and flashing in the crystalline splendour of the Arabian sun, was a glorious sea of rose. The surface, on examination, proved to be covered with a thin brickdust layer of infusoria slightly tinged with orange. Placed in a white glass bottle this changed into a deep violet, but the wide surface of the external sea was of that magnificent and brilliant rose-colour. It was a new and pleasing example of the lustrous, every-varying beauty of the ocean world. It was caused by diatomaceae, minute algae, which, under the microscope, revealed delicate threads, gathered in tiny bundles, and containing rings, like blood-discs, of that curious colouring matter in tiny tubes.

This miracle of beauty is not without its analogies in other seas.

The medusae of the Arctic seas, an allied existence, people the ul-
tramarine blue of the cold, pure sea, with the vivid patches of living green thirty miles in diameter. These minute organisms are
doubly curious from their power of astonishing production and the
strange electric fire they display. Minute as these microscopic creatures are, every motion and flash is the result of volition, and not a
mere chemic or mechanic phosphorescence. The Photocaris light a
flashing cirrus, on being irritated, in brilliant, kindling sparks, increasing in intensity until the whole organism is illuminated. The
living fire washes over its back, and pencils in greenish-yellow light
its microscopic outline. Nor do these little creatures lack a beauty
of their own. Their minute shields of pure translucent silex are
elaborately wrought in microscopic symbols of mimic heraldry.
They are the chivalry of the deep, the tiny knights with lance and
cuirass, and oval bossy shield, carved in quaint conceits and ornamental fashion. Nor must we despise them when we reflect upon
their power of accretion. The Gallionellae, invisible to the naked
eye, can, of their heraldic shields and flinty armour, make two
cubic feet of Bilin polishing slate in four days. By straining sea-
water, a web of greenish cloth of gold, illuminated by the play of
self-generated electric light, has been collected. Humboldt and
Ehrenberg speak of their voracity, their power of discharging elec-
tricity at will, and their sporting about, exhibiting an intelligent enjoyment of the life God has given to them. Man and his works
perish, but the monuments of the infusoria are the flinty ribs of
the sea, the giant bones of huge continents, heaped into mountain
ranges over which the granite and porphyry have set their stony
seal for ever.—*W. W. Harney*.

357.—THE MAJESTIC APPEARANCE
OF THE CEDARS OF LEBANON.
Psalm civ. 16.

℃ The Rev. Hugh Macmillan gives the following beautiful description:—"The cedar is the tree, *par excellence,* of the Bible—
the type of all forest vegetation. Religion and poetry have sounded
its praises so loudly and repeatedly that it has become the most re-
nowned natural monument in the world. For untold ages it covered the rugged slopes of Lebanon with one continuous forest of
verdure and fragrance, and formed its crowning 'glory.' The ravages of man, carried on century after century in the most ruthless

manner, laid its proud honours low; and now only a few scattered groves survive amid the fastnesses of the highest valleys to tell of the splendour that had perished. But what a magnificent relic the one grove of Kadisha is! Each huge trunk, scarred and hoary with the elemental strife of hundreds of years, still spreads out its great gnarled boughs laden with emerald foliage and exquisite cones, 'full of sap' in the freshness of undying youth, so that we cannot wonder at the superstition of the awe-struck Arabs, who attribute to the cedars not only a vegetative power which enables them to live eternally, but also a wise instinct, an intelligent foresight, by means of which they understand the changes of the weather, and provide accordingly. No temple of Nature can be grander than the interior of that grove, where the natives of the neighbouring villages celebrate mass annually in June. It is a spot unique on earth. The sacred associations of thousands of years crowd around one there. In the fragrance of the cedars comes up the richness of Bible memories: each sight and sound suggest some incident alluded to by psalmist or prophet, and a feeling of awe and reverence, such as few other scenes can inspire, fills the soul to overflowing. There, at an elevation of six thousand feet, with their roots firmly planted in the moraines of extinct glaciers, with their trunks riven and furrowed by lightnings, with the snows of Lebanon gleaming white through their dusky foliage, with the stillness of earth's mightiest powers asleep around them, who can fail to feel the force of the Psalmist's words, 'The trees of the Lord are full of sap; the cedars of Lebanon which He hath planted?' "

The number of the trees is variously given by travellers. Mr. William Rae Wilson has taken the trouble to make a *résumé* of their statements, which will now bear an appendix, as his book of travels is dated 1847. In 1550 A.D., the patriarchs were 25; the same sum total is given by Furer, in 1565, and by travellers in 1575. The good missionary Dandini, in 1600 A.D., found 23; in 1657 A.D., Thevenot, 22; in 1696 A.D., Maundrell, 16; in 1737 A.D., Pococke, 15; whilst in 1786 A.D., Volney declared, "There are now but four or five of these trees which deserve any notice." In 1810 A.D., Burckhardt mentions "eleven or twelve of the oldest and best looking cedars," 25 very large, about 50 of middle size, and more than 300 small and young; of the latter some now remain. In 1818, Mr. Richardson reckons seven; in 1832, M. de Lamartine, who did not visit them, also seven; Van de Velde found 12

oldsters surrounded by an aftergrowth of 400 youngsters, more or
less, and he was told by the Maronites that the mystic dozen was
planted by the Apostles. Madame Pfeiffer saw in 1842, "Twenty
very aged, and five peculiarly large and fine specimens, which are
said to have existed in the days of Solomon."

358.—The Rabbinical Account
of the Teraphim.
Zech. x. 2. Marg.

℟ In a previous paragraph we have given Ewald's description of
these household images. A further account of them may be interesting. There is no evidence in the Scriptures that they were
worshipped, but we may assume that they were regularly consulted
as oracles. (See Judges xviii. 5, 6; 2 Kings xxiii. 24; Ezek. xxi.
19–22.)

The Rabbins say that the teraphim were not mere idols, but
idols that really gave oracles and foretold future events. They had
a human shape, and when once they were set up and dedicated,
they spoke and gave answers at certain hours of the day, under the
influence of the heavenly bodies; and this influence was imported
to them by the art of him who made them, provided they were
made of a certain metal, with certain characters, and under given
aspects of the stars.

Zechariah, the prophet, says, "The teraphim speak vain things."
This expression has given one of the Rabbins occasion to assert
that the teraphim really did speak; and he accounts for this, it appears, by the peculiar manner in which they were made, viz., as
follows:—They killed a first-born child, split open its head, and
sprinkled it with salt and oil. They then wrote the name of some
unclean spirit on a plate of gold, and put the plate under the
child's tongue. Thus prepared, the head was placed in a convenient
niche, with lighted lamps before it; then they prayed to it, and received its oracular answers to the questions they proposed.

Other Rabbins maintain that all idolatry came from Egypt, and
that the use of teraphim passed from that country to the East; for
Ham, and his son Mizraim, was the inventor of statues.

They ascribe many virtues to the teraphim in addition to that of
oracular power. They could also reveal the place of hidden or lost

articles, prevent threatened evil, and secure luck, in play or trade, to their possessor.

It is said that when Abraham dwelt in Egypt his domestics became tainted with this kind of idolatry, and carried it with them into Canaan; from them it passed on to the family of Laban.

359.—THE SLAUGHTER OF THE INNOCENTS.
Matt. ii. 16.

❡ Immediately before the massacre of the children of Bethlehem, Herod caused many Pharisees to be put to death for real or supposed conspiracy (*Josephus, Antiquities*, bk. xvii. ch. 2). The murder of the children is recorded by the heathen writer Macrobus, who says: "When Augustus had heard that among the children under two years old whom Herod, King of the Jews, had ordered to be slain, his own son had also been killed, he said, 'It is better to be Herod's hog than his son'" (*Saturnalia*, bk. ii. 4). Herod would have spared his hog, but allowed his son to perish. This cruelty of Herod is mentioned by Justin Martyr, who wrote before A.D. 150. In his *Dialogue with Trypho the Jew*, Sec. 78, he says that Herod, "not knowing the child whom the Magi had come to adore, commanded that all the children in Bethlehem should be slain." Irenaeus, another Christian who flourished in the same century, refers more than once to the cruelty of Herod in slaying the children (*Iren. against Heresies*, bk. iii. ch. 16, 21). Origen also, in his controversy with Celous, the Pagan philosopher, says: "Herod put to death all the little children in Bethlehem, and its borders, with a design to destroy the King of the Jews who had been born there" (bk. i.).

360.—GOING AWAY TO RECEIVE A KINGDOM.
Luke xix. 12.

❡ Our Lord may have taken the form of this parable from an historical event which had recently taken place. Archelaus, the son of Herod the Great, was tetrarch of Judaea at the time when the infant Jesus was brought back from Egypt (Matt. ii. 22). Not being satisfied with the title and dignity which he possessed, he made the journey to Rome in order to induce the reigning Caesar to make him *king* over his father's territories. "But his citizens hated him," and sent Caesar an account of his crimes. They failed at first, but some years later Archelaus was banished by the emperor for his bad rule. It is very probable that this story of Archelaus suggested our Lord's parable, for there was a splendid palace in Jericho which Archelaus had built, or rather rebuilt, which was in sight of the multitude while Jesus was addressing them.

361.—THE BIBLE WORD "DAMNATION."
1 Cor. xi. 29.

¶ As an illustration how words change their meanings in the course of centuries, we give the following from a valuable article by the *Rev. H. F. Woolrych,* author of the *Handbook of Bible Words:*—

DAMN (*v*) and its derivatives—the adjective, with termination *able,* and the substantive, with termination *ation*—are not found in the Old Testament. "Damnable heresies," in 2 Peter ii. 1, is literally "heresies of *destruction,*" the latter noun being the same as that rendered "damnation" in ver. 3—"their damnation slumbereth not." This is evidently "condemnation" in its fullest sense, as it is immediately afterwards compared with that of the angels who sinned and were cast down into hell. This root is that of Apollyon, "destroyer." Damn is generally the translation of another class of words, the root of which is *kri* [whence, in English, *critic, critical, crime*], and undoubtedly generally refers to the final judgment, as in John v. 29, where the resurrection of "damnation" [*krisis*] is contrasted with that of "life." The passage in 1 Cor. xi. 29 is very remarkable, as the Apostle evidently uses the verb in a stronger or weaker sense, and also in a cognate one, in several successive verses, in order to warn his followers from past temporal to future eternal judgment (ver. 29). "For he that eateth and drinketh unworthily, eateth and drinketh—to himself (KRI*ma*) not discerning (*dia*KRI*nōn*) the body of the Lord. For this cause many are weak and sickly among you, and many sleep. For if we had judged (*die*KRI*nomen*) ourselves, we should not have been judged (*e*KRI*nometha*). But when we are judged (KRI*nomenoi*) we are chastened of the Lord that we should not be condemned (*kata*KRI*thōmen*—a stronger form) with the world . . . (ver. 34). And if any man hunger, let him eat at home, that ye come not together unto condemnation (KRI*ma*)." It would appear that the *krima* in the first and last of these verses was the sickness and

death which were to act as a warning voice lest the disciples
should fall into *katakrima.* The Communion Office of the Church
of England likewise includes both these senses of the verb. In the
exhortation to come to the Holy Communion, the people are told
that if unworthy and unrepentant they are to abstain from coming
lest "the devil enter into *them,* as he entered into Judas, and fill
them full of all iniquities, and bring them to destruction both of
body *and soul.*" In another exhortation, when the people are
come, it is said that if we receive the same unworthily, "We eat
and drink our own damnation, not considering the Lord's body;
we kindle God's wrath against us; we provoke Him to plague us
with divers diseases and sundry kinds of death. Judge therefore
yourselves, brethren, that ye be not judged of the Lord." So
closely is the double force of the verb followed. And, again, even
St. Paul's use of the same root in a third sense—that of "dis-cern-
ing"—for he evidently repeated it with a view to the ear as well as
the understanding—is imitated in this service, "not *considering* the
Lord's body." Our word "damn," or "dampne," often only meant
"condemn." Sometimes the context added other words, as in *Piers
Ploughman,* ii. 102—

> *"A dwelling with the devil! and be damned for ever."*

> *"Upon condition Publius shall not live,*
> *Who is your sister's son, Mark Antony.*
> ANT. *He shall not live; look, with a spot I damn him."*
> Julius Caesar, *iv. 1* ("Nare's Gloss.")

Ang.-Sax., *deman,* to "judge," "consider," "doom," "condemn;"
dom, "judgment," "opinion," "sentence;" *dom-boc,* book of decrees; *dom-daeg,* judgment-day.

362.—SWEET-SMELLING FLOWERS IN
MOUNTAIN REGIONS.
Song Sol. iv. 6.

℄ Rev. H. Macmillan observes that sweet-smelling flowers as a
class are found in greatest abundance in mountain regions. A large
proportion of the plants growing on the high pasturages of the
Alps are possessed of aromatic as well as medicinal properties. On
the Scottish mountains there are several odorous plants, such as
the Alpine forget-me-not, blooming amid mists and clouds on the
highest summits, and breathing from its lovely blue flowers a rich

perfume. On the Andes we have the Peruvian heliotrope, whose
purple eyes turn ever toward the sun, and give out an odour so
sweet and ravishing that the Indians regard it as a mystic spell that
opens to them the gates of the spirit world. On the Sikkim
Himalayas, the tiny *Rhododendron nivale,* which grows at a loftier
elevation than any other shrub in the world, scents the air with its
perfumed foliage when the weather is genial. In the highest zone
of the Peak of Teneriffe, far above the clouds, amid the fierce
drought and unmitigated glare of that arid region, there grows a
wonderful bush—found nowhere else in the world—a species of
broom, called by the natives *Retama.* It is a dull, dingy-looking
plant in autumn, harmonising with the dreary desolation around;
but in spring it bursts out into a rich profusion of milk-white blossoms, and fills all the atmosphere with its delicious odour. Beehives are brought up to it by the peasants from the valleys; and
there for a few weeks the bees revel on the nectar, and yield a
highly-prized and fragrant honey. Mount Hybla, in Sicily, is covered with an immense abundance of odoriferous flowers of all
sorts; and Hymettus, a mountain in Attica, has always been celebrated in classic song for the quantity and excellence of its honey,
gathered by the bees from the fragrant plants that luxuriate there.
The costly spikenard of Scripture is obtained from a curious
shaggy-stemmed plant called *Nardostachys Jatamansi,* a kind of
valerian, growing on the lofty mountains in India, between the
Ganges and the Jumna, some of which are for six months covered
with snow.

From these instances it appears that the association of mountains and hills with *fragrance* is a strictly natural and proper one.

363.—IDLERS IN THE MARKET PLACE.
Matt. xx. 6, 7.

¶ Morier in his book of travels gives an illustration of this parable.

The most conspicuous building in Hamadan is the Mesjid
Jumah, a large mosque now falling into decay, and before it a
maidan or square, which serves as a market-place. Here we observed, every morning before the sun rose, that a numerous band
of peasants were collected with spades in their hands, waiting, as
they informed us, to be hired for the day to work in the surrounding fields. This custom, which I have never seen in any other part

of Asia, forcibly struck me as a most happy illustration of our Saviour's parable of the labourers in the vineyard in the twentieth chapter of Matthew, particularly when, passing by the same place late in the day, we still found others standing idle, and remembered His words, *"Why stand ye here all the day idle?"* as most applicable to their situation; for in putting the very same question to them, they answered us, *"Because no man hath hired us."*

364.—THE HAND KISSING THE MOUTH.
Job xxxi. 27, Marg.

℀ This passage is an obscure and difficult one, on which only some side lights can be thrown. The act may have been one of worship offered to some deity, or *the hand itself may have been the object of worship,* and we are not without indications of such a practice. The Talmud asserts that the hand and the foot were both regarded as objects of worship. It says that a broken piece of an idol is not to be considered an idol in itself, since it may be put to some useful purpose: if it be made of metal it may be melted down, and if of earthenware it may be broken up and used again. But the hand and the foot, being objects of worship in themselves alone, whether they are broken from statues or not, are unclean, and must not be touched.

There is a curious relic of hand-worship still preserved in Jerusalem, a rough representation of a hand being always made by the native masons on the wall of a house in the course of erection. This hand-print is made in order to avert the "evil eye." The Jews also take care to make the same mark on a conspicuous part of the exterior of their houses just before a marriage, a birth, or any other festival. At Jerusalem a sign resembling a double arrow is frequently used instead of the hand, the Jews saying that it is a symbol of the five names of God, as are also the five fingers; and either symbol will ward off evil from the place on which it is imprinted.

The cornice of a cistern near Petra, in Arabia, was found, not long since, to be decorated with hands printed in black and red alternately. At the present day both Jews and Mohammedans hang round their children's necks hands rudely cut out of thin plates of silver and gold, and this is done as a charm against the "evil eye."

In Italy the first and last fingers of the hand are used for the same
purpose.

365.—THE DIFFICULTY OF THE FOUR HUNDRED
AND FIFTY YEARS.
Acts xiii. 19, 20.

℘ All kinds of endeavours have been made to reconcile this term
of *four hundred and fifty years* with other Scripture dates; it has
furnished enough material for whole volumes, and this period is
still called *the computation of St. Paul*, in the title of Sir Henry
Ellis's new edition of Blair's *Chronological and Historical Tables*.
Now in the most ancient copies the period of four hundred and
fifty years stands in quite a different connection:—"He destroyed
seven nations in the land of Chanaan, and gave them their land by
lot, about four hundred and fifty years, and afterwards he gave
unto them judges," etc. Attention ought to have been paid to *this*
reading, instead of its being wasted on one more recent.

366.—UNCOVERING THE ROOF.
Mark ii. 1–12.

℘ Various explanations of what was done by these bearers of the
paralytic have been given, but perhaps the most simple and natural
is that found in the well-known work, Thomson's *Land and Book*.

"The houses of Capernaum, as is evident from the ruins, were,
like those of modern villages in the same region, low, very low,
with flat roofs, reached by a stairway from the yard or court. Jesus
probably stood in the open *lewan,* and the crowd were around and
in front of Him. Those who carried the paralytic, not being
able to 'come at Him for the press,' ascended to the roof, removed
so much of it as was necessary, and let down their patient through
the aperture. Examine one of these houses, and you will see at
once that the thing is natural, and easy to be accomplished. The
roof is only a few feet high, and by stooping down, and holding
the corners of the couch,—merely a thickly-padded quilt, as at
present in this region,—they could let down the sick man without
any apparatus of ropes or cords to assist them. And thus, I suppose, they did. The whole affair was the extemporaneous device of

plain peasants, accustomed to open their roofs, and let down
grain, straw, and other articles, as they still do in this country. The
only difficulty in this explanation is to understand how they could
break up the roof without sending down such a shower of dust as
to incommode our Lord and those around Him. I have often seen
it done, and have done it myself to houses in Lebanon; but there is
always more dust made than is agreeable. The materials now employed are beams about three feet apart, across which short sticks
are arranged close together, and covered with the thickly matted
thorn-bush, called *bellan*. Over this is spread a coat of stiff mortar;
and then comes the marl or earth which makes the roof. Now, it is
easy to remove any part of this without injuring the rest. No objection, therefore, would be made on this score by the owners of
the house. They had merely to scrape back the earth from a portion of the roof over the *lewan*, take up the thorns and the short
sticks, and let down the couch between the beams at the very feet
of Jesus. The end achieved, they could speedily restore the roof as
it was before. I have the impression, however, that the covering, at
least of the *lewan*, was not made of earth, but of materials more
easily taken up. It may have been merely of coarse matting, like
the walls and roofs of Turkmen's huts; or it may have been of
boards, or even stone slabs (and such I have seen), that could be
quickly removed. All that is necessary, however, for us to know is,
that the roof was flat, low, easily reached, and easily opened, so as
to let down the couch of the sick man; and all these points are
rendered intelligible by an acquaintance with modern houses in
the villages of Palestine."

367.—THE PICTURESQUE SITUATION OF THYATIRA.
Rev. ii. 18.

¶ Thyatira stands on the Lycus, and is situated on the borders of
Mysia and Ionia, a little to the left of the Roman road from Pergamos to Sardis. It was founded by Seleucus Nicator after the Persian Empire had been destroyed by Alexander the Great. Dr. Tristram thus describes the present city and surroundings, as seen
when approaching from Pergamos:—"Diverging a little to the
right, the broad valley of the Hyllus opens to view, and as we look
down in spring or summer, we see before us a panorama resembling in kind, though not equal in extent and grandeur to the
traveller's first glimpse of Damascus. The eye tracks across the
plain the silver thread which marks the course of one of the

effluents of the Hyllus; and in the centre are the crowded white
roofs of a widespread Turkish city, with here and there a minaret
towering in the midst, and many a clump of tall cypresses raising
their funeral plumes on high; while the whole is girt with a fringe
of orchards, and watered gardens, over which the silver mist,
drawn down by the sun, hangs in a thick quivering cloud. This is
Akhissar, 'the white castle,' the ancient Thyatira."

368.—Birds Lodging in the Mustard-plant.
Matt. xiii. 32.

¶ An Eastern traveller writes:—There was one plant which, although it had little to attract the eye, gave me the deepest interest
—the mustard plant of the text. The herb of our English garden is
but a pigmy in comparison with the giant growth of a richer soil
and a warmer clime. Dr. Hooker measured a mustard plant in the
Jordan valley ten feet high. I myself have seen it in the fork of
land between the Jordan and the Jabbok at least seven or eight
feet in height. Dr. Thomson, in his *Land and the Book,* says that
he has seen the mustard-plant in the plain of Acre, which seems a
favourite abode of the wild plant, as tall as the horse and his rider.
An extract from a traveller of the name of Halket may be of interest to the reader, and strikingly illustrates our Lord's parable.

"As I was riding across the plain of Acre, on the way to Carmel,
I perceived at some distance from the path what seemed to me a
little forest or nursery of trees. I turned aside to examine them. On
coming nearer they proved to be an extensive field of the plant
which I was so anxious to see (the mustard-plant). It was then in
blossom, full grown, in some cases six, seven, and nine feet high,
with a stem or trunk an inch or more in thickness, throwing out
branches on every side. I was now satisfied in part. I felt that such
a plant might well be called a tree, and, in comparison with the
seed producing it, 'a great tree.' But still the branches, or stems of
branches, were not very large, or apparently very strong. Can the
birds, I said to myself, rest upon them? Are they not too slight and
flexible? Will they not bend or break with the superadded weight?
At that very instant, as I stood and revolved the thought, lo! one
of the fowls of heaven stopped in its flight through the air, lighted
down on one of the branches, which hardly moved beneath the
shock, and then began, perched there before my eyes, to warble
forth a strain of the richest music. All my doubts were now
charmed away. I was delighted at the incident."

Other travellers tell us that the smaller birds, such as goldfinches and linnets, settle among the branches in flocks, for the sake of the seed, of which they are very fond.

369.—LEAVEN.
Matt. xiii. 33.

⊄ By this term is to be understood the fermenting matter which, in baking bread, is put into the dough to make it lighter and more tasteful. Hugh Macmillan says, "It consists of myriads of the cells of the common green mould in an undeveloped state. If a fragment of the dough with the leaven in it be put aside in a shady place, the cells of the fungus in the leaven will vegetate, and cover the dough with a slight downy substance, which is just the plant in its complete form. The swelling of the dough, and the commotion which goes on in the leavened mass, are owing to the multiplication of the plant cells, which takes place with astonishing rapidity. By this process of vegetation, the starch and sugar of the dough are converted into other chemical products. But it is only allowed to go to a certain length, and then the principle of growth is checked by placing the dough in the oven, and baking it into bread. Leaven is thus a principle of destruction and construction— of decay and of growth—of death and of life. It has two effects, which are made use of as types in Scripture. On the one side, the operation of leaven upon meal presents an analogy to something evil in the spiritual world, for it decays and decomposes the matter with which it comes into contact. On the other side, the operation of leaven upon meal presents an analogy to something good in the spiritual world, for it is a principle of life and growth, and imparts a new energy and a beneficent quality to the matter with which it comes into contact. Hence we see why Christ, at one and the same time, should bid His disciples beware of the leaven of the scribes and pharisees, and compare the kingdom of heaven to leaven hid in three measures of meal."

370.—EASTERN PRISONS.
Acts xvi. 24.

⊄ The prisons of the East could hardly have been better contrived had they been planned for the purpose of destroying by lingering death. Jeremiah was "cast into the dungeon of Malchiah," into which he was let down with cords. "In the dungeon there was no water, but mire; so Jeremiah sunk in the mire" (Jer. xxxviii. 6). We have seen the "inner prison" at Rome, where the Apostle Paul was let down and Jugurtha died of hunger. These are supposed to be the fruits of a barbarous age, yet the Romans were the most civilised heathen of any age, being surpassed in their time only by the Hebrews. But twenty centuries appear to have produced no change in the East in this matter. We have visited many a prison in the Levant, we have seen maniacs confined in the same dungeon with criminals, and have often wondered how the latter could preserve their reason in such a spot, or how it could remain so full with so large a mortality. The latter is not only the result of intolerable filth and want of ventilation, but also of the lack of rest, the excess of vermin, the heavy chain, and the unmerciful stocks in which the feet are "made fast" (Acts xvi. 24). We may well pity virtuous Joseph if he was indeed cast, as claimed by tradition, into the present dungeon of the citadel of Cairo, which is "composed of dark, loathsome, and pestilential passages, where the prisoners' feet are made fast in the stocks. They are chained to the wall, and cold water in buckets is poured upon them until they have given up all their money to their tormentors." This prison has been called "a hell upon earth" by a humane traveller; but there is scarcely one Turkish prison that does not well deserve the name at this very day (*Thevenot,* p. 141). And yet there are worse places than even these. An Englishman has described the prisons in which Schamyl, so often called the Circassian hero, used to confine his Russian prisoners. They consisted of circular pits dug in the ground for storing grain, and were twenty-five feet deep and ten wide. The top was covered with flagstones, having a small hole for the admission of air, and letting in the rain and snow as well. The prisoners were kept in these dungeons for weeks together, and removed only to cleanse the place, being drawn out and let down again with ropes.—*Van Lennep.*

371.—THE PARTING SCENE OF NAOMI
AND HER DAUGHTERS-IN-LAW.
Ruth i. 8–18.

℃ S. Cox skilfully brings out the point of interest in this most touching scene. "If we would understand the scene, and especially the stress laid on these young widows finding new husbands, we must remember that in the East of antiquity, as in many Eastern

lands to this day, the position of an unmarried woman, whether
maid or widow, was a very unhappy and perilous one. Only in the
house of a husband could a woman be sure of respect and protection. Hence the Hebrews spoke of the husband's house as the
woman's 'menuchah,' or 'rest'—her secure and happy asylum
from servitude, neglect, licence. It was such an 'asylum' of
honour and freedom that Naomi desired for Orpah and Ruth. But,
as she had to explain to them, such an 'asylum,' while it might be
open to them in Moab, would be fast closed against them in
Judah. In marrying them her sons had sinned against the Hebrew
law. That sin was not likely to be repeated by Israelites living in
their own land."

372.—LAWS CONCERNING WITNESSES IN
CASES OF MURDER.
Numb. xxxv. 30.

℃ The Jews were exceedingly careful in judicial trials for murder,
as the following will show. "How is one," say the Rabbis, "to awe
the witnesses who are called to testify in matters of life and death?
When they are brought into court they are charged thus:—
Perchance you would speak from conjecture or rumour, as a witness from another witness—having heard it from 'some trustworthy man,'—or perchance you are not aware that we shall proceed to search and try you with close questions, and searching
scrutiny. Know ye that not like trials about money are trials over
life and death. In trials of money a man may redeem his guilt by
money, and he may be forgiven. In trials of life, the blood, not
only of him who has been falsely condemned, will hang over the
false witness, but also that of the seed of his seed, even unto the
end of the world; for thus we find that when Cain killed his
brother, it is said, 'The voice of thy brother's blood is crying to
Me from the ground.' The word 'blood' stands there in the plural
number, to indicate to you that the blood of him, together with
that of his seed has been shed. . . . But ye might say to yourselves, what have we to do with all this misery here? Remember
then, that Holy Writ has said (Lev. v. 1), 'If a witness hath seen
or known, if he do not utter, he shall bear his iniquity.' But
perchance ye might say, Why shall we be guilty of this man's
blood? Remember then what is said in Proverbs (xi. 10), 'In the
destruction of the wicked there is joy.' "

373.—The Original Home, and Diffusion
of the Vine.
Gen. ix. 20.

¶ The early history of the vine cannot be traced with any certainty. It is first introduced to our notice, in the above passage, as the cause of Noah's shameful drunkenness, and as one of the articles of provision hospitably offered by Melchizedek to Abraham. It was in all probability, a native of the hilly region on the southern shores of the Caspian Sea, and of the Persian province of Ghilan. The tradition of the Jews is that the vine was first planted by God's own hand on the fertile slopes of Hebron. It has been gradually introduced into other countries, and it has been said, that the great revolutions of society may be traced in its gradual distribution over the surface of the globe; for wherever man has penetrated, in that spirit of change and activity which precedes or accompanies civilisation, he has assisted in the dissemination of this useful plant, much more surely and rapidly than the ordinary agencies of nature. Now the range of the vine extends from the shores of the New World to the utmost boundaries of the Old; its profitable cultivation in the open air, however, being still confined to a zone about two thousand miles in breadth, and reaching in length from Portugal to India.

374.—The Promise of a New Name.
Rev. ii. 17.

¶ In the Book of Revelation, one of the promises made "to him that overcometh," is that a white stone will "be given him with a new name written on it." Some have imagined that the name on the stone is the name of Christ; others, that it is a new name given to the person to whom the white stone is presented. The latter supposition is the more accurate of the two, and is supported, not only from expressions in the Old Testament, but by a remarkable custom on the part of the Jews.

In Isaiah, where the prophet speaks of the restoration of the Jews after the captivity, it is declared that the Lord God "shall call His servants by another name," that is to say, a name to indicate that they had been faithful, and were rewarded for their faithfulness. The possession of this "new name" came to be regarded by the pious among the Jews as a demonstration that all sins committed under the old name were forgiven, and all decrees annulled which were issued against the sinner while possessed of his former appellation. Accordingly, at the approach of death the Jews were wont to change the name of the dying person, and the reason of this custom will be perceived from the following prayer offered for the dying, to whom the new name had been given:—"O God, take pity on A (his former name) and restore him to health, and let him henceforth be called B (the new name); and let him be glad in his new name, and let it be confirmed to him. Be pleased, we entreat Thee, O God, that this change of name may abolish all the hard and evil decrees against him and destroy the broad sentence. If death be decreed upon A (the former name) it is not decreed upon B (the new name). If an evil decree was made against A, lo! this hour he is another man, a new creature, and like a child born to a good life and length of days."

This custom affords an interesting explanation of the promise of the "new name" to be given to the victorious Christian, a promise all the more likely to attract the attention of a devout Jew, as containing in it the ideas of the "new birth" and the "new creature," with which it appears from the prayer above cited, the Jews were by no means as unfamiliar as we might suppose. The promise infers that the follower of Christ was to be rewarded by the very blessings for which the Hebrews themselves earnestly prayed, when they begged in behalf of their sick and dying brother that he should have "a new name."

375.—CREATION OUT OF NOTHING.
Hebrews xi. 3.

℘ The expression "God's making all things of nothing," as a definition of creation, though it has a pretty close parallel in Heb. xi. 3, yet appears to be derived from 2 Maccabees vii. 28; "I beseech thee, my son, look up to the heaven and the earth, and all things that are seen in them, and know that *from things that are not* (ἐξ οὐκ ὄντων) God made them, and the race of men thus came into being." The Vulgate renders the phrase "ἐξ οὐκ ὄντων" by "*ex nihilo*," which the Douay follows by "made them out of nothing." Our A. V. renders "made them of things that were not."

376.—FEEDING ON ASHES.
Isaiah xliv. 20.

⟨ Hugh Macmillan has collected the following illustrations of this strange appetite:—"One of the most extraordinary examples of depraved or perverted appetite is the use of earth for food. This propensity is not an occasional freak, but a common custom, and is found among so large a number and variety of tribes, that it may be regarded as co-extensive with the human race. From time immemorial, the Chinese have been in the habit of using various kinds of edible earth as substitutes for bread in times of scarcity; and their imperial annals have always religiously noticed the discovery of such bread-stones, or stone-meal, as they are called. On the western coast of Africa a yellowish kind of earth, called *caouac,* is so highly relished, and so constantly consumed by the negroes, that it has become to them a necessary of life. In the island of Java, and in various parts of the hill country of India, a reddish earth is baked into cakes, and sold in the village markets for food; while on the banks of the Orinoco, in South America, Humboldt mentions that the native Indians find a species of unctuous clay, which they knead into balls, and store up in heaps in their huts as a provision for the winter or rainy season. They are not compelled by famine to have recourse to this clay; for even when fish, game, and fruit are plentiful, they still eat it after their food as a luxury. This practice of eating earth is not confined solely to the inhabitants of the tropics. In the north of Norway, and in Swedish Lapland, a kind of white powdery earth, called mountain meal, found under beds of decaying moss, is consumed in immense quantities every year. It is mixed by the people with their bread in times of scarcity; and even in Germany it has been frequently used as a means of allaying hunger."

377.—PAUL'S NOT RECOGNISING THE HIGH PRIEST.
Acts xxiii. 4, 5.

⟨ Upon inquiry into the history of the age, it turns out that Ananias, of whom this is spoken, was in truth not the high priest, though he was sitting in judgment in that assumed capacity. The case was that he had formerly holden the office and had been deposed; that the person who succeeded him had been murdered;

that another had not yet been appointed to the station; and that during the vacancy he had, of his own authority, taken upon himself the discharge of the office. This singular situation of the high priesthood took place during the interval between the death of Jonathan, who was murdered by order of Felix, and the accession of Ismael, who was invested with the high priesthood by Agrippa, and precisely in this interval it happened that St. Paul was apprehended and brought before the Jewish council.

378.—PASSING THROUGH THE FIRE TO MOLOCH.
Lev. xviii. 21.

℄ The Rabbins say that the idol Moloch, or Molech, god of Ammon, was made of brass, and seated on a throne of the same metal, adorned with a royal crown. His head was that of a calf, and his arms were extended as if about to embrace some one. The image was hollow, and heated from within. When the worshippers offered children to him in sacrifice, the idol was heated to a fierce heat, and then the victims were placed in his arms, where they were quickly consumed. The noise of their shrieks was drowned by the beating of large drums, and the playing of other rude musical instruments.

Others say that the arms of the statue were extended downwards to near the ground, and that when a victim was placed in his arms it immediately fell into a great fire burning at the idol's feet.

Others again say that Moloch was internally divided into seven compartments, into the first of which the worshippers placed meal; into the second turtles; into the third an ewe; into the fourth a ram; into the fifth a calf; into the sixth an ox; and into the seventh a child. This arrangement being completed, the statue was heated, and all the offerings were consumed.

379.—"GET THEE BEHIND ME, SATAN."
Matt. xvi. 23.

℄ This terribly sharp rebuke appears to be a "railing accusation;" and hence commentators have tried various means to weaken the force of the expression, or to divert the point of it from Peter to Satan. The real fault seems to have been a want of discernment on

the part of the translators, whom most of the annotators have
servilely followed. *Satan,* or *Satam,* is a Hebrew word, being first
of all a verb, meaning to attack, to lie in wait for, and to hate. As
a noun it meant originally a foe, or an accuser: every enemy was
a Satan, whether he opposed you in battle, plotted your ruin, accused you of crimes before a judge, or spread false reports about
you. In fact, the Hebrews carried their ideas so far that whoever
opposed another in anything bad or good, was a Satan; thus the
angel who withstood Balaam, when making his way to the court of
Balak, is said to have gone out against the prophet as a *Satan* to
oppose him (Numb. xxii. 22).

These facts will explain the meaning of the rebuke to Peter:
"Get thee behind Me, thou adversary—or thou opponent." This is
the literal meaning of the passage, and, thus read, it ceases to
shock one's best feelings, as the usual translation does.

380.—Corn the Peculiar Provision for Man.
Psalm lxv. 9.

℃ There is a striking difference between corn and other plants.
"All the other plants we use are unfit for their purpose in their
natural condition, and require to have their nutritious qualities developed, and their natures and forms to a certain extent changed
by a gradual process of cultivation. There is not a single useful
plant grown in our gardens and fields but is utterly worthless for
food in its normal or wild state; and man has been left to himself
to find out, slowly and painfully, how to convert these crudities of
nature into nutritious vegetables. But it is not so with corn. It has
from the very beginning been an abnormal production. God gave
it to Adam, we have every reason to believe, in the same perfect
state of preparation for food in which we find it at the present
day. It was made expressly for man, and given directly into his
hands."

It is remarkable that the corn-plants were utterly unknown
throughout all the geological periods. No trace of them is found in
any of the strata until we come to the most recent formations,
contemporaneous with man. Moreover corn has never been found
in a wild state. It has never been known as anything but a cultivated plant. History and observation prove that it cannot grow
spontaneously. It is never, like other plants, self-sown and self-
diffused. Neglected of man, it speedily disappears, and becomes

extinct. "It can only be reared permanently by being sown by man's own hand, and in ground which man's own hand has tilled."

381.—EGYPTIAN WAR WEAPONS.
Exodus xiv. 5–9.

℄ Sir Gardner Wilkinson gives the following list of Egyptian arms and armour:—"The offensive weapons of the Egyptians were the *bow, spear,* two species of *javelin, sling,* a short and straight *sword, falchion, axe* or *hatchet, battle-axe, pole-axe, mace* or *club,* and the *lissan*—a curved stick similar to that still in use among the modern Ethiopians. Their defensive arms consisted of a helmet of metal, or a quilted head-piece, a *cuirass,* or coat of armour—made of metal plates, or quilted with metal bands—and an ample *shield.* But they had no greaves, and the only covering to the arms were a part of the cuirass, forming a short sleeve, and extending about half way to the elbow."

382.—SOWING TARES.
Matt. xiii. 24–30.

℄ Strange as it may appear, this was by no means unfrequent in the East. Roberts says:—"This is still literally done in the East. See that lurking villain, watching for the time when his neighbour shall *plough* his field; he carefully marks the period when the work has been finished, and goes the night following, and casts in what the natives call *pandinellu,* that is pig paddy; this, being of rapid growth, springs up before the good seed, and scatters itself before the other can be reaped, so that the poor owner of the field will be years before he can get rid of this troublesome weed. But there is another noisome plant, called *perum-pirandi,* which is more destructive to vegetation than any other plant. Has a man purchased a field out of the hands of another? The offended says, 'I will plant the *perum-pirandi* in his grounds.'"

383.—"WHO IS THIS KING OF GLORY?"
Psalm xxiv. 8.

℄ Bruce, the Eastern traveller, gives a very interesting account of the coronation of an Abyssinian king, which he had the gratification of seeing. The army present consisted of 30,000 men. The king was dressed in crimson damask, with a large gold chain round his neck, his head was bare, and he rode on a richly caparisoned horse. (To understand some of the allusions in the ceremony, it must be remembered that the royal house of Abyssinia claims descent from Solomon and the Queen of Sheba; and this accounts for the Israelitish air worn by the ceremony.) As the king and his retinue advanced toward the church, they came to a paved covered way, which led directly into the building, and here they were met by a number of girls, daughters of the chief nobility, standing right and left of the court. Two of them held a cord of crimson silk, a little thicker than whip-cord, stretched from one company to the other to stop the approach of the king. It was held about breast-high, and the king advanced curveting, and showing his skill in horsemanship; but when he reached the cord the damsels demanded who he was. He replied, "I am your king; the King of Ethiopia." To this the girls, with one voice, answered, "You shall not pass; you are not our king." The king then retired several paces, but soon returned to the charge. Again the string was drawn tight, and the girls demanded, "Who are you?" He replied, "I am your king, the King of Israel." "You shall not pass; you are not our king," they said. The third time the king advanced to the barrier with assumed sternness and resolution, and when the girls made their demand, he replied, "I am your king, the King of Zion." Then, drawing his sword, he severed the cord, and passed on, the girls shouting as he passed, "It is a truth, you are our king; truly you are the King of Zion." They then began the hallelujah, in which they were joined by the court and the army.

Once in the church, the king is anointed, then crowned; by-and-by he is fumigated with incense, and the whole proceedings are crowned with a festival extending over fourteen days.

384.—THE FEAST OF PURIM.
Esther ix. 20–32.

ℂ Dr. Macduff writes:—"This was the only Jewish feast at which I was present in Jerusalem. I can never forget it. It took place, amid a great noise, in a synagogue near 'The Wailing-Wall'—a well-known spot in the city, of which you have heard, where the Jews go every Friday to weep over the ruins of their old Temple.

"The feast itself, let me tell you, first of all, was not deemed one

of the three great ones; nor was it among those appointed by
Moses. It dates long after, from the time the Jews were living in
exile. Its design was to call to mind the successful pleadings of
Queen Esther with her royal husband, for the Israelites who were
doomed to death; also the story of wicked Haman, who had got
the king to agree to so cruel and wholesale a murder. I remember
well that evening hearing 'The Book of Esther' read. The reader
stood on a desk or raised platform, in the centre of this poor dingy
building, with its bare white walls. There was a goodly number of
boys present, with sticks and clubs in their hands. It was soon evident what use they were going to make of these, for every time
the hated name of Haman occurred, they hissed, and howled, and
scraped with their feet; they beat the seats and floors, and anything in front of them, as if they were flogging the cruel and hard-
hearted man; while old and young clapped their hands in approval,
and joined in a loud blessing, when the name of Mordecai was
mentioned.

"I afterwards bought, near the Jaffa Gate, an old parchment
roll, very tattered and soiled, of 'The Book of Queen Esther,' to
keep me in mind of the feast—at which, doubtless, it must have
been often read; also one of the sweet sugar-cakes with bright
colours upon it, which, in accordance with ancient custom, are
yearly baked for the same occasion. The Feast of Purim I should,
moreover, tell you, always was, and still is, a favourite one with
the people. It was kept as a sort of holiday, with loud clanging
music and dancing; sometimes in the merry way of our own Gun-
powder Plot fifty years ago."

385.—THE WILD GOAT OF THE ROCK.
Job xxxix. 1.

℃ *Burckhardt* describes these animals in his book of travels in
Syria. "As we approached the summit of the mountain (St. Catherine, adjacent to Mount Sinai), we saw at a distance a small flock
of mountain goats feeding among the rocks. One of our Arabs left
us, and by a widely circuitous route endeavoured to get to the lee-
ward of them, and near enough to fire at them. He enjoined us to
remain in sight of them, and to sit down in order not to alarm
them. He had nearly reached a favourable spot behind a rock,
when the goats suddenly took to flight. They could not have seen

the Arab, but the wind changed, and thus they smelt him. The chase of the *beden,* as the wild goat is called, resembles that of the chamois of the Alps, and requires as much enterprise and patience. The Arabs make long circuits to surprise them, and endeavour to come upon them early in the morning, when they feed. The goats have a leader who keeps watch, and on any suspicious smell, sound, or object, makes a noise, which is a signal to the flock to make their escape. They have much decreased of late, if we may believe the Arabs, who say that, fifty years ago, if a stranger came to a tent, and the owner of it had no sheep to kill, he took his gun, and went in search of a *beden.* They are, however, even now more common here than in the Alps, or in the mountains to the east of the Red Sea. I had three or four of them brought to me at the convent, which I bought at three-fourths of a dollar each. The flesh is excellent, and has nearly the same flavour as that of the deer. The Bedouins make water-bags of their skins, and rings of their horns, which they wear on their thumbs. When the *beden* is met with in the plains, the dogs of the hunters easily catch him; but they cannot come up with him among the rocks, where he can make leaps of twenty feet."

386.—THE EFFICACY OF MORNING PRAYER.
Psalm v. 3.

⁋ The efficacy and especial obligation of *morning* prayer is continually dwelt on by Orientals. Thus in the Talmud, we read, "Every one that eateth and drinketh, and after that says his prayers, of him the Scripture saith, 'But Me thou hast cast behind thy back.'" And again, "It is forbidden to a man to go about his business before praying." So too the Koran, "Perform the prayer at the declining of the sun, at the first darkness of the night, and the prayer of day-break, *for the prayer of day-break is borne witness to.*" And so *Hafiz,* the great Persian lyric poet, addressing the beloved in mystical language, says, "In the *morning* hours be on thy guard (lest thou be compelled to hear) if this poor stranger make his complaint." Such instances might be multiplied almost without limit. The habit of going to prayer before taking food will explain the words of St. Peter on the day of Pentecost (Acts ii. 15); the disciples could not have eaten or drunk, for it was still the hour of morning prayer.

387.—THE HORN USED BY EASTERN WOMEN.
1 Sam. ii. 1.

¶ *Van Lennep* says, "The horn, worn almost from time immemorial by the women of Lebanon, both Christians and Muslims, as well as Druses, has lately almost disappeared; but a description of this curious and ancient head-dress will not be inappropriate. It consists of a hollow tube of silver, sometimes chased with gold, and adorned with precious stones, closed at the upper end, and somewhat trumpet-shaped at its base, where it is sewed to a little cushion, and set upon the top of the forehead. It inclines somewhat forward, and its base and cushion are fastened to what is called 'the bridge,' consisting of pieces of cloth, tightly bound together into a cord an inch thick, shaped like an arch; one end of this bridge is sewed to the cushion upon which is fastened the lower end of the horn, while the other end rests upon the crown of the head, having strong cords suspended from it, which hang down the back, and reach to the knees, with huge tassels of red silk weighted with lead. These tassels are a counter-poise to the horn, which would otherwise topple over in front. The whole thing is rendered firm and steady by a net-work of cords, which connect the two ends of the bridge, as well as the little cushion which supports the horn, and by a strong band fastened tightly under the jaws. Surely there can be no stronger example of the tyranny of fashion than this, which has, besides its inconvenience, been repeatedly known to injure particular organs. The veil is worn over the horn in such a manner as to leave its lower half uncovered in front. It is drawn over the face at pleasure, its drapery concealing all but one eye. Indeed the horn is never seen unveiled, even in the house. It is worn day and night, and, to relieve the wearer, a hole is made in the wall by the side of her bed, into which she inserts this incommodious appendage while she sleeps!"

As to the meaning of wearing the horn, Lennep says, "Our own opinion is, that this, in common with various other peculiar head-dresses put on at marriage, and worn during the remainder of life, has no reference whatever to the horns of animals, but is connected with the idea, very prevalent in the East, that the marriage ceremony constitutes the crowning of the virgin, who is thenceforth a queen. She is, indeed, so called in the liturgies of all the Oriental churches, and the head-dress she then puts on for the first time bears a resemblance in varying degrees to a crown."

388.—CHAINS ON PRISONERS.
Acts xxvi. 29.

℘ "To understand the force of this passage we must recollect the
Roman method of fettering and confining criminals. One end of a
chain that was of a commodious length was fixed about the right
arm of the prisoner, and the other end was fastened to the left of
a soldier (see chap. xii. 6). Fettered in this manner, St. Paul delivered his apology before Festus, Agrippa, and Bernice, and it was
this circumstance which occasioned one of the most pathetic and
affecting strokes of true oratory that was ever displayed, either in
the Grecian or Roman senate. What a prodigious effect must this
striking address and conclusion, and the sight of the irons held up
to enforce it, have had upon the minds of the audience!"—*Carpenter*.

389.—LEPROSY OF THE HOUSE AND OF GARMENTS.
Lev. xiii. 49; xiv. 34, 35.

℘ We are indebted to the Rev. Hugh Macmillan for some curious
and interesting information on the subject of leprosy: "A careful
examination of the Levitical narrative in the light of modern science leaves no room to doubt that the conclusions of Sommer,
Kurtz, and other recent authors, who attribute a *vegetable* origin
to the leprosy, are correct. The characteristics mentioned are such
as can belong only to plants. There are some species of fungi
which could have produced all the effects described, and whose
form and colour answer admirably to the appearances presented
by the leprosy. We are, therefore, safe in believing that the phenomena described in the above passages were caused by fungi.

"The leprosy of the house consisted of reddish and greenish
patches. The reddish patches on the wall were in all likelihood
caused by the presence of a fungus well known under the common
name of *dry-rot,* and called by botanists *Merulius lachrymans*.
Builders have often painful evidence of the virulent and destructive nature of this scourge. Most people are acquainted with the
effects of this fungus, but its form and appearance are familiar to
only a few. At first it makes its presence known by a few delicate
white threads which radiate from a common centre and resemble a
spider's web. Gradually these threads become thicker and closer,
coalescing more and more, until at last they form a dense cottony

388.—Chains on Prisoners.

cushion of yellowish-white colour and roundish shape. The size of this vegetable cushion varies from an inch to eight inches in diameter, according as it has room to develop itself, and is supplied with the appropriate pabulum. Hundreds of such sponge-like cushions may be seen in places infected by the disease oozing out through interstices in the floor or wall. At a later stage of growth the fungus developes over its whole surface a number of fine orange or reddish-brown veins, forming irregular folds, most frequently so arranged as to have the appearance of pores, and distilling, when perfect, drops of water, whence its specific name of *lachrymans,* or weeping. When fully matured, it produces an immense number of rusty seeds, so minute as to be invisible to the naked eye, which are diffused throughout the atmosphere, and are ever ready to alight and germinate in suitable circumstances."

By Jewish law notice of the appearance of this plague being given, the house was to be emptied and shut up, and seven days allowed for the true character of the spots to be manifested. If the disease was wide spread and deeply seated, then the corrupted and contagious matter had to be thoroughly cleansed away, and a free circulation of air secured through the house (Lev. xiv. 41–43). Dr. Thomson says that the upper rooms of the houses in Palestine, if not constantly ventilated, become quickly covered with mould, and are unfit to live in.

"In the Levitical narrative we read that in the walls of the affected houses there were *greenish* as well as reddish streaks. These greenish streaks were caused by a much humbler kind of fungus than the *Merulius lachrymans,* or dry-rot, concerned in the production of the reddish streaks. Every one is familiar with the common *green-mould,* or *Penicillium glaucum,* of botanists. This fungus is extremely abundant everywhere, and seems to have been no less general in the ancient world, for we find traces of it pretty frequently in amber, mixed with fragments of lichens and mosses. To the naked eye it is a mere greenish, downy crust, spreading over a decaying surface, but under the microscope it presents a singularly-lovely spectacle. The little patch of dusty cobweb is transformed into a fairy forest of the most exquisite shapes. Hundreds of delicate transparent stalks rise up from creeping, interlacing roots of snowy purity, crowned with bundles of slender hairs, each like a miniature painter's brush. Interspersed among these hairs, which, under a higher power of the microscope, are seen to be somewhat intricately branched, occur greenish, dust-like particles, which are the *sporidia,* or seed cases, containing in their interior the excessively-minute and impalpable spores or germs by which the species is perpetuated.

"The minute regulations for inspecting and cleansing those houses where symptoms of leprosy appeared indicate how complete was the sanitary system under which the ancient Israelites lived.

"The leprosy of *garments* may have been caused by the same fungi. Precisely the same appearances manifested themselves in the one case as in the other. The greenish streaks on the garments may be attributed to the common green mould which grows as readily on clothes as on house walls when left in damp, ill-ventilated, ill-lighted places. The reddish patches may, however, have been produced by the growth of the *Sporendo-nema,* or *red mould,* very common on cheese; or of the *Palmella prodigiosa.* This last-mentioned plant is occasionally found on damp walls in shady places, and on various articles of dress and food. It is usually a gelatinous mass, of the colour and general appearance of coagulated blood, whence it has received the famous name of *Gory-dew.*

"Instances of reddish patches suddenly investing linen and woollen clothes are by no means confined to the Levitical narrative. A whole volume might be filled with similar examples. One instance may suffice. Before the potato blight broke out in 1846, red-mould spots appeared on wet linen surfaces exposed to the air in bleaching-greens, as well as on household linen kept in damp places in Ireland. In ordinary times but few of the fungi are produced, but heir seeds lie around us in immense profusion, waiting but the recurrence of suitable atmospheric conditions to exhibit an extraordinary development."

390.—THE BANDS OF ORION.
Job xxxviii. 31.

ℂ According to the Greek mythology, Orion was a mighty hunter. The Orientals imagined him to be a huge giant, who had warred against God, and was, therefore, bound in chains to the firmament of heaven. The constellation called by his name is therefore supposed to figure a man in hunter's garb. "It is com-

posed of four very bright stars, forming a quadrilateral, higher
than it is broad, with three equi-distant stars in a diagonal line in
the middle. The two upper stars, called Betelgeux and Bellatrix,
form the shoulders; in the middle, immediately above these, are
three small, dim stars, close to each other, forming the cheek or
head. The feet are composed of two very bright stars, called Rigel
and Saiph; the three stars in the middle are called the belt or girdle, and from them depends a stripe of smaller stars, forming the
hunter's sword. The whole constellation, containing seventeen stars
to the naked eye, but exhibiting seventy-eight in an ordinary tele-
scope, occupies a large and conspicuous position in the southern
heavens, below the Pleiades." The point of the reference to the
"Bands of Orion" appears to be this—the three bright stars which
constitute the girdle or *bands* of Orion never change their form:
they preserve the same relative position to each other, and to the
rest of the constellations, from year to year, and from age to age.
They afford, therefore, one of the most striking types of immu-
tability in the midst of ceaseless changes.

391.—ANCIENT CAVES STILL USED AS DWELLINGS.
Job xxx. 5, 6.

⟪ A modern traveller among the Arab tribes describes "Anab as
still inhabited by about one hundred persons; but these all live in
grottoes or caves excavated in the rocks, which are probably more
ancient than any buildings now existing. Their preservation, however, offers the strongest proof that the very earliest of their occupiers must have been men of the ordinary size of the present
generation, and not giants. The size of the caves now inhabited
here, and which are, undoubtedly, of very high antiquity, confirm
the opinion that their original occupiers were of the same size as
their present possessors. These are chiefly shepherds, whose flocks
browse on the steep sides of the hills near them, and who, in the
severe nights of winter, take shelter in the caves, with their attendants. Some of the inhabitants of the caves are, however, cultivators
of the earth, and till and plant such detached plots and patches of
the soil, among the least steep parts of the ascent, as may be most
favourable for the fruits or grain. The grottoes themselves are all
hewn out by the hand of man, and are not natural caverns; but

from their great antiquity, and the manner in which they were originally executed, they have a very rude appearance. Nevertheless, the persons who occupy them fortunately deem them far superior to buildings of masonry, and consider themselves better off than those who live in tents or houses, so that they envy not the dwellers in camps or cities. They are certainly more durable and less likely to need repair, and with the exception of a chimney, or some aperture to give an outlet to the smoke (a defect existing in all the buildings of these parts), they are very comfortable retreats, being drier and more completely sheltered from wind and rain than either house or tent, besides being warmer in winter and cooler in summer than any other kind of dwelling-place that could be adopted."

392.—MEDICINAL USE OF SALIVA.
Mark vii. 31–37.

℘ *Saliva jejuna* was supposed by the ancients to possess general curative properties, and to be especially efficacious in ophthalmia, and other inflammatory diseases of the eyes. Pliny, in his *Natural History,* speaks of this therapeutic virtue in high terms, and both Tacitus and Suetonius record the case of a blind man who was supposed to have been cured of his blindness by the Emperor Vespasian, through the application of an eye-salve, made of spittle. We cannot suppose that our Lord used it because of its medicinal value. His was wholly a symbolical action, indicating that as it was the man's tongue that was bound, so the moisture of the tongue was to be the sign of its unloosing, and the means by which it would be enabled to move freely in the mouth, and to articulate words.

Trench, writing on this miracle, says: It is not "hard to perceive why He should especially have spat, etc., in the case of one so afflicted as this man was; almost all other avenues of communication, save by sight and feeling, were of necessity closed. Christ, by these signs, would awaken his faith, and stir up in him the lively expectation of a blessing. The fingers are put into the ears as to bore them, to pierce through the obstacles which hindered sounds from reaching them. Then, as it is often through excessive drought, that the tongue cleaves to the roof of the mouth, so the Lord gives here, in what secondly He does, the sign of the removal of this evil by the unloosing of the tongue."

393.—That Woman Jezebel.
Rev. ii. 20.

⁋ "Outside the walls of Thyatira stood a small temple dedicated to a sibyl, a woman who was supposed to have the gift of prophecy. This temple or church was in the midst of an enclosure called the 'Chaldaean's Court,' and the sibyl, who was called *Sanbethe,* is sometimes said to be Jewish, sometimes Chaldaean, and sometimes Persian. The inference to be drawn from this is, that some corrupted Jews of the disputed tribes had introduced from Chaldaea or Persia a religion which was a mixture of Judaism and heathenism.

"It is not improbable that this Sanbethe, or her school, had at Thyatira a place dedicated to the promulgation of a religion which was an admixture of Orientalism and Judaism, with some importations from the Greek and Roman rites, and even with some kind of appropriation of Christian ideas, forming altogether a system similar to those which the various sects of the Gnostics soon afterwards held. And this supposition being correct, it is then easy to see how Jewish Christians of the Church of Thyatira might be affected with this heresy, and not offer to it the opposition which it ought to have received from a Christian community. This would explain the charge against the angel of the Thyatiran Church: 'I have a few things against thee, because thou sufferest that woman Jezebel, who calleth herself a prophetess, to teach and seduce my servants to commit fornication, and to eat things offered to idols.' "—*R. V.*

394.—Sealing Prisons, Tombs, etc.
Daniel vi. 17.

⁋ Not letters or documents only were, in ancient times, sealed with a seal. "Whatever was intended not to be opened was guarded by this species of talisman. The ancient Egyptians sealed the doors of the tombs of their ancestors, whom they venerated to a degree equalled only by the modern Chinese. Many of these stamps in clay have been found in modern researches. The Jews, who believed in the immortality of the soul and the resurrection of the body, guarded the tombs of their dead with the same jealous care as the modern Orientals, and they doubtless sometimes sealed them with a signet, as was done in the case of our Lord. The

sealing of the mouth of the lion's den, into which the Prophet
Daniel was cast, still further explains the purpose of such an act,
and shows that the custom extended to Chaldaea. At the present
day, when an Oriental dies, his property is sealed by the authorities, and the seal is not removed until the judge is ready to divide
the inheritance. Bags of money are sent by private or public post,
with the simple precaution of stamping them with the owner's seal,
which none but highway robbers dare to violate."

395.—PRE-CHRISTIAN TRACES
OF DEATH BY CRUCIFIXION.
Gal. iii. 13.

¶ *Dr. Zoeckler* has collected valuable information concerning the
practice of impalement or crucifixion, and the sentiments associated with it. "For the extraordinarily wide-spread, yea, almost
unlimited prevalence of the punishment of the cross in the widest
sense, among the better-known pre-Christian peoples, evidence is
afforded by the, to a large extent, well-supported ancient accounts
which attest it. For the Indians there are those referring to a time
so early as that of the conquests of Semiramis, who (in *Diodorus*
ii. 18) scornfully threatens the Indian king, Stabrobates, with a
nailing to the cross; for the Turanian people of the Scythians, to
the north of Media, those referring to a period six hundred years
before Christ, at the time of the Median King, Cyaxares: as concerns the Medes and Persians, there are those vouching for its existence among them under the kings of the line of Achaemenides,
in the sixth and fifth centuries; for the people of Magna Graecia,
its presence is attested in Sicily at the time of the Elder Dionysius,
of Syracuse, about the year B.C. 400, and often after that time; for
the Macedonians, under Alexander the Great and his successors;
even for the ancient Britons and the Frieslanders, whose custom,
attested by Tacitus, for the first century of our era, of hanging
their captives upon crosses or gibbets, unquestionably points back
to an existence thereof in earlier ages. As concerns the Romans,
crucifixions in the wider sense present themselves even in the history of their kings. The account in Livy, given in connection with
the history of the Horatii, of a hanging upon a 'tree of ill omen,'
no doubt refers to one which was effected by means of a cord, not

by nailing, but, nevertheless, implies clearly enough an execution
bearing the character of a punishment on the gallows—a shameful
death by hanging. And as it reminds of the 'hanging upon the tree'
of the Old Testament, so, also, does the proceeding of Tarquinius
Priscus, of which Pliny bears testimony, who, in the construction
of the Cloaca Maxima, caused the bodies of those who had committed suicide in order to escape the labour imposed upon them to
be attached to the cross as a warning to other labourers, in some
degree resemble the ancient Hebrew custom. In its later prevailing
form, as an execution carried out mainly upon slaves and of those
guilty of the graver offences—such as mutinous soldiers, subjects
taken in revolt, highway robbers, etc., but never upon Roman citizens—crucifixion amongst the Romans declares with sufficient
clearness its Punic origin, as a custom which had extended to them
by virtue of the commercial relations with Carthage during the
first ages of the republic. And it is precisely this Roman custom of
crucifixion, adopted from the Carthaginians, which first brings out
with great distinctness the use of the four-armed cross, † properly
so called, to which we thus owe the idea and name of that which
we now term crucifixion in the narrower sense."

396.—BLASTING AND MILDEW.
Haggai ii. 17.

⁋ These scourges were very frequent in Bible lands and times,
and were generally regarded not merely as a visitation of God, but
even as a special product of God's creative power. Modern science
has shown that blasting and mildew are produced by *plants*—they
are the diseases occasioned by the growth of minute *fungi*. These
vegetable parasites appear in greater or less abundance every year:
they take a great variety of forms; are oftentimes exceedingly
beautiful both in form and in colour; and accomplish important
service in the economy of nature; the functions of vegetable nature are reversed in them, their pores inhale oxygen, and exhale
carbonic gas, like animals.

Rev. Hugh Macmillan gives a careful account of the four diseases in corn produced by fungi, and known in this country as
smut, bunt, rust, and *mildew*.

"About the beginning of July, when the ear is protruding
through the sheath, a black head may be noticed among the green

ones, covered with a soot-like dust, which comes away freely, and stains the hands. This is known as smut, or dust-brand. Under the microscope the black powder is found to consist of a collection of spores, or round seed-cases, containing sporules or seeds in their interior. It is, therefore, a parasitic plant—a true fungus, capable of reproducing and extending itself indefinitely. Botanists have given it the name of *Ustilago sequetum.* When germinating, this fungus first attacks the interior portions of the flower, and renders them abortive. It then seizes upon the little stalks of the florets, and causes them to swell and become fleshy. At length it consumes all the reproductive organs, and converts the whole nutritious grain into vile dust and ashes.

"Another species of 'blasting' is known as *bunt.* Botanists call it *Ustilago foetida,* on account of the intolerable odour, like that of putrid fish, which it exhales. It confines its ravages entirely to the grain. Externally, the infected ear presents no abnormal appearance. The infected ears continue growing, and appear even plumper, and of a richer and darker green, than the sound ones. The very stigmata of the flowers remain unaltered to the last. Stealthily and secretly the process of poisoning is accomplished; and not, in many cases, till the harvest is reaped and the wheat ground for flour, is the discovery made, by the odour and colour, that the produce is unfit for human food. Under this external mask of health all fecundation is rendered impossible; there is no development of the parts of fructification; no embryo whatever can be detected; the whole interior of the seed when broken or bruised is found to be filled with a black, foetid powder, which contains, on chemical analysis, an acrid oil, putrid gluten, charcoal, phosphoric acid, phosphate of ammonia, and magnesia, but no traces of starch, the essential ingredient in human food. Under a high power of the microscope, this powder consists of a mass of round spores or seed-vessels, considerably larger than those of smut; and instead of being plain and smooth, as in that species, their surface is beautifully reticulated. They are also mixed with a number of delicate branched threads, called the mycelium or spawn. The seeds contained in the spore-cases are of a greasy, oily nature, and consequently adhere to the skin of the sound grains, so that the disease may be propagated at any time by inoculation or contagion.

"Another species is known as *rust,* or *red-robin;* botanists call it *Trichobasis rubigo-vera.* It is found upon the wheat plant at all stages of growth. Early in the spring it attacks the young blades; later in the season it breaks out on the glumes and paleae of the ear, even after the grain is formed. So long as it is confined to the leaf, it is comparatively harmless. In appearance the corn rust is a mere patch of reddish-yellow powder, bursting like an eruption through the skin of the leaves and culms of the growing corn.

"The fourth species of blight is *mildew*. By the Hebrews this term was employed in the most general sense, to designate all the diseases of vegetables caused by fungi, and often included very different plants. The term should, however, be restricted to that disease of corn which is caused by the fungus known to botanists as the *Puccinia graminis*. It is derived from the Saxon words, *Mehl-thau,* meaning *meal-dew.* It makes its appearance in the corn-fields in May or June, and first takes possession of the lower green leaves, which become sickly, and break out through the skin round them in blisters, into rusty patches, as though the corn-stalk had been powdered with red ochre. It is like rust at first, but when the corn is nearly or fully ripe, the straw and the culm are profusely streaked with blackish spots, ranging in length from a minute dot to an inch. Its effect seems to be to intercept the sap intended to nourish the grain, which, consequently becomes shrivelled and deficient in nutritive matter, yielding a super-abundance of inferior bran."

397.—THE EXCEEDING VALUE OF WISDOM.
Prov. iv. 7.

❧ Hillel had a wise disciple whose name was Maimon. In natural gifts he greatly delighted. But soon Hillel perceived that his youthful friend trusted too much in his own wisdom, and wholly discarded the aid of prayer. The youth said in his heart, "Why should we pray? Does the Almighty need our words in order to aid and bless us? Then He is human. Can man's sighs and petitions change the counsels of the Eternal? Will not the All-merciful of Himself bestow what is good and needful?" Such were the young man's thoughts. But Hillel was grieved in his soul that Maimon considered himself wiser than the Divine Word, and he determined to reprove him. One day when Maimon went to Hillel, he found him sitting in his garden, leaning his head upon his hand, and he said, "Master, where are thy thoughts?" Then Hillel raised his head and answered in these words, "I have a friend who lives upon the produce of his lands, which until now he has cultivated with care, and has been richly rewarded for his pains. But now he has thrown aside plough and mattock, and no more cultivates his field. Thus he will soon come to poverty, and lack the necessaries of life." "Has a spirit of ill-humour seized him, or has he become a fool?" asked the youth. "Neither," answered Hillel; "he is well skilled in all human and sacred wisdom. But he says, the Lord is almighty, so that He can easily supply my wants without my bending my head to labour. He is good, so that He will open His kind hand to bless my table. And how can it be contradicted?" "How?" said the youth; "is it not tempting the Lord God? Hast thou not told him so, master?" Then Hillel smiled, and said, "I will do so now. Thou, my beloved Maimon, art the friend of whom I spake." "I!" said the youth, in amazement. "Ay," said the old man; "dost thou not tempt the Lord? Is prayer less than labour? and are spiritual gifts less than the fruits of the field? And is He who commands thee to labour for earthly goods other than He who bids thee to raise thy heart to heaven to implore heavenly blessings? O my son, be humble, believe and pray!" So spake Hillel, and Maimon went away to pray, and henceforth his life was a godly one.

398.—PHYSICAL QUALITIES SOUGHT IN A CHIEF.
1 Sam. xvi. 7.

ℂ The prevalence of the feeling of regard for personal bulk and stature is seen in the sculptures of ancient Egypt, Assyria, and Persia, and even in the modern paintings of the last-named nation, in which the sovereign is invested with gigantic proportions in comparison with the persons around him. . . . . . It appears to have been usual with the ancient Orientals, as well as with the Greeks and Romans, to choose persons to the highest offices of the magistracy, whose personal appearance was superior to that of others; and this is what ancient writers often take notice of as a recommendation of them in princes. Herodotus, after recounting the numbers of men in the army of Xerxes, makes the remark that among this vast host there was not one who appeared by his comeliness and stature more worthy than he to fill the throne. The same writer also informs us that the Ethiopians deemed the man who was strongest and tallest of stature fittest to be their king. In Virgil, Turnus is another Saul in the superiority of his person to others, whom he by a whole head overtops. It is not surprising

that, as Quintus Curtius remarks, barbarians made part of the
royal majesty consist in the outward form and goodly figure of
their princes; but it does excite some surprise to hear a man so
cultivated and refined as Pliny the younger naming qualities of
this sort among those which entitled his hero, Trajan, to the
supreme rank to which he had been elevated. There is a curious
passage in Homer, where, in order to secure greater respect for
Ulysses from the Phaeacians, upon whose island he was cast,—

> *"Pallas o'er his head and shoulders broad*
> *Diffusing grace celestial, his whole form*
> *Dilated, and to statelier height advanced,*
> *That worthier of all reverence he might seem*
> *To the Phaeacians."*—Odyssey, viii., 20, 24.

He had been before announced as—

> *"A wanderer o'er the deep,*
> *But in his form majestic as a god."*

This latter intimation lets us into the secret of the extraordinary
estimation of stature in ancient times among, at least, the Gentiles.
They had a notion that such persons came nearer to the deities,
and looked more like them. So Diana is described in Ovid as superior in stature to the nymphs and inferior goddesses by whom she
is surrounded.—*Kitto.*

399.—THOSE FEEBLE FOLK, THE CONEYS.
Prov. xxx. 26.

❡ The creature named the *Coney* in Scripture is called the *Wabar*
by the Arabs, and the *Hyrax Syriacus* by naturalists, and it has
been seen by recent Eastern travellers, and described by them. Dr.
Wilson thus describes his discovery of these very interesting little
creatures. "When we were exploring the rocks in the neighbourhood of the Convent of Mar Saba, I was delighted to point attention to a family or two of the *Wabar*, engaged in their gambols
on the heights above us. Mr. Smith and I watched them narrowly,
and were much amused with the liveliness of their motions, and
the quickness of their retreat within the clefts of the rocks when
they apprehended danger. We were, we believe, the first European
travellers who actually noticed this animal (now universally admitted to be the *Shaphan,* or coney, of Scripture) within the proper
bounds of the Holy Land; and we were not a little gratified by its

discovery. . . . . We climbed up to see its nest, which was a hole in the rock comfortably lined with moss and feathers, answering to the description given of the coney. The specimen thus obtained, when stuffed, I have had an opportunity of examining in England. The preparer of the skin mistook it for a rabbit, though it is of stronger build, and of a duskier colour, being of a dark brown. It is entirely destitute of a tail, and has some bristles at its mouth, over its head, and down its back, along the course of which there are traces of light and dark shade. In its short ears, small, black, and naked feet, and pointed snout, it resembles the hedgehog."

Though in external form this little animal resembles the *Rodentia,* it really belongs structurally to a very different order, the *Pachydermata,* which comprises the elephant, rhinoceros, hippopotamus, etc. Its dental system almost exactly agrees with that of these animals, and its skeleton might easily be mistaken for that of a rhinoceros in miniature.

400.—CALL THE POOR.
Luke xiv. 13.

℘ Pococke informs us that an Arab prince will often dine before his door, and call to all that pass, even to beggars, in the name of God, and they come and sit down to table, and when they have done retire with the usual form of returning thanks. It is always customary among the Orientals to provide more meats and drinks than are necessary for the feast; and then, the poor who pass by, or whom the rumour of the feast brings to the neighbourhood, are called in to consume what remains. This they often do in an outer room, to which the dishes are removed from the apartment in which the invited guests have feasted; or otherwise, every invited guest, when he has done, withdraws from the table, and his place is taken by another person of inferior rank, and so on, till the poorest come and consume the whole. The former of these modes, however, is the most common.

401.—ALL THINGS COMMON.
Acts iv. 32.

℘ The same fact is recorded in chap. ii. 44, 45. The expressions are too strong to permit us to suppose that all that is meant is

merely that the disciples were extremely generous and liberal—
that they gave freely of their substance. There was, in some sense,
an actual community of goods. Yet we must not suppose that all
property ceased among the Christians; that they sold all their possessions and goods, and placed them in a common fund, out of
which all were supported. The words certainly at first sight would
seem to imply as much; but there are several considerations which
render such a meaning improbable.

1. This community of goods, whatever is meant by it, was entirely confined to Jerusalem. There is no trace of it elsewhere. 2. It
does not seem to have continued long in Jerusalem. It was instituted to meet existing emergencies, when the Church was poor,
weak, and feeble; and when the circumstances of the case were altered it was abandoned. 3. This community of goods was perfectly
voluntary on the part of the disciples. There was no law in the
Church, no apostolic injunction, which bound believers to sell
their lands, and to place their money in a common fund (Acts v.
4). This community of goods was not a matter of law, but of love.
4. It does not appear that this community of goods was a universal
custom, so that all the disciples (not of constraint, but voluntarily)
disposed of their possessions, and put the proceeds into one common fund. If this had been the case, the goods of the Church
would soon have been consumed; nor would the instance of Barnabas have been adduced as anything remarkable. We read, also,
afterwards of Mary, the mother of Mark, possessing a house in
Jerusalem (Acts xii. 12).

But although not a universal custom, yet it was probably pretty
general. Many, though not all, actuated by a spirit of love which
impelled them to regard the necessities of their brethren as their
own, sold their houses and possessions, and put the money in a
common fund, which was placed at the disposal of the Apostles.
Out of this fund the wants of the poor were supplied; there was a
daily distribution to the widows (chap. vi. 1); there were none
among the disciples that lacked (chap. iv. 34). Perhaps, also, the
expenses of the *agapae* (love-feasts) were defrayed out of it, for
we find that afterwards it was the custom of the rich to bring of
their provisions to supply the wants of their poorer brethren. Thus,
in the first glow of Christian life, the disciples put into actual practice the precept of our Lord, Luke xii. 33.

In every age of the Church there have been imitations of this
community of goods, such as the various orders of monks, the

mendicant friars, etc.; but they have all failed, because they interpreted that as an institution of permanent and universal obligation,
which was only designed to meet a present emergency; and because, moreover, they attempted to regulate by law that which, to
succeed at all, must proceed from, and be dictated by, voluntary
love. But although the external practice of community of goods is
by no means to be imitated, yet the spirit of love which gave rise
to it is to be imbibed. Like these early Christians we should regard
our possessions as not our own, but as given us by God, to be employed in the service and for the good of our brethren.—*Dr.
Gloag.*

402.—THORNS A PART OF THE CURSE ON MAN.
Gen. iii. 18.

℃ Rev. Hugh Macmillan says, "It is a remarkable circumstance
that whenever man cultivates Nature, and then abandons her to
her own unaided energies, the result is far worse than if he had
never attempted to improve her at all. There are no such thorns
found in a state of nature as those produced by the ground which
man has once tilled, but has now deserted. In the waste clearings
amid the fern brakes of New Zealand, and in the primeval forests
of Canada, thorns may now be seen which were unknown there
before. The nettle and the thistle follow man wherever he goes,
and remain as perpetual witnesses of his presence, even though he
departs; and around the cold hearthstone of the ruined shieling on
the Highland moor, and on the threshold of the crumbling log-hut
in the Australian bush, these social plants may be seen growing,
forming a singular contrast to the vegetation around them."

No country in the world, now that it has been so long let out of
cultivation, has such a variety and abundance of thorny plants, as
the once favoured heritage of God's people, the land flowing with
milk and honey. Travellers call the Holy Land "a land of thorns."
Giant thistles, growing to the height of a man on horseback, frequently spread over regions once rich and fruitful, as they do on
the pampas of South America; and many of the most interesting
historic spots and ruins are rendered almost inaccessible by
thickets of fiercely-armed buckthorns. Entire fields are covered
with the troublesome creeping stems of the spinous *Ononis* or rest-
harrow, while the bare hillsides are studded with the dangerous

capsules of the *Paliurus* and *Tribulus*. Roses of the most prickly
kinds abound on the lower slopes of Hermon; while the sub-
tropical valleys of Judaea are choked up in many places by the
thorny *Lycium,* whose lilac flowers and scarlet fruit cannot be
plucked, owing to erect branches armed at all points with spines.
The feathery trees of the *Zizyphus spina Christi,* or Christ's thorn,
that fringe the banks of the Jordan, and flourish on the marshy
borders of the Lake of Gennesaret, are beautiful to look at, but
terrible to handle, concealing as they do, under each of the small
delicately formed leaves of a brilliant green, a thorn curved like a
fish-hook, which grasps and tears everything that touches it. Dr.
Tristram mentions, that in passing through thorny thickets near
Jericho, the clothes of his whole party were torn to rags . . . In
short, thorny plants, the evidences of a degenerate flora, and of
deteriorated physical conditions, now form the most conspicuous
vegetation of Palestine, and supply abundant mournful proof of
the literal fulfilment of prophecy. "Upon the land of my people
shall come up thorns and briers; yea, upon all the houses of joy in
the joyous city."

403.—THE DAY OF PENTECOST.
Acts ii. 1.

⁋ The time of the festival was calculated from the second day of
the Passover, the 16th of Nisan. The fifty days formally included
the period of grain-harvest, commencing with the offering of the
first sheaf of the barley-harvest in the Passover, and ending with
that of the two first loaves which were made from the wheat-
harvest of this festival. It was the offering of these two loaves
which was the distinguishing rite of the day of Pentecost. They
were to be leavened. Each loaf was to contain the tenth part of an
ephah (*i.e.,* about three and a half quarts) of the finest wheat
flour of the new crop. The loaves, along with a peace-offering of
two lambs of the first year, were to be waved before the Lord, and
given to the priests . . . The question on what day of the week
this Pentecost fell must, of course, be determined by the mode in
which the doubt is solved regarding the day on which the Last
Supper was eaten. If the Supper was eaten on the thirteenth, and
our Lord crucified on the fourteenth, Pentecost must have occurred on the first day of the week.

404.—A STORY LIKE THAT OF JONAH.
Jonah i. 17.

℃ A story is told by Herodotus, the "Father of History," which bears a striking likeness to that connected with the name of the prophet Jonah. If the history of it could be traced, it might be discovered that both had the same original. Somewhat abridged it is as follows:—"Arion, the Mithymnaean, who, in the days of Periander, King of Corinth, resided for some time in that city, is said to have been carried to Taenarus on the back of a dolphin. He went to Italy, and there acquired a large fortune, apparently by the exercise of his unrivalled talents as a harpist. Wishing to return to Corinth with his wealth, he embarked at Tarentum in a Corinthian vessel; but as soon as they were out at sea, the sailors determined to murder him for the sake of his money. Perceiving their intention, he offered them all he had to save his life, but the men were determined to be rid of him. Reduced to extremity, he entreated that they would at least allow him to put on his most valuable dress, and also permit him to give them a specimen of his musical powers, promising that as soon as he had finished he would destroy himself. They complied, retiring to the centre of the ship while he made his arrangements. Having dressed to his taste, Arion stood with his harp upon the side of the vessel, where he sang them a quick, spirited song, and then leaped into the sea. The ship pursued her course to Corinth, but Arion, so the fable relates, was taken up by a dolphin, and carried on its back to Taenarus. He hastened away at once to Corinth, and told his strange adventure to Periander, who would not believe him until he was confronted by the sailors with whom he had sailed, who, when they saw him, confessed their crime."

405.—THE SKILFUL QUESTION OF THE SANHEDRIM.
Acts iv. 7.

℃ More literally, "In what sort of power, or in what sort of name, did you do this?"—an interrogation so framed as to entangle them, if possible, into an admission which should criminate themselves. To understand its phraseology it must be remembered that at that time, as for long before, there existed a numerous class (among Jews not less numerous than among Gentiles) who pretended by magical formulae, and the invocation of names of more than mortal might, to expel demons, cure diseases, or in other ways to change the course of nature. Such practices had been branded by the Mosaic law as profane, and made punishable by death (Exod. xxii. 18; Lev. xix. 26, etc.), but they were never extirpated from Jewish soil. It is in this light that we must read the question of the Sanhedrim. A wonder is confessed. The doers of it are assumed to have done it in some ghostly "power," or by the charm of some compelling "name;" and they are adjured to say in what sort of "name" or "power," divine or magical, good or evil. Of course it is not obtruded on their attention that by virute of the old Mosaic statute they might be stoned to death if they confessed to having used any other name than that of Jehovah; but equally, of course, this fact was present to their own recollection not less than to the mind of the examiners. It was, if the court chose to make it such, a question of life and death.

Hence the courage of Peter's reply is to be estimated by the double danger which he ran. By avowing that in the name of Jesus, and not nominally in that of "Jehovah," the cure had been effected, he ran the risk of being condemned for sorcery. By preaching to their face the resurrection of Jesus, or the authentication of His Divine power, he braved the strongest and most implacable party in the court. He shrank from neither danger.— *Dykes*.

406.—WHERE SATAN'S SEAT IS.
Rev. ii. 13.

⁋ "The tutelary deity of Pergamos was Aesculapius, the god of healing. He was honoured by the name of 'Saviour,' and his characteristic emblem was the serpent. There is a legend to the effect that, on one occasion, he was in the house of Glaucus, whom he was to cure, and while he was standing absorbed in thought, a serpent entered, and twined around his staff. He having killed this, another serpent came in, carrying in its mouth a herb with which it recalled to life the one that had been killed. And, the story says, Aesculapius henceforth made use of that same herb with the same effect upon man. This was the explanation given of the fact that serpents were everywhere connected with the worship of this deity. Not only was a peculiar kind of tame serpent kept in his

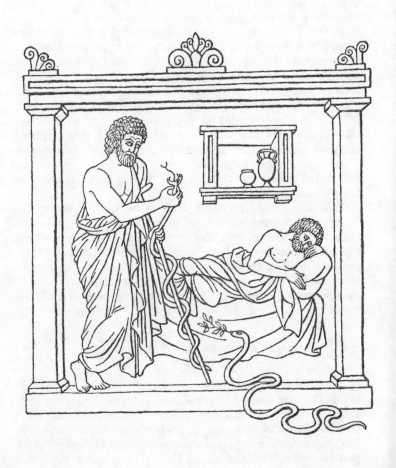

406.—Where Satan's Seat Is.

temple, but the god himself was frequently represented in the form of a serpent. Probably, however, this prominence of the serpent in the worship of the god of health was because it was a symbol of prudence and renovation. The worship of this deity was prominent in Pergamos at the time when John addressed the epistle to the Christian church there. The symbol of the wreathed serpent must have been an object with which the Christians of Pergamos were familiar. As the peculiar emblem of a worship full of lying pretensions and deceptive practices, it would naturally suggest the Jewish and Christian idea of the serpent, the father of lies. This, together with the fact that the city was a sort of focus of idolatrous worship, would render the description of it as the place 'where Satan's throne is' most appropriate."—*R. V.*

407.—CURSING THE DAY.
Job iii. 8.

⁋ The translation of this passage is wrong, so far as the second clause is concerned, though the margin of our Bibles gives the word 'leviathan' instead of 'mourning.' Rendered literally the text would run—"Let the curse of the day curse *it*—they who are skilled to raise up leviathan." Leviathan is the dragon, an astro-mythological being, which has its place in the heavens. Whether it be the constellation still known by the name "draco," or dragon, or whether it be serpens, or hydra, constellations lying further south, it is not possible to decide. But the dragon, in ancient popular opinion, had the power to follow the sun and moon, to enfold, or even to swallow them, and thus cause night. Eastern magicians pretended to possess the power of rousing up the dragon to make war upon the sun and moon. Whenever they wished for darkness they had but to curse the day, and hound on the dragon to extinguish for a time the lamp that enlightened the world. Job, in his bitterness, curses the day of his birth, and utters the wish that those who control leviathan would, or could, blot that day and its deeds from the page of history.

408.—TRADITION CONCERNING THE WOMAN
WHO TOUCHED CHRIST'S GARMENT.
Matthew ix. 20–22.

⁋ A curious tradition is preserved by Eusebius connecting the city of Caesarea Philippi with the woman of faith, who was cured of her inveterate disease by touching the border of Jesus' garment. The words of the early historian are:—"But, as we have mentioned this city, I do not think it right to pass by a narrative that deserves to be recorded for posterity. They say, that the woman who had an issue of blood, mentioned by the Evangelists, and who obtained deliverance from her affliction by our Saviour, was a native of this place, and that her house is shown in the city, and the wonderful monuments of our Saviour's benefit to her are still remaining. At the gates of her house, on an elevated stone, stands a brazen image of a woman on her bended knee, with her hands stretched out before her, like one entreating. Opposite to this there is another image of a man erect, of the same materials, decently clad in a mantle, and stretching out his hand to the woman. Before her feet, and on the same pedestal, there is a certain strange plant growing, which, rising as high as the hem of the brazen garment, is a kind of antidote to all kinds of diseases. This figure, they say, is a statue of Jesus Christ, and it has remained even until our times, so that we ourselves saw it whilst tarrying in that city."

409.—CUSTOM OF PRAISING THE RETURNING CONQUERORS.
1 Sam. xviii. 6, 7.

¶ This is quite characteristic of the manners of the East. Everywhere in that part of the world the people are accustomed in this manner to hail the arrival of those who have been any time absent from them. More especially do they do so on the return of a victorious army. Multitudes then issue from the towns and villages through which they are expected to march, in order to form a triumphal procession to celebrate their valour; the principal part being composed of women and children who band together, and, as they go along, gratify the heroes with dancing, music, and songs in honour of their martial deeds, particularly of such of the chiefs as have greatly distinguished themselves. We find this custom in Persia, Turkey, etc. Mr. Campbell, the missionary, witnessed it even in Africa. When he was leaving the city of Lattakoo, he fell in with a party of men who were returning from a distant expedition, after an absence of several months. The news of their approach had reached the town, and the women were hastening to meet them. On joining the party the females marched at their

head, clapping their hands and singing with all their might, till
they arrived at their homes in the town.

410.—NO BALM IN GILEAD.*
Jer. viii. 22.

⚏ "The word *treacle* is derived from the Greek word *therion,*
which primarily meant a wild beast of any kind, but was afterwards more especially applied to animals which had a venomous
bite. By many Greek writers the term was used to denote a serpent
or viper specifically. In this sense it is employed in the last chapter
of the Acts of the Apostles, where we are told that 'when Paul had
gathered a bundle of sticks, and laid them on the fire, there came
a viper out of the heat and fastened on his hand. And when the
barbarians saw the venomous beast hang on his hand, they said
among themselves, No doubt this man is a murderer, whom,
though he hath escaped the sea, yet vengeance suffereth not to
live. And he shook off the beast into the fire, and felt no harm.'
The Greek word translated *beast* in the fourth and fifth verses is
therion; and though the word rendered *viper* in the preceding
verse is different, being *echidna,* it nevertheless specialises the
meaning of *therion,* and proves that it refers to this species of serpent. But what connection, it may well be asked, can there be between a viper and treacle? How came such a sweet substance to
have such a venomous origin? Here we are introduced, in the way
of explanation, to one of those strange superstitions that were exceedingly common in ancient times, when little else but foolish
marvels filled the pages of natural history. It was a popular belief
at one time that the bite of the viper could only be cured by the
application to the wound of a piece of the viper's flesh, or a decoc-
tion called *viper's wine,* or *Venice treacle,* made by boiling the
flesh in some fluid or other. Galen, the celebrated Greek physician
of Pergamos, who lived in the second century, describes the custom as very prevalent in his time. At Aquileia, under the patronage of the Emperor Marcus Aurelius, he prepared a system of
pharmacy, which he published under the name of *Theriaca,* in allusion to this superstition. The name given to the extraordinary
electuary of viper's flesh was *theriakē,* from *therion,* a viper. By

---

* In old version no *treacle.*

the usual process of alteration which takes place in the course of a few generations, in words that are commonly used, *theriakē* became *theriac*. Then it was transformed into the diminutive *theriacle*, afterwards *triacle*, in which form it was used by Chaucer. (Chaucer says of our Lord, 'Christ, which that is to every harm triacle'); and finally it assumed its present mode of spelling as early as the time of Milton and Waller. It changed its meaning and application with its various changes of form, signifying first the confection of the viper's flesh applied to the wound inflicted by the viper's sting; then any antidote, whatever might be its nature, or whatever might be the origin of the evil it was intended to cure. Afterwards medical prescriptions came to be prepared in some vehicle intended to cover their nauseous taste, or disagreeable look; and this vehicle was generally some kind of sweet syrup or sugary confection to which the name of *treacle* was applied. When the viscous substance known as 'molasses' was imported from the West Indies, it formed a welcome addition to the old limited list of vehicles for medicine; and so completely did it usurp the name of treacle, that very few are aware that the word ever had any other meaning or application."

The above interesting and curious information has been taken from Hugh Macmillan's *Ministry of Nature*.

411.—THE ROSE OF SHARON.
Song Sol. ii. 1.

¶ The wild rose grows in abundance all over Western Asia, and the cultivated species are very abundant and varied, but it is now generally admitted that the flower referred to in the above passage is not the rose, but one coming from a bulbous root. The varieties of bulbous plants are not numerous, and if we except the tulips and their cognates, they all offer but little attraction to an Eastern mind, on account of the paleness of their tints. Exceptions, however, may be made in favour of the hyacinth and the narcissus, both of which are attractive by reason of their beauty and perfume. Some versions use the word "narcissus" in the above passage, and this is probably the more correct translation.

412.—NINE HEBREW WORDS FOR A CHILD.
Exod. ii. 3, etc.

℧ These nine words describe the various possible stages of the child's life, from its birth to manhood. 1. The word *ben,* son; feminine *bath,* daughter; this is the general term for a child of any age. 2. The more characteristic and specific *yeled,* the newly-born child (Ex. ii. 3, 6, 8), indicating by its name the fact of its arrival. 3. The word *yonek,* or suckling (Psalm viii. 2; Jer. xliv. 7; Lam. iv. 4; Joel ii. 16). 4. Still referring to the nursing period, but denoting the age at which a child is about to be weaned, we find the word *Olel* (Lam. ii. 20). 5. *Gamul,* the weaned (Isa. xi. 8), marks the period when the child has become independent of his mother. 6. *Taph,* the quickly-stepping, a very suggestive word, indicating how the little lad must almost run to keep pace with his parents (Jer. xl. 7; Esther iii. 13). 7. *Elem,* the strong, so far developed as to be able to assist his parents in their labours, though not prepared for independent action (1 Sam. xx. 22). 8. *Naar,* the free, the grown-up youth, able in some measure to walk about freely, and defend himself. 9. *Bachur,* the matured, the ripe, having attained his majority, and become marriageable, and also fit for military service.

413.—BALAAM.
Numb. xxii. 21.

℧ The Rabbins say that Balaam was at first one of Pharaoh's counsellors, and that he was the father of Jannes and Jambres, the two noted magicians who withstood Moses when he went to Pharaoh to demand the release of Israel. They further add, that Balaam was lame, and afflicted with a squint. They affirm, too, that he was the author of that passage in the book of Numbers which gives his personal history; and that Moses merely inserted it in the book, as he did other documents in his works, without making himself responsible for what they contained. It is probable that the Rabbins resort to this hypothesis to avoid accepting the account of the ass speaking.

414.—THE MODERN DAY OF ATONEMENT.
Lev. xxiii. 26–32.

℄ The persistence under altered names of popular festivals is among well-known facts; but perhaps in the survival for a long time of minute observances there is nothing more striking than the fast which is solemnised by Jewish congregations under the name of the Day of Atonement or Atonements. The ceremonial will be found laid down in the 16th chapter of Leviticus, and the observance of the day is commanded also in Exodus xxx. and Leviticus xxiii. "Ye shall afflict your souls," is one of the directions in Leviticus, and in part fulfilment of an ancient interpretation of this passage, the worshippers eat no food and drink no liquid during a period of more than twenty-four hours, from sunset to sunset. There are other fasts in the rabbinical year which are observed by a few with equal strictness. This, however, is the only one for which the explicit authority of the Pentateuch can be invoked, and it is observed as a fast by an overwhelming proportion of religious Jews. That abstention from food was a part of religious observance at a very early period is clear from passages in the prophets. Thus Isaiah quotes and rebukes the complaint: "Wherefore have we fasted and thou hast not seen it? Wherefore have we afflicted our souls and thou has not heeded it?" In Leviticus the priest is commanded to have the linen breeches upon his flesh and to be girded with a linen girdle, and with the linen mitre to be attired; and still on this day the readers of the synagogue (the "angels" of Revelation ii. 2) are clothed in white linen. The liturgy used has much that is solemn and much that is affecting amid a vast collection of prayers that occupy the whole day from six in the morning till the stars appear at nightfall. Both in the evening, and in the morning unto the next even, the white and banded scarf of prayer or Tallith, which has often been represented in painting and sculpture, is worn by male worshippers. Many also remove the boots from their feet, to signify that the place whereon they stand is holy ground. It was on this day that the trumpet sounded for jubilee, at the end of the cycle of seven times seven years, and a horn is now intoned every year with certain traditional notes. There are now no sacrificial priests, and, of course, the "scapegoat," or goat of Azazel, is not sent into the wilderness. But the ordinance is repeated to preserve the memory of the ceremony, and a traditional account of the way in which the high priest performed the duties of the day when the temple was standing is also recited. At the entry of the priest into the holy place within the rail, before the mercy-seat is reached, the priest's confession ending with the name of God is recited. It is also recited how, at the sound of that name, which was heard on no other day, the priests and the people who stood in the court bent the knee, bowed down, and fell upon their faces. At the moment of recital the whole of the modern congregation bend the knee, bow down, and turn their faces to the earth, the voice of the reader pealing above them in his measured repetition of the passage. The greater solemnity attaches to this act of devotion because on no other day except New Year, which is really an outwork of this day, do the worshippers in Hebrew synagogues kneel. At another time a long general confession of sins is made by the congregation, and the reader answers with the consoling text, "And the Lord said, I have pardoned according to thy word." The scrolls of the law are twice during the day taken out of the ark, and the Book of Jonah is read at another period of the service as an instance of the efficacy of repentance.

415.—DAVID A MAN AFTER GOD'S OWN HEART.
Acts xiii. 22.

¶ Canon Perowne gives the following beautiful summary of the character of David: "That character was no common one. It was strong with all the strength of man, tender with all the tenderness of woman. Naturally brave, his courage was heightened and confirmed by that faith in God which never, in the worst extremity, forsook him. Naturally warm-hearted, his affections struck their roots deep into the innermost centre of his being. In his love for his parents, for whom he provided in his own extreme peril—in his love for his wife Michal—for his friend Jonathan, whom he loved as his own soul—for his darling Absalom, whose death almost broke his heart—even for the infant whose loss he dreaded—we see the same man, the same depth and truth, the same tenderness of personal affection. On the other hand, when stung by a sense of wrong or injustice, his sense of which was peculiarly keen, he could flash out into strong words and strong deeds. He could hate with the same fervour that he loved. Evil men and evil things, all that was at war with goodness and with God, for these he found no abhorrence too deep, scarcely any imprecations too strong. Yet he was, withal, placable and ready to forgive. He could exercise a prudent self-control, if he was occasionally impetuous. His true courtesy, his chivalrous generosity to his foes, his rare delicacy, his rare self-denial, are all traits which present themselves most forcibly as we read his history. He is the truest of heroes in the genuine elevation of his character, no less than in the extraordinary incidents of his life. Such a man cannot wear a mask in his writings. Depth, tenderness, fervour, mark all his poems."

416.—THE CAMEL NOT TO BE EATEN.
Lev. xi. 4.

℄ Among the forbidden beasts is the camel; and it is singular to find in the *Institutes of Menu,* the ancient lawgiver of the Hindoos, whose probable date is between Homer (962 B.C.), and the Roman Twelve Tables (about 449 B.C.), directions on the same subject, which in some respects resemble those of Moses. He forbids the Brahmin to "eat the flesh of the camel, or any quadruped *with the hoof not cloven.*" None were clean to the Israelites which did not divide the hoof (Lev. xi. 3). Menu also orders to be shunned carnivorous birds; birds that strike with the beaks, the heron, the raven; also hogs, and fish of every sort were forbidden.

The distinction between clean and unclean animals is exceedingly ancient, and dates from before the flood. The distinction is nowhere explained, for even in the history of the flood it is introduced as a thing well known. In India, as well as in Palestine, the origin of the two classes of animals was early lost, and even as early as Menu speculations had been rife on the subject, for he himself says:—"No doubt in the primeval sacrifices by holy men, and in oblations by those of the priestly and military tribes, flesh of such beasts and birds as may legally be eaten was presented to the deities." There can be no doubt that the distinction originated in the sacrificial rites of primeval man, but whether through revelation, or otherwise, it is impossible to decide.

417.—THE TOWER OF BABEL.
Gen. xi. 4.

℄ In Babylonia there are at present the remains of three stupendous ruins, each of which has been claimed by different travellers

as occupying the site of the Tower of Babel. One of these especially has much to support its claim. The Temple of Belus was in
all probability erected on the site of the Tower of Babel, so the arguments which settle the position of one of these erections serve to
fix the other. Rawlinson says of these particular ruins:—"It is an
oblong mass, composed chiefly of unbaked bricks, rising from the
plain to a height of one hundred and ten feet, and having at the
top a broad flat space, with heaps of rubbish. The faces of the
mound are about two hundred yards in length, and thus agree with
Herodotus's estimate. Tunnels driven through the structure show
that it was formerly covered with a wall of baked-brick masonry;
many such bricks are found loose, and bear the name of Nebu-
chadnezzar." The difficulty of identifying the site of the Scripture
Babylon arises chiefly from the fact that the materials of which it
was built have at various times been removed for the construction
of the great cities which have successively replaced it. Nebuchad-
nezzar either repaired Babylon, as many suppose, or built it anew
upon a neighbouring site with the remains of the more ancient
Babel.

The kind of building which was erected, and known as the
Tower of Babel, may be best understood by the description of the
great temple of Nebo at Borsippa, known to moderns as the *Birs-
Nimrud*. It was a sort of oblique pyramid, built in seven receding
stages. "Upon a platform of crude brick, raised a few feet above
the level of the alluvial plain, was built of burnt brick the first or
basement stage—an exact square, two hundred and seventy-two
feet each way, and twenty-six feet in perpendicular height. Upon
this stage was erected a second, two hundred and thirty feet each
way, and likewise twenty-six feet high; which, however, was not
placed exactly in the middle of the first, but considerably nearer to
the south-western end, which constituted the back of the building.
The other stages were arranged similarly—the third being one
hundred and eighty-eight feet, and again twenty-six feet high; the
fourth one hundred and forty-six feet square, and fifteen feet high;
the fifth one hundred and four feet square, and the same height as
the fourth; the sixth sixty-two feet square, and again the same
height; and the seventh twenty feet square, and once more the
same height. On the seventh stage there was probably placed the
ark or tabernacle, which seems to have been again fifteen feet
high, and must have nearly, if not entirely, covered the top of the
seventh story. The entire original height, allowing three feet for

the platform, would thus have been one hundred and fifty-six feet, or without the platform, one hundred and fifty-three feet. The whole formed a sort of oblique pyramid, the gentler slope facing the N.E., and the steeper inclining to the S.W. On the N.E. side was the grand entrance, and here stood the vestibule, a separate building, the *débris* from which having joined those from the temple itself, fill up the intermediate space, and very remarkably prolong the mound in this direction."

418.—ACHOR AND HOPE.
Hosea ii. 15.

℀ The Easterns prefer a figure that is suggestive but at the same time hazy and indistinct, and this passage belongs to such a class. The Valley of Achor runs up from Gilgal towards Bethel. There Achan was stoned, and the Divine indignation removed. The word *Achor* means *trouble, affliction;* and it is just possible that from it we get our word *ache.* Thus the valley of affliction was the door through which Israel first entered the land of Canaan. And so again, by Hosea, the Lord promised to lead Israel to peace and rest through the valley of trouble. The very indistinctness makes this mode of speaking the more suggestive.

419.—"EAT AND NOT BE SATISFIED."
Lev. xxvi. 26.

℀ A curious illustration of the way in which the body may be wasted even when the appetite appears to be satisfied, and the stomach to be content, is found in the sad story of the Australian explorers, Burke and Wills. There is a singular plant, known as the *nardoo,* having clover-like leaves, and closely allied to the fern-tribe, which grows in the deserts of Central Australia. The seeds of this plant formed almost the only food for the explorers during several months. The food appeared to stay their hunger, it produced a pleasant feeling of comfort and repletion. The natives were accustomed to eat it in the absence of their usual roots and fruits, not only without injury, but apparently with positive benefit to their health. It did not, however, feed Messrs. Burke and Wills. Day after day they became more emaciated. Their flesh wasted

from their bones, their strength was reduced to an infant's
feebleness, and they could only painfully crawl a mile or two a
day, perishing at last of starvation. When analysed, the *nardoo*
bread was ascertained to be destitute of certain nutritious elements
indispensable to the support of a European, though an Australian
savage might for a time find it beneficial as an alterative.

It is said that "the peasant women of Styria are in the habit of
eating a certain quantity of arsenic, in order to enhance their personal charms. It imparts a beautiful bloom to the complexion, and
gives a full and rounded appearance to the face and body. For
years they persevere in the dangerous practice, but if they intermit
it for a single day, they experience all the symptoms of arsenical
poisoning. The complexion fades, the features become worn and
haggard, and the body loses its plumpness and becomes angular
and emaciated. Having once begun, therefore, to use this cosmetic,
they must in self-defence go on, constantly increasing the dose to
keep up the effect. At last the constitution is undermined; the evil
effects cannot be warded off any longer; the limit of safety is
overpassed; and the victim of foolish vanity perishes miserably in
the very prime of life."

420.—GRINDING AND WOOD CARRYING.
Lam. v. 13.

℧ In the East may now be seen long files of women and children
carrying on their heads heavy bundles of wood. But it is the
severest kind of drudgery, especially trying to the young girls. Yet
daily these loads have to be brought from the mountains into
Jerusalem. To carry water, also, is very laborious and fatiguing.
The fountains are sometimes far off, in deep wadies with steep
banks, and it is painful to see the feeble and the young staggering
up long and weary ways with large jars of water on their heads. It
is the work of slaves, and of the very poor, whose condition is still
worse. Grinding at the hand-mill is a low, menial work, assigned
to female slaves, and therefore utterly humiliating to the young
men of Israel. The picture of this and the delicate children of Zion
falling under loads of hard, rough wood, along the mountain
paths, calls for the pathetic lamentations of the prophet.

421.—The Perils of a Winter Flight.
Matt. xxiv. 20.

℄ There can be little doubt that our Lord referred in this passage to the destruction of Jerusalem by the Romans under Titus, whatever wider and more general significance we may think should be attached to His words. Exactly what is meant by the "abomination of desolation" cannot be decided. Some apply it to the standards of the Roman legions gathered round the devoted city. Others to the faction-fights, murders, and outrages which took place within the city. But it is evident that something which would act as a warning to the Christian disciples is meant; something which would induce them to seek a sudden flight into the open country. Such a flight would involve much hardship. They would have to forsake their property, and, probably with young children and delicate women, gain temporary shelter in mountain caves. The Romans would be sure to scour the country round the besieged city, and make it difficult for refugees to gain safety and shelter. Our Lord intimates the perils to which His disciples would be exposed by the prayers He teaches them to offer. The perils from exposure, damp, and cold would be greatly increased if their flight had to be made in the winter. And this prayer appears to have been graciously answered; for the siege and destruction of Jerusalem took place in summer time, in the months of August and September, when the dangers of living in mountain caves, and in the open country, were reduced to the narrowest limits. There are indications that the time of the siege and final attack was altered, men may say, on account of national emergencies, but the Christian disciples might say, in Divine response to their earnest prayers, and in the overrulings of Divine Providence. Josephus relates that Titus at first resolved to reduce the city by famine. He therefore built a wall around it, to keep any provisions from being carried in, and any of the people from going out. The Jews, however, drew up their army near the walls, engaged in battle, and the Romans pursued them, provoked by their attempts, and broke into the city. The affairs of Rome also at that time demanded the presence of Titus there; and contrary to his original intention he pressed the siege, and took the city by storm, thus shortening the time that would have been occupied in reducing it by famine. Titus appeared before the city early in the year A.D. 70.

422.—ANXIETY TO SECURE JUST JUDGMENT.
Deut. xvi. 18.

℃ Among the Jews, says the late Mr. Deutsch, "the care taken of human life was extreme indeed. The judge of capital offences had to fast all day, nor was the sentence executed on the day of the verdict, but it was once more subjected to the scrutiny of the Sanhedrim the next day. Even to the last the favourable circumstance that might turn the scale in the prisoner's favour was looked for. The place of execution was at some distance from the court in order that time might be given to a witness, or the accused himself for naming any fresh fact in his favour. A man was stationed at the entrance to the court, with a flag in his hand, and at some distance another man, on horseback, was stationed, in order to stop the execution instantly if any favourable circumstance should come to light. The culprit himself was allowed to stop four or five times, and to be brought back before the judges, if he had still something to urge in his defence. Before him marched a herald, crying, 'The man N. N., son of N. N., is being led to execution for having committed such and such a crime; such and such are the witnesses against him; whoever knows aught to his favour, let him come and proclaim it.' Ten yards from the place of execution they said to him, 'Confess thy sins; every one who confesses has part in the world to come; for thus it is written of Achan, to whom Joshua said, "My son, give now glory to the God of Israel."' If he 'could not' offer any formal confession, he need only say, 'May my death be a redemption for all my sins.' To the last the culprit was supported by marks of profound and awful sympathy. The ladies of Jerusalem formed a society which provided a beverage of mixed myrrh and vinegar, that, like an opiate, benumbed the man when he was being carried to execution."

423.—THE VINE IN EGYPT, ETC.
Psalm lxxviii. 47.

℃ De Wette and Hupfeld assert that the writer of this Psalm, as a native of Canaan, ascribes too much prominence to the vine, the cultivation of which was but little attended to in Egypt, and which is not said in the Pentateuch to have suffered. But this is an unfounded assertion. Mr. R. S. Poole shows that "Vines were extensively cultivated in Egypt, and there were several different kinds of wine, one of which, the Mareotic, was famous among the Romans." Pharaoh's chief butler dreams of the vine (Gen. xl. 9–11); and the vines of Egypt, as well as the figs and pomegranates, are thought of with regret by the Israelites in the wilderness (Num. xx. 5). The mural paintings at Thebes, at Beni-Hassan, and in the Pyramids, contain representations of vineyards. Boys are seen frightening away the birds from the ripe clusters, men gather them and deposit them in baskets, and carry them to the wine-press.

The mode of treating the vine, and the various uses made of its fruit, may here be added. An Eastern traveller gives the following description:—

"In the winter season the vines are cut back, so that only three or four thrifty arms remain, and these the three or four nearest the root, which are to give the new wood and fruit of the approaching season. These arms are supported by crotched sticks a cubit or two long, which keep the vines from the ground and give them room for ventilation and for putting forth their clusters. The soil in the vineyards is kept loose and free from weeds. The vines are planted from eight to ten feet apart. The heavy dews from April to October furnish the vines and fruit with sufficient moisture, for they get no rain during this season. The clusters grow to an enormous size. I have measured them half a yard long, reminding one of the grapes of Eshcol, which the spies had to carry on a staff between them to avoid breaking the cluster. The varieties are as many and the qualities as varied as among our own grapes.

"In July the natives begin to use the green grape in making sherbet, which means 'a drink.' The sherbet of the winter and spring, made of orange blossoms, is very sweet, rich in perfume, and pleasant to the native palate, but not very refreshing. Besides, the hot July weather compels the stomach to crave an acid, and the green grape pounded to a pumice in a mortar, strained, sweetened, and diluted with water, furnishes a drink which rivals our best lemonade, and which the mountaineer employs as a substitute. When the grapes ripen, which they begin to do in August, the natives eat them with their dry bread, and they become a staple article of daily food.

"The grape season lasts through August, September, October, and November. The grapes of Syria being so saccharine are easily converted into raisins, which, when dry, are pressed into cheeses, and then cut and eaten with bread as we cut and eat our cheese. But we must hasten to the wine-press, and see the Arabs manufacturing the juice of the grape. And, first of all, the press deserves attention. Either cut out of the solid rock or built with large stones and cement upon the surface of the soil in the vineyard, it is a simple affair. The vats are usually four, six, or eight feet square, and one foot deep, slightly inclined to one end, where a small trough conducts the expressed juice into a receptacle of masonry, holding fifteen to twenty-five gallons. The grapes are placed in the vat, and a native or two with bare feet tread the grapes, and the juice runs off into the cistern, whence it is carried in jars or leathern bottles to the home. The process of extraction is very simple and primitive—the vats just the same as those used two thousand years ago. The juice thus extracted is converted into molasses, wine, vinegar, and jelly.

"Molasses, called by the natives 'dibs,' and in Hebrew 'debesch,' is grape juice boiled to a syrup. The natives often make their evening meal upon bread dipped into a bowl of 'dibs.'

"The wine is made by the grape juice being placed in skins (in the New Testament called bottles), and the smallest possible vent allowed for fermentation to keep the skins from bursting. The wine is generally reduced with water. There are many different wines in Syria, generally called after the place where they are made. During my two years' residence in the land I never saw a native intoxicated.

"The vinegar is similar to our wine vinegar, and is mostly made from the pumice of the grape after the juice has been extracted. Besides its ordinary table use a pleasant drink is made by mixing it with sweetened water. The jelly is simply the juice boiled down, and by the addition of a little sugar it makes a very nice condiment. Besides being served as a compote it is not unfrequently presented as a sherbet, after being dissolved in water."

424.—NICOLAITANES.
Rev. ii. 15.

℄ Much difficulty has been found in explaining who are intended by this term. The most simple suggestion is that the word Nicolaus is the Greek equivalent for Balaam, and consequently the term

Nicolaitanes means Balaamites, or those holding doctrines, and teaching them, which led to others being drawn into corrupt and immoral principles. "Through the counsel of Balaam the Moabites and Midianites united to tempt the children of Israel by idol worship connected with female devotees thereto. The Jewish people were induced to commit fornication and to eat of the idol sacrifices, for we are told that 'the people ate and bowed down to their gods,' namely, to the gods of the Moabites."

We may therefore suppose that the Nicolaitanes were Jews and other members of the Christian Church who held, however little they might themselves see its consequences, a doctrine in regard to heathenism which led precisely to a similar result of licence and immorality. If they themselves were better than their creed many would gladly take full advantage of the liberty which their creed allowed.

425.—MARRIAGE LAWS AMONG THE HINDOOS.
Matt. xxiv. 38.

℘ Marriages in the East differ in many respects from the marriages with which we are familiar; and several kinds of giving in marriage were anciently recognised. According to the Gentoo Law Code of Ancient India there were formerly eight different modes of contracting marriage recognised as valid in that portion of the East. Those presenting some parallel to Bible customs deserve mention. The third form is called *Aesh*, from the custom of the girl's parents receiving a bull and a cow from the bridegroom on his marrying their daughter. This may recall several cases mentioned in Scripture. Shechem, when desirous of marrying Dinah, the daughter of Jacob, said, "Ask ye never so much dowry and gift, and I will give according as ye shall say" (Gen. xxxiv. 12). When it was proposed that David should marry Michal, the daughter of Saul, he was given to understand that the king required no dowry, except that the bridegroom should make war upon the Philistines (1 Sam. xviii. 24–26). The fourth form is called *Kundehrub;* in this case a man and woman, by mutual consent, interchange their necklaces or strings of flowers, and both make agreement in some secret place; as, for instance, the woman says, "I am become your wife;" and the man says, "I acknowledge it." It is just possible that Tamar considered herself as married to

425.—Marriage Laws Among the Hindoos.

Judah in some such manner as this when she took his signet, bracelets, etc. (Gen. xxxviii. 12–18). The seventh form, *Rakhus*, is when a man marries the daughter of a man he has conquered in war. This kind of marriage was practised and legal among the Jews (Deut. xxi. 10–14). The eighth form is *Peishach*, when a man in woman's dress debauches a girl, and the parents afterwards give her to him in marriage. This is almost parallel to the case provided for in Exod. xxii. 16.

426.—"SHE CRIETH AFTER US."
Matt. xv. 23.

℄ The endeavour to obtain redress by long-continued crying, and by mere force of importunity,—to extort by these means a boon or a right which is expected from no other motives, is quite in the spirit of the East. It is mentioned in Chardin's *Travels in Persia* that the peasants of a district, when their crops have failed, and they therefore desire a remission of the contributions imposed on their villages, or when they would appeal against some tyrannical governor, will assemble before the gates of the shah's harem, and there continue howling and throwing dust in the air; and they will not be silenced or driven away till he has sent out and demanded the cause, and thus given them at least an opportunity of stating their griefs; or sometimes they would beset him in the same manner as he passed through the streets of the city, and thus seek to gain, and often succeed in gaining, their point, not from his love of justice, but from his desire to be freed from annoyance.

427.—PETER'S NIGHT VISIT TO MARY'S HOUSE.
Acts xii. 13–17.

℄ The incidents of this narrative are thoroughly Oriental. Any one acquainted with the manners and customs of the modern Syrians must be struck with this. Dr. Kitto is wrong when he says that "there are no knockers to Eastern doors." On the contrary, every house in the towns, and even large villages in Palestine, has a knocker, generally a rude massive iron ring. The mode of knocking is very different from ours. On going to a door one gives two or three loud knocks, and then pauses for a moment to listen. If

there is no response he repeats them, and again listens. He thus
goes on until some one from within calls, "Who?" The door is
never opened, under any circumstances, without such a question
being put. The person without, if his voice is known to those
within, answers, "I—open." If there be any doubt within a further
question is put, "Who art thou?" The name or title is then given in
reply. If the name be unknown another question is not unfrequently asked, "What do you want?" and a report must be made
to the master or mistress of the house ere the door is opened. During the absence of the servant or attendant making such report,
the person *continues knocking,* just as Peter did. On more than
one occasion, when I returned after a lengthened journey to my
own house at Damascus, I have known my servant, on recognising
my voice at the door, to run away before opening and com-
municate the glad news to the members of my family. So did the
damsel Rhoda, "When she knew Peter's voice she opened not the
gate for gladness, but ran in and told how Peter stood before the
gate."

428.—MODERN FORMS OF IDOLATRY.
1 John v. 21.

℄ In the Russo-Greek Church solid images are not permitted,
and the symbols of faith are generally worthless pictures, made to
represent images as much as permissible, by having stuffs wrought
in thin gold or silver stuck upon the painting. The celebrated gate
in the wall of the Kremlin is famous because a picture of this sort,
"The Redeemer of Smolensk," as it is called, is suspended above
the high archway of brick. With an opera-glass one can discern a
representation of the typical face of Christ decked in golden garb
and nimbus. Even in these degenerate days it is scarcely permitted
that any one shall pass under this archway except uncovered. Jews
and Mohammedans generally find some less sacred gate when they
wish to enter the Kremlin—the Acropolis of Moscow. The Czar
himself never passes by any other way, and never with his hat
upon his head. But it is upon the outer side of the Voskreneski
Gate, in the Kitai-Gorodi, or "Chinese town" of Moscow, that the
most remarkable exhibition of religious feeling may be witnessed.

Before the stout wall of brickwork which separates the outgoing
from the incoming way is the Iberian Chapel (Iverskaya Chasov-

nia), architecturally nothing but a large-sized hut of stone, on a platform raised by two steps above the roadway. From morning till night this platform is thronged, and the chapel overflows with a crowd chiefly composed of men, pressing, all bare-headed, and all with money in their hands, toward the narrow doorway of the little sanctuary.

We were some time getting into the chapel, which will hold about ten people abreast, and is lighted by the flickering glare of a score of candles. There is a step at the further end, and the wall opposite the door is resplendent with shining metal, except where the object of this extravagant devotion looks grimy through its framework of gold. On the left side of "the Iberian Mother of God," which is the name given to this commonplace daub, supposed to possess miraculous powers, stands a long-haired priest—now and then relieved by another long-haired priest—who, hour by hour, in the name of the tinselled and jewelled picture, and with blessings, consecrates the prayers and offerings of the faithful. Only the face of the Madonna is visible, and it is not easy to distinguish her features beneath the dust of years. But not a minute passes in which the rattle of money falling to the uses of the Russian Church is not heard, or in which lips are not pressed upon the framework or upon the rudely-wrought robes of beaten gold which conceal the picture to the neck. Surely no lower depth of superstitious degradation was ever reached in connection with Christian worship!

One cannot be surprised that to a Turk a Russian seems to be an idolatrous worshipper of pictures. The refining explanation which the most enlightened fathers of the Greek Church offer concerning this exhibition is precisely of the sort, and differs only in degree, from that which might be offered for the idol worshippers of more southern and eastern lands. The picture has no historic reputation. It was brought from Mount Athos, that pleasant wooded hill peopled with monkish drones. A sum of about £ 12,000 a year is collected, and from this the salary of the Metropolitan of Moscow is paid.

Time was when in the ceremonies which precede Easter the Czar used to lead the donkey upon which the Patriarch of Moscow rode, carrying a sacred chalice and a copy of the four Gospels. Nowadays that ceremony is neglected, but we are given to

understand that the Czar never enters Moscow without assisting
the revenues of this high ecclesiastical officer by praying at this
shrine of "the Iberian Mother of God."—*Fraser's Magazine.*

429.—THE CENSUS CONNECTED
WITH OUR LORD'S BIRTH.
Luke ii. 1; 2.

℩ This passage has given rise to endless discussion, and it can
hardly be said that any absolutely certain explanation has been obtained. The following judicious and complete summary of the
principal facts is taken from the writings of Prof. Plumptre:—

"The word 'taxed' is used in its older English sense of simple
'registration,' and in that sense is a true equivalent for the Greek
word. What Augustus decreed was a general census. It may be admitted that no Roman or Jewish historian speaks distinctly of such
a general census as made at this time. On the other hand, the
collection of statistical returns of this nature was an ever-recurring
feature of the policy of Augustus. We read of such returns at intervals of about ten years during the whole period of his government. In B.C. 27, when he offered to resign, he laid before the senate a *rationarium,* or survey of the whole empire. After his death,
a like document, more epitomised—*a breviarium*—was produced
as having been compiled by him. There are traces of one about
this time made by the emperor, not in his character as censor, but
by an imperial edict such as St. Luke here describes. Just before
the death of Herod, Josephus reports that there was an agitation
among the Jews, which led him to require them to take an oath of
fidelity, not to himself only, but to the emperor, and that 6,000
Pharisees refused to take it. He does not say what caused it, but
the census which St. Luke records, holding out, as it did, the prospect of future taxation in the modern sense, sufficiently explains it.
It may be noted that none of the early opponents of Christianity—
such as Celsus and Porphyry—call the accuracy of the statement
in question. And as an educated man St. Luke would hardly ven-
ture to set down, as matter of fact, what could be so readily
refuted if untrue.

"Publius Sulpicius Quirinus ('Cyrenius' is the Greek form of the
last of these three names) was Consul B.C. 12, but he is not named

as Governor of Syria till after the deposition of Archelaus, A.D. 6, and he was then conspicuous in carrying out a census which involved taxation in the modern sense; and this was the 'taxing' referred to in Gamaliel's speech (Acts v. 37) as having led to the revolt of Judas of Galilee. Our knowledge of the governors of Syria at this period is imperfect. The dates of their appointments, so far as they go, are as follows:—B.C. 9, Sentius Saturninus; B.C. 6, T. Quintillius Varus; A.D. 6, P. Sulpicius Quirinus. It was, however, part of the policy of Augustus that no governor of an imperial province should hold office for more than five or less than three years, and it is in the highest degree improbable that Varus (whom we find in A.D. 7 in command of the ill-fated expedition against the Germans) should have continued in office for the twelve years which the above date suggests. One of the missing links is found in A. Volusius Saturninus, whose name appears on a coin of Antioch about A.D. 4 or 5. The fact that Quirinus appears as a *rector,* or special commissioner attached to Caius Caesar, when he was sent to Armenia, at some period before A.D. 4, the year in which Caius died—probably between B.C. 4 and 1—shows that he was in the East at this time, and we may therefore fairly look on St. Luke as having supplied the missing link in the succession, or, at least, as confirming the statement that Quirinus was in some office of authority in the East, if not as *praeses,* or *proconsul,* then as *quaestor,* or imperial commissioner. Tacitus, however, records the fact that he triumphed over a Cilician tribe (the Homonadenses) after his consulship; and as Cilicia was, at that time, attached to the province of Syria, it is probable that he was actually 'governor' in the stricter sense of a term somewhat loosely used. St. Luke, on this view, is as accurate in his history here as he is proved to be in all other points where he comes in contact with the contemporary history of the empire, and the true meaning is found by emphasising the adjective, 'His enrolment was the first under Quirinus's government of Syria.' He expressly distinguishes it, that is, from the more memorable 'taxing' of which Gamaliel speaks. Justin Martyr, it may be added, confidently appeals to Roman registers as confirming St. Luke's statement that our Lord was born under Quirinus." And Zumpt has shown that as Cilicia was joined to Syria at this time, Quirinus, as governor of Cilicia, was also virtually governor of Syria.

430.—THE EARTH SWALLOWING UP KORAH, ETC.
Numb. xvi. 32.

℀ The Jews and other Eastern people have a curious tradition respecting Korah, which runs substantially as follows:—Korah was the most beautiful of the Israelites, and he also so far surpassed them all in opulence that his riches became a proverb. He built a large palace, which he overlaid with gold, and made the doors thereof of massy gold. On account of his riches he became very insolent, and raised a sedition against Moses. The precise nature of the sin for which he was destroyed, however, is variously given by different writers. Some say he refused to give alms, as Moses had commanded, and that this ultimately led to a quarrel between them, which ripened into sedition on the part of Korah. Others relate that one day when Moses was preaching to the people he uttered the command that adulterers should be stoned. Korah asked him what would be done if he [Korah] happened to be the culprit. Moses replied that he would be punished just as any other man. Korah then procured an abandoned woman, and instigated her to charge Moses with the crime he had just condemned. At this injustice Moses complained to God, who directed him to command the earth to do whatever he pleased, and it should obey him. Moses thereupon said, "O Earth, swallow them up!" And immediately the earth opened under Korah and his confederates, and swallowed them up with the palace and all his riches. A further tradition says that Korah himself sank gradually into the earth, first to his knees, then to his waist, then to his neck; and that he cried out four separate times—"O Moses, have mercy on me!" But Moses continued to say, "O Earth, swallow them up!" till at last Korah totally disappeared. God then said to Moses, "Thou hadst no mercy on Korah, though he asked pardon of thee four times; but I would have had compassion on him if he had asked pardon of Me but once."

431.—EARLY HUMAN SACRIFICES.
Gen. xxii. 2.

℀ Knobel points out that human sacrifices, especially of children, were customary among the pre-Hebraic nations of Palestine, among the kindred Phoenicians, among their descendants the

Carthaginians, among the Egyptians, among the tribes related with Israel, the Moabites and Ammonites, who honoured Moloch with them. They appear also in the Aramaic and Arabian tribes, but were forbidden by the Jewish law, and sternly opposed by the Jewish prophets. They were thus generally spread through the *cultus* of the nations in contact with Israel, but were entirely foreign to its legally established religion.

Stanley says, "The form taken by the Divine trial or temptation of Abraham was that which a stern logical consequence of the ancient view of sacrifice did actually assume, if not then, yet certainly in after ages, among the surrounding tribes, and which cannot therefore be left out of sight in considering the whole historical aspect of the narrative. Deep in the heart of the Canaanitish nations was laid the practice of human sacrifice; the very offering here described, of 'children passing through the fire,' 'of their sons and daughters,' 'of the firstborn for their transgressions, the fruit of their body for the sin of their soul.' On the altars of Moab, and of Phoenicia, and of the distant Canaanite settlements in Carthage and in Spain, nay even at times within the confines of the chosen people itself, in the wild vow of Jephthah, in the sacrifice of Saul's sons at Gibeah, in the dark sacrifices of the Valley of Hinnom, under the very walls of Jerusalem—this almost irrepressible tendency of the burning zeal of a primitive race found its terrible expression."

Kurtz says, "The human sacrifices are, indeed, a fearful madness, but a madness of doubt as to the true sacrifice, of hopelessness as to finding the true atonement."

From the *Speaker's Commentary* the following sentences are taken:—"The conclusion of the history is as clear a condemnation of human sacrifice as the earlier part might have seemed, had it been left incomplete, to sanction it. The intervention of the angel, the substitution of the lamb, the prohibition of the human sacrifice, proved that in no case could such an offering be acceptable to God, even as the crowning evidence of faith, devotion, and self-sacrifice."

F. W. Robertson points out that Abraham's sentiment respecting offering his son as a sacrifice would greatly differ from the sentiments upon the matter which we cherish now, in the fuller but milder light of Christianity. "Abraham lived in a country where human sacrifices were common; he lived in a day when a father's power over a son's life was absolute. He was familiar with the idea; and just as familiarity with *slavery* makes it seem less horrible, so familiarity with this as an established and conscientious mode of worshipping God removed from Abraham much of the horror that *we* should feel."

It may also be suggested that in those days the only way in which a thing could be devoted wholly to God was by offering it in sacrifice, making it a burnt-offering.

432.—THE FATE OF SIMEON AND LEVI.
Gen. xlix. 7.

℘ These two tribes were charged with immoderate revenge. "Cursed be their anger, *for it was cruel.*" Had they not felt anger, had they not avenged, they had not been men. That responsibility which is now shared between judge, jury, the law, and the executioner, was necessarily in early ages sustained alone by the avenger of blood. That instinct of indignation which is now regularly expressed by law was then of necessity expressed irregularly. They are not to be blamed for doing the avenger's justice. But they slew a whole tribe. The sin committed by one man was avenged on the whole nation; they let their fury fall on the innocent cattle, for the expression "they digged down a wall" is better given in the margin, "they houghed oxen," *i.e.* hamstrung, or cut the sinews of the beasts. The penalty therefore which fell on them was of a peculiar kind. They were both to be "divided and scattered." Yet the curse was fulfilled in very different ways, and in each case was closely connected with blessing. The dispersion of the Levites arose from their holding the place of honour in the nation, and being spread, for the purposes of education and worship, broadcast over the face of the country. In the case of Simeon the dispersion seems to have arisen from some corrupting element in the tribe itself, which first reduced its numbers, and at last drove it from its allotted seat in the country. Simeon was the weakest of all the tribes, having at the second census only 22,200, against 76,500 of Judah (Numb. xxvi. 14, 22). But there is a Jewish tradition which intimates that in the case of Simeon also the curse was intimately connected with blessing. This tradition is given in the *Jerusalem Targum,* and is to the effect that multitudes of Simeon's posterity were scattered among the other tribes in the capacity of teachers; so that the He-

brews were accusomed to say that every poor scribe and school-
master was a Simeonite.

433.—OLD JERUSALEM.
2 Sam. v. 6–9.

ℭ Another advance has been made in the topography of Ancient
Jerusalem. It comes in the shape of a series of four maps, drawn
by Dr. Carl Zimmermann, after the designs of Schick. The first
and principal map of the series—to which the other three are no
more than accessories, or aids for its better understanding—gives
the results of measurements and investigations in several hundred
localities of the substratum of the modern city down to the "hard-
pan." This map, therefore, is intended to lay bare the virgin soil of
Salem-Jebus, which must have been the foundation of Old Jerusalem. He lays down the principle that all hypothetical restorations
have to be abandoned which locate entire quarters of the city in
localities where there are little or no accumulations of *débris*.
Thus, he says, the hypothesis which places the Palace of David to
the north of the Haram is utterly at fault. In 1 Kings viii. 4, we
are told that they "brought up the ark of the Lord;" while, from
the configuration of the original soil, it appears that, if David's
Palace stood where it is supposed to have been, the ark had to be
brought *down*. In general, then, it may be accepted that whatever
cannot be proved to have been built upon the virgin soil of Salem-
Jebus has to be removed as having been erected on the *débris* of
tradition. Yet we must not rely entirely on the testimony of this
virgin soil when the site of edifices erected after the exile has to be
determined. From various traces, it seems certain that the Chaldaean destruction of the city was so complete that even the
Jerusalem of the time of Nehemiah must have stood on a foundation different from that of the city before the exile. This appears
especially from the principal vertical section of the region near the
north-western margin of the valley, though not as plainly from a
section of the interior of the city, or the Tyropoeon. Dr. Zimmermann should, also, have told us what we are to understand by the
term Old Jerusalem, which properly designates only the Jerusalem
before the exile, and not all the way down to the time of Herod.
His system of indicating the curves of the equidistances every ten
feet by red lines, so that the highest points are always indicated by

the smallest of these concentric curves, is excellent; and the delicate tracings of the modern buildings, which will prove of great assistance for personal investigations, do not interfere with the artistic impression and lucidity of the map. In the letter-press annex is furnished a good account of the history of Jerusalem research, in which due prominence is given to the labours of De Vogué and De Saulcy; of Wilson, Warren, and Conder, since 1865, in the service of the English "Palestine Exploration Fund;" and of the "American Palestine Exploration Society."

434.—Man's Traditions Injuring God's Word.
Mark vii. 13.

℃ The Talmud, to which these paragraphs have several times referred, is the modern collection of the traditions of the elders: and it gives us a good idea of the evil influence exerted by human traditions in the time of our Lord. The Talmud is the basis and rule of all present Jewish customs; but it was not written until after the destruction of Jerusalem by Titus, and the consequent dispersion of the Jews. So far as can be ascertained, it was begun in the second century, and completed in the sixth or seventh. It professes to contain the traditions of the elders respecting the right interpretation of the Old Testament, as well as oral precepts never before committed to writing. Our Saviour declared respecting these traditions, when as yet they must have been less objectionable than afterwards, that they made the "Word of God of none effect." There seems reason for thinking that the principal object of the Talmudists was so to pervert the Old Testament as to destroy the force of its argument for Christianity, and so keep the Jews from abandoning the religion of their fathers. It may be truly said that the Talmud has, among modern Jews, wholly supplanted the Old Testament. There is a striking fact which illustrates the influence of the Talmud in destroying or modifying the old practices of Judaism; it is the existence of the sect of the Karaïtes, who reject the Talmud, and all traditionary teachings, and receive the Old Testament alone, without note or comment. Their religious practices and customs materially differ from those of other Jews, but their numbers are small, and they are confined to a few districts of Poland, Gallicia, and Crim Tartary, owing chiefly to the bitter persecutions they endure from the rest of the nation.

435.—THE EVIL EYE.
Prov. xxiii. 6.

℄ It is probable that a belief in *ocular* fascination, such as that in Virgil's

"Nescio quis teneros oculus mihi fascinat agnos,"

was extensively prevalent among the Hebrews, and the following passages have been cited with this view:—Deut. xviii. 10, Micah v. 11, Isa. ii. 6, Lev. xix. 26. Gesenius regards the verb in these passages, however, as rather signifying "cloud-augury." The Targum of Palestine paraphrases Gen. xlii. 5, thus: "But Benjamin, Joseph's brother, Jacob sent not down with his brethren; for he said, Behold he is a youth, and I fear lest death should befall him. And the sons of Israel went every one by one door, lest the evil eye should have sway over them, as they went together to buy among the Canaanites," etc. The date of this Targum is placed by many before Christ. In Egypt, and other countries frequented by Arabs, charms are practised to ward off from children the obnoxious influence of the evil eye, and if their beauty is praised before them the mother will immediately spit on the ground or in the child's face. "Is thine eye *evil* because I am good?" (Matt. xx. 15). This is compared with Prov. xxiii. 6, "Eat thou not the bread of him that hath an evil eye, neither desire thou his dainty meats. For as he thinketh in his heart so is he: Eat and drink, saith he to thee, but his heart is not with thee." No doubt this spirit of *malevolence* was the evil eye with which Saul regarded David. The sense of the passage in Matt. vi. 23 is somewhat different, and the evil eye is there a distorted, depraved character, opposite to the "single" or honest one, and indicative of a double mind, such as the Pharisees and other deceitful men of the period possessed. Lastly, the "eye" of God is said to be turned towards persons generally in a good sense, but not always.

436.—CYRUS THE PERSIAN.
Isaiah xlv. 1.

℄ The personal history of this founder of the Persian Empire cannot be accurately traced. The Bible narrative is only concerned

with him so far as he was the Divine agent in the judgment of the
nation that carried Israel captive; and in the restoration of that
captive people. So far as the facts can be recovered they are these.
He was the son of Cambyses, a Persian of the royal Achoemenian
race, by Mandane, daughter of Astyages, King of Media. His
grandfather ordered him to be put to death, because, in consequence of a dream, he apprehended danger from him. He was
secretly preserved, and brought up in obscurity under the name of
Agradates. Discovered by the spirit he showed, he was placed at
the head of the Persians. He took Media, B.C. 559; conquered
Lydia; took Babylon, B.C. 538; and fell in battle with the Scythians, B.C. 529.

Dean Stanley forms a very high estimate of this king. "He, first
of the ancient conquerors, appears in other than a merely despotic
and destructive aspect. Both in Greek and Hebrew literature he is
represented as the type of a just and gentle prince. He belongs to
the only nation in the then state of the world which, in any sense
at all approaching the Israelite, acknowledged the unity of the
Godhead. The religion of the Persians was, of all the Gentile
forms of faith, the most simple and the most spiritual. Their abhorrence of idols was pushed almost to fanaticism. 'They have no
images of the gods, no temples, no altars, and consider the use of
them a sign of folly.' This was Herodotus' account of the Persians
of his own day, and it is fully borne out by what we know of their
religion and of their history."

The relation of Cyrus and the Persian nation to the kingdoms
that have occupied foremost places in modern civilisation is very
remarkable. With Cyrus we "enter on an epoch when the Semitic
race is to make way for the Aryan or Indo-Germanic nations
which, through Greece and Rome, are henceforth to sway the des-
tiny of mankind. . . . Of all the great nations of central Asia Persia alone is of the same stock as Greece and Rome and Germany.
It was a true insight into the innermost heart of this vast movement which enabled the prophet to discern in it not merely the
blessing of his own people, but the union of the distant isles of the
western sea with the religion hitherto confined to the uplands of
Asia. It was one of those points of meeting between the race of
Japheth and the race of Shem, that have been truly said to be the
turning-points of human history."

437.—HAND TO HAND.
Prov. xi. 21.

℟ This is literally "hand to hand," the italicised words being added by our translators; and interpreters differing about the meaning of the phrase "hand to hand." Fürst looks upon it as a formula of assurance, "the hand upon it;" but Gesenius, comparing the Arabic, considers it a formula of succession, "for all generations;" and so De Wette renders, "Von Geschlecht zu Geschlecht bleibt der Böse nicht ungestraft." What our translators meant is seen in the note of the Genevan version, which preceded theirs, and was the same rendering: "Though they make never so many friends, yet shall they not escape." The Septuagint turned the phrase somewhat differently: "He that unjustly strikes hands shall not be punished." Others take the Hebrew word as meaning "blow." "Blow after blow the wicked will not be amended." It may be objected to the interpretation of Gesenius and De Wette that "from generation to generation" is expressed in various other ways, principally by *Dōr*. On the other hand, the Authorised Version is in accordance with Oriental usage: "When two persons make a contract, they bring the palms of their hands into contact, and then raise them to their lips and foreheads" (*Paxton*).

438.—THE SACRAMENT OF BROTHERHOOD.
Luke xxii. 15.

℟ The following illustrations, taken from Hamlin's book *Among the Turks*, may help to explain the action of our Lord in instituting the Feast of the Supper:—

"In the evening the bey had his dinner in the highest style of an Oriental prince. . . .

"I gave my travelling companion notice that we should probably have not less than fifteen courses of food; and, as we must taste of all, we must act accordingly; and so we did. But we had *twenty-two* courses, and it need not be said that the latter part of the dinner dragged. After dinner, pipes, and a small cup of strong, black coffee; and we were soon disposed to sleep.

"While eating, the bey asked me if it was true that in Frankistan we all eat at high tables, sitting on high stools, and having every man his plate, knife, fork, spoon, and his food doled out to him as

we do to prisoners? I explained and defended our table habits as
well as I could; except the drunkenness, which does sometimes disgrace them.

" 'But how would you do an *ikram* to a guest?' (an act of
honour and regard). 'Now *this* is what we do;' he said, as he detached a piece of roast mutton with his fingers, and passed it to
me, which I took with my fingers from his and ate. 'Now do you
know what I have done?'

" 'Perfectly well. You have given me a delicious piece of roast
meat, and I have eaten it.'

" 'You have gone far from it. By that act I have pledged you
every drop of my blood, that while you are in my territory no evil
shall come to you. For that space of time we are brothers.'

" 'But does it not make a difference whether you eat with a
Moslem, a Christian, a Jew, or a pagan?'

" 'We don't eat with pagans. They are kitabsiz and dinsiz (book-
less and faithless). But as to Moslems and kitablis (all who have
a revelation) it makes no difference. We are all brothers of the
dust.'

"He expressed a very strong dislike to Frank modes and fash-
ions at table. He thought them *uncivilised,* and not susceptible of
expressing kindness and good-will. 'If they only once knew our
customs,' he said, 'they would adopt them for ever.' This sacred
regard to eating and drinking is such a peculiar trait of the Eastern world, that it will repay a little attention. It has evidently been
a kind of sacrament, from very ancient times. It was a sacrament
of brotherhood. The bey expressed it, in saying, we are all
brothers of the dust, made out of the same clay; but he illiberally
excluded the pagan from it. It seems, at this day, to be in greater
force among the Moslems than others. The sacrament of the
Lord's Supper has taken the place of it among Christians, so that
it has almost disappeared from their social life.

"I was once coming from Smyrna, and we had on deck two
hundred and fifty raw recruits from the interior, for the Turkish
army. They were strong and healthy young men, from the fields
and vineyards of Asia Minor; and they were going to tread the
wine-press of God's wrath in war. Just before reaching port, some
fifteen or so of these recruits threw off their look of stolid resigna-
tion, cleared a place on the deck, as I supposed, for a country
dance; and I looked on with interest. I could see, by their costumes, that they were all from the same village, or villages closely

associated. Generally the mode of wearing the turban, more than anything else, indicates neighbourhood. They stood in a ring, each man's right hand upon his neighbour's left shoulder. Soon one came to take a vacant place, with a *semeet* (a ring of bread) in his hand. He broke it into bits, and they all ate of it, saying a few words of prayer, probably the first chapter of the Koran. It was a religious act, plainly. About to separate, and be dispersed into the army, they bound themselves to be faithful in memory, and in aid, should it ever become possible. It was to them a kind of sacrament, an oath of brotherhood.

"I was once, under peculiar circumstances, in the island of Rhodes, spending the night in a solitary house, with a coloured man as the only companion. He was a giant in form and strength. Born in African heathenism, and thoroughly tattooed, he had been made a slave, but became, by the piety of his master, a soldier, to serve Abdel Kader in his wars with France. When his master was taken, he fled to Turkey, and had become a butcher, thus adhering, so far as he could, to his old trade of blood.

"I felt I must test him, and see whether I could trust him. His aspect was huge and rough, but not positively forbidding. I arranged our evening meal, and invited him to partake of it with me. He took food from my hand and ate it, and he returned the compliment. After dinner, I made two cups of Turkish coffee, poured them out in his presence, and gave him one. He rolled up a cigarette and gave me, and we drank and smoked together. I felt perfectly safe with him. We had become 'brothers of the dust.' We were 'of one blood.' At a very late hour there was a knock at the door. I went down; it was a cawass and note from Mr. Kerr, the English consul, a noble and generous-hearted man, telling me that man would put his knife through me for a shilling, and I must come directly to his house. I felt his kindness and thoughtfulness, but I assured him, in reply, that I could not be safer under his own roof. And so the event proved. He served me with a brother's fidelity, and I have often prayed that the Lord would remember him for good. I have no doubt he would have defended me to the last drop of his blood. He had bound himself by the oath of human brotherhood to do it. Every other feeling of obligation might fail, but this never. To break this would be to consign himself to Gehenna, without redemption. I would not hesitate to risk my life upon it at any time.

"Our Lord, in instituting the Supper, took hold of an institution as old as the human race. David recognised it in saying, 'Yea, mine old familiar friend, *who did eat of my bread,* hath lifted up his heel against me!' The Saviour makes the same charge against Judas; and it is also said that *after the sop,* after he had himself sealed the oath of brotherhood, he yielded himself to Satan, and betrayed the Master who had pledged His own life for him.

"The Sacramental Supper was not only commemorative of our Lord's sufferings and death, but was also a sacrament of brotherhood. It was in this vein that he said to the chosen disciples, 'With desire have I desired to eat this passover with you before I suffer.' Having loved His own as brethren and friends, 'He loved them unto the end.'"

439.—SITE OF ANCIENT JERICHO.
Josh. vi. 1; 2 Kings ii. 19–22.

¶ "At the foot of a mound on the northern side of Wady Kelt, about a mile from the base of the mountains, a fine fountain of clear sweet water bursts forth, which there is every reason to believe is the scene of Elisha's miracle, and the site of ancient Jericho. It is known as the Ain-es-Sultan, or Fountain of the Sultan. Except in the immediate neighbourhood there are no other springs, and it is the only natural site for a city in the surrounding country. The spring seems once to have been enclosed by a sort of reservoir of hewn stones, but this is now broken, and the water finds its way at random over the plain, covered here with a dense thicket of *Zakkum* and *Spina Christi.* The ruin at the spring appears to be that of a small Roman temple; but there are other ruins to the north, and in the thorny copse below are many foundations, low mounds, etc., which may have been connected with the ancient city. The site of Ain-es-Sultan, in close proximity to *Jebel Kuruntul* (Quarantania), where the spies may have taken refuge, meets all the requirements of the Biblical Jericho, and we can only account for the displacement of the city by the perpetual curse laid upon him who should attempt to rebuild its walls. On the southern side of Wady Kelt stood the Roman city of Jericho, but it has entirely disappeared with the exception of a few mounds and the fine reservoir, Birket Musa, 190 yards long and 160 wide, which was fed by aqueducts from the neighbouring mountain springs."—*Wilson.*

440.—THE IDOL-GOD BAAL.
Numb. xxii. 41.

℃ In the Scriptures Baal makes his first appearance Numb. xxii.
41. Balaam lending himself to Balak to curse Israel, was taken by
the contractor "up into the high places of Baal, that thence he
might see the utmost part of the people." In Judges ii. 13 the second mention occurs, and *Ashtoreth* is here beside him. About
twenty-five times the name of the god recurs, always as "under the
wrath and curse of God." The prophet (Zeph. i. 4) has this "word
of the Lord"—the last in Scripture: "and I will cut off the remnant of Baal from this place," which is said to refer "to the final
extirpation of the devotees of Baal." Variations and compounds
with the name are about equally numerous, as Baalim, Baali, Baal-
Peor, Baal-Zephon, Baal-Zebub, etc. Ashtoreth was the name of a
city first noticed in Genesis xiv. 5—the capital of Og, king of
Bashan (Deut. i. 4), and given to Gershom (1 Chron. vi. 71), the
name "supposed to be derived from the goddess Astarte, adored
there."

In the later mythologies both these deities represented the ab-
stract attributes of *good fortune* and *love,* but human sacrifices
were offered to Baal, and "bread, liquors, and perfumes" were the
offerings to Ashtoreth. While bloody rites formed the worship to
him, "dissolute licentiousness" was regarded as "consecrated to
her."

This most ancient idolatry shows remnants of itself even in
modern times. The Druids in the British Isles planted it so deeply
that the rootlets remain. In Perthshire is the town *Tillie-beltane—*
i.e., the hill of the fire of Baal. The remains of a Druidical temple
and a well, held in considerable veneration, are near it. On *Beltane*
morning a procession used to be formed, the members of which
would drink of this well and march nine times around it and the
temple. *Beltane,* or *Bal-tein* morning is May 1st. One ceremony
was to cut a circle or trench in the green sod, kindle a line of fire
in it, make an oatmeal cake which was divided by lot in equal
pieces; the last was called the "black bit." He drawing it was to be
"sacrificed to *Baal,*" to make the year productive. But instead of
being sacrificed "he is compelled to leap three times through the
flames." This leaping through a circular flame was a ceremony in

Ireland and Wales, and the "St. John's fire" is well known in Norway, Sweden, and Germany. The rites are relics of that early idolatry which these two names represent.

441.—IDLE AND MOCKING YOUTHS.
2 Kings ii. 23–25.

❡ Needless difficulty has been felt in explaining this incident in
consequence of a somewhat defective translation. The path of the
prophet Elisha lay through the district of Bethel, the stronghold of
idolatry in Israel (1 Kings xii. 28–33), where, as in Dan, stood
one of the golden calves set up by Jeroboam. In this place insult
offered to Jehovah's prophet would be intended as insult to
Jehovah, and, so regarded, it was properly met by an immediate
and terrible punishment. It appears that there was a number of
idle young men on the outskirts of the town, lawless, rude, and
amusing themselves with rough play. They are called "children,"
but the same Hebrew word is used in 1 Kings xii. 8, 10, 14, where
it is applied to young men of the same age as King Rehoboam. In
all the languages of the East the words "child" and "children"
often denote simply a social relation, and are constantly applied to
full-grown persons, as in the New Testament.

"No one who has travelled in the East can have failed to notice
the extreme lawlessness of a certain class of boys and young men
living on the outskirts of a town, especially toward a Jew, a Christian, or a European, who should happen to be passing by alone or
unprotected. Let him go, for instance, to the castle hill of Smyrna,
and, if it be a holiday and the 'boys' (oghlans) are out, he will
perceive stones whizzing past him, and will hear the shouts of
'Frank,' 'hat-wearer,' 'Giaoor,' rallying the rowdies of the vicinity,
and warning him to beat a hasty retreat."

442.—EMBROIDERED BEDS.
Prov. vii. 16.

❡ Baron du Tott gives a remarkable account of such a bed as is
indicated in this passage. "The time for taking our repose was now
come, and we were conducted into another large room, in the
middle of which was a kind of bed, without bedstead or curtains.
Though the coverlet and pillows exceeded in magnificence the

441.—Idle and Mocking Youths.

richness of the sofa, which likewise ornamented the apartment, I foresaw that I could expect but little rest on this bed, and had the curiosity to examine its make in a more particular manner. Fifteen mattresses of quilted cotton, about three inches thick, placed one upon another, formed the groundwork, and were covered by a sheet of Indian linen, sewed on the last mattress. A coverlet of green satin, adorned with gold embroidered in embossed work, was in like manner fastened to the sheets, the ends of which, turned in, were sewed down alternately. Two large pillows of crimson satin, covered with the like embroidery, in which there was no want of gold or spangles, rested on two cushions of the sofa, brought near to serve for a back, and intended to support our heads. The taking of the pillows entirely away would have been a good resource if we had had any bolster; and the expedient of turning the other side upwards having only served to show that they were embroidered in the same manner on the bottom, we at last determined to lay our handkerchiefs over them, which, however, did not prevent our being very sensible of the embossed ornaments underneath."

443.—PRAISE—BLESS.
Psalm cxlv. 10.

¶ Matthew Henry indicates the distinction between these terms, and the appropriateness with which each is used. "All God's *works* shall *praise* Him. They all minister to us matter for praise, and so praise Him according to their capacity; even those that refuse to give Him honour He will get Himself honour upon. But His *saints* (beloved ones) do *bless* Him, not only as they have peculiar blessings from Him, which other creatures have not, but as they praise Him actively, while His other works praise Him only objectively. They bless Him, for they collect the rent or tribute of praise from the inferior creatures, and pay it into the treasury above. All God's works do *praise* Him, as the beautiful building praises the builder, or the well-drawn picture praises the painter; but the saints *bless* Him as the children of prudent tender parents rise up and call them blessed. Of all God's works, His saints, the workmanship of His grace, the firstfruits of His creatures, have most reason to bless Him."

444.—ANTIOCH.
Acts xi. 26.

℟ Antioch was a famous city of ancient times, the capital of the Greek kings of Syria, finely situated on the left bank of the Orontes, about twenty-one miles from the sea, in a beautiful and fertile plain. It was founded by Seleucus Nicator in 300 B.C., and was named after his father Antiochus. It was four miles in circumference, and famed for the number and splendour of its public buildings, the Seleucid monarchs having vied with each other in embellishing their metropolis, and the Roman emperors having also done much to adorn it. It was called the "Queen of the East" and "The Beautiful," and it was advantageously situated for trade, being easily approached by the caravans of the East, and through its port Seleucia having maritime communication with the West. Its inhabitants were celebrated for their luxury and effeminacy, their love of frivolous amusements, and their propensity to ridicule and scurrilous wit. Antioch is frequently mentioned in the New Testament, and it was here that the disciples of our Saviour were first called Christians (Acts xi. 26). Few places have undergone so many calamities as Antioch. In B.C. 65, on the breaking up of the kingdom of Syria, it was captured by Pompey; in A.D. 115 it was almost utterly destroyed by an earthquake; in 260 it was captured by the Persians under Sapor; and in 540 it was thrown into a heap of ruins by the Persians under Chosroes. It was restored by the Emperor Justinian, but never quite recovered this last blow. In the first half of the seventh century it was taken by the Saracens, and remained in their possession for upwards of three hundred years, when it was recovered by the Greek Emperor Nicephorus Phocas. In 1084 it was again taken by the Saracens and remained with them till 1089, when it was taken by the Crusaders. They established the principality of Antioch, of which the first ruler was Boemond, and which lasted till 1268, when it was taken by Bibas, the Mameluke Sultan of Egypt. In 1516 it passed into the hands of the Turks. The modern Antioch, or Antakick, occupies but a small portion of the site of the ancient Antioch. It is a poor place, with narrow, dirty streets, and houses mostly of one story. The population is variously given, the figures ranging between 6,000 and 8,000. It has some manufactures of silk, stuffs, leather, and carpets, and has some trade in these articles, and in goat's wool, beeswax, etc. The neighbourhood of Antioch abounds in fig, olive, and mulberry trees, and in vines, but is indifferently cultivated.

445.—The Eagle Renewing its Youth.
Psalm ciii. 5.

℄ The fable of the eagle's renewing its youth has received different embellishments. The version of *Saadia,* given by *Kimchi,* is as follows:—The eagle mounts aloft into heaven till he comes near to the seat of central fire in the sun, when, scorched by the heat, he casts himself down into the sea. Thence he emerges again with new vigour and fresh plumage, till at last, in his hundredth year, he perishes in the waves. Augustine's story is more elaborate and far less poetical. According to him, when the eagle grows old, the upper curved portion of the beak becomes so enlarged that the bird is unable to open its mouth to seize its prey. It would die of hunger, therefore, did it not dash this part of its beak against a rock till the troublesome excrescence is got rid of. Then it can devour its food as before, vigour is restored to its body, splendour to its plumage, it can soar aloft; a kind of resurrection has taken place. Thus it renews its youth.

Some have supposed that the reference is to the mythical Egyptian bird, the *Phoenix,* which was supposed to live a thousand years, and at the end of that time burn itself in its own nest, that a new and young phoenix might spring from the ashes.

It is sufficient to regard the passage as a poetical reference to the annual moulting of these, as of other birds.

446.—Vow on Recovery from Sickness.
Acts xviii. 18.

℄ On his deliverance from the imminent danger to which he had been exposed, Paul had taken the Nazarite vow in testimony of his thankfulness. It was usual, as Josephus informs us, for the Jews on their recovery from severe disease, or deliverance from any great peril, to take the vow binding themselves to abstain from wine, and let their hair grow for thirty days. By the law on the subject, as stated in the Book of Numbers, the vow might be of shorter or longer duration; and at the expiration of the time the devotee shaved his head and offered certain appointed sacrifices; but as these could not be offered out of Jerusalem those who took

this vow in foreign parts made their offerings at their next visit to
the holy city. At the eastern port of Cenchrea, where he prepared
to embark for Asia, the days of Paul's vow expired, and he shaved
his head, necessarily deferring his offerings till he should reach
Jerusalem. Some have seen so much difficulty in this transaction
that they transfer the vow to Aquila. But, besides that the vow
was not in itself improper, it might be an object with Paul, now
proceeding to Jerusalem, to show, by the offerings which he had
by this act rendered himself liable to make there, that he did not,
as injuriously reported, despise their law, but was himself, as a
Jew, disposed to conform to it on every proper occasion.—*Kitto*.

447.—Breaking the Legs of the Crucified.
John xix. 31.

℄ This was done by means of blows from clubs, and was a
Roman punishment, known by the name of *crurifragium*, which
sometimes accompanied crucifixion, and appears also to have been
used as a separate punishment. Death by crucifixion was ordinarily
exceedingly slow; sometimes the sufferer would linger for several
days, and at last die of hunger. We cannot wonder, therefore, that
occasionally certain lenitives to the terrible lot of the crucified
should be applied by the Romans. The rendering of the sufferer
partly insensible by the giving of wine mingled with myrrh is not
mentioned in the classical writers. They do, however, refer to the
custom of breaking the legs in order to bring about death by exhaustion more rapidly. This accelerating of death would be
regarded by one wearied out with pain as a benefit; but it was a
very barbarous mode of doing a kind act. Origen mentions the
other practice, which was much less common, but was applied in
the case of Christ, of a thrust with a spear in the side. The objection to this mode of expediting the death would be that the man
would then be really put to death in some other mode than that
which his judicial sentence had indicated.

448.—The Wedding Garment.
Matt. xxii. 11.

℄ Archbishop Trench, in discussing the views entertained on this
passage, remarks upon the practice of bestowing gifts upon guests
on festal occasions, and proceeds:—"If the gift took the form of

costly raiment, it would naturally be expected that it should be worn at once, as part of the purpose of the distribution would else be defeated, which was to testify openly to the magnificence and liberality of the giver, and also to add to the splendour and glory of the festal time; not to say that the rejection of a gift or the appearance of a slight put upon it, is ever naturally esteemed as a slight and contempt not of the gift only, but also of the giver.

"So strongly," he adds in a note, "is this felt, that we are not without example in the modern history of the East (and Eastern manners so little change that modern examples are nearly as good as ancient), of a vizier having lost his life through this very failing to wear a garment of honour sent to him by the king. Chardin mentions the circumstances:—The officer through whose hands the royal robe was to be forwarded, out of spite, sent in its stead a plain habit. The vizier would not appear in the city arrayed in this, lest it should be taken as an evidence that he was in disgrace at court, and put on in its stead a royal habit, the gift of the late king, and in that made his public entry into the city. When this was known at court, they declared the vizier a dog, that he had disdainfully thrown away the royal apparel, saying, 'I have no need of Sha Sefi's habits.' Their account incensed the king, who severely felt the affront, and it cost the vizier his life. (*Burder's Orient. Liter.,* vol. i., p. 94. See Herodotus, ix., 111, for an example of the manner in which the rejecting of a monarch's gift was resented.) Olearius (*Travels,* p. 214) gives an account of himself, with the ambassadors whom he accompanied, being invited to the table of the Persian king. He goes on to say, 'It was told us by the *mehmander,* that we, according to their usage, must hang the splendid vests that were sent us from the king over our dresses, and so appear in his presence. The ambassadors at first refused; but the *mehmander* urged it earnestly, alleging, as also did others, that the omission would greatly displease the king, since all other envoys observed such a custom, and at last they consented, and hanged, as we did also, the splendid vests over their shoulders, and so the cavalcade proceeded.' This passage, besides its value as showing us how the rejection of the garment of honour, or rather the failing to appear in it, would be felt as an insult, clears away any difficulty which might have occurred to any from the apparent unfitness of the king's palace as a place for changing of apparel; in fact, there was, strictly speaking, no such changing of apparel, for the garment of honour was either a vest with loose sleeves, which hang down (for the arm is not put into them), drawn over the other garments, or a mantle hung on the shoulders. Schulz, in his *Travels*, describes that given to him as a 'long robe, the white ground of which is goat's hair, mixed with some silver, but the flowers woven in are of golden-coloured silk:' and his account of the necessity of putting it on before appearing in the presence of the Sultan agrees with that given by the earlier traveller."

Every guest invited to the wedding at the royal marriage of Sultan Mahmoud, a few years ago, had made expressly for him, at the expense of the Sultan, a wedding garment. No one, however dignified by his station, was permitted to enter into the presence-chamber of that sovereign without a change of raiment. This was formerly the universal custom in the East. But inasmuch as these garments were very costly, and some of the guests invited might plead poverty, and thus appear unclad in the guest-chamber of the king, the cost was defrayed at Sultan Mahmoud's expense. To each guest was presented a suit of wedding garments.

449.—VINEGAR.
Matt. xxvii. 48.

⟨ The Hebrew word (*chomets*) translated "vinegar," was applied to a beverage consisting generally of wine or strong drink turned sour; but sometimes artificially made by an admixture of barley and wine, and thus liable to fermentation. The Old Testament allusions to vinegar are found in the following passages:—Num. vi. 3; Ruth ii. 14; Ps. lxix. 21; Prov. x. 26, xxv. 20.

The Roman word (*acetum*) was applied to a thin sour wine generally used by the soldiers, either in a pure state or, more usually, mixed with water, when it was called *posca*. Probably it was this wine and water that was offered to the Saviour, and it would be refreshing to one suffering as He was with exhaustion and thirst. Earlier in our Lord's sufferings He refused this vinegar, because it was then mingled with myrrh, which was intended to deaden the sense of pain. The sponge had probably served instead of a cork to the jar in which the soldiers had brought the drink that was to sustain them in their long day's work. One of them had evidently heard our Lord's cry, "I thirst," and so, prompted by a rough pity, stretched out a cane, or stalk of hyssop, with the sponge that had been dipped in the vinegar fastened to the end of it. The act gives us some indication of the height to which the

cross was raised above the ground, a stalk of hyssop being not
more than two feet long.

450.—Sentiment concerning Removal
of Garments.
2 Sam. vi. 14.

⚏ The common people of the East wear a loose shirt, large trousers, long jacket, and a girdle round the loins. Others add a waist-
coat, and a flowing robe under the girdle. Over all is a loose mantle (the coat of Scripture) with short but wide sleeves, and open in
the front, though capable of being wrapped round with the arms
in cold weather. This cloak is the full dress, and is usually laid
aside in the house when a person wishes to be at his ease. It is also
very inconvenient to work in the wide under-garment, and hence
the peasants and servants do not adopt it. But in taking it off, the
girdle must necessarily be first removed.

"David was girded with a linen ephod;" and Michal said, "How
glorious was the king of Israel to-day, who uncovered himself!"
(ver. 20, etc.). David took off his robes, and girt his under-gar-
ments with a linen ephod, for a description of which see Exod.
xxxix. 5. Now the great men of the East will not let even their feet
be seen whilst they are sitting with their legs under them. King
David had assumed the costume of a working man, having only
put the priest's girdle over it, but without the sacerdotal coats. It
was this, and the act of dancing, that offended Saul's daughter,
who had been brought up in all the regal pride which prevailed in
the court of her father.

451.—The Philistines.
Gen. x. 13, 14.

⚏ This people inhabited the south-west seaboard of Canaan.
Their origin and race-character have been much disputed, some
contending that they were an *Hamitic,* while others think that they
were a Semitic people. They are said to have emigrated from
Caphtor, probably the Island of Crete, or the coast of Asia Minor.
Professor Wilkins argues that three distinct emigrations can be
traced: the first from Casluhim, the second and chief from Caph-
torim; the third from the Cherethim: and the last one appears to

have taken place about the middle of the age of the judges, from
which time we observe a decided accession of Philistine power.
Compare Gen. x. 14; Deut. ii. 23; Jer. xlvii. 4; Amos ix. 7; 1 Sam.
xxx. 14.

Their geographical position and their relation to neighbouring
nations will account for the growth of the Philistine power. Between the times of Abraham and Joshua the Philistines had
changed their quarters, and had advanced northwards into the
Shephelah, or plain of Philistia. This plain has been remarkable in
all ages for the extreme richness of its soil. The crops which it
yielded were alone sufficient to ensure national wealth. It was also
adapted to the growth of military power; for while the plain itself
permitted the use of war chariots, which were the chief arm of
offence, the occasional elevations which rise out of it offered
secure sites for towns and strongholds. It was, moreover, a commercial country; from its position it must have been at all times
the great thoroughfare between Phoenicia and Syria in the north,
and Egypt and Arabia in the south. Ashdod and Gaza were the
keys of Egypt, and commanded the transit trade.

"Unlike the rest of the inhabitants of Canaan, they were uncir-
cumcised, and appear to have stood on a lower level of civilisation. They were almost, it may be said, the laughingstock of their
livelier and quicker neighbours, from their dull, heavy stupidity;
the easy prey of the rough humour of Samson, or the agility and
cunning of the diminutive David. Throughout sacred history they
seem to be the butt of Israelitish wit and Israelitish craft."

452.—HEBREW FIGURE FOR EARNESTLY PROTESTING.
Jer. xi. 7.

⊄ These are the words of the Lord, and in order to understand
this and similar passages we must bear in mind that the Hebrew
verb had come to be used merely as a strong adverb. One of the
most remarkable cases of this usage is found in 1 Sam. xvii. 16.
"And the Philistine drew near morning and evening," where
"morning" and "evening" are properly infinitives and might have
been rendered "rising early and coming late." Thus in the passage
of the prophet "protesting earnestly" would have conveyed the
meaning. *Shacham,* the verb in question, is properly applied to
loading a camel's back, in one of its conjugations, and this was

done at dawn, and hence the metaphor is peculiarly Oriental, being taken from the daily life of the sons of the desert.

453.—THE VALUE OF SLEEP.
John xi. 12.

⟪ Rev. Hugh Macmillan writes: "Sleep is one of the most wonderful phenomena of rejuvenescence. It is through sleep that worn-out nature is recruited and renews its youth. As the French proverb says: 'He who sleeps, eats.' Our bodies return in sleep every night to the ante-natal state, in order that our exhausted energies may be concentrated and refreshed, and, obtaining a new draught from the great Source of all life, we may issue every day from the womb of the morning new creatures. We sink to a low condition of development analogous to that of the vegetable, that we may rise to a more perfect animal condition than before. The inner formative processes do not rest during this depression and retreat, but rather act the more vigorously, as they do in the plant, because of the absence of all the distractions and interferences of self-consciousness. So, too, the mind in sleep relaxes its hold of the outward world, and becomes a mere passive mirror to reflect its images and sensations in dreams; but in this state of passivity it gathers itself into new force—into a renewed recollection of its specific purpose—and rearranges in an orderly manner all the confusions and perplexities of its waking state. It is also through the soft soothing sleep which occurs at the crisis of severe diseases that the rejuvenescence of the body occurs. The patient falls into the same state as the caterpillar when it prepares the rejuvenised body for its future resurrection into the butterfly. In this pupa-sleep—this chrysalis state as it were—all his exhausted energies are gathered in and restored, and he afterwards emerges into a freer and more mobile existence."

454.—PETER'S SHADOW.
Acts v. 15.

⟪ From what is said in the verse following it would appear that cures actually ensued. The act itself of bringing the sick and laying them in the streets showed *faith,* and it might please God to bless such an act in a special manner at that time, in order to give additional authority to the doctrine preached by the Apostles, and to show that they were in an extraordinary degree filled with the Holy Ghost recently poured out on them on the day of Pentecost. There was no cause for fear lest the people should regard the Apostles as *sources* of Divine power and not as *channels,* for Peter and the rest took care to obviate any such supposition. (See chap. iii. 13, xiv. 15.) They assumed nothing to themselves, and ascribed all their efficiency to Christ. Indeed, these signs of a special out-pouring of Divine effluence were proofs of Christ's ascension, and were manifestations of *His* glory. They showed that He had re-ceived gifts to give to men; and that He had sent what He prom-ised. These miracles, therefore, were confirmatory of the faith and courage of the Apostles. They showed that though absent from them in person, Christ was present with them in power (Matt. xxviii. 20). Christ, when on earth, had shed forth Divine virtue on those who touched with faith the hem of His garment (Matt. ix. 20; Mark vi. 56; Luke viii. 44). And now that He is glorified in heaven, He works by the shadow of Peter, and by the handker-chiefs of Paul (chap. xix. 12). So He fulfils His own prophecy, that they who should believe in Him when glorified should do greater works than He had done on earth (John xiv. 12).— *Wordsworth.*

455.—"WITH HIS COAT RENT."
2 Sam. xv. 32.

⫷ If the ancient customs were like the modern ones, the "rending of garments" was a much less serious and more formal matter than has been generally supposed. And the characteristic distinc-tions between the flowing garments of the East and the tightly-fitting garments of the West need to be carefully estimated. Van Lennep says of the present habits of the people in Asia Minor— "The rending of the garment consists in ripping open the seams on each side of the *kuftan,* or robe, in front, where the gored pieces are sewed on to enable the edges to overlap each other, so that, there being no real tearing, the damages can easily be repaired by a few stitches. The 'entary,' or woman's garment, corresponding to the kuftan of the men, is rent in the same manner as a sign of mourning. It is now the custom for the priest in charge of the obsequies at a funeral to go round to the chief mourners and rip

open the front seam of each one's kuftan for him three or four
inches down from the waist, and so as not to injure the garment."

456.—THE CLOVEN TONGUES OF PENTECOST.
Acts ii. 3.

⁋ The Greek word used in this passage does not indicate that the
tongues were *cloven,* or cut, as the Authorised Version gives it.
The true sense is that the tongues were *distributed,* or divided
among the disciples, in such a manner that each received one. It is
also manifest from the Greek that only one tongue was allotted to
each disciple, for the original expression is "it," that is the particular tongue, "sat upon each of them." Dr. Dykes says: "With the
sound came a brightness, as of a fiery stream, *which parted itself
to each,* so that each brother or sister saw on every other's head a
flame-like tongue-shaped thing, which seemed to alight there and
rest." This is the view of Dr. Gloag also. But Calvin and Alford
maintain that the translation given in our version is correct, and
that the word "cloven" must refer not to the *apportionment* of the
tongues, but to something peculiar in their *appearance.*

457.—SITTING AT THE FEET OF THE TEACHER.
Luke x. 39.

⁋ Describing the School for Theological Instruction, established
at Tocat, in Asia Minor, Van Lennep says: "During term time,
our most interesting exercise was held in my study every Sunday
evening, our principal church members and the members of our
families, with all the students, being present. They sat cross-legged
in two rows upon the floor, and related whatever interesting con-
versation they had held during the week on the subject of the
great salvation with persons as yet ignorant of it. These narratives
were interspersed with suggestions, advice, and consultations respecting the best mode of prosecuting the work in its application
to the cases in hand."

The *Abbé Huc,* traveller in Thibet and China, describes a similar attitude taken by the Lama students in the Lamaseries, or col-
leges, of Thibet. In their case, however, they sat in the open air,
whatever the weather might be.

458.—SITTING AT THE RIGHT HAND.
Psalm cx. 1.

℃ This was regarded both among the Greeks and Orientals as entailing the greatest dignity; it was the position of the highest honour, and even involved participation in the royal dignity and power; and in the psalm a permanent, not a merely occasional, honour is evidently referred to, for Jehovah is to aid the king in effecting the subjugation of his enemies; he is to sit at Jehovah's right hand till that subjugation is effected.

As an illustration from classical writings we may cite Pindar, who speaks of Minerva as at the right hand of Zeus, associated with him in his sovereignty, and receiving his commands for the other gods. And Callimachus says that Apollo is able to reward the chorus, if they sing to please him, because he sits at the right hand of Zeus.

As an illustration from Eastern life we quote a passage from Eichhorn. Ibn Cotaiba says: "The *Ridafat* is the dignity of sitting next to the king. But the Radaf (he who holds rank after the king) sits on his right hand, and if the king drinks, the Radaf drinks next, before all others; and if the king goes out upon an expedition, the Radaf sits on his seat, and acts in his room till he returns; and if the king's army goes forth to war, the Radaf receives a fourth part of the booty."

459.—A PLACE WHERE TWO SEAS MET.
Acts xxvii. 41.

℃ The following interesting letter appeared in a weekly journal: the name of the writer was not given:—Being at Malta lately, and finding that my stay there would be of considerable duration, I hired a small cutter for the purpose of amusing myself. I had sailed with the north-west wind (Euroclydon) very many times into the bay which tradition points out as the spot where St. Paul was wrecked, and had always wondered why the ship's captain allowed her to run ashore at the traditional spot, which is very rocky, instead of running the ship aground at the top of the bay— an undertaking attended with danger neither to the ship nor to the passengers. One day, however, while trying to solve the difficulty, as I entered the bay, I perceived to my astonishment what ap-

peared to be a small land-locked bay with a sandy beach about
sixty yards to the right of the traditional spot. I had never
remarked this on any previous occasion, and the thought struck
me that I must be on the exact spot where the ship anchored during the night. It is plain, then, that the captain, at daylight, seeing
this little sandy bay about 400 to 600 yards distant, determined to
"run his ship aground" there, instead of sailing up to the top of
the bay, about two miles distant. He accordingly took up the
anchors and put the ship before the wind, and in about five minutes, to his horror, he perceived the charming spot was not a
land-locked bay, but that what he before took for a headland was
really an island, with the wind sweeping furiously down the narrow channel between it and the mainland, bringing a heavy sea
with it; accordingly he "fell into a place where two seas met," and
owing to the altered direction of the wind coming down the funnel
or channel, he could not haul close and make the sand in time, but
was carried to the rocks on his left. This, sir, I feel certain is the
true interpretation, and St. Luke has described the spot exactly.
Therefore, it cannot reasonably be doubted that St. Paul was
wrecked at Malta.

460.—THE GREEK WORDS WHICH ARE
TRANSLATED DAMNATION.
Rom. iii. 8.

¶ The word *damn* only occurs twelve times in the New Testament.
The Greek words which it is presumed to represent are κρίνειν
(Krinein) and κατα-κρίνειν (Kata-Krinein). *Krinein* properly means
"to part, to separate, to discriminate between good and bad, to
judge." *Kata-Krinein* properly means "to give judgment against,
to condemn." The word *Krinein* occurs more than a hundred and
seventy times in the Greek Testament; more than one hundred and
fifty times it is rendered in the English version by our verb "to
judge," so that our translators evidently knew its plain meaning
and use. Seven times they render the word by the term "to condemn," twice by "to accuse," and only eight times by "to damn."
That is to say, our English translators render this word in the sense
of "to damn" only eight times out of nearly one hundred and
eighty. The similar thing may be observed concerning the other
word, *Kata-Krinein*, which means "to condemn." With its derivatives it is used twenty-four times in the New Testament, and only

twice is it rendered by the verb "to damn;" in every other case our translators abide by its true meaning, "to condemn."

Rev. S. Cox thus traces the origin and meaning of the English word "damn." It probably came from an old Teutonic word, *deman,* to deem. It is at least closely related to the words "deem" and "doom." It meant to *deem* any one guilty of any kind of offence, and to *doom* him to its appropriate punishment. Thus, for example, a man might be *damned* to prison, *i.e.* *deemed* worthy of it, and *doomed* to it; or his gods might be damnified, *i.e.* injured or condemned; or a play might be damned, *i.e.* hissed off the stage, *deemed* too poor for further representation, and *doomed* never to appear again.

461.—THE LEGEND OF THE CEDAR OF LEBANON.
Psalm civ. 16.

⁋ This ancient legend—the dream, perhaps, of a Syrian hermit—shows that the Cedar of Lebanon, the timber tree of the Temple built on Zion, was held in highest estimation, and exercised the fancy. The story proceeds that Seth received from the angels three seeds of that tree which he beheld still standing upon the spot where sin had been first committed, but standing there blasted and dead. He carried the seeds home, placed them in the mouth of the dead Adam, and so buried them. Their future history is curious. Growing on the grave of Adam in Hebron they were afterwards most carefully protected by Abraham, Moses, and David. After their removal to Jerusalem, the Psalms were composed beneath them; and in due time, when they had grown together, and united into one giant tree, they, or it—for it was now one tree, a Cedar of Lebanon—was felled by Solomon for the purpose of being preserved for ever as a beam in the Temple. But the design failed; the king's carpenters found themselves utterly unable to manage the mighty beam. They raised it to its intended position, and found it too long. They sawed it, and it then proved too short. They spliced it, and again found it wrong. It was evidently intended for another, perhaps a more sacred office, and they laid it aside in the Temple to bide its time. While waiting for its appointed hour, the beam was on one occasion improperly made use of by a woman named Maximella, who took the liberty of sitting on it, and presently found her garments on fire. Instantly she raised a cry, and feeling the flames severely, she invoked the aid of Christ, and was immediately driven from the city and stoned, becoming in her death a pro-Christian martyr. In the course of an eventful history the pre-destined beam became a bridge over Cedron, and being then thrown into the Pool of Bethesda, it proved the cause of its healing virtues. Finally it became the Cross, was buried in Calvary, exhumed by the Empress Helena, chopped up by a corrupt Church, and distributed.

462.—YE SHALL NOT CUT YOURSELVES.
Deut. xiv. 1.

℅ Among the Orientals the custom of cutting the flesh was practised on various occasions, and that too from the most remote periods of which we have any record. The priests of Baal, in their contest with Elijah, "cut themselves after their manner with knives and lancets, until the blood gushed out upon them" (1 Kings xviii. 28). This might have been done in order to show their affection for their god, as lovers regularly did the same thing to attract the pity of their mistresses. Mr. Aaron Hill, the poet and traveller, who lived some time in Turkey early in the last century, says of the Turks, "The most ridiculous and senseless method of expressing their affection is their singing certain amorous and whirling songs, between every line whereof they cut and slash their naked arms with daggers: each endeavouring in their emulative madness to exceed the other by the depth and number of the wounds he gives himself. Some Turks I have observed, when old and past the follies which possessed their youth, show their arms all gashed and scarred, from wrist to elbow, and express a great concern, but greater wonder, at their past simplicity."

One of the songs runs thus:—

> "Could I, dear ray of heavenly light,
> Who now behind a cloud doth shine,
> Obtain the blessings of thy sight,
> And taste thy influence all divine.

> "Thus would I shed my heart's warm blood,
> As now I gash my veiny arm;
> Would'st thou but like the sun think good
> To draw it upward, by some charm."

The custom of cutting the flesh is referred to frequently in the Old Testament, e.g. Jer. xlviii. 37, xvi. 6. This prophet also relates

462.—Ye shall not Cut Yourselves.

that on a certain occasion "there came from Samaria fourscore men, having their beards shaven, and their clothes rent, and having cut themselves, with offerings and incense in their hand, to bring them to the house of the Lord." It appears from these passages that the prohibitions given by Moses against this foolish custom had proved ineffectual, for the prophet refers to it as quite a common thing.

It appears that the Baalites were not the only idolaters who lanced themselves at their worship. Herodotus says that the Carians cut their foreheads with knives when sacrificing to Isis; and Lucian relates that the Syrians in worshipping the same deity cut their arms and tongues with swords. It is possible that the Mosaic prohibition was also directed against tattooing, by which men indicated their allegiance to a given deity, just as soldiers and slaves marked themselves to shew their allegiance to their commanders and masters. This branch of the custom is referred to in Ezek. ix. 4. The Apostle Paul declares (Gal. vi. 17) that he "bears in his body the marks of the Lord Jesus"—tattoo marks that showed his owner. His meaning seems to be, "I am the slave of Jesus, and since I belong to Him, and have the marks to shew, let no man interfere with me while I am about my Master's business." In the Book of Revelation the "mark of the beast" is mentioned, which is to be understood in a similar manner.

463.—PERMISSION TO MAKE STREETS
A TERM OF ANCIENT TREATIES.
1 Kings xx. 34.

℀ When Ahab of Israel had conquered Benhadad of Syria, the latter became a suppliant for his life, and among other promises made to the conqueror was this:—"Thou shalt make streets for thee in Damascus, as my father made in Samaria." This appears to mean that at a former period, when Benhadad's father had conquered Israel, he had settled a sort of colony of Syrians in the capital of the conquered country; and those colonists dwelt in streets, either expressly built for them, or from which Israelitish inhabitants had been expelled in order to make room for them. Now, Benhadad, in turn being subdued, agrees that Ahab shall either build or seize certain streets in the Syrian capital to be occupied by Israelites. The transaction receives a good illustration in the history of Constantinople. When that city had been besieged by Bajazet, the Turkish Sultan, for about two years, about the end of the fourteenth century, Emmanuel, the Greek Emperor, sent out ambassadors to the Grand Turk to sue for peace. At length a treaty was concluded, and peace restored, on the condition, among others, that the Turks should have liberty to dwell in one street, with free exercise of their own religion and laws, and under a judge of their own nation. This was agreed to, and a large number of Turks forthwith took up their residence at the capital.

464.—THE POSSIBILITY OF ALL ISRAEL HEARING THE LAW AT EBAL.
Josh. viii. 34.

℘ Having satisfied myself more than once during my stay at Nablûs of its feasibility, a party of us resolved to make the experiment. We had pitched our tent in the valley near the foot of Gerizim, on the line between the two mountains, where I suppose the Ark to have formerly stood. I clambered up Gerizim and Mr. Williams up Ebal, Mr. Edwards remaining with the men at the tent. Having reached the lower spur, I found myself standing, as it were, upon a lofty pulpit, and my friend found himself similarly situated on Ebal. Having rested awhile, I opened my Bible, and read the command concerning the blessings in Hebrew, and every word was heard most distinctly by Mr. Edwards in the valley, as well as by Mr. Williams on Ebal. Mr. Williams then read the cursings in Welsh, and we all heard every word and syllable. Before we descended, Mr. Edwards requested us to sing, and gave out, "Praise God from whom all blessings flow," etc. I commenced it upon the tune Savoy, or the Old Hundredth, but I pitched the tune in a key too high for them to join me. I was determined, however, to sing it through; and if I ever sang well and with spirit, I did so then on Gerizim, and was heard most distinctly by all. And it was our impression, and still is, that if the whole area before and around us had been filled with the hundreds of thousands of Israel, every soul amongst them would have heard every note and word with perfect clearness.—*Mill's "Nablûs."*

465.—THE WEIGHTY AMMONITE CROWN.
2 Sam. xii. 30.

℞ In the chapter from which this verse is taken there is an account of David's capture of *Rabbah,* a very important city of the Ammonites. It is stated that he took from the head of their king a crown of gold, set with precious stones, the weight of which was *one talent;* and this heavy diadem is said to have been placed on David's own head. So runs the translation, but there must be some misconception of the precise meaning of the original words. A talent weighs, according to the lowest computation, from 90 lbs. to 100 lbs., and no human head could possibly wear a crown so heavy. The difficulty, it has been suggested, may be thus explained:—In the Hebrew "their king" is expressed by one word, viz., *Malcom,* which is also the name of the great idol of the Ammonites; and although no living man could wear a crown of 100 lbs. weight, a god of metal, wood, or stone, might support a headdress much heavier. It is probable, then, that the crown was taken from the head of Malcom, or Moloch, the Ammonite god, not from the Ammonite-king.

But the question must still arise, how could David's head sustain so great a weight, for it is said that the ponderous crown was put upon him? The translation says that the crown was ornamented with precious stones; but the Hebrew mentions *only one* stone. Possibly, there was one large stone set in the huge crown, and this stone was transferred to the royal crown of David.

466.—NIGHT WATCHES IN THE TEMPLE.
Psalm cxxxiv. 1.

℞ From a Targum we learn that "the custom in the Second Temple appears to have been this. After midnight the chief of the doorkeepers took the key of the inner Temple, and went with some of the priests through the small postern of the Fire Gate. In the inner court this watch divided itself into two companies, each carrying a burning torch; one company turned west, the other east, and so they compassed the court to see whether all were in readiness for the Temple service on the following morning. In the bakehouse, where the *Mincha* (meat-offering) of the High-priest was baked, they met with the cry 'All well.' Meanwhile the rest of the priests arose, bathed themselves, and put on their garments. They then went into the stone-chamber (one half of which was the hall of session of the Sanhedrin), and there, under the superintendence of the officer who gave the watchword and one of the Sanhedrin, surrounded by the priests clad in their robes of office, their several duties for the coming day were assigned to each of the priests by lot."

467.—"GO, SEEK THE ASSES."
1 Sam. ix. 3.

❡ The search appears to have been conducted without any settled plan, and among the Tartars such journeys appear to be frequent. Everyone has a private mark upon his beasts, and when they stray their ownership is easily ascertained. A Tartar with a large extent of plain before him will set out at sunrise, not knowing which way to go, but choosing the direction from any chance that inclines him, this way or that. He rides on till sunset, and then dismounts, fastens his horse, and gets his supper. He carries with him in a bag six lbs. of the flour of roasted millet, which is sufficient to last him thirty days. Day after day he goes on, observing the marks of all the herds he meets, and receiving information from any who, like himself, are in search of stray cattle. Very likely the search of Saul was somewhat similar.

468.—ONE OF THE PHOENICIAN GODS.
1 Kings xviii. 24.

❡ The Phoenician religion has been defined thus,—a deification of the powers of nature, which naturally developed into an admiration of the objects in which those powers seemed most active. Baal, Moloch, and Astarte were their gods, and a sad and cruel worship was rendered to them. The immoralities and falsities connected with this worship were very difficult of extirpation, and are even lamented by such fathers of the Church as Tertullian and Augustine, long after the Phoenician Carthage might have been supposed to pass away.

But there was one god whose worship seems to have been much more genial, and much more spiritual, than the rest.

"This god was Melcarth, that is, Melech-Kirjah, or the King of the City. He is called by the Greeks 'the Phoenician Hercules,' and his name itself has passed, with a slight alteration, into Greek mythology as Melicartes. The city of which he was pre-eminently the god was Tyre. There he had a magnificent temple, which was visited, for antiquarian purposes, by Herodotus. It contained two splendid pillars, one of pure gold, the other, as Herodotus believed, of emerald, which shone brilliantly at night; but there was no image of the god to be seen. The same was the case in his famous temple at Thasos, and the still more famous one at Gades, which contained an oracle, a hierarchy of priests, and a mysterious spring, which rose and fell inversely with the tide; but still no image. At Carthage, Melcarth had not even a temple. The whole city was his temple, and he refused to be localised in any particular part of it. He received, there is reason to believe, no sacrifices of blood; and it was comparatively pure and spiritual worship which, as we see repeatedly in Carthaginian history, formed a chief link in the chain that bound the parent to the various daughter-cities scattered over the coasts and islands of the Mediterranean."

469.—WATERING WITH THE FOOT.
Deut. xi. 10.

⟪ Egypt owes not only her fertility, but even her very existence as an agricultural country, to the risings of the River Nile. Far back in Palaeontological periods the Nile flowed through a barren district, and lower Egypt was covered by the Mediterranean waters. But the mighty river was ever bearing down from the interior of Africa precious freights of fine rich mud, which were deposited, age after age, in the channel through which the stream flowed, till by and by the estuary was filled up, and lower Egypt and the Delta rose above the waters. The same river that had thus transported a whole country from the inland regions, continued every year to fertilise the same by periodical flooding, and the deposit of a fresh thin layer of earth. Those who first settled in Egypt found much ready to hand; but necessity soon showed them that continued prosperity could be assured only by labour. The

land was annually flooded for a short period; but for the rest of
the year it was parched by a cloudless sun. Hence irrigation became necessary, and they soon learned the art of raising the water
from the Nile for purposes of agriculture. Very early in the history
of the country the methods of irrigation were as perfect as they
have ever been. By some simple machinery the water was first
raised from the river to a height rather above the elevation of the
most distant fields to be watered. From the Nile banks the water
was then conveyed by sluices, or small rude aqueducts, to reservoirs, situated in the fields and gardens; and from these reservoirs
the precious liquid was eventually drawn off to every plant which
required its aid.

In the present day, as in the time of Moses, the plants and seed
are watered by the foot. The water-furrows run through the garden, but do not reach every plant; the *fellah,* however (as the
modern Egyptian hind is called), walks down the rows of maize,
or cotton, and tracks in the loose soil, with his big toe, a small
runlet from the water-furrow to the root of each plant, and when
the plant is sufficiently watered the soil is smoothed over again.
Thus the *fellah* waters his seed "with his foot," as the Israelites did
thousands of years before him.

470.—THE OLDEST LIGHTNING CONDUCTORS.
Job xxviii. 26.

℃ Arago, the celebrated French astronomer, writes the following:
—"The temple of the Jews at Jerusalem existed for a period of
nearly one thousand years; for the temple of Solomon existed
nearly four hundred years, and the second temple about six hundred years. This temple was, by its situation, more particularly exposed to the very frequent and violent thunderstorms in Palestine.
Nevertheless, neither the Bible nor Josephus mentions that it was
ever struck by lightning. The cause of this is very simple. By a for-
tuitous circumstance, the temple of Jerusalem was provided with a
lightning conductor, which came very near that discovered by
Franklin, and used by us. The roof of the temple, similar to those
found in Italy, was covered with thickly gilt wood. Lastly, beneath
the fore court of the temple, there were cisterns into which flowed
the water coming from the roof, by means of metal pipes. Here
we find such a multitude of lightning conductors, that Lichtenberg
was right when he maintained that the mechanism of the like con-

struction in our days is far from presenting an apparatus so well
adapted to produce the desired effect."

471.—ABYSSINIAN ACCOUNT OF THE VISIT
OF THE QUEEN OF SHEBA.
2 Chron. ix. 1.

⁋ The exact location of the country of Sheba has always been a
matter of uncertainty, but the following tradition, brought by
Bruce, the traveller from Abyssinia, is full of interest, and may to
some extent help towards the settlement of the difficulty.

She was the Queen of Saba, Azah, Azaba, that is "Queen of the
South," or Ethiopia. "Pagan, Arab, Moor, Abyssinian, and all the
countries round," says Bruce, "vouch for the story pretty much in
the terms of Scripture." Her name, the Arabs say, was *Belkis,*
though the Abyssinians call her *Macqueda.* The annals of Abyssinia say that when she left Azah she was a pagan, but became a
convert to Judaism through the influence of Solomon. They further state that she remained for some time in Judaea, where she
bore a son to Solomon, and called him Menilek. The Abyssinians,
both Jews and Christians, believe that the 45th Psalm is a prophecy of this queen's journey to Jerusalem. The psalm speaks of the
glory of some king, probably Solomon; refers to kings' daughters
as being among his honourable women, the queen being present in
gold of Ophir; and the "daughter of Tyre being there with a gift"
(verses 9–12). The reference to the daughter of Tyre is explained
by the statement that King Hiram's daughter accompanied the
Queen of Sheba from Tyre. The 16th verse of the psalm says: "Instead of thy fathers shall be thy children, whom thou mayest make
princes in the earth." This is said to be a direct allusion to
Solomon's son by Belkis, or Macqueda, who succeeded her in the
kingdom. This son she took back with her on her return to Azah,
but in a few years she sent him to Jerusalem to be instructed by
his father. Solomon is said to have discharged his duty well, and
when the prince's education was finished, he was anointed and
crowned King of Ethiopia in the temple at Jerusalem, and at his
inauguration assumed the name of David. He returned home, taking with him a colony of Jews, with many doctors of the Mosaic
Law, and particularly one doctor from each tribe to be made
judges in his own land. The present judges of Abyssinia claim de-

scent from these immigrants. In addition to those already named,
Menilek was also accompanied by Azarias, son of Zadok the
priest, who carried with him a Hebrew copy of the Law, and bore
the title of High Priest. This honour is continued, they say, in his
descendants, who are still the keepers of the church at Axum.
When the young king arrived, the whole country was very soon
converted, and the government was remodelled according to that
of the Jews. Of the race of Abyssinian kings descended from
Solomon and Belkis the heraldic device is a lion passant, proper,
upon a field of gules, and their motto, *Mo Anbasa am Nizilet
Solomon Negadé Jude,* "The lion of the race of Solomon and tribe
of Judah hath overcome."

472.—MIGRATIONS FROM KIR.
Amos ix. 7.

℄ "The most competent authorities teach us to conceive of successive waves of population, issuing from the mountainous country
near the sources of the Euphrates and the Tigris, to which the narrative of Genesis points as the cradle of the human race, and to
which the Mosaic accounts of the Deluge bring us back as the
centre from which the children of Noah went forth again to people the earth. Of all the migrations from the land of Kir, to the regions that lay south-west of it, that which is of the greatest importance in the history of man is undoubtedly the one which the Bible
connects with the name of Terah. But this was so far from being
the first of the movements in this direction, that it is much more
likely to have been the last. The anthropomorphic language of the
Mosaic record is certainly not intended to hinder us from the
quest of secondary causes for the change of abode, which it ascribes to the direct command of the Deity. It was probably partly
in consequence of the barrenness of the upper valley of the
Euphrates that rendered it little fitted for the home of a pastoral
tribe; partly from the establishment of a powerful non-Semitic empire upon the banks of the Tigris, leading, according to an old tradition, which may be accepted in its general meaning, even if its
details bear the stamp of later invention, to the persecution of
those who clung to the purer faith, that the family of Abraham
found its way into the more fertile and peaceful land of Canaan.
But the same causes which had urged him on we may believe to

have been powerful with kindred tribes. All evidence that we have
confirms the supposition that, long before the days of Abraham,
Semitic tribes had pressed along the path by which the Divine
guidance was to lead him, to the land that should afterwards be
possessed by his descendants, as the sand that is by the sea-shore
for multitude."—*A. S. Wilkins.*

473.—HABITS OF SWALLOWS.
Psalm lxxxiv. 3.

⁋ Swallows are in the East allowed the freedom of the house.
They make their nests not only in the verandah, but in the rooms
themselves, within the mosques, and in the sacred tombs. It is one
of the most useful of birds. It is impossible to reckon the number
of flies, gnats, mosquitoes, and other small insects he destroys,
which would otherwise render life insupportable. It has been calculated by an Eastern missionary that over the gateway of a single
farm-house no less than 800 swallows had been bred in a single
season. If we allow but ten flies and mosquitoes as the daily fare
of each swallow, we have a daily consumption of 8,000 insects,
which could, in the space of an hour or two, worry the life out of
the owner of the property, his family, attendants, and cattle.

474.—ORMUZD, THE PERSIAN GOD.
Ezra i. 1, 2.

⁋ Two things are specially remarkable in this passage—the
strongly marked religious character, very unusual in heathen documents, and the distinctness with which it asserts the unity of God,
and thence identifies the God of the Persians with the God of the
Jews. Both these points receive abundant illustration from the Persian cuneiform inscriptions, in which the recognition of a single
supreme god, Ormuzd, and the clear and constant ascription to
Him of the direction of all mundane affairs, are leading features.
In all the Persian monuments of any length, the monarch makes
the acknowledgement that "Ormuzd has bestowed on him his empire." Every success that is gained is "by the grace of Ormuzd."
The name occurs in almost every other paragraph of the Behistun
inscription. No public monuments with such a pervading religious

spirit have ever been discovered among the records of any heathen nation as those of the Persian kings; and through all of them, down to the times of Artaxerxes Ochus, the name of Ormuzd stands alone and unapproachable as that of the supreme Lord of earth and heaven. The title "Lord of heaven," which runs as a sort of catchword through these Chaldee translations of the Persian records, is not indeed in the cuneiform monuments distinctly attached to him as an epithet; but the common formula wherewith inscriptions open sets him forth as "the great God Ormuzd, who gave both earth and heaven to mankind."—*Rawlinson*.

475.—ABRAHAM LIKE A BEDOUIN SHEIKH.
Gen. xii. 4.

℧ Every English pilgrim to the Holy Land, even the most reverential and the most fastidious, is delighted to trace and to record the likeness of patriarchal manners and costumes in the Arabian chiefs. Such as we see them now, starting on a pilgrimage, or a journey, were Abraham and his brother's son, when they "went forth" to go into the land of Canaan. All their substance that they had "gathered" is heaped high on the backs of their kneeling camels. The "slaves that they had bought in Haran run along by their sides. Round about them are their flocks of sheep and goats, and the asses moving underneath the towering forms of their camels. The chief is there, amidst the stir of movement, or resting at noon within his black tent, marked out from the rest by his cloak of brilliant scarlet, by the fillet of rope which binds the loose handkerchief round his head, by the spear which he holds in his hand to guide the march, and to fix the encampment. The chief's wife, the princess of the tribe, is there in her own tent, to make the cakes and prepare the usual meal of mill and butter; the slave or the child is ready to bring in the red lentile soup for the weary hunter, or to kill the calf for the unexpected guest. Even the ordinary social state is the same: polygamy, slavery, the exclusiveness of family ties; the period of service for the dowry of a wife; the solemn obligations of hospitality; the temptations, easily followed, into craft or falsehood. The likeness between a Bedouin chief of our day and such a chief as Abraham is complete, except in the force of the religious faith which probably raised Abraham's

tribe altogether above those who have been described as the
godless, grasping, foul-mouthed Arabs of the modern desert."—
From Dean Stanley.

476.—THE GODS OF THE STRANGERS PLANTED IN SAMARIA.
2 Kings xvii. 29–31.

℄ Shalmaneser, King of Assyria, who conquered the kingdom of
Israel, and carried off the ten tribes into captivity, also peopled the
desolate land with Gentile tribes brought from various parts of his
empire. To screen themselves from the attacks of wild beasts, the
Gentile immigrants adopted the worship of Jehovah, but simultaneously worshipped also the gods of their several tribes.

Thus the Babylonian settlers made and worshipped *Succoth-
benoth.* This compound word occurs nowhere else in the Bible,
and it is doubtful whether it signifies a god or tents set up for the
obscene worship of some god. Sir H. Rawlinson thinks it is the
Hebrew name of the Babylonian goddess, *Zirbanit,* the wife of
the god Merodach, whose worship was very popular among the
Babylonians.

Nergal, whom the men of Cuth worshipped, was a deity corresponding to the Greek *Ares,* and the Roman Mars, probably also
identical with the planet Mars. His name signifies the "great man,"
or "great hero." The titles given him on the Assyrian sculptures
are "the storm-ruler," "the king of battle," "the champion of the
gods," "the strong begetter," "the tutelar god of Babylonia," and
"the god of the chase." Some think he is the same as Nimrod. He
was probably adored under the form of the "man lion," so familiar to all who visit the British Museum.

Ashima is not so readily identified, though he is probably the
same as the *Pan* of the Greeks. He was possibly the god of medicine.

Nibhaz has not yet been identified, though speculations have
been sufficiently plentiful respecting him. *Tartak* also is an unknown god.

Adrammelech and *Anammelech* were probably a male and female deity, representing the double power of the sun. The Sephar-
vites burnt their children in sacrifice to those idols, which at once
identifies them with Moloch. In confirmation of this view, it may

be mentioned that the city of Sepharvim was called "The City of the Sun," and there can be no doubt that Moloch, the fire-god, was really the orb of day.

477.—A NIGHT IN A SYRIAN INN.
Luke ii. 7.

⁋ I found the house consisted of only one very lofty room, about eighteen feet square. The roof, of heavy beams, blackened with smoke, was supported by two wide-spreading arches. The walls were of roughly hewn blocks of stone, not plastered in any way. Just within the door a donkey and a yoke of oxen stood; and I soon perceived that rather more than one-third of the room was set apart for cattle, where the floor, which was on a level with the street, was of earth, and partially strewn with fodder. We were led up two stone steps on to a daïs, twenty-two inches high, where fragments of old mats and carpets were spread. . . . In the meantime the mule was led in and unladen, and our two horses were unsaddled and lodged in the lower part of the room. . . . Nearly in the middle of the raised floor the large fire, made of piled-up wood and thorns, and resinous evergreen shrubs, was burning briskly. Three deep troughs, or mangers, about three feet by one, were hollowed out of the broad stone coping at the edge of the daïs. Mohammed, our groom, filled these troughs with barley, and our tired animals enjoyed their evening meal. . . . A large cat, walking gently and cautiously over my head, startled me out of a dreamy and restless sleep. I roused myself, and looked about: it was midnight; the lamp was still burning, and by its dim light I could make out the strange groups around. . . . The armed guide and our kawass, rolled up in their cloaks and carpets, were lying on the edge of the daïs, their saddle-cloth serving as pillows. The muleteer, resting on the luggage, and our groom, Mohammed, on a heap of fodder, were just below with the tethered horses. The air of the room was heated and oppressive, and dense with tobacco smoke. There was no window, but over the closed door there were five small round holes. In the stone wall close to my resting-place was the trap-door of a corn granary. I could hear rats and mice within nibbling and scratching, and the grey cat again and again returned to post herself on my pillow. I sat up; my horse started out of his sleep, neighed, and shook himself, walking as far as his halter would let him, disturbing the repose of all the rest, and es-

pecially of the donkey. . . . Suddenly the idea entered my mind
that it must have been in such a house as this that Christ was
born. . . . I imagined Joseph anxiously seeking rest and shelter for
her (Mary) after her long journey. All the guest-chambers were
already filled, and there was no room in the inn; that is, there was
no room for them in the "house of rest for wayfarers" (the place
of unlading). The raised floor was crowded with strangers, who
had, like them, come to be taxed. But Joseph and Mary may have
taken refuge from the cold in the lower part of the room. . . .
The manger was very likely close by her side, hollowed out at the
edge of the daïs, and filled with soft winter fodder. I raised my
head and looked at one of the mangers, and I felt how natural it
was to use it as a cradle for a newly-born infant. Its size, its shape,
its soft bed of fodder, its nearness to the warm fire always burning
on the daïs in midwinter, would immediately suggest the idea to an
Eastern mother.—*Mr. Rogers' "Domestic Life in Palestine."*

478.—THE OLD ENGLISH WORD HELL.
Matt. v. 29.

❡ "The word 'hell' comes from an old English or Teutonic word,
hel-an, to cover; and, in the ancient use of it, it signified any covered place. In our early English literature it is used of any obscure
dungeon, or covered spot; even of the dark hole into which a tailor threw his shreds and clippings; nay, even of the retired and
bosky shade to which the lads and lasses caught in a game called
Barley-break were led to pay the forfeit of a kiss."

479.—THE VOW OF THE NAZIRITE.
Numb. vi. 1–8.

❡ Ewald gives a full account of the significance of this vow; from
his work on Jewish antiquities the following interesting particulars
are taken:—"The Nazirites, *i.e.* the Consecrated, were those who
had devoted themselves by a vow exclusively to Jehovah, and had
given themselves up, along with the whole of their bodies, to be
owned by Him. In them an urgent desire was awakened to devote
themselves more purely and more strongly than the ordinary people to Jehovah alone—to present Him with their whole bodies and
their greatest pleasures. Thus the vow to abstain from wine, which

certainly existed here and there long before their time, received under their efforts a new and more rigid application. To the priests it had been forbidden from the days of Moses to drink anything of an intoxicating nature before the commencement of their public functions. Such ancient sacred prohibitions, however, are easily carried to excess by those who are anxious to acquire a special sanctity, and this was what happened in the case of the Nazirites. He who had once taken this vow of consecration to Jehovah might never again taste the least drop of wine or any part of the vine, neither pure nor mixed wine, neither sweet nor sour drink of any kind prepared from the vine, no form whatever of the juice of the grape; neither fresh nor dried grapes, no dish of any kind which was made of unripe grapes, or of the pressed-out skins. So long as the Nazirite lived true to this vow, free from the infection and even free from the touch of the intoxicating growths, he was deemed a consecrated, pure being; but since, from the moment of his exit out of the world of ordinary enjoyments, he was deemed, along with the whole of his body, to be consecrated to God, no further alteration even of his body might be made. Accordingly the hair of his head might not be reduced, still less shaved; and if this laid on him a new burden and hardship, on the other hand the luxuriant growth and waving locks of this inviolable adornment of the head served, for himself and for the world, as the visible token and as the mighty spell of his own unbroken divine power and complete consecration."

480.—THE ANOINTING OF SAUL.
1 Sam. x. 1.

℄ Curious Oriental traditions have gathered round this simple incident. It is said that when Samuel made his report to God that the Israelites were resolved to have a king, God gave him a vessel, or horn, full of oil, and a staff, telling him that the man in whose presence the oil should boil, and whose stature should be found equal to the length of the staff, was the one whom he had chosen to be king. No sooner was this revelation published than all the chiefs of the tribes hurried away to Samuel, each one hoping to find the staff answer to his own height, and that the oil would boil as he approached. But in this all the princes suffered a grievous disappointment. Saul also, otherwise called Shareh, and surnamed Talout, who was no more than a carrier of water, or dresser of

480.—The Anointing of Saul.

leather, went to the prophet along with the rest: and immediately as he approached the oil began to boil, and it was found that the miraculous staff exactly corresponded with his height. Samuel thereupon declared Saul to be king; but the princes, especially the princes of Judah, to which tribe the royal dignity had been promised, expostulated against the choice, saying, "How can this man be our king, who has no estate? How can he support the dignity and expense of royalty?" Samuel replied that the Lord, who, according to His will, disposed of kingdoms, had chosen this man to be king over His people. Still the murmurers refused to submit, and insisted on some further sign that he was the chosen of God. The ark of God was at that time a trophy of war in the hands of the Philistines, and Samuel told the princes that the ark should be brought home by angels, and that should be the sign that Saul was God's choice. When the Philistines heard that Israel had a king, fearing perhaps that the first expedition of the new monarch would be undertaken for the recovery of the ark, they hid the sacred chest in a dunghill. For this they were smitten by some dreadful and loathsome disease, and therefore resolved to send the ark back to the frontiers of Israel. No sooner had it reached the boundaries than the angels of the Lord took it up, and carried it to the tabernacle at Shiloh. This miracle secured the crown to Saul.

Such a story as this may serve to illustrate how legends are woven out of history; and they help us to distinguish sharply between the simple historical records of Holy Scripture and the extravagant traditions which, in later times, men have associated with the Sacred Word.

481.—STATE OF THE POPULATION OF CANAAN IN ABRAHAM'S TIME.
Gen. xii. 6.

℘ When Abraham was brought by the guidance of God into the land of Canaan, he found himself in the midst of a population which could not be regarded as wholly alien. Nor do the inhabitants appear to have been of a character which would repel all intercourse. They had already abandoned, at least to a certain extent, their original pastoral and nomadic habits, and we find them gathered into cities, leaving the open country principally to the occupation of friendly strangers, such as Abraham. Their civilisation was, however, but little developed; for good and for evil, they

seem to have retained much of their primitive character. Where
kings are mentioned, they approach more nearly to the patriarchal
heads of tribes than to the barbarous despots of later days. We
come across no traces of the fearful moral corruption that afterwards made "the land spue out" its inhabitants, except, indeed, in
the wealthy and luxurious cities of the plain. There the degeneracy
that was afterwards to bring the Divine judgments upon all the nations of Canaan had rapidly run its fatal course. But the rest of
the land was still comparatively uncorrupted.

Later on we find the numerous cities of the land, excluding such
as were still held by the warlike and savage aborigines, loosely
grouped into four main divisions. There are the Amorites, or
Highlanders, a fierce people—apparently the furthest removed
from the Canaanites proper—that dwelt in the mountains, from
the Scorpion Range, south of the Dead Sea, to the hills of Judah.
The Hittites are their neighbours, dwelling in the valleys, lovers of
refinement at an early period, and living in well-ordered communities possessing national assemblies. The fertile lowlands by the
course of the Jordan, and along the coast of the Mediterranean,
are held by the Canaanites, who, as possessors of the choicest of
the land, and by far the best known by foreigners, often gave their
name to the whole of the population of the country. These also
were much more addicted to commerce than to war, in this
resembling the fourth main division, the Hivites of the midland region, whose principal city seems to have been the flourishing,
wealthy, but timorous Gibeon.

In these early times the Philistines seem to have been but weak
and under the yoke of the alien Canaanites, to whom they were always bitterly hostile.—*A. S. Wilkins.*

482.—DOGS EATING JEZEBEL.
2 Kings ix. 10.

❡ It may cause some surprise that the body of this queen should
have been so quickly devoured; but in the East dogs are very
numerous, and, living for the most part without masters, they
prowl about the cities in gangs, and live entirely upon the offal
flung into the streets.

In *Bruce's Travels* there occurs a passage which may serve to illustrate the dreadful fate of Jezebel. "In Abyssinia," he says, "the
bodies of those killed by the sword were hewn to pieces, and scat-

tered about the streets, being denied burial. I was miserable and
almost driven to despair at seeing my hunting-dogs, twice let loose
by the carelessness of my servants, bringing into the courtyard the
heads and arms of slaughtered men, which I could no way prevent
but by the destruction of the dogs themselves."

483.—Customs Similar to Circumcision.
Jer. ix. 26, marg.

℃ "Sometimes large communities, or even nations, will pledge
themselves to a universal corporal offering of such a kind, that
every member shall constantly bear about its mark on himself, and
so make his personal appearance or condition a perpetual witness
for the special religion whose vows he has undertaken. In such a
case the external form this offering assumes becomes less and less
burdensome, till every one is able to adopt it without much trouble, and it becomes a mere token (symbol, sacrament), and becomes as little conspicuous as possible. Several Arabian tribes living not far from the Holy Land adopted the custom, as a sign of
their special religion (Herodotus says after the example of their
god), of shaving the hair of their heads in an extraordinary
fashion—viz., either on the crown of the head or towards the temples, or else of disfiguring a portion of the beard (see Lev. xix.
27). This custom was extremely ancient, and in the above very old
legal passage such mutilations of the hair of the head are entirely
forbidden; reference to mourning customs being only introduced
Lev. xix. 28, we may assume that v. 27 indicates a more general
law. Jeremiah designates these races by the hereditary nickname of
'those who are shorn on the temples.' In other cases it was deemed
sufficient merely to brand or tattoo the symbol of a particular god
on the skin, on the forehead, the arm, or the hand. The earliest
traces of the practice of circumcision are found among the Egyptians and Ethiopians, and from them it passed to the Israelites.
The essential idea of the rite appears to be this. It cannot be performed without loss of blood, and there is, no doubt, a possibility
that the patient may die of the wound; it is, therefore, essentially a
bloody sacrifice of one's own body, difficult to render, such as man
may regard with shuddering fear. But he who has offered up to his
god this flesh of his own body and this blood, and bears circumcision on his person as a permanent token of this hardest sacrifice,
becomes thereby for the first time a man well pleasing to his god.

Circumcision was accordingly an offering of one's own flesh and blood sacrificed to a god. It was a perpetual reminder carried about on a man's person that he was consecrated to a higher being."

484.—THE PHARAOH OF THE EXODUS.
Exod. v. 1.

℄ This king probably belonged to the nineteenth dynasty, which marks the Augustan age of Egypt, but closes in gloom and darkness. Rawlinson says, "Not only have the stately structures ceased to arise, the expanding walls to be decorated with processions of tribute-bearing kings and nations, but there is a significant silence in the existing monuments: the names and titles of their kings, in their characteristic cartouches, are no longer lavishly inscribed upon them; but there are signs of erasure, of studious conceal-ment, as of something which they would shrink from committing to imperishable memory. Some disaster seems to have fallen upon the realm, which rather than commemorate, the records break off and are mute." The solution of the mystery is furnished only by the Mosaic narrative. The name of this king was *Mirenptah*, or *Amenophis*, and he was the son of the great oppressor.

485.—ANTICIPATIONS OF CHRIST'S TEACHINGS.
Matt. v.–vii.

℄ It appears that many of the most admirable sayings in the Ser-mon on the Mount had been more or less perfectly anticipated by heathen moralists and poets, and by Jewish teachers. Confucius anticipated the Golden Rule when he summed up the whole duty of man in the single word "Reciprocity." Rabban Hillel anticipated it still more exactly, for while the Lord Jesus said, "All things whatsoever ye would that men should do to you, do ye even so to them; for this is the law and the prophets," Hillel said, "Do not unto another what thou wouldest not have another do unto thee; this is the whole law, the rest is mere commentary." If Christ bade us love, not "our brethren" only, but all men, even "the evil and the unthankful," the Greek sage Menander said, "I am a man, and therefore nothing human is alien to me." Cicero, the Roman ora-tor, said, "Men were born for men, that each should assist the rest;" and, again, "Nature ordains that a man should wish the good of every man, whoever he may be, for the simple reason that he is a man;" and Seneca both bade us "confer benefits even on the unthankful," and "give aid even to our enemies," and laid down the rule, "Let us give as we would wish to receive." If Christ bids us "do the will of our Father who is in heaven," Epictetus affirms that then only is a man truly good and free "when whatever is the will of God is his will too, and whatever is not God's will is not his will."

486.—TARTARUS.
2 Peter ii. 4. Greek.

℃ This is the only passage in the New Testament in which this word occurs. "It is a purely heathen word, and embodies a purely heathen conception. As they pried into the future the Greeks and Romans saw nothing clearly, although the 'initiated,' perhaps, had been quickened into an intense yearning for, if not a bright and vivid hope of, a life to come. The world beyond the gates of death was, for them, 'a world of shades.' Their utmost hope even for the good was that some thin shadow of the former man would survive to enjoy some faint shadow of his former honours and pursuits. The utmost they foreboded for the wicked was that their thin, wavering, unsubstantial ghosts would be doomed to hopeless tasks, or consumed by pangs such as men suffer here. Sometimes they gave the name Tartarus to the whole of this land of shadows; but more commonly they divided the underworld into two provinces— the Elysian fields, in which the spirits of their heroes and their sages, with all who loved goodness, wandered to and fro, illumined by a pale reflection of their former joys; reserving the name *Tartarus* for that dismal region in which the ghosts of the wicked were tasked, and tantalised, and tormented. . . . But the Tartarus of Peter by no means answered to our hell, as it is usually conceived. Our plain duty is to read the above passage just as it reads in the original Greek, 'God spared not angels who sinned, but cast them into Tartarus.' "—*Salvator Mundi*.

487.—SITTING DOWN AMONG THE ASHES.
Job ii. 8.

℃ We must suppose that Job sat outside the house, or the city, as is usual with the leprous. The Septuagint have a word instead of

"ashes," which literally means "dung," and there is some reason to
think that this would be the more correct. Wetzstein describes the
heaps of dry dung found outside every town and village in the
Hauran, and he specially noticed that persons smitten with loathsome diseases are accustomed to lie on these heaps both day and
night.

Sitting down among the ashes is, however, frequently mentioned
in Scripture as an act expressive of repentance and humiliation; it
may, therefore, have been a voluntary act on Job's part, not one
necessitated by his sad and suffering condition. Job himself seems
to have regarded it in this way, for towards the close of his book
we find him saying to God, "I abhor myself, and repent in dust
and ashes." The heathen, in times of great mourning, used to
sprinkle themselves with ashes, and even sat down in them, as see
Jonah iii. 6; Isa. lxi. 3.

488.—CUTTING A COVENANT.
Jer. xxxiv. 18.

℘ In this passage there is a curious and exceedingly ancient custom referred to, which prevailed not only among the Israelites, but
in most nations of antiquity. When covenants were made among
the ancients they were usually ratified by others, and an animal
was slain, probably as an imprecation, each party in effect praying
God, or the gods, that his fate might be that of the slaughtered
beast if he broke the terms of the covenant. Usually the victims
were divided, and the contracting parties passed between the parts.
The oldest case of the kind mentioned in history is that recorded
in Genesis xv. 10–18. There Jehovah orders Abraham 'to take a
heifer three years old, a she-goat, and a ram of the same age, a
turtle-dove, and a young pigeon. At the Divine command Abraham slaughtered the beasts and birds, divided the former, and
placed the pieces opposite each other; and when the darkness
came on, a smoking furnace and a burning lamp passed between
the divisions of the carcases; and that day Jehovah made a covenant with Abraham. There can be little doubt that the furnace and
the lamp were symbols of Jehovah, who thus, by act instead of
speech, confirmed the covenant by an oath.

The same custom is alluded to in *Homer,* who, by a figure of
speech, puts the victims for the oaths, and speaks of the ceremony
as "cutting the faithful oaths" (*Iliad* ii. 124, iii. 105). Both the
Greeks and Trojans, however, used lambs or sheep for those pur-

poses; but the Romans, according to Virgil, slaughtered swine on such occasions. An ancient writer relates that Agamemnon, the leader of the Greeks, at the siege of Troy, "to confirm his faith sworn to Achilles, ordered victims to be brought. He took one, and with his sword *divided it in the midst,* placed the pieces opposite to each other, and holding his sword, reeking with the blood, passed between the separated pieces." Livy, the Roman historian, relates that in the time of Philip of Macedon, father of Alexander the Great, it was the custom at the lustration, or purification of the armies, to cut off the head of a dog, and then make the whole army file between the head and trunk.

An old traveller, who knew the Algerines of North Africa well, relates that when those pirates were overtaken by a storm at sea, or were hotly pursued by a too powerful enemy, they first of all were in the habit of calling upon some one of their saints for succour; and if that failed, they sacrificed a sheep, or even two or three if their danger happened to be excessive; and after extracting the entrails, they divided the body, and threw half over the right side of the ship and its other half over the left, thus making the vessel pass between the parts.

489.—CORBAN.
Mark vii. 11, 12.

¶ As this passage stands it conveys no distinct impression to a reader unfamiliar with Jewish customs. The text would be better translated thus:—"If a man say to his father or mother, 'Corban (that is, a votive offering) as regards anything whatever by which you might derive assistance from me,' etc." The explanation is simple. Corban denotes anything offered to God or the service of the temple. Almost every possession a man had might be rendered Corban by him, even his own person; and when once offered to God the article was sacred, and could on no account be turned to a secular use until redeemed. All that was necessary was that a man should say respecting a given thing, "May this be as the temple to me;" or, "as the altar," etc.; or, "as the (sacred) fire," etc.; or, "as the sacrifice to me." Thereupon a man, being displeased with his aged or poor parents, might free himself from all obligation to support them by merely pronouncing one of these forms; and then, when either father or mother appealed to him for aid, he would say, "Whatever I might have bestowed upon you is now Corban." And the Pharisees, as Christ complains, insisted on the fulfilment of this execrable vow, even though it necessitated the violation of natural instinct, as well as the command, "Honour thy father and thy mother." In fact, there was no duty a villain might not shun by this infamous procedure.

490.—THE TURTLE.
Jer. viii. 7.

¶ The turtle-dove—Hebrew, *tor*—belongs to the *Columbidae,* or dove family. Two species appear to be mentioned in Scripture— the true Syrian dove, or collared pigeon (*Turtur risorius*), and the turtle-dove proper (*Turtur auritus*). The former is a permanent resident in Palestine; the latter is migratory. The collared pigeon is that generally kept in cages in this country, and known as the turtle-dove. *Turtur auritus* visits the south of England in spring, and retires to the north of Africa in September. It visits Palestine, and nests there at the spring season. The migratory habits of this bird appear to be taken into account in the alternative presented to the poor, in regard to their offering (see Lev. i. 14). It was either to consist of turtle-doves or young pigeons; the former to be taken at the season when they visited Palestine, the latter at any time.

The collared turtle (*Turtur risorius*) occurs in great numbers near the springs and streams on the shores of the Dead Sea where trees grow; and here it resides throughout the year. In the summer it spreads northwards up the Jordan valley, and may be seen in the woods of Mount Tabor and Gilead. Dr. Tristram says that Palestine appears to be almost the western limit of this bird. It is very common in India, but is not found in a wild state in Europe.

The return of the turtle-dove (*Turtus auritus*) is one of the most marked epochs in the ornithological calendar. Dr. Tristram says: "Search the glades and valleys even by sultry Jordan at the end of March, and not a turtle-dove is to be seen. Return in the second week in April, and clouds of doves are feeding on the clovers of the plain. They stock every tree and thicket. At every step they flutter up from the herbage in front; they perch on every tree and bush; they overspread the whole face of the land. So universal, so simultaneous, so conspicuous, is their migration, that the

prophet may well place the turtle-dove at the head of those birds
which 'observe the time of their coming.' "

491.—MEMORIAL STONES.
Gen. xxviii. 22.

❡ The practice of setting up a stone as a memorial of mercies received is still common in the East. Mr. Morier describes what he
witnessed in ascending the rock of Istakhar, in Persia:—"We ascended on the north-west side, winding round the foot of the rock,
and making our way through narrow and intricate paths. I
remarked that our old guide every here and there placed a stone
on a conspicuous bit of rock, or two stones, one upon the other, at
the same time uttering some words, which I learnt were a prayer
for our safe return. This explained to me what I had frequently
seen before in the East, and particularly on a high road leading to
a great town, whence the town is first seen, and where the Eastern
traveller sets up his stone accompanied by a devout exclamation,
as it were, in token of his safe arrival. A stone on the road placed
in this position, one stone upon another, implies that some
traveller has there made a vow or a thanksgiving. Nothing is so
natural in a journey over a dreary country as for a solitary
traveller to sit himself down fatigued, and make a vow similar to
that of Jacob—'If God will be with me, and keep me in this way
that I go, so that I reach my father's house in peace, then will I
give so much in charity;' or, again, that on first seeing the place
which he has toiled so long to reach, the traveller should sit down,
and make a thanksgiving, in both cases setting up a stone as a memorial."

492.—MESHA'S SON MADE A BURNT OFFERING.
2 Kings iii. 27.

❡ The story of Mesha, king of Moab, is one of the most extraordinary records found in the Bible. At one time he was subject to
the yoke of Israel, and paid to Ahab a large tribute. But he subsequently rebelled, and for a time maintained his independence.
When, however, Jehoram, son of Ahab, ascended the throne, he
leagued with Jehoshaphat, king of Judah, and the king of Edom,
for the chastisement of Moab. The way the three kings carried on
the conquest of Moab was the most infamous imaginable. Mesha

was worsted on all sides, and the conquerors covered his fields
with stones to render them barren, and filled up his wells to make
the land uninhabitable. By-and-by, Mesha, in desperation, led 700
of his chosen men against the combined army; but was once more
repulsed. He next appears to have retired with the ruins of
his army to some stronghold, probably Kirharaseth, where he
was closely besieged by the allies; and here followed a scene
which has no parallel in Scripture, and is very difficult to understand. Mesha took his eldest son and heir to the crown, and
offered him up as a burnt offering upon the ramparts, apparently
in the sight of the besiegers. Meanwhile, it appears the Moabites
were foaming with rage and indignation against their enemies who
had driven them to such terrible shifts. This horrible story is
matched in the main particulars by several events related by Lord
Teignmouth as having occurred in India. There were two Brahmins, named Beechuk and Adher, brothers, who had a quarrel
with a man named Gowry. The emissaries of the latter stole forty
rupees, the property of the two brothers, from the apartments of
their women. When Beechuk understood what had happened, he
took his mother to the bank of the rivulet which ran through the
village, and there was also met by Adher, his brother. This was in
the grey of the morning, and they called aloud to the people of the
village that the forty rupees must be returned. No answer being
given, Beechuk drew his scimetar, and deliberately struck off his
mother's head. This was done that the mother's spirit, excited by
the beating of a large drum during forty days, might ever haunt,
torment, and pursue to death Gowry and his associates. The last
words the mother uttered were, "I will blast Gowry and those concerned with him." Possibly this deed and its motive may explain
the action of Mesha. It is not said to whom he offered his son, nor
what was his object; but the probability is that he intended thus to
awe the allies by the superstitious fear of being haunted and
cursed by the ghost of his son. It is worthy of note that the
besiegers at once retired.

It should be further mentioned that, though the above is a possible explanation of Mesha's motive, his act may have been intended
to propitiate some god or demon. A parallel case in some respects
is mentioned by Sanchoniathon, the Phoenician historian, who
relates that "Cronos, in a time of pestilence, made his only son a
whole burnt offering in compliance with an ancient custom of
princes so to do: such sacrifices being offered as redemption offer-

ings, to appease avenging demons, and drive off general destruction."

493.—PRECIOUS STONES OF THE BIBLE.
Ezek. xxviii. 13, etc.

⊄ The Bible contains three lists of precious stones, besides those mentioned separately in various parts of the sacred volume. 1. The description of the four rows of three stones each, with the names of the children of Israel engraved upon them, which composed the breast-plate of judgment (Exod. xxviii. 17–21, xxxix. 10–14). 2. The list of the ornaments of the king of Tyre, comprising nine stones, viz., sardius, topaz, diamond, beryl, onyx, jasper, sapphire, emerald, and carbuncle (Ezek. xxviii. 13). 3. The Apocalyptic vision of the heavenly Jerusalem, in which the twelve stones named jasper, sapphire, chalcedony, emerald, sardonyx, sardius, chrysolite, beryl, topaz, chrysoprasus, jacinth, and amethyst, figure as the foundations of the heavenly city (Rev. xxi. 19–21).

There has been much confusion in the translation of the names of some of these stones, and the Authorised Version is often incorrect. Thus, there is every reason to believe that the diamond was confounded with the white sapphire or corundum. Chrysolite was the same as our Oriental topaz, and the topazion was the peridot, a yellowish-green stone.

"The twelve precious stones mentioned in St. John's vision are not arranged in the order of those on the breast-plate, but according to their shades of colour; and here and elsewhere the writer of the book of Revelation exhibits an intimate acquaintance with the colours and qualities of jewels. Gems and precious stones have been offered to the gods from the earliest times, and these valuable objects were to be seen in ancient temples, arranged with the greatest profusion. The contents of the treasury of the Parthenon are enumerated in Boeckh's *Inscriptions,* but the Greek temples seem poor when compared with the shrines of imperial Rome."

494.—DIFFERENT FORMS OF THE
GIFT OF TONGUES.
Acts ii. 4; 1 Cor. xiv. 2.

⊄ The gift of tongues bestowed on the Day of Pentecost does not seem to have been the same as that described in 1 Cor. xiv. There the speaking with tongues was unintelligible to the hearers; he that spoke in an unknown tongue, spoke not to men, but to God, for no man understood him: the man could not interpret what he himself said; an interpreter was necessary to explain what was spoken, and sometimes there was no interpreter present in the assembly; the gift is compared with the tinkling of a cymbal, the indistinct sound of an instrument, and the speech of a barbarian; Paul himself spoke with tongues more than they all, but he says that he would rather speak five words with his understanding, that he might teach others, than ten thousand words in a tongue; and he forbids any to speak with tongues in the church unless there be an interpreter. Certainly there does appear to be a difference between this speaking with tongues and that mentioned in the Acts. Both were spiritual gifts—supernatural manifestations; in both the mind of the speaker was controlled by the Spirit; both are described as speaking with tongues. But the speech of the disciples of Pentecost was directly intelligible to the hearers; whilst the speech of the Corinthians required the medium of an interpreter to be understood. The speaking at Pentecost was evidently a speaking in foreign languages; whilst it is not so evident that this was the case with the converts at Corinth. Moreover, in 1 Cor. xiv. there is only mention of speaking with tongues, whereas in Acts ii. the disciples are said to speak with other tongues.

495.—THE DESTRUCTIVE WORK OF MOTHS.
Isaiah l. 9.

❡ It is in the larval state that moths fret the garments. They furrow the thick parts of woollen clothes, and furs, and in these furrows pass from the larval into the chrysalis state. Mr. Kirby says: "Perhaps you imagine that these universal destroyers spare at least our garments, in which you may at first conceive there can be nothing very tempting to excite even the appetite of an insect. Your housekeeper, however, would probably tell you a different story, and enlarge upon the trouble and pain it costs her to guard those under her care against the ravages of the moths. Upon further inquiry you would find that nothing made of wool, whether cloth or stuff, comes amiss to them. There are five species described by Linné, which are more or less engaged in this work— *Tinea vestianella, tapetzella, pellionella, Laverna sarcitella,* and *Galleria mellonella.* Of the first we have no particular history, ex-

cept that it destroys garments in the summer; but of the others
Reaumur has given a complete one. *T. tapetzella,* or the tapestry
moth, not uncommon in our houses, is most injurious to the lining
of carriages, which are more exposed to the air than the furniture
of our apartments. These do not construct a movable habitation,
like the common species, but, eating their way in the thickness of
the cloth, weave themselves silken galleries, in which they reside,
and which they render close and warm by covering them with
some of the eroded wool. *T. pellionella* is a most destructive insect, and ladies have often to deplore the ravages which it commits
in their valuable furs, whether made up into muffs or tippets. It
pays no more respect to the regal ermine than to the woollen
habiliments of the poor; its proper food, indeed, being hair,
though it devours both wool and fur. This species, if hard pressed
by hunger, will even eat horsehair, and make its habitation, a movable house or case in which it travels from place to place, in
search of this untractable material. These little creatures will shave
the hair from a skin as neatly and closely as if a razor had been
employed. The most natural food of the next species, *L. sarcitella,*
is wool; but in case of necessity it will eat fur and hair. To
woollen cloths and stuffs it often does incredible injury, especially
if they are not kept clean and well aired. *Galleria mellonella* commits its devastations in our beehives, and if it cannot come at wax,
it will content itself with woollen cloth, leather, or even paper. Mr.
Curtis found the grub of a beetle (*Ptinus fur*) in an old coat
which it devoured, making holes and channels; and another insect
of the same order (*Attagenus pellio*), Linné tells us, will sometimes entirely strip a fur garment of its hair. A small beetle of the
Capricorn tribe (*Callidium pigmaeum Fabr.*) I have good reason
to believe devours leather, since I have found it abundant in old
shoes."

496.—TEMPERING THE HEAT
WITH A CLOUD-SHADOW.
Isaiah xxv. 5.

❡ Bonar writes of his travels in the East:—About midday, when
the heat was very oppressive, a small cloud, scarcely observable by
the eye, passed over the disc of the burning sun. Immediately the
intense heat abated, a gentle breeze sprung up, and we felt

refreshed. "Thou shalt bring down the noise of strangers [ene-
mies] as the heat in a dry place [a sandy desert], even the heat
with the shadow of a cloud."

497.—SEALED AS A SACRIFICE.
John vi. 27.

⁋ This remarkable passage refers, no doubt, to the custom of
marking or sealing an animal for sacrifice. Among the Egyptians it
was the custom for the priests to select with the utmost care the
bulls to be offered to Apis. Herodotus, respecting this matter, says,
"One of the priests appointed for the purpose searches to see if
there is a single black hair on the whole body [of the bull], since
in that case the beast is unclean. He examines him all over, standing on his legs, and, again, laid upon his back, after which he
takes the tongue out of his mouth to see if it be clean; he also in-
spects the hairs of the tail to see if they grow naturally. If the animal is pronounced clean in all these various points, the priest
marks him by twisting a piece of papyrus round his horns, and attaching these to some *sealing-clay, which he then stamps with his
own signet-ring.* After this the beast is led away, and it is forbidden, under penalty of death, to sacrifice an animal which has not
been *sealed* in this way."

There can be no reason to doubt that the Jews, too, had some
way of *sealing* the animals devoted to sacrifice. We know that they
were to be without blemish. The priest would naturally be the
judge of the fitness of the animal, and he probably sealed it in
some way when it had passed through his hands. It is not necessary to dwell upon the application of the *sealing* as applying to the
case of Christ, who was *sealed* by God the Father as a fit and perfect sacrifice for the sins of the world (see Heb. vii. 26–28; Eph.
v. 27; 2 Peter iii. 14).

498.—ANCIENT NINEVEH.
Gen. x. 11.

⁋ From the various facts or fables we gather something like the
following account of Nineveh:

It was founded by Ninus about 1,000 years before the Trojan
war, or 2,183 years before Christ, a date which does not differ
very materially from that given in Scripture. Ninus is universally

represented as a man of great power, courage, and ambition, "a mighty hunter," and a lover of war. He is stated by Berosus to have been the first king who sought to bring neighbouring states beneath his power. Joined with the Arabians, he made incursions into Babylonia, Armenia, Media, Bactria, and other kingdoms, reducing one after the other to submission. During these campaigns he laboured hard to complete the defences of the city which he had founded. He enclosed for this purpose a tract of land no less than seventy-four miles in circumference, throwing up lofty walls around it 100 feet high, defended by still loftier towers, of which there were 1,500, each 200 feet in height. The city being thus fortified, he prepared for the entire subjugation of the Bactrians, whose mighty mountain fastnesses had hitherto defied his efforts, but whom he now completely conquered.

Ninus was thus an avowedly great monarch, and may be counted greater than any of his predecessors or contemporaries, while his city must have been one of the largest that has ever been erected; that is, taking the number of square miles it covered. Upon his death he left his empire to his queen, Semiramis—a fit wife for such a king while he lived, and a no less fit successor when he died.

Her son Ninygas proved himself an idle and voluptuous prince, of whose successors we hear nothing till we come to Sardanapalus, a yet more debased and luxurious king. This monarch is spoken of as dressing like a woman, speaking in a soft and squeaking voice to imitate a female, and living in the indulgence of the silliest habits and the most abominable practices.

At last, one of his disaffected warriors plotted against his life, and headed a revolution to dethrone him. Sardanapalus, roused by the impending danger, took the field, and in three several engagements beat back his foes; but the Bactrians joining, Arbaces drove back the royal forces, and laid siege to the city. For two whole years did Sardanapalus bear the siege; when, remembering an old prediction, that when the river became the enemy of the city, his empire should be at an end, and believing, as it had overflowed its banks and washed down a part of the city walls, that the prediction was now fulfilled, he grew desperate, and resolved on self-destruction. Accordingly he caused an immense wooden stage or building to be erected, and gathering together his wives and concubines, his children, and his great men, with all his treasure, he ordered the whole to be set on fire. For fifteen days did this vast

pile burn, the people outside the walls believing it to be a great
sacrifice to the gods, little thinking that it was in reality the funeral
pile of Sardanapalus and his empire.

Thus, about the year 606 B.C., Nineveh was overthrown; and
since that time nothing has been seen of her save the heaps of
ruins, which, like mighty gravestones, have silently marked the
place where she lay entombed.

Winer gives the conquest of Nineveh at 606 B.C., but it may
have occurred earlier, perhaps in 625 B.C. Mr. Galloway, imagin-
ing that it was at the time of an eclipse, identifies this eclipse with
the one known to have happened in 585 B.C.

499.—Eastern Mode of Washing Hands.
2 Kings iii. 11.

⁋ Kitto carefully explains the Eastern custom; he says:—"The
Easterns, in washing, never, if they can help it, dip their hands in
the water, unless it be running water, as they abhor the idea of
using in this form water which has been already soiled. To pour
the water upon the hands from a vessel requires the assistance of
another; and this is usually the office of a servant, and the most
frequent one he has to render to his master—which makes the
phrase, 'who poured water upon the hands,' appropriately descriptive of a personal attendant. Friends, neighbours, and fellow-
travellers often, however, pour water on each other's hands in the
absence of a servant, as it is exceedingly inconvenient to fill one
hand repeatedly with water held in the other, and which is laid
frequently down to be taken up again. No one washes thus who
can find any one willing to pour water on his hands. Indoors, a
ewer and basin of tinned copper are commonly used. The water
poured from the ewer upon the hands falls into the basin held
below, which generally has a perforated false bottom, through
which the used water passes out of sight. The same kind of ewer
and basin as are now in use we find represented on the most ancient monuments of Egypt."

Van Lennep further describes the attitudes and actions of the
servant who waits at the table; he says:—"When waiting upon his
master, the servant stands upon the farthest edge of the raised
platform, having left his shoes at the door; his hands are folded,
and rest upon the centre of his girdle; and he watches closely
every movement of his master, prompt to attend to all his wants,

which are expressed by a nod or a sign. He fills his pipe, and hands him his coffee; he sets his food before him, and it is his special duty to 'pour water on his hands' to wash. Should he happen to be missing when wanted, his master summons him by clapping his hands so effectually that the sound is heard throughout the house, especially as the doors and windows generally stand open." The servant *girds* himself when at work, as he often has occasion to roll up his sleeves and to draw up his sharwar, tightening it with his girdle; he also sometimes binds an apron around his waist.

500.—THE STORING HABITS OF ANTS.
Prov. vi. 6–8.

℧ Dr. F. B. White reports his own observations made at Capri in 1866. "A colony of ants," he writes, "afforded us amusement. These insects had a regular road, made by cutting away the grass and other plants in their way. This road led to a large clump of plants in seed. Along it a train of ants was seen travelling to the nest, bearing with them pods of leguminous plants, and the seeds of grasses and *Compositae*. The perseverance with which a single ant would tug and draw a pod three or four times its own length was very interesting; sometimes four ants would unite in carrying one burden." Also in Indiana Mr. Charles Horne noted a similar habit in several species. Some of their pathways were thirty feet in length. The quantity of seeds was sometimes so great that five or six handfuls could be collected from one nest.

501.—THE SPARROW.
Psalm lxxxiv. 4.

℧ The sparrow has so excessively multiplied in Syria that its name seems to be generally applied to all small chirping and singing birds. The country being deprived of its woods, and overrun with birds of prey, is very poor in singing birds. The Heb. name for the sparrow (*dûrî*) signifies properly "that which is found or dwells in the farmyards," and it is a thoroughly characteristic appellation for the sparrow, which inhabits the villages in immense flocks, where the standing corn, and the corn lying on the threshing-floors in the open fields, feed it for one half of the year, whilst it finds its food during the other half in the courts of the houses. It builds its nest in the walls by digging out the mortar between the air-dried bricks. These holes are stopped up once a year, because they injure the walls; and the birds that are then taken out always furnish an abundant repast—the only one of the kind, however, in the year, for no one takes the trouble to make a sport of shooting sparrows.

502.—THE MIRACULOUS RELEASE OF THE APOSTLES.
Acts v. 19, 20.

⁋ Dr. Dykes says: "The design of this miraculous rescue is not at first sight apparent. That Jesus sent a messenger from Heaven to liberate His witnesses was certainly not due to any intention to extricate them out of a difficulty, for it did not postpone their trial for a day. His main purpose could only be to encourage their confidence in the gracious concern He felt for them, and in His power to protect them if He chose. At the same time, I cannot help thinking that this strange rescue of prisoners was designed to carry its lesson also to the Sanhedrim. I recall that very strange incident at the arrest of our Lord in the garden, when, before the silent meek majesty of the Man who a few moments earlier had been prostrate in sorrow, the band of temple police and Roman soldiery 'went backward and fell to the ground' (John xviii. 6). That was no vulgar attempt to escape from apprehension. Their victim waited till they recovered, and held out His wrists to be bound. Neither was it obtrusively a miracle; no prayer from His lips called anger out of heaven to beat His assailants back. It was a secret, silent hint only of a power above their own, into the origin of which no man cared too curiously to look. Very similar was the incident before us. That it was an angel who had opened the prison the Sanhedrim could not know unless they chose (and they did not choose) to inquire. Yet there was enough of wonder about the occurrence to suggest whose hand had possibly undone the bolts. This, too, was no vulgar rescue, for the men stood quietly in the temple to be recaptured. Miraculous aid was the first explanation which would occur to any Jew of that day whose mind was habituated to miracle, and who knew that these men's Master had spent His ministry in doing miracles, and that they themselves were filling Jerusalem still with miracles done in their Master's name. It follows that had the authorities even now been only tolerably open to spiritual warnings, this very midnight deliverance, wrought for His servants by the Man whom they had slain, might

have warned them back from the fresh persecution which they
were already plotting against Jesus and His cause."

503.—CAIN'S MARK.
Gen. iv. 15.

⁋ It is impossible to know what the mark set upon Cain was, or
on what part of his person it was placed. An extract from the
Laws of Menu, one of the oldest books extant, will show that in
ancient India it was customary to set upon flagrant criminals
"marks," which denoted the crime of which they had been guilty.
The following marks were set upon persons who had committed
the crimes to which they are annexed:—

> *"For drinking spirits, a vintner's flag;*
> *For stealing sacred gold, a dog's foot;*
> *For murdering a priest, the figure of a headless corpse.*
> *With none to eat with them,*
> *With none to be allied by marriage to them;*
> *Abject, and excluded from all social duties,*
> *Let them* wander over the earth;
> *Branded with indelible marks,*
> *They shall be deserted by their paternal and maternal*
>   *relations.*
> *Treated by none with affection;*
> *Received by none with respect.*
> *Such is the ordinance of Menu."*

The doom of such a wretch seems even worse than that of Cain.
The marks were branded by a hot iron on the forehead.

504.—THE MEDICAL ART.
Jer. viii. 22.

⁋ Medical art was, among the Hebrews, practised from early
times by a special profession—the Ropheim—and is already mentioned in the ancient Book of the Covenant, which embodies the
oldest fundamental laws (Exod. xxi. 19). They may possibly have
derived much of their knowledge from the Egyptians, famous for
their discovery of remedies from remote ages (Hom., *Od.* iv.
229–232), and for their medical skill generally (Herod., ii. 84, iii.
1, etc.; "embalming physicians" are mentioned in Gen. l. 2); and
during their sojourn in Egypt they had Hebrew midwives (Exod. i.
15–20). Their art seems, for the most part, to have been limited to

surgery and the cure of external injuries (comp. Isa. i. 6; Ezek. xxx. 21; 2 Kings viii. 29, ix. 15); but the physicians, many of whom belonged to the prophetic order (2 Kings iv. 33–36, v. 10, viii. 7, xx. 7; Isa. xxxviii. 21), enjoyed great respect and confidence, and were very generally employed, especially after the time of the exile, when even the smaller towns had their medical practitioners (Jer. viii. 22; Sirach xxxviii. 1–15, a remarkable passage; Joseph., *Vita*, 72, etc.), though the priestly book of Chronicles severely blames king Asa for "not having consulted God, but the physicians" (2 Chron. xvi. 12). In later times the priests and Levites, who officiated barefooted at the temple, had a special physician ("medicus viscerum") to cure the colds to which they were liable; the Essenes particularly were celebrated for their knowledge of medicine and the natural sciences (Joseph., *Bell. Jud.* 11, viii. 6).

The remedies used by the ancient Hebrews were chiefly ointments (especially of balsam, Jer. viii. 22, xlvi. 11, li. 8), leaves of trees (Ezek. xlvii. 12), cataplasms (especially of figs, 2 Kings xx. 7), mineral baths (Joseph., *Antiq.*, 17, vi. 5; *Vita*, 16), river baths (2 Kings v. 10), oil baths (Joseph., *Bell. Jud.* 1, xxxiii. 5), animal warmth for restoring the circulation (1 Kings i. 2–4; 2 Kings iv. 34, 35). Music was employed for dispelling melancholy (1 Sam. xvi. 16); fish-gall put on the eye to cure blindness (Tob. vi. 4). Of inward medicines, honey only is mentioned in the Old Testament (Prov. xvi. 24); several others occur in the Mishna and Talmud, where also many chirurgical manipulations are alluded to, even the insertion of artificial teeth (Mishn., Shabb., vi. 5).

As a kind of sanitary police, the law (*i.e.*, the Levitical law) appointed the priests, not so much to practise, but to exercise the inspection and control over the sick and persons suspected of some endemic malady, especially leprosy; and it gives, in this respect, directions which seem to prove very careful observation (Lev. xii., xiii., xv.). The laws of purification had, of course, an important sanitary influence (Lev. xii. etc.). The dietary laws also were partially, though by no means exclusively, suggested by sanitary considerations.—*British Medical Journal.*

505.—SILVER SHRINES FOR DIANA.
Acts xix. 24.

℀ There was a sacred month in Ephesus—the month of Diana, when a great religious gathering took place to celebrate the public game in honour of the goddess. It was the pleasant month of May. Trade was brisk then at Ephesus, not only from the large temporary increase of population, by the presence of provincials and strangers from more distant parts, but from the purchases they made in the shops and markets. Among the tradesmen of Ephesus there were none who depended more upon the business of this month than the makers and dealers in such holy trinkets, which votaries took home as memorials of their visit to sacred places. These were, at Ephesus, chiefly silver models and medallions representing the shrine and image of the goddess. Many of the latter exist in public and private cabinets.—*Kitto.*

506.—MODERN TRACES OF KIBROTH-HATTAAVAH.
Numb. xi. 33–35.

℘ "A little further on, and upon the watershed of Wady el Hebeibeh, we came to some remains which, although they had hitherto escaped even a passing notice from previous travellers, proved to be among the most interesting in the country. The piece of elevated ground which forms this watershed is called by the Arabs Erweis el Ebeirig, and is covered with small enclosures of stones. These are evidently the remains of a large encampment, but they differ essentially in their arrangement from any others which I have seen in Sinai or elsewhere in Arabia; and on the summit of a small hill on the right is an erection of rough stones surmounted by a conspicuous white block of pyramidal shape.

"The remains extend for miles around, and, on examining them more carefully during a second visit to the peninsula with Mr. Drake, we found our first impression fully confirmed, and collected abundant proofs that it was in reality a deserted camp. The small stones which formerly served, as they do in the present day, for hearths, in many places still showed signs of the action of fire, and on digging beneath the surface we found pieces of charcoal in great abundance. Here and there were larger enclosures, marking the encampment of some person more important than the rest; and just outside the camp were a number of stone heaps, which, from their shape and position, could be nothing else but graves. The site is a most commanding one, and admirably suited for the assembling of a large concourse of people.

"Arab tradition declares these curious remains to be 'the relics of a large Pilgrim or Hajj caravan, who in remote ages pitched their tents at this spot on their way to 'Ain Hudherah, and were soon afterwards lost in the desert of Tíh, and never heard of again.'

"For various reasons I am inclined to believe that the legend is authentic, that it refers to the Israelites, and that we have in the scattered stones of Erweis el Ebeirig real traces of the Exodus.

"Firstly, they are said *taku,* to have 'lost their way,' the Arabic verb from which the name Tíh, or 'Wilderness of the Wanderings,' is derived. Secondly, they are described as a Hajj caravan; at the first glance this would seem an anachronism, as the word is employed exclusively by the Muslims, and applied to their own annual pilgrimage to Mecca. But this very term owes its origin to the Hebrew *Hagg,* which signifies 'a festival,' and is the identical word used in Exodus (x. 9) to express the ceremony which the children of Israel alleged as their reason for wishing to leave Egypt; namely, 'to hold *a feast* unto the Lord' in the wilderness. It could not apply to the modern Mohammedan Hajj caravan, for that has never passed this way, and would not under any circumstances find it necessary to go to 'Ain Hudherah; but the children of Israel did journey to Hazeroth, and the tradition is therefore valuable in determining the latter site, as well as their subsequent route on leaving the peninsula. The length of time which has elapsed since the events of the Exodus furnishes no argument against the probability of this conclusion, for there are other monuments in the country in even better preservation, and of a date indisputably far anterior. It is a curious fact that, if you ask twenty different Arabs to relate to you one of the national legends, they will do so in precisely the same words, thus showing with what wonderful precision oral tradition is handed down from generation to generation among them."—*"The Desert of the Exodus," by E. H. Palmer.*

507.—JOHN BAPTIST'S IMPRISONMENT.
Mark vi. 17.

℃ Josephus gives some interesting particulars respecting the imprisonment and murder of the Baptist which are not supplied in the Gospel history. Herod Antipas, son of Herod the Great, was at that time tetrarch of Galilee and Peraea, and had married the daughter of Aretas, an Arabian king, whose territories abutted upon his own. When he was at Rome, however, he stayed at the house of his half-brother Philip, whose wife, Herodias, he con-

507.—John Baptist's Imprisonment.

ceived a passion for. Antipas made known his passion, and
Herodias readily enough consented to leave Philip and go with
him. The daughter of Aretas was divorced, and Herodias duly in-
stalled in her place. John the Baptist had the courage to denounce
this infamous marriage; and by-and-by Herod Antipas, under pre-
tence that he feared John's popularity with the multitude might
lead to disturbances, apprehended and imprisoned him. John was
sent to Machaerus, or M'khaur, on the eastern side of the Dead
Sea, where Herod had both a city and fortress. The site and ruins
of Machaerus were identified by Canon Tristram in his visit to the
Land of Moab in 1872. It was from this spot, then, that John sent
two of his disciples to Christ to ask, "Art Thou He that should
come, or do we look for another?" And it was here that Salome,
"the daughter of Herodias," danced before Antipas, and won for
her infamous mother the head of John the Baptist.

508.—HOUSES OF IVORY.
Amos iii. 15.

⁋ These appear to have been houses whose internal decorations
consisted chiefly of ivory—panels of ivory on their walls—couches
of ivory on which the inmates reclined, and, if palaces, a throne of
ivory for the king. Beds of ivory are mentioned in Amos vi. 3, 4.
Solomon, leaving the royal simplicity of his father, took to imitat-
ing the luxurious arrangements of neighbouring courts, and made
a great throne of ivory, and overlaid it with the best gold (1 Kings
x. 18).

Ivory is described by Homer as used in the decoration of the
Palace of Menelaus:—

> "Above, beneath, around the palace shines
> The sumless treasure of exhausted mines:
> The spoils of elephants the roofs inlay,
> And studded amber darts a golden ray" (Odys. iv.).

Mr. Layard met with many traces of the skill of the Assyrians in
working in ivory when examining the ruins of Nineveh and
Babylon.

Ivory is attained from the tusks, which answer to the incisive
teeth of the elephant. It was long believed that this animal periodically sheds its tusks; the impression, however, is erroneous. The
beast must be destroyed in order to get possession of the tusks.

The permanent tusks are, like the other teeth, preceded by "milk tusks." After these are shed, the permanent tusks cut the gum a month or six weeks later. They are dark-coloured, and ragged at the ends when they first appear, following thus the characteristics of the other teeth, but are worn smooth by use, and soon lose all traces of roughness. The annual importation of ivory into Great Britain alone, for the last few years, has been about one million pounds; which, taking the average weight of a tusk at sixty pounds, would require the slaughter of eight thousand three hundred and thirty-three male elephants.

509.—Puteoli.
Acts xxviii. 13.

⁋ This place was, and still is, the most sheltered part of the celebrated Bay of Naples. At that time it was the chief port south of Rome, and specially frequented by the Alexandrian corn-ships. A large mole of twenty-five arches, with a lighthouse thereon, extended far into the waters; and alongside of it the corn-ships unladed their precious burdens. A number of the piers of this structure still remain. Seneca has left an interesting and graphic description of the arrival of a fleet of corn-ships into Puteoli. He says that "all ships entering the bay were obliged to strike their topsails except wheat-ships, which were allowed to carry theirs;" and that "it was the practice to send forward fast sailing vessels to announce the speedy arrival of the fleet." He then proceeds to describe the inhabitants excitedly flocking down to the pier in large numbers to greet the ships. We may fairly picture such a scene when Paul stepped from the deck, and we see the crowd part to let the soldiers pass through with their prisoners in chains. The scenery around the bay was even more beautiful then than now, though Nature had not yet put on her new spring dress. Herculaneum and Pompeii were then standing, and the slopes of Vesuvius were covered with vines. No intimation was apparent of the devastation and ruin which shortly after occurred.

510.—Form of Easter Invitations.
Luke xiv. 17.

⁋ When a person of respectable rank in society proposes to celebrate a feast in his house, he forthwith circulates his invitations to the friends he wishes to be of the party, either by card or by a verbal message, carried by a servant of the house, or a person hired for the purpose, and superbly decked, according to the rank of his employer. The following is a specimen of the form of invitation: —"Such a person [naming him] sends best compliments to such another person [naming him also], and begs to inform him that as to-morrow there is a little gaiety to take place in his house, and he wishes his friends, by their presence, to grace and ornament with their feet the house of this poor individual, and thereby make it a garden of roses, he must positively come and honour the humble dwelling with his company."

Having after this fashion gone to all the houses, and returned with assurance from the invited friends of their intention to come next day, a messenger is again despatched for them at the appointed time, to inform them that all the preparations for the banquet are completed. This second invitation is included by our Lord, and is very characteristic of Eastern manners.

When Sir John Malcolm was invited to dine with the eldest son of the Shah, the invitation was given two days before, and one of the prince's attendants was despatched at the hour appointed for the banquet to tell him that all things were ready. And Morier also informs us, that having been engaged to dine with a Persian khan, he did not go till his entertainer had sent to the English ambassador and his train, to say that supper waited. After the same manner, the invitations to the great supper described in the parable seemed to have been issued a considerable time before celebration; and as the after invitation was sent, according to Eastern etiquette, to the guests invited, they must be understood as having accepted the engagement, so that the apologies they severally made were inadmissible, and could be regarded in no other light than as an affront put upon the generous entertainer, and an ungrateful return for all the splendid preparation he had made for their reception.

511.—THE SOOTHING, HEALING POWER OF MUSIC.
1 Sam. xvi. 23.

℄ Buretti declares music to have the power of so affecting the whole nervous system as to give sensible ease in a large variety of disorders, and in some cases a radical cure. Particularly he instances sciatica as capable of being relieved by this agency.

Theophrastus is mentioned by Pliny as recommending it for the hip gout; and there are references on record by old Cato and Varro to the same effect. Aesculapius figures in Pindar as healing acute disorders with soothing songs.

> *"Music exalts each joy, allays each grief,*
> *Expels diseases, softens every pain,*
> *Subdues the rage of poison and of plague:*
> *And hence the wise of ancient days adored*
> *One power of physic, melody, and song."*

512.—THE HEBREW WORD, MAANAH, OR FURROW.
Psalm cxxix. 3.

℃ This word signifies a strip of arable land which the ploughman takes in hand at one time, at both ends of which consequently the ploughing team always comes to a stand, turns round, and begins a new furrow. The length of the *maanah* is of course the same as the length of the furrows. Since the ordinary ox of Palestine is smaller and weaker than ours, and easily becomes tired under the yoke, which presses heavily on its neck, and confines its neck, they are obliged to give it time to recover its strength by frequent resting. This always takes place at the termination of a furrow, when the peasant raises the unwieldy plough out of the earth, and turns it over, clearing off the moist earth with the small shovel at the lower end of the goad, and hammering the loosened edges and rings tight again; during which time the team is able to recover itself by resting. They do not, therefore, make their furrows of great length. If the field is under two hundred feet long, it forms only one *maanah;* but when, in level districts, the long parcels of ground of the separate peasant farmers of a village frequently extend to the distance of a mile and a half, the ploughman is compelled to divide his parcels of ground into several *maanahs,* each of which is ploughed by itself. The furrows, that is to say, cannot be made breadthwise, because the small plots are mostly far too narrow, and because the fields of his neighbours on either side that might be already tilled would be injured by it; for the boundaries of the fields are not formed, as with us, by rows, but only by isolated heaps of stones, of which two larger ones lie between every two fields. Cross-ploughing would be rendered difficult by these boundary stones, and the plough would often be seriously injured.

The figure of the above passage is explained by the overexhaustion of the oxen, if the furrow, through which they had to drag the plough, was made over-long.

513.—THE JEWISH COMMUNITY AT ROME.
Acts xviii. 2.

⸿ The Jewish community established in Rome had its first beginnings in the captives brought by Pompey after his Eastern campaign. Many of them were manumitted, and thus a great proportion of the Jews in Rome were freedmen. Frequent accessions to their numbers were made as years went on, chiefly from the mercantile relations which subsisted between Rome and the East. Many of them were wealthy, and large sums were sent annually for religious purposes from Italy to the mother country. Even the proselytes contributed to these sacred funds. It is difficult to estimate the amount of the religious influence exerted by the Roman Jews upon the various heathens around them; but all our sources of information lead us to conclude that it was very considerable. So long as this influence was purely religious, we have no reason to suppose that any persecution from the civil power resulted. It was when commotions took place in consequence of expectations of a temporal Messiah, or when vague suspicions of this mysterious people were more than usually excited, that the Jews of Rome were cruelly treated, or peremptorily banished. Yet from all these cruelties they recovered with elastic force, and from all these exiles they returned; and in the early years of Nero, which were distinguished for a mild and lenient government of the empire, the Jews in Rome seem to have enjoyed complete toleration, and to have been a numerous, wealthy, and influential community.—*Conybeare and Howson.*

514.—ROMAN EXAMPLES OF EXCESSIVE DRINKING.
Eph. v. 18.

⸿ The early sobriety of the ancient Romans formed a striking contrast to their subsequent excesses. In the first ages of the Commonwealth no one was permitted to drink wine until he had attained his thirtieth year. Whether it was the scantiness of the liquor, or the more probable motive of attention to the morals of the people, which gave rise to this severe prohibition, does not appear;

but from whatever cause it proceeded, it is certain that the ancient sobriety of the Romans ceased as soon as the grape became abundant, and excess in wine became so prevalent in Rome, that Pliny speaks of men in polite society who, after drinking to repletion, have sought to create new means of continuing their revelry. Of this number was Mark Antony, who published an account of drunken revels, and the younger Cicero, who acquired great celebrity by the quantity he could drink at a draught, "as if," says Pliny, "he wished to deprive Anthony, the murderer of his father, of the glory of being the greatest drunkard of the age." It is recorded of the Emperor Tiberius that he passed two whole days and nights at table with Pomponius Flaccus and Lucius Piso, whose convivial qualities he afterwards rewarded, the one with the government of Syria, the other with the prefecture of the city; and so far was he from concealing the motive for their advancement, that the patents of their appointments expressed it. So dissipated, indeed, was Tiberius, that Seneca says he was only drunk once in his life—that was from the moment he first became intoxicated to the day of his death. Cossus, prefect of the city under Tiberius, was in the constant habit of going in a state of intoxication to the senate, whence he was frequently carried in so sound a sleep as not to be awakened by the motion of his removal. It does not appear that the Romans were acquainted with the distillation of ardent spirits; but Pliny speaks of a kind of beer that was made by fermenting several species of grain with water, and mentions it as an instance of the depravity of the times, that men, not satisfied with wine, contrived that even water should contribute to inebriate them.

515.—HAMAN HANGED ON HIS OWN GALLOWS.
Esther vii. 10.

℩ As an illustration of the working of the law of retribution which brought Haman to the end which he had devised for Mordecai, we may cite Mr. de Quincey, who, in his memorable narrative of the revolt of the Tartars, or flight of the Kalmuck Khan and his people from the Russian territories to the frontiers of China (1771), relates in conclusion how Zebek-Dorchi, the author and originator of this great Tartar *exodus*, perished after a manner specially gratifying to those who compassed his ruin; the Chinese morality being exactly of that kind which approves in everything the *lex talionis*. "Finally, Zebek-Dorchi was invited to the imperial lodge, together with all his accomplices; and under the skilful management of the Chinese nobles in the emperor's establishment, the murderous artifices of these Tartar chieftains were made to recoil upon themselves, and the whole of them perished by assassination at a great imperial banquet."

516.—RABBINICAL RULES RESPECTING THE SABBATH.
Matt. xii. 2.

⁅ In their bigoted reverence for the Sabbath some of the Jews asserted that the day was first of all kept in heaven, and that the Jewish nation had been chosen for no other end than to preserve it holy upon earth. The extent to which they carried their scruples excites one's ridicule and contempt. To preserve life on that day was to violate it, and to kill a flea was as bad as to kill a camel. On the Sabbath you must not cross a stream on stilts, for in so doing you carry the stilts; a woman must not go out with her ribbons about her, unless they are part of her dress; a false tooth must not be worn; a person with toothache must not rinse his mouth with vinegar, though he might hold it awhile in his mouth and then swallow it; no one was to write two letters of the alphabet; the sick might not send for a physician; a person suffering from lumbago must not rub or foment the part affected; a tailor must not carry a needle out on Friday night, lest he should forget it, and so break the Sabbath by carrying it about on that day; a cock must not wear a piece of ribbon round its leg on the Sabbath, for it would be carrying something. Shammai, one of the two great rabbis of our Saviour's day, would not entrust a letter to *a pagan* to be carried to its destination later than Wednesday, lest it should not be delivered before the Sabbath. It is said that he spent the whole week in thinking how best to keep the Sabbath. His followers held that Sabbatism applied—(1) to men; (2) to beasts; (3) to things. The Hillelites, the opposite sect at the same period, denied the third, and did not think it necessary to extinguish a lamp that had been lit previous to the Sabbath, or to remove fish-nets that were cast, or to prevent the dropping of oil in a press. A curious story is told in illustration of the extent to which Pharisaic scruples might be carried. The Rabbi Kolonimos was innocently accused of having murdered a boy. It appears that he knew the assassin, and to prevent himself being torn to pieces, he

wrote the name of the culprit on a piece of paper, and laid it upon
the lips of the corpse. By this means the rabbi saved his own life,
and the real murderer was exposed. But, alas! Kolonimos had written that name on the Sabbath-day, and he spent the rest of his life
in penance. Not content with this long atonement for his sin, the
rabbi gave orders that for one hundred years after his death every
one who passed by should fling a stone at his tomb, because every
one who profaned the Sabbath ought to be stoned!

517.—LEAPING ROUND BAAL'S ALTAR.
1 Kings xviii. 26.

℃ Baal, whose idolatrous worship is here referred to, was the
same as Apollo, or the sun. Callimachus has given us a remarkable
instance of the universal veneration which was paid by the ancient
pagans at his altar, in the temple of Delos. Among other ceremonies in the worship of this idol it was customary to *run round*
his altar, *to strike it with a whip;* and with their hands or arms
bound behind them, *to bite the olive.* For of Delos the poet
says,—

> *"Thee, ever-honoured isle, what vessel dares*
> *Sail by regardless? 'Twere in vain to plead*
> *Strong driving gales; or, stronger still than they*
> *Swift-wing'd necessity. Their swelling sails*
> *Here mariners must furl; nor hence depart*
> *Till round the altar, struck with many a blow,*
> *The maze they tread; and, backward bent their arms,*
> *The sacred olive bite."*—Hymn to Delos.

The former part of this ceremony plainly alludes to singing and
dancing round the altar; the latter part seems to accord with what
is said of Baal in 1 Kings xviii. 26–28, where we read of the
priests of Baal, who *leaped* upon the altar they had made: which
the Septuagint renders *"run round;"* and they "cried aloud, and
cut themselves after their manner with knives and lances, till the
blood gushed out upon them." This running round the altar
signified the annual rotation of the earth round the sun; striking
with a whip the altar, cutting themselves with knives and lances,
and crying aloud to their deity were symbolical actions, denoting
their desire that he would show forth his power upon all nature in

general, and that sacrifice in particular then before him. Having thus surrounded the altar of Apollo, and, by these actions, declared their belief in his universal power, they used to bend their own arms behind them, and so take the sacred olive into their mouths, thereby declaring that not from their own arm or power, which was bound, but from his whose altar they surrounded, they expected to obtain that peace whereof the olive was always a symbol (Gen. viii. 11). There are some evident allusions to these abominable idolatrous practices in the Old Testament; and the Jews are severely reprimanded by the prophets for following such absurd and wicked ceremonies. "Thus saith the Lord concerning the prophets, that make My people err, that bite with their teeth, and cry peace" (Micah iii. 5). And respecting Ashdod, the prophet says, "I will take away his blood out of his mouth, and his abomination from between his teeth" (Zech. ix. 7).

518.—Joseph's Shaving Himself.
Gen. xli. 14.

℄ The following paragraph is taken from Kitto:—"Carefully considered, this is one of many passages in which the truth of the Scripture narrative is attested by an incidental and slight allusion to remarkable customs, which no mere inventor would think of noticing, or notice without explaining. Shaving was a remarkable custom of the Egyptians, in which they were distinguished from other Oriental nations, who carefully cherished the beard, and regarded the loss of it as a deep disgrace. This was the feeling of the Hebrews; but here Joseph shaves himself in conformity with an Egyptian usage, of which this passage conveys the earliest intimation, but which is confirmed, not only by the subsequent accounts of Greek and Roman writers, but by the ancient sculptures and paintings of Egypt, in which the male figure is usually beardless. It is true that in sculptures some heads have a curious rectangular beard, or rather beard-case, attached to the chin; but this is proved to be an artificial appendage by the same head being represented sometimes with and at other times without it; and still more by the appearance of a band which passes along the jaws, and attaches it to the cap on the head, or to the hair. It is concluded that this appendage was never actually worn, but was used in sculpture to indicate the male character."

519.—THE PRODUCTIONS OF CYPRUS.
Acts xiii. 4.

℃ Mr. James Bell, a well-known and careful geographical compiler, gives the following summary of the productions of this island:—"Copper is the chief metallic wealth of Cyprus; it is said to have once produced gold, silver, and emeralds. What is called the diamond of Paphos, is a species of rock-crystal, found near that place. In this same vicinity is produced the celebrated *amianthus,* or mineral cloth, famed among the ancients for its incombustibility, flexibility, whiteness, and delicate fibrous structure. Red jasper and amber are also productions of Cyprus. The slopes of the mountains are thickly clad with woods of oak, pine, cypress, beech, and elm, together with groves of olives, and plantations of mulberries. Myrtles, various evergreens, and innumerable sweet-scented flowers, adorn the northern sides of the range and the narrow belt at its foot. Hyacinths, anemones, ranunculuses, the single and double flowered narcissus grow spontaneously, and deck the hill slopes, valleys, and plains, giving the country the appearance of an immense flower-garden, and regaling the sense of smelling with delightful odours. The vegetable productions are vines, olives, cotton, lemons, oranges, apricots, and others congenial to the climate and soil. Cyprus has always been famous for its wines, which are of two kinds, red and white, made from grapes superlatively rich and luscious, their juice resembling a concentrated essence. These wines, however, are unpalatable to British taste, by their sickly sweetness, which it requires almost a century to remove. They are strongly aperient, and must be drunk with caution. In colour, sweetness, and other properties, Cyprian wine strongly resembles Tokay wine. It is supposed to be perfect at forty years old, when kept in casks covered at the bung-hole with a thin sheet of lead. Its qualities are then considered as truly balsamic. All the valuable kinds are white, and the red is the common wine. Sugar-canes were anciently very abundantly cultivated, till they were all burned by a Turkish pasha. The silk of Cyprus is of two kinds, yellow and white, but the former is preferred. The cotton is the finest in the Levant. Of the cerealia, wheat is the chief, and of superior quality; but there is little or no capital in the hands of the peasantry, and the exportation of wheat is a monopoly, shared between the moutsellim and the Greek archbishop, who export or retail at an advanced price the whole annual produce, which they

purchase at an arbitrary valuation. More than once during the war
in Spain, the whole of the grain produce was purchased of the persons above mentioned by the merchants of Malta, and exported,
leaving the people without a morsel of bread. Game abounds in
this island, as partridges, quails, woodcocks, and snipes; but here
are no wild animals, except foxes and hares, but many kinds of
serpents, especially the asp, whose bite is said to have caused the
death of the infamous Cleopatra. All kinds of domestic animals
and fowls are bred here, where the natives boast that the produce
of every land and every clime will not only flourish, but attain
even the highest point of perfection. Cyprus is noted for its manufactures of leather, printed cottons, and carpets. The first is remarkable for its brilliant and lively colours; and the second for the
permanency of their colours, which become brighter by washing.
The carpets are of excellent workmanship, and though barely large
enough for an English hearth, bring from 40 to 50 piastres a
piece."

520.—Scorn of Jesus as a Carpenter.
Mark vi. 3.

¶ When Jesus began to preach to the people in His own town,
where He spent most of His life—in Nazareth—His neighbours in-
dignantly demanded, "Is not this the carpenter?" This fact, in their
esteem, was sufficient reason why they should rather insult Him
than listen to anything He might say. Had He previously been
recognised by the Jewish doctors, His humble birth and occupation
would have been no bar to His popularity, for the Jews were ever
ready to honour labour, provided it were accompanied by learning, and learning they would readily respect, provided it bore the
stamp of the rabbis. A quotation from the apocryphal book entitled
Ecclesiasticus will show in what light the Jews regarded the ar-
tisan:—"The wisdom of a learned man cometh by opportunity of
leisure, and he that hath little business shall become wise. How
can he get wisdom that holdeth the plough, and that glorieth in
the goad, that driveth oxen, is occupied in their labours, and
whose talk is of bullocks? He giveth his mind to make furrows,
and is diligent to give the kine fodder. So every carpenter and
workmaster that laboureth night and day, and they that cut and
grave seals, and are diligent to make great variety, and give themselves to counterfeit images, and watch to finish a work; the smith

also sitting by the anvil and considering the iron-work, the vapour
of the fire wasteth his flesh, and he fighteth with the heat of the
furnace. The noise of the hammer and anvil is ever in his ears,
and his eyes look still upon the pattern of the thing he maketh; he
setteth his mind to finish his work, and watcheth to polish it perfectly. . . . All these trust to their hands, and every one [of them]
is wise in his work. . . . They shall not be sought for in public
council, nor sit high in the congregation; they shall not sit on the
judges' seat, nor understand the sentence of judgment; they cannot
declare justice and judgment, and they shall not be found where
parables are spoken" (*Eccles.* xxxviii. 24–33). Notwithstanding
this, when once a working man had exhibited wisdom and was
recognised by the rabbis, his path was henceforth clear, and whatever his occupation he was respected for his learning.

521.—EASTERN SILK.
Ezekiel xvi. 10.

℃ The Hebrew word translated "silk" is *mēshī*. It is mentioned as
an article with which the people were well acquainted, and it is almost certain that silk was known in Palestine at a date long anterior to the time of Ezekiel. Every attempt to trace the history of
the use of silk as an article of clothing leads us to the North of
China. The inhabitants of that district were acquainted with it
from time immemorial. It would reach Syria and Egypt by way of
India, both in its raw state, and as woven into garments. In its
progress from China to Western Asia, it has been traced through
India, Assyria, and Persia in its manufactured state, until it
reached the land of the Pharaohs. Thence it found its way into
Greece, and ultimately to the nations of Western Europe bordering on the Great Sea. It is clear that the fabric was known long
before the nations of the West were acquainted with the source
whence the thread was obtained. Some imagined that it was the
entrails of a spider. Virgil speaks of "Ethiopia growing white with
soft wool" (cotton?), and of the Seres "who draw the tender
threads from leaves" (*Geor.* ii. 120).

"The mode of producing and manufacturing this precious material was not known to Europe until long after the Christian era,
being first learned, about the year 550, by two monks, who
procured in India the eggs of the silkworm moth, with which, concealing them in hollow canes, they hastened to Constantinople,

where the moths speedily multiplied, and were subsequently introduced into Italy, of which country silk was long a peculiar and staple commodity."

Van Lennep says:—"One of the most interesting insects to be
met with in Western Asia, unknown indeed to the ancients, but
decking the moderns in glossy garments, and creating an industry
which supports thousands of people on the slopes of Lebanon, and
hundreds of thousands in other portions of the lands of the Bible,
is the silkworm. Its produce appears to have been unknown in the
West until the conquests of Alexander. At a later period silk was
made in Persia; but the silkworm was not introduced in Western
Asia until the reign of the Emperor Justinian, *i.e.*, in the latter half
of the sixth century. Silk was at one time so great a luxury in
Rome that it was sold for an equal weight of gold. There are few
persons now who do not wear more or less silk. The cultivation of
the mulberry tree, the cutting of its branches and leaves, the gradual growth of the worm, the formation of the cocoon, the issuing
forth of the butterfly, and the laying of the tiny eggs, are episodes
in the process of silk-making which we have often watched with
intensest interest. Silkworms are now reared from Persia to the
Egean, and almost to the Red Sea. Much of the silk thus obtained
is consumed at home; but large quantities go to Europe, the value
of the article compensating the heavy cost and insecurity of trans-
portation."

522.—SCENE OF THE DEATH OF ABEL.
Gen. iv. 8.

¶ The present reading of this text is much embarrassed. The Hebrew word which our translators have rendered "talked," will not
bear this meaning; but, not finding anything that was spoken on
the occasion, they have ventured to intimate that there was a con-
versation indefinitely. In the most correct editions of the Hebrew
Bible there is a hiatus, a deficiency marked, which is supplied in
the ancient versions, and in the Samaritan text. According to
these, the text is clear and consistent, thus:—"And Cain said unto
Abel his brother, Let us go out into the field; and it came to pass,
when they were in the field, that Cain rose up," etc.

522.—Scene of the Death of Abel.

523.—THE EXPRESSION, "TAKE NO THOUGHT."
Matt. vi. 25.

¶ When the earlier versions of the New Testament into English were made, the expression "to take thought" signified what we now mean by such words as vexing, worrying, fretting, being anxious, full of care, and the like. This is its meaning in our translation. But, like many other words and phrases which have fallen out of common use, "taking thought" has become obsolete. Hence the blunder which is now so common.

The Greek verb and its derivatives occur twenty-two times in the Greek Testament, and they always denote an anxious condition of mind. This will be seen by a reference to the passages.

The noun, meaning anxiety, occurs in the following places:— Matt. xiii. 22; Mark iv. 19; Luke viii. 14, xxi. 34; 2 Cor. xi. 28; 1 Pet. v. 7.

The verb occurs in the following texts of the Greek Testament: —Matt. vi. 25, 27, 28, 31, 34, x. 19; Luke x. 41, xii. 11, 22, 25, 26; 1 Cor. vii. 32, 33, xii. 25; Phil. ii. 20, iv. 6.

If the reader will refer to all these texts, he will see that anxiety or care must be meant in every one, and that the mere act of thinking is nowhere indicated.

The adjective, meaning "without anxiety," occurs in Matt. xxviii. 14; 1 Cor. vii. 32. In the first of these places the Greek may be literally translated, "and will make you without anxiety," or "will free you from anxiety." Our version, "will secure you," represents the old meaning of the word "secure," which is "free from or without care."

Every dictionary explains the words in accordance with the above statements. Every version, ancient and modern, so far as we can find, conveys the same idea. No critic or commentator will be found to understand the words of mere thinking.

Christianity was meant to make men think, and it is common to speak of a religious man as a thoughtful man. Christians are of course anxious, but it is not right for them to be full of care, nor to be without full confidence in the grace and providence of God.

We are also reminded that the phrase "to take thought," in the sense of being anxious, occurs in the Old Testament at 1 Sam. ix. 5. Saul said, "Come and let us return, least my father leave caring for the asses and take thought for us." Some time had elapsed since Saul and the servant had left home in search of some lost asses, and it is worse than childish to suppose that Saul imagined that his father had forgotten him all the while, and that it was so desirable that he should not think of him, that it would be better to go home without the asses than incur the risk of being thought of by Kish. The original Hebrew word here translated "take thought" is explained in Fürst's Lexicon "to fear, to be concerned, to be distressed;" and in 1 Sam. x. 2 it is rendered, in our version, "sorroweth for you." The ancient Greek, Latin, Syriac, and Arabic, as well as the Chaldee Targum, all give, substantially, the same meaning.—*Christian Evidence.*

524.—CHAIRS USED IN EGYPTIAN HOUSES.
Gen. xliii. 33.

℧ Wilkinson tells us, "The house of a wealthy person in Egypt was always furnished with chairs. Stools and low seats were also used, the seat being only from eight to fourteen inches high, and of wood, or interlaced with thongs: these, however, may be considered equivalent to our rush-bottomed chairs, and probably belonged to persons of humble means; and many of the *fauteuils* were of the most elegant form; they were made of ebony and other rare woods, inlaid with ivory, and very similar to some now used in Europe. The legs were mostly in imitation of those of an animal; and lions' heads, or the entire body, formed the arms of large *fauteuils,* as in the throne of Solomon (1 Kings x. 19). Some, again, had folding legs, like our camp stools."

525.—ZION PLOUGHED AS A FIELD.
Micah iii. 12.

℧ It has been remarked that when this prophecy was delivered it must have seemed a most daring utterance; to those who heard it an utter impossibility. David, having made Zion the capital of his kingdom, greatly strengthened its fortifications, and this hill appears to have been densely crowded with the best and strongest edifices in Jerusalem. It was difficult indeed to imagine it turned into a common wheat-field where, generation after generation, the husbandman should quietly gather rich harvests; and yet this prophecy has been most literally fulfilled. Luxuriant crops of grain may now be found growing on all the south-eastern face of the mount.

526.—SMELLING THE GARMENTS.
Gen. xxvii. 27.

⟪ From Roberts's Oriental illustrations we take the following interesting notes:—The natives of the East are universally fond of having their garments strongly perfumed; so much so, that Europeans can scarcely bear the smell. They use camphor, civet, sandal-wood, or sandal oil, and a great variety of strongly-scented waters.

It is not common to *salute*, as in England; they simply *smell* each other; and it is said that some people know their own children by the smell. It is common for a mother or father to say, "Ah, child, thy smell is like the *Sen-Paga-Poo*." The crown of the head is the principal place for smelling.

Of an amiable man it is said, "How sweet is the smell of that man! the smell of his goodness is universal."

That delightful traveller, Captain Mangles, R.N., informed me that while on a short visit at the house of Mr. Barker, our consul at Aleppo, he heard Mrs. Barker, who was a Greek lady, say something to her child, accompanied by signs of great endearment. Mr. Barker said to Captain Mangles, "You do not understand her; she says, 'Come hither, my darling, and let me smell thee.'"

527.—LOCUSTS AFFECTED BY THE COLD.
Nahum iii. 17.

⟪ "Paxton and others have remarked that there is much difficulty in this passage; but to anyone who has attentively watched the habits of the locusts, it is not only plain but very striking. In the evenings, as soon as the air became cool, at Abeîh, they literally camped in the hedges and loose stone walls, covering them over like a swarm of bees settled on a bush. There they remained until the next day's sun waxed warm, when they again commenced their march. One of the days on which they were passing was quite cool, and the locusts scarcely moved at all from their *camps*, and multitudes remained actually stationary until the next morning. Those that did march crept along very heavily, as if cramped and stiff; but in a hot day they hurried forward in a very earnest, lively manner. It is an aggravation of the calamity if the weather continues cool; for then they prolong their stay, and do far more damage."—*Thomson.*

528.—OFFERING WORSHIP TO WEAPONS AND IMPLEMENTS.
Hab. i. 16.

℃ Roberts tells us that, strange as it may appear, the Hindoos make offerings to their weapons of war, and to those used in hunting. Fishermen offer incense to the bag in which they carry their fish, and to the net; and whilst the incense is burning, they hold the different implements in the smoke. The opulent sacrifice a sheep or a fowl, which is said to make the ceremony more acceptable to Varuna, the god of the sea. Should the tackle thus consecrated not prove successful, they conclude that some part of the ceremony has not been properly performed, and therefore must be repeated. But, in addition to this, they often call for their magicians to bless the waters, and to intercede for prosperity. Nor is this sacrificing to implements and weapons confined to fishermen, hunters, and warriors; for even artisans do the same to their tools; as also do students and scholars to their books. Thus at the feast called *nava-ratere,* that is, "the nine nights," carpenters, masons, goldsmiths, weavers, and all other tradesmen may be seen in the act of presenting offerings to their tools. Ask them a reason for their conduct, and they will say, "The incense and ceremonies are acceptable to Sarusa-pathi, the beautiful goddess of Brahma."

529.—PERSONAL APPEARANCE OF CHRIST.
Isaiah lii. 14.

℃ Publius Lentulus, who was governor of Judaea in the time of Christ, wrote to Tiberius Caesar thus of our Saviour:—

"There has a man appeared here who is still living, named Jesus Christ, whose power is extraordinary. He has a title given to Him of the Great Prophet: His disciples call Him the Son of God. He raises the dead and heals all sorts of diseases. He is a tall, well-proportioned man; there is an air of serenity in His countenance

which attracts at once the love and reverence of those who see
Him. His hair is of the colour of new wine; from the roots to His
ears and from thence to the shoulders it is curled and falls down
to the lowest part of them; upon the forehead it parts in two after
the manner of the Nazarenes. His forehead is flat and fair, His
face without any defect, and adorned with a very graceful vermil-
ion; His air is majestic and agreeable; His nose and mouth are
very well proportioned, and His beard is thick and forked, of the
colour of His hair; His eyes are grey and extremely lively; in His
reproofs He is terrible, but in His exhortations and instructions
amiable and courteous. There is something wonderfully charming
in His face, with a mixture of gravity. He is never seen to laugh,
but He has been observed to weep. He is very straight in stature;
His hands are large and spreading; His arms very beautiful. He
talks little but with great gravity, and is the handsomest man in
the world."

530.—SYENE.
Ezek. xxix. 10.

℄ "Syene itself being the last town of Egypt towards the frontier
of Ethiopia, this version does not convey the sense of the original,
which is correctly given by Newcome—'From Migdol to Syene,
even to the border of Ethiopia.' Migdol, rendered 'tower' in our
version, but which should be preserved as a proper name, was in
the north of Egypt, while Syene was at its southern frontier; so
'from Migdol to Syene' is an expression for describing the whole
extent of the country, analogous to 'from Dan to Beersheba.' The
cataracts (or rather the first cataract) of the Nile, which occur
above this place, and the difficult navigation of the river, make a
natural boundary line, so that Syene (now called Assouan) has
under all governments been considered the frontier-town of Egypt
in this direction. Speaking more strictly, the boundary may be said
to be formed by the mighty terraces of that peculiar kind of
reddish granite, called *syenite,* from the name of the place. These
terraces, shaped into peaks, stretch across the bed of the Nile, and
over them the great river rolls its foaming stream, forming the cataracts so often mentioned in every description of Egypt. It was
from the quarries at this place that the Egyptians obtained the
stone so frequently employed by them in their obelisks and colossal statues. The town of Syene long retained its importance, with a

very considerable population. Ruins of works and buildings by the
successive masters of the land, the Pharaohs, the Ptolemies, the
Romans, and the Arabians, are still seen on and around the site of
the old town, which the present town so closely adjoins on the
north, that the northern wall of the old town forms the southern
one of the new. The removal is said to have been made in the year
1403 A.D. (806 A.H.), in consequence of a plague which destroyed
21,000 of the inhabitants; from which the importance of the place,
down to comparatively later times, may be estimated. The scenery
in this part is very striking:—'The river is rocky here, and the
navigation, by night at least, dangerous. At the pass of Assouan,
ruin and devastation reign around. This pass, which nature has so
well fortified, seems ill-treated by man. Hardly anything was to be
seen but the vast remains of the old town of Syene, with mud-built
walls and hovels on every side. Rocks, forming islands, were in the
middle of the stream, upon which shrubs were growing. The scene
altogether was wild and forlorn.' "—*Madox*.

531.—THE SIROCCO SUGGESTING PROPHETIC FIGURES.
Joel ii. 30, 31.

℄ Dr. Thomson writes:—"We have two kinds of Sirocco—one
accompanied with vehement wind, which fills the air with dust and
fine sand; and one of a quieter kind, which yet is often more over-
powering. I have often seen the whole heavens veiled in gloom
with this sort of sand-cloud, through which the sun, shorn of his
beams, looked like a globe of dull smouldering fire. It may have
been this phenomenon which suggested the strong prophetic figure
of Joel, quoted by Peter on the Day of Pentecost:—'Wonders in
the heaven above, and signs in the earth beneath; blood, and fire,
and pillars of smoke; the sun shall be turned into darkness, and
the moon into blood.' The pillars of smoke are probably those columns of sand and dust raised high in the air by local whirlwinds,
which often accompany the sirocco. On the great desert of the
Hauran, I have seen a score of them marching with great rapidity
over the plain, and they closely resembled 'pillars of smoke.'"

532.—GIVING UP IDOLS.
Hosea xiv. 8.

℄ The Rev. W. Pool, missionary in Madagascar, sends a report
which may serve to illustrate the spirit of the above passage.

"On the 8th September last, the Chief Secretary of State, with others high in rank, were sent to the village where the royal idols were kept, with orders to burn them. They started at about half-past three in the afternoon, well armed, and hasted to Ambohimanambolu, a distance of seven miles, to execute the queen's commands. On arriving at the village, the first thing to do was to read the Prime Minister's letter, and secure possession of the idol's house. This done, a fire was kindled with the materials of the fence which surrounded the house, and had been pulled down by the queen's orders on the day she laid the corner-stone of the Chapel Royal. Then first the long cane, called Tsoutsonaraka, which usually preceded the idol in processions or journeyings, was cast into the fire; then twelve bullocks' horns, from which the sacred sprinklings were made; three scarlet umbrellas followed, and the silk lamba or loose-flowing garment which concealed the idol when suspended on the person of its keeper when it travelled. The idol's case succeeded; this case was made of a small tree hollowed, having a lid or cover fitted to it; and, lastly, the idol itself. This idol consisted altogether of two thicknesses of scarlet silk, about three feet long and three inches wide, having a small piece of wood, about the length and size of a finger to the second joint, inserted in the middle between the silks, in such a manner that, by turning the silks a little way, the point of the wood could be made to touch water or anything else that was to be sanctified: at either extremity of the silk a silver chain was sewed or fastened, equal in length to the width of the silk. On seeing the idol, the people said, 'You cannot burn him, he is a god!' to which the Christian officer replied, 'If he be a god he will not burn; we are going to try;' and when enveloped in flames, one of them held it up on a stick, to show it was burning. On the day following four others were burned, and on the 10th September two more. One of those burnt was the sovereign's private idol, which was found to consist of a small quantity of sand tied in a cloth."

533.—THE DESOLATION AND DEGRADATION OF EDOM.
Obadiah 8.

℄ The publication, in 1838, by Laborde and Linant, of their great work, *Voyage de l'Arabie Petrée,* with its splendid engravings, has presented before the mind a bird's-eye view of the utter desolation of the country of Esau, such as would be beyond the power of mere verbal description. The topographical view of the land, taken from El Nakb, gives at a glance a most striking view of the land of Edom as it is, "most desolate," the "desolation of desolations"—a once fertile region made bare, the line of confusion, and the stones of emptiness stretched over it.

When He whose prerogative it is to define the bounds of our habitation gave to Esau his inheritance, it was thus described through the lips of the patriarch Isaac:—"Behold, thy dwellings shall be the fatness of the earth, and the dews of heaven from above;" and that it was such a land the allusions and descriptions of the Book of Job give abundant evidence (Job xix. 23, 24, xxxi. 35, 36, xiii. 26). It was a land exalted as high as wealth and art could raise it, the abode of a high state of civilisation and commerce, and a country in which the arts had made considerable progress (Job xxxiii. 1–11).

But the sons of Edom transgressed, and woes were denounced against them and their territory, which have been as strikingly fulfilled as those beneath whose tremendous weight Nineveh, and Babylon, and Tyre, and Bethsaida, and Capernaum lie prostrate and forgotten. "Behold, O mount Seir, I am against thee, and I will make thee most desolate. Because thou hast had a perpetual hatred, and hast shed the blood of the children of Israel by the force of the sword in the time of their calamity" (Ezek. xxxv. 3, 5).

Now "wisdom is departed from Teman, and understanding has perished out of the mount of Esau," and the wanderers in that region are sunk in the grossest folly, regarding the ruins around them as the work of evil spirits (Obadiah 8). Travellers assert that the minds of the Bedouins are as bare and uncultivated as the deserts they traverse. "Our Sheikh, Hassan," says Dr. Robinson, "has never known a Bedouin who could read; he had only heard that there were some in the far east."

All modern travellers unite in the declaration that it is one broad plain of barrenness and desolation, and that its present state could not be more graphically described than it is in the words of the prophetic writers. "These portray," says Dr. Olin, "a state of desolation and ruin the most absolute and irretrievable, such as probably no portion of the globe once populous and fertile now exhibits." The fearful denunciations of the prophets against this once rich and beautiful region and its highly civilised inhabitants, and their fulfilments, furnish an invulnerable argument in favour of the inspiration of the Holy Scriptures. In the words of a modern writer, "Read here in the word of prophecy what desolations

are foretold—look there, over the land of Edom, how all is
fulfilled, and can you but confess that this book is from God?"
(Compare Isaiah xxxiv. 11; Jer. xlix. 10; Ezek. xxxv. 9.)

534.—THE HISTORY OF CYPRUS.
Acts xiii. 4.

℃. The colonisation of Cyprus dates from the earliest age, and the
mainland furnished it with men. It lies contiguous to three continents, and Phoenicia probably supplied the first swarm that settled on its shore. Then came an early Egyptian expedition or conquest, and its Phoenician settlers figure as tributaries from the isles
of the Great Sea, or Mediterranean, to the Pharaoh Thothmes III.,
about the fifteenth century, B.C. Later than this, Greek adven-
turers, who pried into every nook of the Mediterranean, wafted
themselves and Homeric legends to the shores of Cyprus. According to their tales, after the Trojan war Agamemnon visited the island in no friendly spirit, although its monarch, Cinyras, had given
a valuable and artistic corselet to conciliate the favour of the King
of men. Teucer, the archer *par excellence* of the Greek hosts,
founded with his vagabond companions another Salamis, and
other Greeks alighted upon the coasts later than the days of
Cinyras—a name suggestive of Semitic origin. The early worship
of Aphrodite, carried on in a manner almost Babylonian, has left
traces of its origin to the present day in the ethnographical type of
its inhabitants. When the Assyrians, protected by iron armour, dis-
ciplined by a severe drill, and led by skilled officers, overran Syria
and Phoenicia, the petty kings of Cyprus, terrified at the Assyrian
march, proffered a hasty submission, and propitiated by daughters
instead of armour the goodwill of the triumphant monarch. Sargon, about B.C. 720, was recognised by four or seven kings; and,
recorded on a tablet found at Citium, his sway over the island.
Ten other petty princes sent tribute to Assurbanipal, or Sardanapalus, the grandson of Sennacherib, for the conquest of Tyre
had rendered Cyprus an easy prey to the victor. The next century
and a half found Cyprus a dependency of Egypt, and so it
remained till conquered by Cambyses, and added as one more sa-
trapy to Persia. But the island still had its local princes, although
under Persian sway. At Citium and Idalium the monarchs, if not
Phoenicians, as their names show, were a suite of kings, named
Azbaal, Baalmelek, Abdemon, Melekiatun, Pumiathon, who
flourished, although Evagoras and Nicocles had a short interval of

independence, and made for a while a successful stand, and introduced a culture purely Hellenic into the hearts and literature of
Cyprus. The island, in fact, was divided into several kingdoms,
and their mutual discord ultimately led to its fall. They assisted
Alexander the Great, and were subdued by Ptolemy, and finally
became an appanage of Egypt and a convenient mint. The
Romans, then, on a slight affront, annexed it to the empire,
whence, after an ephemeral transfer to Cleopatra, it remained till
the fall of the Byzantine empire, and passed from the Arabs to
Dukes in the tenth century A.D. After that it was conquered by
Richard I. in the twelfth century, sold to the Templars, then transferred to Guy of Lusignan, a French crusader. Venicè subsequently acquired it; but Selim II. conquered it in the sixteenth
century A.D., inflicting unheard-of cruelties on the defenders. With
the Turks it has remained ever since, and experienced the usual
administration of a pasha.

535.—THE PRACTICAL VALUE OF THE OLIVE.
Habakkuk iii. 17.

℄ "The fruit of this tree is indispensable for the comfort, and
even the existence of the mass of the community. The Biblical references to this matter are not at all exaggerated. The berry, pick-
led, forms the general relish to the farmer's dry bread. He goes
forth to his work in the field at early dawn, or sets out on a journey, with no other provision than olives wrapped up in a quantity
of his *paper-like* loaves, and with this he is contented. Then almost
every kind of dish is cooked in oil, and without it the good wife is
utterly confounded; and when the oil fails, the lamp in the dwelling of the poor expires. Moreover, the entire supply of soap in this
country is from the produce of the olive. Habakkuk, therefore,
gives a very striking attestation of his faith in God in the expression found in the above passage."

536.—THE RIVER OF EGYPT.
Gen. xv. 18.

℄ "As the traveller pursues his weary way from Egypt to Palestine, he crosses the broad channel of a river, bounded still by its
well-marked banks, but destitute of water. When the rivers of
Judah flowed with water, this was the southern boundary of the

country, dividing it from the land of Ham, and hence it is often
alluded to as the 'River of Egypt.' On one side is a parched desert
of sand, spotted here and there with little verdant patches, where a
few bushes of palm-trees grow, and flowers show their smiling
faces to the scorching rays of the sun that pour down as if from a
glowing furnace; but, in general, dreary, waste, and bare, with
nothing to relieve the eye, almost blinded by the glare of the white
sand, but occasional heaps of stones, that tell of ruin and desolation. Here and there the flat sands are covered with an incrusta-
tion of fine salt, the very symbol of barrenness. The wild ass,
whose 'house' God has 'made the wilderness, and the barren land
(Heb., the salt places) his dwellings,' here ranges, far from the
haunts of men, 'searching after every green thing.'

"On the eastern side of this ancient channel, once a considerable
river, since it is not less than six hundred feet in breadth, the
country changes. Low sand hills, running in ranges parallel to the
shore of the Mediterranean, which is close at hand, for a while
struggle for supremacy with the increasing verdure of grassy slopes
and eminences, and with advancing cultivation."—*P. H. Gosse.*

537.—THE VALLEY OF HINNOM.
2 Kings xxiii. 10.

⸿ An Eastern missionary writes:—I remember a similar place in
Calcutta, called the *Burning Ghat.* It was naturally a pleasant spot
on the bank of the wide, deep Hoogly; but the bodies of the dead
were here burned—often very imperfectly—and so there was always the smouldering flame, the heavy black smoke, the noisome
smell of burning, corrupting flesh; while crowds of lazy, bloated
vultures were lounging about, oppressed with their heavy meal. It
was a painful, humbling, disgusting sight; but it put me in mind of
the valley of Hinnom at Jerusalem, and showed me how it came
to be regarded by the Jews as an image of the place of the lost,
Gehenna, or the valley of Hinnom, as hell is called in the New
Testament.

538.—DAGON, THE PHILISTINE FISH-GOD.
Judges xvi. 23.

⸿ Dagon appears to have been the favourite national idol of the
Philistines. The name is evidently formed from the word *dag,* a

fish. A description of the figure of Dagon is given in 1 Sam. v. 4,
and this has been observed to agree exactly with the representations of a fish-god which have been found on the walls of
Khorsabad, on slabs at Kouyunjik, and on sundry antique cylinders and gems. In these, however, the form of the figures somewhat vary. Some have the human form down to the waist, with
that of a fish below the waist; while others have a human head,
arms, and legs, growing, as it were, out of a fish's body, and so arranged that the fish's head forms a kind of mitre to the man's
head, while the body and fins form a kind of cloak, hanging down
behind. "The name Dagon seems to be preserved in the *Odacon* of
Berosus. Diodorus Siculus describes the idol at Ashkelon, under
the name of Derceto, as having the face of a woman and the body
of a fish, and gives the legend of her fishy shape, and makes her
the mother of Semiramis, Ninus's wife, thus connecting the Philistine and Assyrian mythologies. Horace was probably describing
what he had seen when he speaks of a picture in which 'the beautiful form of a woman terminated in a hideous fish.' The fish was
a natural emblem of fruitfulness for people dwelling on the sea
coast."

The Babylonians had a tradition, according to Berosus, that at
the very beginning of their history an extraordinary being, called
Oannes, having the entire body of a fish, but the head, hands, feet,
and voice of a man, emerged from the Erythroean sea, appeared
in Babylonia, and taught the rude inhabitants the use of letters,
arts, religion, law, and agriculture; that, after long intervals between, other similar beings appeared, and communicated the same
precious lore in detail, and that the last of these was called
Odacon. Selden is persuaded that this Odacon is to be identified
with the Philistine god Dagon.

539.—THE BODILY LOCATION OF THE
MORAL SENTIMENTS.
Phil. i. 8, etc.

¶ Every reader of the Bible has been struck with the curious use
of the names of the different parts of the body, when the affections and feelings are referred to. Thus we read (Job xvi. 13),
"His archers compass me round about, He cleaveth my *reins*
asunder," and also (Ps. vii. 9) "the righteous God trieth the hearts
and *reins*." The word reins is derived from the Lat. *renes*=kid-

neys. This part of the human frame the Hebrews thought was the
seat of knowledge, joy, pain, pleasure, and various other mental
and moral sentiments and affections.

By the old anatomists, compassion was supposed to be lodged in
the bowels. Hence we read (Phil. i. 8), "For God is my record,
how greatly I long after you all in the *bowels* of Jesus Christ." It
was a common thing 200 years ago to allude to the *bowels* when
one was speaking of pity or compassion. Such curious usages of
language in the Bible, and in old books, are rendered much clearer
when this old belief concerning the localising of mental and moral
qualities is borne in mind.

540.—GENNESARET LAKE, AS IT NOW IS.
Luke v. 1.

¶ Palestine contains two beautiful sheets of water—one in the
north called the Sea of Galilee, the other in the south called the
Salt Sea. The latter is now usually known as the Dead Sea, a title
which it richly deserves, since its waters are so briny that even fish
cannot live in them. The former might well bear the same name,
though for very different reasons. Its waters are fresh and sparkling, bright flowers fringe its shores, and birds of various hue
warble on its banks or skim over its surface. All nature is gay and
animated. But the hum of men is absent. Not a sail whitens the
sea. Occasionally the keel of a single row-boat vexes the placid
waves, and at one end a few fishermen spread their nets, but for
all practical purposes the sea is dead. Its bold shores, instead of
being lined with villas and populous towns, are deserted, save in
two instances. One of these is the city of Tiberias, not the stately
and brilliant capital founded by Herod Antipas, in the beginning
of the first century, which has long since disappeared; but a modern town, once fortified with lofty walls and a castle, but afterwards shattered by an earthquake, and now occupied only by
some indolent Turks and beggarly Jews. The latter are drawn
hither by the reputation of the city as a holy place, since it was in
former ages the seat of a great Jewish school, and furnished the
scholars from whom came the Masora. They come hither to be
supported, while they live, by the alms of their richer brethren
elsewhere, and when they die, to have their bones laid beside the
dust of the honoured Rabbis, whose tombs are in the adjoining
hill-side. The other is the Arab village of Mejdel, a miserable

rockery of stones and stalks and mud, with a smell equal to the concentrated essence of a thousand stables. Yet it is generally agreed that this wretched collection of huts stands on the site of the ancient Magdala, the town from which came that Mary of the Gospel, whose fame is second only to that of the mother of our Lord. The tradition of Christendom has dishonoured her name by appropriating it to fallen women who have been restored, whereas there is not the smallest reason for inferring from the records of Scripture that she was ever anything but a virtuous, although a deeply afflicted woman.

Decayed Tiberias and filthy Mejdel, then, represent the present population around the shores of this famous sea, and whatever visitors (except Howadgis from other continents) resort to the former, are drawn, not by the lake, but by the hot baths hard by. Three or four springs send forth an ample stream of water, impregnated with sulphur, at a very high temperature, which is considered very efficacious for all manner of rheumatic complaints. In the eyes of the surrounding populations all the glorious memories of Gennesaret count for nothing compared with the benefits of a bathing establishment! There are many points on this sea from which a man might look out for days and weeks together and see no more signs of life than he would if standing by the Salt Sea. Both are dead, the one by nature, the other by human misrule and neglect. This is most apparent in the north-western corner, where there is an extensive plain, unequalled anywhere for its exuberant fertility, as is manifested from the small portion now under culture. The remainder is overgrown with gigantic weeds and thistles, the bridle-paths through which are alike disagreeable to the horse and his rider. Purling brooks cross it in several directions, one of which once was utilised for a mill; but the mill is a ruin, and indeed ruins abound everywhere. Nature lives, no richer oleanders and altheas are seen anywhere, but all else breathes the air of decay and death. No houses, no roads, no enclosures, here and there a fellah carrying a rude sickle, or a shepherd going before a flock of sheep or goats, a vast silence brooding over land and water, no angler casting his line, no sportsman pointing his gun— not the untrodden wilderness of the new world conveys such a sense of absolute and unrelieved desolation.

This is made more apparent by contrast. Only a few days before coming to Tiberias I had crossed the plain of Esdraelon, and was surprised to meet eight two-horse wagons loaded with hay after the manner of our own country, while off in the distance were the white tents which sheltered the reapers who cut the grass. These wagons were taking their loads by a good road which twice bridged the Kishon (the only bridges I suppose built in Palestine for a century) to Haifa, the port at the foot of Mount Carmel, where a considerable colony, mainly of Germans, who expect the second advent to be made in the Holy Land, have made a thriving settlement, and are introducing the improved methods of agriculture. Gennesaret is as rich as Jezreel in every respect, but it shows no wagons, no white tents, not the least sign of progress or even stir. Yet the time was when this very region was the centre of a social and political life of the greatest interest. The harvests of the land, and the still greater harvests of the sea, nurtured many considerable cities; manufacturing industry found a large and steady market, and the favour of the ruler attracted a constant stream of visitors from surrounding nations. Not only the plains but the slopes of the hills which elsewhere come close to the water, were turned to profitable account. The lake and its confines were the garden of Galilee, as Galilee was the garden of Palestine.

But its greatest distinction was that fact which now draws to its shores every year a crowd of visitors from all parts of the world—it was the home of our Lord Jesus Christ. He was born in Bethlehem. He was reared in Nazareth, but He lived in Capernaum, which is called by Matthew "His own city." From this as a centre He went forth upon His missionary journeys, and to this He regularly returned. Here He performed most of His mighty works. Here He delivered many of His noblest discourses. The great light which illuminated the world shed its brightest beams upon "the sea coast in the borders of Zebulon and Naphtali." The capital saw Him only occasionally, but Capernaum had Him for a resident. Its inhabitants beheld habitually the life that was without sin, and heard repeatedly the words that were full of wisdom and grace. Yet the record, is that the very communities which were most favoured in this respect made the least improvement of their privileges. The only human career which has successfully defied criticism in every age was without effect on those who had it before their eyes. Publicans and harlots, Samaritans and lepers, were won to the great Teacher; but Capernaum, Chorazin, and Bethsaida were more impenitent than Tyre and Sidon, more insensible than Sodom and Gomorrah. The truthful Saviour "upbraided" them for their sin; and their present condition is a fearful commentary upon

His words. They have perished so completely that even their sites are matters of uncertainty and dispute. The sea is the same as when Christ once with a word calmed its waves, the shore is the same as when He uttered the exquisite series of parables recorded in Matthew's Gospel; but the cities, the centres of population and influence, are gone, utterly gone. An alien race of another faith now roam in ignorant unconcern over the very ground consecrated by the footsteps of the Son of God, while the original inhabitants are known and remembered only as the rejectors of that divine Saviour. Sitting in darkness they saw a great light, but scornfully despising it, they relapsed into a yet blacker darkness, and the desolate shores of Gennesaret are witness to-day that there is no greater curse than a privilege abused.—*T. W. Chambers.*

INDEX OF SUBJECTS

The numbers in this Index allude to the numbers of the Paragraphs,
not to those of the pages.

INDEX OF TEXTS

xix. 35, 127
xxiii. 10, 537

1st Chronicles
ii. 16, 118

2nd Chronicles
ix. 1, 471
xviii. 10, 326
xxvi. 15, 349
xxxii. 3, 4, 278
xxxv. 20, 202

Ezra
i. 1, 2, 474
iv. 8, 95
v. 14, 185

Nehemiah
iv. 1, 298
viii. 8, 179

Esther
i. 1, 215
iii. 13, 67
vii. 10, 515
ix. 20–32, 384

Job
i. 15, 85
ii. 8, 487
iii. 8, 407
vii. 9, 174
ix. 25, 128
xv. 33, 330
xxiv. 16, 15
xxvii. 18, 59
xxviii. 26, 470
xxx. 5, 6, 391
xxxi. 27, 364
xxxi. 31, 32, 200
xxxviii. 7, 189
xxxviii. 31, 260, 390
xxxix. 1, 385
xlii. 10, 38
xlii. 17, 201

Psalms
v. 3, 386
xv. 209
xviii. 30, 274
xxiv. 8, 383
xlv. 1, 325
xlv. 8, 322
lxv. 9, 380
lxxviii. 47, 423
lxxxiv. 3, 473
lxxxiv. 4, 501
ciii. 5, 445
civ. 16, 357, 461
cix. 10, 210
cx. 1, 457
cxx. 4, 281
cxxix. 3, 512
cxxxiii. 3, 83
cxxxiv. 1, 466
cxli. 7, 111
cxlv. 10, 443

Proverbs
iv. 7, 396
vi. 6–8, 500
vi. 13, 235
vii. 16, 442
ix. 2–4, 246

xi. 21, **437**
xiv. 23, 141
xix. 24, 143
xxiii. 6, 435
xxv. 1, 228
xxx. 17, 225
xxx. 26, 399
xxxi. 10–31, 149
xxxi. 15, 314

Ecclesiastes
ii. 6, 218
v. 11, 318
x. 16, 302

Song of Solomon
ii. 1, 411
ii. 11, 12, 175, 239
iv. 6, 362
iv. 13, 24
v. 1, 123

Isaiah
i. 8, 211
ii. 20, 227
iii. 20, 21, 307
viii. 1, 113
x. 29, 136
xi. 11, 161
xiii. 19, 40
xiv. 9–20, 50
xix. 223
xix. 7, 256
xxii. 1, 339
xxii. 22, 310
xxii. 23, 319
xxv. 5, 496
xxv. 11, 49
xxviii. 24, 76
xxxv. 2, 130
xl. 3, 4, 231
xli. 8, 23
xli. 19, 212
xliv. 20, 376
xlv. 1, 436
xlviii. 2, 244
xlix. 16, 262
l. 9, 495
li. 23, 133
lii. 14, 529
lvii. 6, 328
lviii. 11, 265
lx. 8, 213

Jeremiah
i. 1, 353
i. 11, 12, 207
ii. 13, 167, 327
ii. 32, 305
viii. 7, 490
viii. 22, 410, 504
ix. 26 marg. 483
xi. 7, 452
xvii. 1, 168
xxv. 24, 64
xxxiv. 18, 488
xlvi. 15, 268

Lamentations
v. 13, 420

Ezekiel
v. 5, 266
ix. 3, 113
x. 20–22, 122

xiii. 10, 11, 336
xvi. 10, 521
xxvii. 9, 206
xxvii. 16, 226
xxviii. 13, 493
xxix. 10, 530
xxxvi. 24–28, 222
xxxvii. 1–10, 214

Daniel
v. 12, 110
v. 25, 82
vi. 17, 394

Hosea
ii. 15, 418
xiv. 8, 532

Joel
ii. 30, 31, 531

Amos
iii. 15, 508
ix. 7, 472

Obadiah
8, 533

Jonah
i. 17, 102, 404
iii. 10, 170

Micah
iii. 12, 525

Nahum
iii. 17, 527

Habakkuk
i. 16, 528
iii. 17, 535

Haggai
ii. 17, 396

Zechariah
iii. 10, 355
x. 2 marg. 358

Matthew
i. 1, 98
ii. 1, 2, 354
ii. 16, 359
iii. 4, 68, 184, **311**
iii. 11, 120
iv. 13, 332
v., vii. 272, 485
v. 29, 478
v. 46, 129
vi. 1–4, 6
vi. 7, 333
vi. 25, 523
vi. 34, 315
ix. 17, 105
ix. 20–22, 408
x. 2–4, 17
xi. 7, 99
xii. 2, 516
xii. 40, 56
xiii. 24–30, 220, 382
xiii. 32, 368
xiii. 33, 369
xiii. 44, 146
xiii. 47–49, 182, 346
xv. 23, 426